By Matthew Goodman

The City Game: Triumph, Scandal, and a Legendary Basketball Team

Eighty Days: Nellie Bly and Elizabeth Bisland's History-Making Race Around the World

The Sun and the Moon: The Remarkable True Account of Hoaxers, Showmen, Dueling Journalists, and Lunar Man-Bats in Nineteenth-Century New York

Jewish Food: The World at Table

THE CITY GAME

THE

CITY

GAME

Triumph, Scandal,
and a Legendary
Basketball Team

Matthew Goodman

BALLANTINE BOOKS · NEW YORK

Published in the United States by Ballantine Books, an imprint of Random House, a division of Penguin Random House LLC, New York.

BALLANTINE and the HOUSE colophon are registered trademarks of Penguin Random House LLC.

Hardback ISBN 978-1-101-88283-2
Ebook ISBN 978-1-101-88284-9

Printed in the United States of America on acid-free paper

2 4 6 8 9 7 5 3 1

First Edition

Book design by Susan Turner

For my grandfather, Jack Rothenfeld
(1904–1944)

———

"Jack Rothenfeld, all-league forward and probably the cleverest player in the circuit in years . . ."

—New York *Daily News*, April 4, 1926

Urbs Coronata

(Song for the City College of New York)

O youngest of the giant brood
Of cities far-renowned;
In wealth and power thou hast passed
Thy rivals at a bound;
And now thou art a queen, New York;
And how wilt thou be crowned?

"Weave me no palace-wreath of pride,"
The royal city said;
"Nor forge an iron fortress-wall
To frown upon my head;
But let me wear a diadem
Of Wisdom's towers instead."

And so upon her island height
She worked her will forsooth,
She set upon her rocky brow
A citadel of Truth,
A house of Light, a home of Thought,
A shrine of noble Youth.

Stand here, ye City College towers,
And look both up and down;
Remember all who wrought for you
Within the toiling town;
Remember all they thought for you,
And all the hopes they brought for you,
And be the City's Crown.

—HENRY VAN DYKE, June 1909

CONTENTS

PREFACE

The few films that still exist of the City College Beavers playing basketball in the late 1940s are black and white, grainy, soundless. By today's standards the players don't look very athletic: Few of them are muscular, some are too skinny or stocky, and all wear shorts that seem impossibly short and are held up by belts. But more striking still is the team's style of offense, which features lots of passes, very little dribbling, a profusion of shots rarely seen anymore—set shots and hook shots and underhand foul shots—and nearly constant movement by all five players. Back and forth the ball flies, heading this way and that, the players moving swiftly around the edges of the court, circling around behind one another, occasionally breaking free for a rush toward the basket. At times the action proceeds in a regular, predictable rhythm, and then it abruptly turns staccato, the passes becoming shorter and quicker, the movement broken up with feints, shifts, stops, and starts.

Unlike most college teams of the era, the Beavers ran very few set plays. At its essence the offense was improvisatory, created by the players themselves during the course of a game: built from a sideways glance, a nod, a quick tilt of the head that told a teammate in which direction a pass would go. At a time when bebop was just coming into its own, the City College of New York basketball team operated something like a five-man jazz combo, with each player improvising off a few basic patterns, sometimes deferring to another player and sometimes taking the lead, the group momentarily breaking down into duets or trios before building back up again, together creating something fast and complex and unpredictable.

The team's assistant coach, Bobby Sand, liked to refer to this style of offense as "spontaneous play." On the court, he advised, a player should be alert at all times, moving and watching his teammates and anticipating what they are likely to do, responding intelligently to each new situation as it develops.

"Every play in basketball," Sand once wrote, "is a constant revelation in skill, speed, and judgment."

They were a college basketball team unlike any that had ever been assembled. They played not for a powerhouse state school such as Kentucky, Kansas, Indiana, or Oklahoma A&M, but for a tuition-free, merit-based college in Harlem known far more for intellectual achievement than athletic prowess. Only two years after Jackie Robinson broke the color line in Major League Baseball—and at a time when the newly formed National Basketball Association included not a single black player—the 1949–50 CCNY starting five comprised two black and three Jewish players, the first such team ever to play at tournament level. Of the fifteen players on the varsity team, eleven were Jewish and four were black. They were, every one of them, the children of immigrants, from Eastern Europe and the West Indies; they were only a generation or two removed from the bonds of peasantry and servitude, and for them City College represented the opportunity to move into the mainstream—to become, as the saying went, as American as the Americans.

Their fathers worked mostly as laborers, many in jobs with a distinctly Old World flavor. One was a window washer, another a house painter; one drove a seltzer truck, one plied his trade as a blacksmith, shoeing horses that still pulled wagons along the streets of Brooklyn. Among the four black players on the team, three had mothers who worked as domestics for wealthier families; the other was an orphan.

They played most of their home games not in the small City College gym but at Madison Square Garden, where the stands rose up from the court sheer and high and each night were filled with eighteen thousand spectators, many of them serious gamblers who cared less about whether a particular team won than whether it had covered the point spread. Among team sports in New York in those days, only baseball was more widely watched and passionately debated than college basketball. Football was still a decade away from truly capturing the popular imagination, and the National Basketball Association was in its infancy. On nights when the Garden had scheduled a college doubleheader, the New York Knicks were relegated to the small, dilapidated 69th Regiment Armory down on Twenty-Fifth Street; the college game was by far the bigger attraction. "The way college basketball draws," Garden promoter Ned Irish was once heard to say, "the Knicks are nothing but a tax write-off anyway."

When the game was over the players would return home on the subway, back to tenements and walk-up apartments and two-family houses in crowded, boisterous neighborhoods trimmed with ragged shrubbery, ringed by factories and pocked with empty lots. The City College players inhabited the same city as their fans—not the downtown city with its soaring stone skyscrapers but the New York of low-slung brown brick apartment houses and chained-in playgrounds and tiny candy stores where the proprietor was oftentimes happy to handle a bet on a local sporting event. They were a bunch of kids from the outer boroughs, not all of them poor but none of them rich, and together they achieved extraordinary, even unparalleled success. They were celebrated from one end of the city to the other, lauded in banner headlines, feted at testimonial banquets, invited onto radio programs, hailed by the mayor as "our athletes." For a while they seemed to embody the city's brightest hopes for itself—of racial harmony, civic virtue, the triumph of the outsider. Later, though, their names would appear on the front pages of the newspapers again, under equally astonishing circumstances, and almost overnight they came to represent only disappointment and disillusion. Once they had been the most celebrated basketball players in New York; now they were the most notorious.

For decades, members of the team would live in the shadow of scandal, building their lives away from the glare of public scrutiny, haunted by the notion that a potential employer had said no because he recognized a name, or that the whispering in the far corners of restaurants and cocktail parties was about them; forever after, most would maintain unlisted phone numbers. They lived with dignity but also with a lingering sense of shame and anger and frustration. Their story, they always believed, was far larger than they were.

That story begins, though, with basketball: in a small gymnasium in a college on a hill, where a head coach and his assistant are watching fifteen players practice. Overhead a spiderweb of steel trusses spans the entire ceiling, giving the room an industrial feel; gray afternoon light pours down from the Gothic windows, making bright rectangles on the varnished yellow hardwood. Sounds echo in the vaulted space, the gym almost silent but for the ragtag music of the game: an occasional grunt or exhalation of breath, the squeak of sneakers, the dull percussive thud of a ball being dribbled, and then a brief pause and the cymballine *swish* of the shot.

PART ONE

Harvard-on-Hudson

The George Washington Gate at the City College of New York, one of three such gates designed for the campus by architect George B. Post. Archives, The City College of New York, CUNY

CHAPTER 1

On a warm October afternoon, in the hours after a rain, the oldest buildings on the City College campus glisten and shimmer in the light. Their stone walls are heavy and dark and rough hewn, flecked throughout with crystalline mica (the same ingredient that gives sparkle to the city's sidewalks), and in a college open only to residents of New York City the stone itself is as local as can be, having spent the entirety of creation on that very spot.

In the latter years of the nineteenth century, the trustees of the College of the City of New York* realized that the school's rapidly growing population, then crammed into a single building downtown on Lexington Avenue, required a new, larger campus. A site was purchased on St. Nicholas Heights, a steep, rocky bluff overlooking western Harlem, where the wind sweeps in from the Hudson River, and in 1897 the commission was awarded to the distinguished New York architect George B. Post. Setting quickly to work, Post hit on an ingenious cost-saving measure: The Manhattan schist that would have to be excavated from the site, he realized, could be used to construct the buildings themselves. The college was thus to be made from its own bedrock, painstakingly quarried and shaped and raised into the sky, and the amount removed for the foundations turned out to be almost exactly the amount that was needed for the walls. "Nature herself seemed to have been aware that

---

* In 1927 the name was altered slightly, to the City College of New York.

the College of the City of New York was to locate there and provided accordingly," marveled the reviewer for *The American Architect and Building News*. "Had the rock been planned to order it could not have been better suited to the purpose."

After two years of design, three of delay, and four of construction, City College's new uptown campus finally opened in 1907. The campus that George Post had created—five large buildings grouped around a central quadrangle—was built in the style then known as Collegiate Gothic, a medieval dreamscape of turrets and gables and parapets, inscribed crests, arched doorways, and leaded glass in broad mullioned windows. Many of the excavated stones had emerged from the earth streaked and stained with rust; rather than set those aside, however, Post ordered that the most heavily discolored ones should be reserved for the exterior walls. It was a mandate that bewildered and maddened the Italian stonemasons who had been hired for the job, but Post was adamant, insisting that the imperfections would provide welcome variations in color and tone. Perhaps most striking of all, he had trimmed the dark-gray schist not in the more traditional fashion, with a lighter-colored stone such as lime or sandstone, but instead with smooth terra-cotta glazed the snowiest white. It was a daring choice, and little appreciated by the critics of the time. Writing in *The Architectural Record*, Montgomery Schuyler called Post's mix of materials "violent and disturbing" and "a serious blemish on the artistic result," and further expressed the hope that Manhattan's sooty air would eventually darken the terra-cotta. (In 1939, however, thirty-two years after CCNY opened its uptown campus, the *WPA Guide to New York City* reported: "The schist has aged and blackened, but the terra cotta remains a pristine white.")

Something else, though, is odd about that terra-cotta. A sharp-eyed observer walking past any of Post's original buildings will notice an unexpected assemblage of creatures cavorting on the trim overhead: gargoyles and grotesques, more than six hundred of them in all, dragons and owls and shrieking harpies, and a host of whimsical little men robed and cowled like medieval monks (or the scholarly ancestors of Disney's movie dwarfs), laughing, scowling, leering, beckoning with crooked fingers to the pedestrians below. George Post himself had overseen the design of all the grotesques; each was different, and each had been crafted to reflect the activities of the building on which it was placed. On the Chemistry Building the little men seem to be conducting experiments, stirring beakers and grinding ingredients with a mortar and pestle. The Mechanics Arts Building features laborers: They hammer and drill, beat on anvils, fan bellows; one struggles to turn a gigantic bolt that seems to be emerging from the building itself. In Wingate Hall, home of the school gymnasium, the front doorway is framed by a pair of recumbent lions, but the heroic effect at street level is undercut by the scene going on above, where a squad of grinning tumblers use the building's cornice as a kind of gymnastic bar, throwing themselves into a variety of acrobatic contortions.

Inside Wingate on this particular day, Wednesday, October 5, 1949, City College's basketball team was conducting its first practice of the season—an event scarcely noticed by the rest of the campus. Cars honked on rain-slicked Convent Avenue, the thoroughfare that bisected the campus; the ginkgo trees along the avenue were tinged now with

gold, their leaves like delicately tinted Japanese fans, providing a burst of color in a landscape otherwise mostly bare. The young men hurrying through the quadrangle wore cardigan sweaters and button-down shirts and pressed slacks; some of the older ones, mostly World War II veterans in school on the GI Bill, preferred jackets and ties. The women wore low-heeled pumps, and sweater sets with pleated skirts, bought at discount stores like Loehmann's or Alexander's in the Bronx or, downtown, Best & Company or S. Klein. Some of

City College students in conversation on the campus quadrangle in 1951. The Main Building rises in the background. Archives, The City College of New York, CUNY

the more scholarly-looking of the men wore horn-rimmed glasses in black or tortoiseshell, the women cat's-eye glasses in black or white or silver. Those who weren't on their way somewhere stood on the sidewalk in front of the Main Building, or in clusters by the statue of General Alexander Webb, hero of the Battle of Gettysburg and the college's second president. They tossed raincoats over their arms, looking up doubtfully at the unsettled sky; many of them smoked cigarettes and talked.

A reporter from *The Saturday Evening Post*, observing City College students a couple of years earlier, had written that a visitor to the campus "will hear them talking like social workers determined to correct all the injustices of a harsh world by next Tuesday." But that was just an easy quip meant for a middle-American readership; far more likely, a visitor on this afternoon would have heard them talking about parties or dates from the previous weekend, or about plans for the upcoming one. Several of the Brooklyn movie theaters were showing the Cary Grant comedy *I Was a Male War Bride;* afterward, if things went well, there might be a burger and a malted at Garfield's cafeteria or a slice of cheesecake at Junior's. Up in the Bronx, the Ritz was showing *My Favorite Brunette,* another good date film, while guys who were on their own could catch Jimmy Cagney in *White Heat* at the Fordham. Some of the students likely talked about the latest news of the mayoral race (William O'Dwyer, the Democrat, seemed to be cruising to reelection), or, if their families owned a television set, the Milton Berle show from the night before, or perhaps their classes or one of the lectures upcoming that week. Professor Henry Leffert's comparative literature class was always popular; later that month there would be a lecture titled "Novels of the Forties" by a promising young writer named Gore Vidal. (Professor Leffert was himself a notable figure on the campus. He wore a beret, collected modern art, and frequented the opera and the ballet, and though he was a fierce advocate of higher culture he also admitted to reading the novels of Mickey Spillane. When a student once asked him why, he replied, "Well, it's good to see how the other half lives. After all, there are so many of you.")

Surely much of the talk, too, was about the first game of the World Series, played in Yankee Stadium earlier that afternoon between the Yankees and the Dodgers. The game had been a tense, tautly contested pitchers' duel—scoreless until the bottom of the ninth—and for those two and a half hours the city had come almost to a halt. Commuters on their way to Grand Central or Penn Station missed their trains to duck into a local tavern to drink a beer and watch the game; in the garment district, racks of dresses and furs clogged sidewalks, left there by shipping clerks clustered around radios in the doorways of office buildings. For days, most of the papers had been running previews of the Series not on the sports pages but the front page; the headline of that morning's *Daily Mirror* had read YANKEES 3 TO 2 TO WIN OPENER. It seemed to no one especially remarkable that one of the city's major newspapers would devote its front page to a presentation of the latest gambling odds.

That was the way things were in New York in 1949.

From the tiled sidewalk near the entrance to the Main Building came a distinctive squawk; it belonged to a man whose name was Raymond Haber but who was known to everyone on campus simply as Raymond the Bagel Man. A squat figure wearing a long white apron and cloth flat cap, Raymond was never seen without the rickety wooden pushcart that he piled high with a single product, a combination bagel and pretzel of his own invention. He hawked his "pragels" to all who passed by, extolling their virtues with a string of random adjectives that combined to make a kind of bebop scat. "They're homogenized, radiatized, ostracized!" he would cry in a raspy voice. "Liberally sprinkled with cerebral salts!"

Many of the students rushing into the Main Building were carrying stacks of textbooks, the economizing among them having bought the books downtown at a Fifth Avenue store specializing in used textbooks, called Barnes & Noble. Late on a Wednesday afternoon, they might have been heading to a four o'clock session of analytic geometry, or perhaps chemistry, or public speaking. Every student who attended City College was required to take no fewer than four terms of public speaking, the first course being Vocal Expression, in which, the course bulletin indicated, "speech that is careless or too narrowly provincial is corrected, and a clear, easy, unaffected American English encouraged." Everyone understood what that really meant: to extirpate, as much as was possible, the "Noo Yawk" from the speech of the school's young New Yorkers.

Even in 1949, City College's primary mission remained what it was when the school moved its main campus uptown in 1907: to assimilate and to elevate—to take the brightest of New York's high school students whose families could not afford to send them to a private college and to provide them, free of charge, with an undergraduate education equal to any in the nation. Unlike the schools of the Ivy League, most of which favored the children of alumni and maintained strict ethnic quotas, entrance to City College was resolutely meritocratic, open to any high school student who had achieved a sufficiently high grade point average and passed a rigorous entrance exam. (Of course that meritocracy, it must be said, was itself for many years discriminatory: Women were barred from City College until 1930, and for many years afterward they were segregated almost entirely in the School of Education, the area of study deemed most appropriate for the female student. Women were not permitted into the general program of study for the College of Liberal Arts and Sciences until 1951.) City College was the sort of place where the inked markings on the wooden tables of the cafeteria, left there by generations of former students, were not initials or declarations of love but mathematical formulas. "Probably no group of college students of comparable size has a higher level of academic aptitude," declared a report on CCNY chaired by a professor at Columbia University, which seemed only to confirm the boastful wisecrack sometimes heard around St. Nicholas Heights: that when a City College student flunked out and transferred elsewhere, he raised the academic level of both places.

City College was commonly referred to as "the working-class Harvard," "the Harvard of the Proletariat," or simply as "Harvard-on-Hudson." The most important difference between the two schools, of course—as Samuel Middlebrook, a City College professor, once noted—"may be a matter of which end of the family tree you represent: Are you the roots of a family's prestige, as at CCNY; or are you its fruits, ripening in the quadrangles of New Haven or Cambridge?" As late as 1944, the last time anyone had measured this, nearly half the fathers of City College students were classified by New York City under the rubric "unskilled laborers, on relief, unemployed, not living with the family, or deceased"; only 17 percent of the fathers, and 23 percent of the mothers, had even been born in the United States.

Those who attended City traced their arrival at the country's shores not in centuries to the *Mayflower* but in years or decades to an immigrant ship, to a landing site that was not Plymouth Rock in Massachusetts but Ellis Island in New York Harbor. With admission to City College,

the process of upward social mobility that might otherwise have required a generation or more could now be accomplished in only a few
years, and it's not hard to imagine the sense of wonder that must have
coursed through a mother or father who had come to the United States
in the belly of an immigrant ship, who had dreamed simply of escaping
the crowded streets of the Lower East Side for the slightly less crowded
streets of Brooklyn or the Bronx, who now walked with a child through
the high iron gates of City College, beneath the arch inscribed with the
Latin motto RESPICE, ADSPICE, PROSPICE ("Look to the past, look to the
present, look to the future"), into a cluster of Gothic halls where, but for
the tenements lining the nearby streets, one might imagine oneself in
Oxford or Cambridge.

In *World of Our Fathers,* his magisterial account of the lives of Eastern European Jewish immigrants, Irving Howe (CCNY class of 1940)
described the deep attachment that New York's Jews felt toward City
College: "Of all the institutions they or their children might encounter
in the new world, City College came closest to fulfilling Emerson's prom-
ise that 'this country, the last found, is the great charity of God to the
human race.'" The school's Jewish students, Howe observed, "loved the
place, loved it utterly, hopelessly, blindly." Here was a college that didn't
care what religion they practiced (or didn't practice), didn't care how
little money they had. Moreover, the college seemed to prize the attri-
butes that they themselves prized, scholarship and argumentation; and,
most remarkably, it would reward the most bookish among them with a
tuition-free education. City College had been founded in 1847 for the
sons of the city's merchant class, but the mass Jewish immigration that
began in the late nineteenth century changed the school's composition
utterly and forever: As early as 1903, when the college still occupied a
single building downtown, upward of 75 percent of the student body
was Jewish. By the 1930s the number was closer to 90 percent, and the
joke making the rounds was that CCNY stood for Circumcised Citizens
of New York. (Others preferred "Christian College Now Yiddish.")

In those years City College had, in the words of one historian, "the
most militant student body of any college at the time," and indeed another nickname for City in those years was "the Little Red Schoolhouse."
The college's cafeteria, it was often said in jest and tribute, was the only
place in the world where a Trotskyite could freely debate a Stalinist. On

leather-covered benches in the little alcoves that ringed the room, the debates would rage for hours (often, as in a relay race, one of the arguers would pass off his side to a companion so that he could attend class and return later), working through the implications of the Moscow Trials or the French Popular Front, parsing the finer points of the latest New Deal program or Comintern dictate. The more skillful of the debaters would draw crowds several deep, the onlookers murmuring and nudging one another in admiration whenever an especially well-delivered point was made, as they might at a schoolyard basketball game. Thus did innumerable City College students educate themselves and their classmates, in heated debates or long, digressive conversations over a chessboard or one of the games of bridge or pinochle that went on no matter the hour, and decades later many City College alumni would say, looking back on their undergraduate career, that in truth they had majored in cafeteria.

Despite the grandeur of George B. Post's original buildings, entering its fifth decade, much of the City College campus had taken on a worn, dingy quality, the inevitable outcome of too many students crammed into too small a space for too many hours a day. In the intervening years the college had purchased a few of the buildings that surrounded the campus to house academic departments and had moved the business students into an office building downtown, but still the campus was not nearly sufficient for an enrollment that now numbered more than 34,000, making City the third-largest academic institution in the world. A writer for *Newsweek* once calculated that City College provided 98 square feet per student, which might seem sufficient until one noticed that in comparison, the number at Princeton was 15,672.

Throughout the college, the electrical system ran on direct current generated by the school's own antiquated dynamo, and a light turned on anywhere on campus hesitated for several seconds, as though considering its options, and then cast only a dim, flickering glow. "The college's lighting system," admitted the school's director of planning and design, "is not only inadequate, but has constituted a positive menace to the eyesight of our students, faculty and administrative workers." The heating system, too, was original to Post, and much of the school day was carried on alongside a cacophony of banging pipes and hissing radiators; the classrooms always seemed too warm, no matter the weather outside, and in the winter months the locker room at the stadium was so cold that the student athletes referred to it as Pneumonia Gulch. In a basement lavatory of Townsend Harris Hall, some enterprising reporters for the *Observation Post*, one of the school's student newspapers, had measured the water streaming from taps at 167 degrees Fahrenheit, and with it had successfully parboiled a couple of eggs.

That profile of City College in *The Saturday Evening Post* had been titled "College Without Frills or Fun," and in truth, CCNY offered not much in the way of typical campus life. For one thing, almost no one actually lived on campus: The college provided only a few dozen dorm rooms, mostly reserved for returning veterans. Most of the school's students arrived after a lengthy ride by bus or subway—or, for students coming from more far-flung neighborhoods, bus *and* subway—and as no permanent lockers were available, they had to schlep their coats and textbooks and paper-bag lunches around with them as they proceeded, burdened like peddlers, from class to class, until they returned home at the end of the day; many of them also worked part-time jobs, which further reduced the time available for extracurricular activities such as clubs or sports.

There was a stadium at City College, where the baseball and football teams played; Lewisohn Stadium* was one of the architectural glories of the campus, a vast amphitheater in the classical Greek style, ringed by sixty-four Doric columns. The athletic events that went on there, though, were always something of an afterthought—Lewisohn was far better known for the hundred or so concerts held there each year, where for as little as twenty-five cents New Yorkers could listen to the Philharmonic Orchestra or the Metropolitan Opera Company perform under the stars. Marian Anderson and Lily Pons sang arias inside Lewisohn Stadium, Jascha Heifetz played the violin there, and George Gershwin introduced a new composition he had just written, called *Rhapsody in*

---

* Named for the philanthropist Adolph Lewisohn, the stadium was not built until 1915, eight years after the rest of the school. In his review of George Post's new campus in *The Architectural Record*, Montgomery Schuyler lamented the lack of both a school library and an athletic field, though the latter omission seemed to him a bit more understandable—because, after all, so many of the college's students were Jewish: "The all work and no play which makes Jack a dull boy does not seem to have the same effect on Abraham."

Blue, accompanying the orchestra himself on piano. (Among those who regularly attended the performances were the jazz greats Thelonious Monk, Dizzy Gillespie, and Ben Webster; recalled another member of the group, Milt Hinton, "On Sunday nights we'd go to Lewisohn Stadium when the symphonic session was on. 'We're going to church,' we used to say.") The concerts attracted as many as twenty thousand spectators, who filled the stadium's twenty-four tiers of stone benches and many more temporary rows of seats set up on the playing field. One of the college's baseball or football games might draw, on a good day, perhaps a few hundred.

At its best the City College baseball team was undistinguished; the football team was, by general acclaim, the worst in the country. *Life* magazine once observed that "almost any good Nebraska high school team can beat City at football," and if anything, that seems a bit of an understatement. From 1943 through 1946 the CCNY football team ran off a string of twenty-three consecutive defeats; in a long, dismal history the year 1944 was a special low, as the team finished the season not only without a win but without having managed to score a single point. At the beginning of the 1950 football season a popular City College student by the name of Milton Luchan set up a tent in front of the school flagpole and vowed to stay there until the team won a game. Luchan had packed a suitcase with all of the essentials, from toothbrush and vitamins to a pair of long johns he had dyed lavender, the school color. Within the week, though, the college dean had ordered the tent to be taken down, not only, as he put it, to preserve the dignity of the school, but also out of concern for Milton's health: Given the football team's history, the administration did not think he should remain outside for the entire winter.

The football team inspired jokes, the baseball team not much of anything at all. Still, even at a subway school like City College, where rah-rah college spirit was at a minimum, there was one team that for a time united the school more than anything else athletic or academic or political ever did, that managed to gladden the hearts of even those students who otherwise cared nothing for sports. It was the team that spent afternoons in the gym inside Wingate Hall, where the little men on the terra-cotta performed their elaborate contortions. "Our best sports," recalled one graduate, "basketball and talk, were indoor."

CHAPTER 2

The success of the City College basketball team, almost everyone on campus believed, could be attributed to one man: the team's long-time head coach, Nat Holman. By 1949 Holman was widely considered to be the greatest basketball player who had ever lived. "He was more than just a star," note the authors of a history of American street basketball. "Holman shaped the sport in much the same way Beethoven shaped the evolution of music: He routinely did the unthinkable, making the impossible suddenly seem possible."

Holman had learned the game as a boy on the streets of Manhattan's Lower East Side, playing one-on-one against other neighborhood kids in the Seward Park playground for a nickel or a dime or sometimes an ice-cream cone; by the age of fourteen he had joined a club called the Roosevelt Big Five, where he played in gyms and dance halls in the Adirondacks, Catskills, and Berkshires for six dollars a night. At Commerce High School, in addition to starring for the basketball team, he pitched and played second base for the baseball team, halfback for the football team, and goalie for the soccer team; even a century later, he remains the only person in the history of New York City high schools to be named All-City in four sports. From 1921 through 1929, he was the featured player for the Original Celtics, a touring team that over the course of Holman's career compiled a staggering record of 720 wins against only 75 losses. When he first signed with the Celtics he was paid $12,500 for the season, which at the time was more money than anyone had ever received for playing basketball. Over the years his hard-wood feats assumed a certain legendary quality, such as the night in Fort Wayne, Indiana, when Holman blew kisses to jeering fans with one hand while sinking the winning free throw with the other. The story was often told of how Holman, as a young head coach, was short a man at practice and suited up to scrimmage with his players; a scout for one of CCNY's upcoming opponents, sitting in the bleachers, watched the practice for a while and then sent a wire to his team's coach. City College was going to be very tough, the scout warned, because "they have the greatest forward I've ever seen on a college team."

Nat Holman was one of those rare sports figures who evolve from athlete into icon; throughout the 1930s and 1940s he appeared in magazine advertisements for products such as Wheaties cereal, Lifebuoy soap, and Planters peanuts, in all of which he is presented as a paragon of basketball and, more generally, of clean, healthy living. ("Take a tip from Nat Holman—drink Cocomalt for a strong and sturdy body.") A 1944 photograph taken during a War Bond rally at New York's Waldorf-Astoria Hotel presents a tableau of American sports heroes from the early decades of the twentieth century. The participants had been asked to come in the attire of their respective sports, and so, among others, Babe Ruth has on the Yankee pinstripes, golfer Gene Sarazen a sweater and tweed knickers, Sid Luckman a football warm-up outfit, and Eleanor Holm a two-piece swimsuit. Representing basketball, in his

A typical magazine advertisement featuring City College head coach Nat Holman, this one for Vitalis Hair Tonic and its "60-Second Workout." Archives, The City College of New York, CUNY

Celtics pullover, gym shorts, and black high-top sneakers, is Nat Holman.

Unmarried until nearly fifty, Holman was single-minded about basketball and indifferent, even oblivious, to much of the rest of daily life. (His nephew Bruce recalls one incident when Nat asked him to come over and fix his record player, which he could not get to work; upon arrival Bruce immediately saw that it was simply unplugged.) When Holman appeared on the cover of *Newsweek* he was identified as Mr. Basketball, the nickname by which he was known to fans throughout the country. For his own part Holman preferred a different moniker, the Master, and sometimes used it when referring to himself: "The Master was proud of you tonight, boys," Holman might say to his players after a victory. "He couldn't have done it better himself."

Anyone talking basketball with Nat Holman was immediately struck by what Stanley Frank, a writer and City College alumnus, called his "natural assumption of superiority." New York's sportswriters revered Holman as an icon of the sport and often went to him for quotes; still, while they might be mildly amused when he would receive them at home wearing a smoking jacket and puffing on a pipe—there weren't many basketball coaches who could pull off that effect—they also bristled at the imperious tone he often adopted in interviews: He seemed less to be answering questions than conducting a lecture. Leonard Ansell, the basketball writer for *The Sun,* once observed that Holman "sometimes gives the impression he is perpetually posing for a portrait," while Jimmy Cannon, the dean of the city's sportswriters, complained in a *New York Post* column that Holman addressed him as though he were the audience at an alumni banquet.

In 1949, Holman had been the head basketball coach at the City College of New York for thirty years. When he first took the job, in 1919 (for the next fourteen years he continued to play professional basketball on the side), he was twenty-three years old, the youngest college basketball coach in the nation; now he was fifty-three, but everyone who met him for the first time invariably remarked that he looked as if he could still play. Trim and handsome and dapper, with perfectly coiffed salt-and-pepper hair and a jutting jaw, Holman dressed in tailored double-breasted suits always accessorized with crisply folded pocket squares. Though he had been born to a poor Jewish grocer on the Lower East

Side, he spoke in the honeyed tones of a romantic leading man, with broad *a*'s and a broguish roll to his *r*'s. In a typical phrase such as "our game against St. John's," the second word would be drawn out to *geem*, the third into *agaynst*. His players, who had little experience in parsing upper-class distinctions, usually referred to Holman's diction simply as British, but in fact it was closer to that of the homegrown boarding-school aristocracy, the transatlantic accent most closely associated in the public mind with President Franklin D. Roosevelt. Holman's older brother Jack, with whom Nat owned a summer camp, enjoyed making fun of this particular affectation. "Where did he get this phony accent?" he would ask friends with a laugh. "I grew up in the same neighborhood he did."

Nathan "Noosty" Holman, who had grown up in a tenement on Norfolk Street where the toilet was in the hallway, was now Nat Holman, who lived in a high-rise apartment house on Madison Avenue and could walk hardly a block without being greeted by a stranger or asked for his autograph. In April 1947, Holman was scheduled to appear as a celebrity contestant on the WOR radio show *Twenty Questions*. A few days before the show his nephew Alexander came over for a family visit; at one point he went looking for something in the apartment and noticed on his uncle's desk a card on which was scrawled *Rose of Washington Square*, the title of a movie musical that had been popular several years earlier. Alexander didn't ask about it, but he was not surprised when, later that week, *Rose of Washington Square* turned out to be the answer to one of the questions—an answer that, to all indications, had been provided to Holman ahead of time. His uncle, Alexander understood, was not going to appear on that show without being forearmed; Nat Holman, who had so painstakingly cultivated his own image, would do almost anything to avoid looking a fool.

In his thirty years as head basketball coach of City College, Nat Holman had compiled an impressive 359–127 record. In that time, though, the college had gotten no closer to a national championship than an opening round victory in the National Invitation Tournament in 1941. In both the 1942–43 and 1943–44 seasons the team had endured losing records, the first of Holman's career, and around town one began to hear whispers that Mr. Basketball had lost his edge, that the game was passing him by. Holman's was a style of basketball he'd learned on small courts in low-ceilinged gymnasiums, played by men rarely more than six feet tall; it was a game of feinting, screens, and constant passing. The jump shot had not yet been invented, and most players used a two-handed set shot in which the ball was pushed from chest level; that was an easy shot for a defender to block, so a player usually needed to be unguarded to get the shot off. Without a shot clock to compel a team to shoot within a prescribed length of time,* a team could patiently pass the ball around, probing the defense until one of the players had worked himself free for a shot.

More than anything else, Nat Holman abhorred careless play, and he was deeply suspicious of the new style of running basketball that had transformed the college game. The fast break—in which an offense rushes the ball upcourt, trying to shoot before the defenders can get into position—brought many more scoring opportunities but also many more turnovers; it was the antithesis of Holman's deliberate style, and he resisted it with the furious, losing energy of a householder bailing as the floodwaters rise around him. During those difficult years, *Sport* magazine once noted, Holman "had many a brush with impetuous youngsters who felt he was too old-fashioned, too set in his ways, too prone to dismiss everything new as foolish and unreliable." Yet as the 1940s moved along, City College's fans began to notice that something unexpected had happened: The team was beginning to incorporate the fast break into its offense. At the end of the 1946–47 season, City College finished strongly enough to receive its first invitation to the National Collegiate Athletic Association tournament, and two years later, to the National Invitation Tournament. As the 1949–50 season began, Nat Holman seemed to have regained his touch.

• • •

* The NBA first adopted a 24-second shot clock in the 1954–55 season. Men's college basketball did not begin using a shot clock until 1984, when a 45-second clock was introduced.

For the first practice of the year the players wore gray CCNY T-shirts, dark gym shorts, and black high-top canvas sneakers, mostly the Spalding Double-S model or the Chuck Taylors made by Converse.* Nat Holman wore a fresh white T-shirt, pressed slacks, and black-and-white saddle shoes rather than sneakers. A silver referee's whistle dangled around his neck; it was an Acme Thunderer, the best that could be bought, but often, when he saw something he didn't like, he simply put two fingers to his mouth and unleashed a shrill whistle, at which point the gym grew immediately still. "What are you *doing?*" he would cry, gray eyes flashing, and then dart over to the offending player. "Right way," he would say, demonstrating the correct technique, "wrong way. Right way, wrong way."

In a corner of the gym, intently watching the action, stood the team's assistant coach, Bobby Sand. Sand had heavy eyebrows and a round face like a fellow City College graduate, Edward G. Robinson; he had a perpetual five o'clock shadow (he had begun shaving even before his bar mitzvah), and his clothes, no matter how new or recently ironed, always seemed rumpled. At five foot seven he was shorter than the young men he coached, and stockier, and his voice was redolent of his Brooklyn upbringing, in which the game they played was "*bask*-uh-ball," and Madison Square Garden was located on "Fawty-Ninth" Street. He read voraciously, everything from monographs on agricultural credit (the subject of his Columbia doctoral dissertation) to Transcendentalist essays and hard-boiled detective stories; he also had a prodigious memory, be it for languages—he was fluent in five and could read four more—or economic statistics or whatever other subject happened to interest him and could be broken down into discrete bits of information. Sand was himself a former City College basketball player, a member of the 1937–38 team nicknamed the Mighty Midgets. Basketball had been an official sport at City College since 1905, and in the intervening

---

* In 1921 the Converse Rubber Shoe Company of Malden, Massachusetts, had offered Nat Holman fifty dollars a month to make appearances for the company in sporting goods stores. Holman declined, and the offer was subsequently made to another professional basketball player, Chuck Taylor. Taylor proved to be an outstanding sneaker salesman, eventually becoming so identified with the Converse brand that the company put his name on the sneakers.

years hundreds of young men had played for the varsity team; yet in all that time, only a single City College basketball player had ever been elected to the Phi Beta Kappa society, and that was Bobby Sand.

As an undergraduate, Sand had majored in economics, and after graduation he went on to earn a master's degree in education. In 1940 the economics department hired him to teach an introductory section of American economic history; that year, newly married, he and his wife, Sylvia, moved with her parents and her brother into a small apartment in the Brownsville section of Brooklyn. They made do as best they could, but before long they had a new anxiety: Sylvia's health went into decline. She started having heart problems, the aftermath of several childhood bouts of rheumatic fever; she was often fatigued and was constantly in and out of doctors' offices. In 1943 Sylvia gave birth to their first child, Wendie. At the age of six months, Wendie was stricken with tuberculosis, which eventually cleared up but left her with severely weakened lungs, and for a long time afterward it seemed that every time she caught a cold it turned into pneumonia and she ended up in a hospital oxygen tent.

A 1947 profile in the City College student newspaper *The Campus* called Bobby Sand "one of the few men here who is [*sic*] admired and respected by students and faculty alike." Smiling and amiable, Sand was a familiar, comforting presence around City College; the word everyone used to describe him was *mensch*. By the fall of 1949, though, he was a man stretched very thin. He was thirty-two years old—a bit slump-shouldered now—and he had an invalid wife and a sickly daughter, with whom he tried to spend as much time as he could. In the mornings, before he left for school, he set out Wendie's clothes and made her breakfast with orange juice that he squeezed by hand; sometimes, when Sylvia was feeling especially tired, he brought Wendie with him, seating her in the back of the classroom as he lectured. Many days, when basketball practice was over, he would race downtown to the business campus for an evening-session class before finally heading home to Brooklyn for the next day's class preparation and a few hours' sleep.

On the subway he would take out the yellow legal pad he always carried in his briefcase and design plays, the pages growing dark with penciled swirls of arrows and squares and triangles. It was Bobby Sand, of course, who had finally convinced Nat Holman that the team needed to incorporate the fast break. Indeed, he had developed theories on every imaginable aspect of the game: the five times when dribbling should be used, the three most dangerous scoring positions for the pivot man, the basic principles of movement to maintain proper spacing on the court. At home, eating an orange, he'd move pits and pieces of peel around on the counter, lost in thought; he was working out long progressions of moves, imagining the opponents' responses for each and the most effective counterresponse in turn, like a chess player trying to read the future from the position of the board.

During varsity games Sand sat next to Holman on the bench, scribbling notes for him while also devising the team's game strategy: when to press on defense, when to run and when to stall, even which players to put on the floor. It was common knowledge among City College basketball players (though not among the public at large) that Bobby Sand suggested most of the team's substitutions. "I think it's time for that guy to come out, Nat," he would murmur to him on the bench—just loud enough, amid the roar of the arena, for only Holman to hear.

Unlike most of the other leading basketball coaches in New York, Nat Holman did not involve himself in high school recruitment; that task had now fallen primarily to Bobby Sand—and so whenever he could, he haunted the gyms and playgrounds where the best players competed, leaning for hours on the chain-link fence at Lincoln Terrace Park in Brooklyn, at Creston Junior High in the Bronx, on the Colonel Young playground in Harlem, sitting in the bleachers of the YMCAs and the YMHAs. He was looking for intelligent, aggressive players, players who moved well without the ball, who would rather pass than shoot and were willing to work hard on defense: those who refused to play a schoolyard game even in a schoolyard.

Each year, Sand seemed to bring in ever more talented players, culminating in the freshman team of 1948–49, which, everyone agreed, had been the best recruiting class in the college's history. Right from the start he could see that these players had the chance to be something special. If they worked hard, Sand had told them, and sacrificed, and were willing to play as a team, when they graduated they would represent the United States in Helsinki, at the 1952 Olympic Games.* "Nobody believed him," one of the players on the freshman team would recall. "None of us could rise to that thought. But Bobby saw it as clear as day."

Four of the players on that freshman team had been especially promising, and now, as sophomores, they had graduated to the varsity.

Floyd Layne was six foot three and gangly, all arms and legs, a whirlwind on defense; he wore kneepads when he played, because in guarding his man he sometimes got so low that his knees actually scraped the floor. He had large eyes in a narrow, angular face, and a smile that lit up the gym.

Broad and barrel-chested, Al Roth was known to everyone as Fats, a name that he had picked up on the junior high schoolyard and that had followed him ever since. He wore his hair brushed back in a pompadour, and he had the eyes of a playmaker, cool, always seeming to calculate the angles.

Ed Warner was the most muscular member of the team, with sinewy legs and impressively developed biceps. He was the only one of the players who wore a mustache, and he had thick eyebrows and a long nose in a round, pleasant face that would quickly cloud when he felt he had been crossed. An orphan, he lived with two of his aunts in a dilapidated tenement across West 135th Street—a short walk but a world away from the Gothic towers of City College.

Ed Roman stood six feet six inches tall and weighed, at least officially, 225 pounds. He had a pear-shaped body, narrow across the shoulders and very broad in the beam, and a distinctively large-featured face with a poor complexion. He looked nothing at all like an athlete, until he held a basketball in his hands.

Bobby Sand watched them practice and wondered how they would adjust to life on the varsity. As freshmen they had been known only to their teammates and some of their more basketball-mad classmates;

---

* At that time the United States Olympic basketball team was put together primarily from two teams, each of which had won its bracket in the Olympic qualifying tournament. One bracket consisted of the nation's four top college teams; the other bracket was made up of the two finalists from the American Athletic Union and the two finalists from the YMCA national tournament.

now their names and pictures would be in all the papers, their strengths and shortcomings dissected after each game. If they did poorly they would be booed and heckled, just as any of the pro players were. And if they played well enough to be invited to one of the two postseason tournaments, they would be competing against serious basketball programs, with recruiters who were able to make the sorts of offers to high school students that Sand, at City College, never could.

The more prestigious of the two competitions, the National Invitation Tournament, was held each year at the beginning of March in Madison Square Garden; a week after the NIT concluded, the National Collegiate Athletic Association began its tournament. It was possible for a team to be invited to both, but that had happened only four times, most recently with the University of Kentucky, which during the previous season had lost in the quarterfinal round of the NIT before going on to win the NCAA championship.

Indeed, in the four seasons from 1945–46 through 1948–49, Kentucky had won the NIT championship once and the NCAA championship twice, compiling over that time a record of 130 wins against only 10 losses. The team's head coach, Adolph Rupp, had called the 1947–48 team "the greatest team ever assembled in college sport," but now he was telling friends around Lexington that the current one might be even better.

No team had ever accomplished college basketball's Grand Slam—winning both the NIT and the NCAA tournaments in the same year—but if anyone was going to do it, the smart money was on Kentucky.

A major part of Adolph Rupp's confidence stemmed from the fact that the University of Kentucky now had possibly the most dominant center in the nation, a seven-foot sophomore by the name of Bill Spivey. Spivey, though, was by no means the only imposing big man on the horizon. Closer to home, City College's most formidable intracity rivals were St. John's University and Long Island University (which, despite its name, was located in Brooklyn). At center, St. John's had a six-foot-six sophomore named Bob Zawoluk, who was so central to the team's offense that coach Frank McGuire would admit to a reporter, "When I have to take Bobby out, I'd like them to douse the Garden lights and let us play in the dark." LIU's center, Sherman White, stood six foot eight and was widely considered to be the most promising young player in America.

Now, at last, City College had a big man too; if City was going to advance through the postseason, it would be up to Eddie Roman to hold his own against the best other teams had to offer. "It's more or less an established fact among the basketball cult that Eddie Roman holds the balance of power for the 1949–50 cagers," wrote Dick Kaplan, the sports columnist for one of City College's student newspapers, the *Observation Post*. Before the season began, Nat Holman gave an interview to Leonard Ansell of the New York *Sun*. While admitting that he was "concerned over Roman's stamina and the fact he is unnaturally heavy in the seat," Holman praised his deft shooting, his unselfishness, and his court savvy; Roman, he declared, would be "the wheel upon which we will work."

Or, as Kaplan cleverly summarized the situation: "All roads lead to Roman."

CHAPTER 3

In the fall of 1945, Eddie Roman was fifteen years old and, with one exception, was much like all of the other sophomores wandering the halls of William Howard Taft High School in the Bronx. He had grown up, as they had, with nighttime air raid drills, rooms darkened and shades pulled down tight while, outside, searchlights roamed the sky; and gold-star banners that hung like crepe in the front windows of houses where a son had been lost; and maps in *The New York Times* with heavy black arrows tracking the progress of the war; and the raucous impromptu V-J Day parade that had snake-danced its way down the Grand Concourse to the sound of church bells, the girls kissing every soldier in sight.

The Bronx, with nearly one and a half million residents, often seemed like a small town. Eddie noshed on cold cuts from the delicatessen and cupcakes from the bakery, boxed up and tied with red-and-white string pulled so tight it could be plucked like a guitar. He bought chocolate marshmallow strips and licorice at a candy store a block from his house. (Almost every block had its own candy store—"Oh, I know that guy," one kid might say of another, "he lives three candy stores down.") Sometimes on weekends he went to the movies, and afterward ate banana splits with his pals at the Sugar Bowl; weeknights he did his homework at the dining room table, big band music playing from the kitchen radio. He worked as an aide in the high school biology lab and cheered the blue and gold at pep rallies. His homeroom teacher had a

Delaney card that Eddie had filled out with his name and address on the first day of school, his card lined up in an alphabetized row in the daily attendance book, just like all of his classmates'.

There was, though, one thing that differentiated Eddie Roman from everyone else in the school: He stood six feet four inches tall, and, to all indications, he was still growing.

Eddie had always been large—not just tall, but *large*. He had large hands, and large feet, and large ears, and a rear end that his City College teammate Floyd Layne laughingly described as "the biggest keister you ever saw." He and his parents and his two brothers lived on the downstairs floor of a brown-shingled two-family house on Teller Avenue, the second in a row of five identical houses. The house seemed too small for someone his size, and inside Eddie was often bumping into things, his hip accidentally grazing a table or chair as he went by. By high school Eddie had already developed the stoop-shouldered walk of many big men self-conscious about their height, wanting not to call attention to themselves. He had blue eyes and a crooked nose and wavy black hair that he brushed straight back from a forehead often dotted with pimples; his voice in those years was slightly nasal, the result of a sinus problem that caused his nose to run all the time. He had narrow shoulders that widened out to broad hips and powerful thighs; the top half of his body seemed out of proportion to the bottom, and later on, in regard to his unusual shape, his college teammates would playfully dub him Goose, a nickname that he always disliked and that he eventually persuaded them to stop using.

Eddie was soft-spoken and friendly (one journalist would use the phrase "genial giant" in writing about him) and everyone agreed that he was intelligent, and certainly dedicated to his studies; he would work till all hours of the night, unwilling to hand in an assignment until he could find nothing left to improve. Starting in his sophomore year at Taft, Eddie was moved into advanced placement classes, and in his four years of high school he would earn a cumulative average of 87, which was excellent for his time and far better than was necessary to gain entrance to City College, where the minimum grade average required for acceptance was usually about 81. With his friends he had a big grin and a braying laugh, but outside his immediate circle he tended to be shy and self-conscious, especially around girls, and though his friends often encouraged him to date, he never had a girlfriend in high school. On weekends, instead, he and a few of his buddies might shoot pool or eat hot dogs in front of the deli, joking and laughing for hours (Eddie's imitation of Frankenstein's monster was thought to be especially hilarious); most of the time he hung around with guys who were louder than he was, more self-confident, more successful with girls, as though some of their swagger might rub off on him. Says Ron Schechter, one of his closest friends from that period: "Some of us would steal a piece of halvah off the counter, or a Nestlé's bar, or walk out of the deli without paying, and Eddie was the guy who would stand there and say, 'Hey, you gotta pay for that! You're gonna get me in trouble.' Of all the guys that we hung with, he was really the only hundred-percent honest guy. Everybody else had a bit of larceny in them."

One day in a hallway of Taft High School, Marty Force, the school's interim basketball coach, happened to notice the immense kid with the shambling gait. The Taft basketball team—known as the Presidents—won more often than it lost, but that was primarily due to the excellence of the team's star, Irwin Dambrot. Now, though, Dambrot was in his senior year and the team would need to replace him as best they could. Force called Eddie into his office and suggested that he join the basketball team, telling him, "I can make a ballplayer out of you."

He wouldn't play that year, the coach explained, though he anticipated that eventually Eddie would. "But there are two things," Marty Force warned him. "It's going to be difficult—you're going to have to work very hard. The second thing is that people are going to laugh at you. Eventually you'll get to the point where they'll realize that you're a good player, but in the beginning they'll laugh. I want you to think about it and tell me what you decide."

Eddie had never been especially athletic, beyond the games of curb ball in which all of the neighborhood boys took part. Once when he was twelve, the gym teacher had made the class line up on the basketball court and shoot free throws. Though he had barely touched a basketball before, Eddie sank five in a row, one right after the other. It was a remarkable thing, but instead, the other boys laughed at him; he had done it, they teased, only because he was so tall—he had an unfair advantage because he was so much closer to the basket. (That hurt never entirely went away: Even years later, long after he had established himself in basketball, he would make a couple of free throws and his mind would flash back to that afternoon and he would wonder if those in the crowd still felt that way about him.) Now Eddie began to consider the possibility that through basketball he might turn a deficit into an asset, make a name for himself in his school, and in so doing silence the remarks he had long endured, the endless unfunny variations on "How's the weather up there?" The next day he returned to the gym and said to Marty Force, "I'll do it."

So Eddie Roman joined the Taft Presidents in his sophomore year, and the perfectionism that he had brought to his schoolwork he now applied to basketball. Every day when practice was over Eddie would remain in the gym, the school having long since emptied out, practicing one thing that the coach had shown them that afternoon, repeating the action over and over again, sometimes with a friend, much of the time by himself. Taking a shot, he would hold his arms out in front of him, the basketball balanced lightly on the fingertips of his right hand, his left hand resting on the ball, acting as a kind of guide; then his knees would bend slightly, like a spring tensing, and the shot would be released from just above his right temple, the ball lofted into the air with a deceptively gentle flick of his wrist. Sometimes he practiced jump shooting, though he could never get very high in the air and his legs splayed out at crazy angles beneath him. He began to develop a hook shot—as a big man he knew he had to have this—his back to the basket and his arm describing an arc above him like a lever. From the pivot he also worked on a turnaround shot, one quick dribble and then the spin, adjusting his footwork until it became a kind of pirouette; eventually he found that he could often make a shot without even looking at the basket, just from knowing where he was on the court. Sometimes, when he had a ball in his hands, he felt almost graceful.

Weekends he practiced in the playground of his old elementary school, PS 53, where the backboard was screwed directly into the brick wall of the building. Other times he played in the schoolyard of Creston Junior High, the very spot where he had first been laughed at when shooting free throws; there the baskets were just rims, the nets having long since disappeared, and the metal backboards were rusted and dead in spots and he had to adjust his shooting touch to compensate, like a golfer correcting for the quirks of a green. He practiced almost every day, no matter the weather. ("I remember going to see him once, and it was raining," says his Taft teammate Bernie Cohen. "You know where I saw him? Shooting baskets on the court near his house. In the rain!") In the wintertime, when the court was covered with snow, he would shovel it clear, then light a fire in a trash can to keep his hands warm and practice for hours.

"The day just isn't long enough," he told a *New York Post* reporter once, referring to his basketball practice, though in truth he didn't let sundown stop him either. In Claremont Park, just up the hill from his house, lights had been installed for a National Guard unit that had been stationed there during World War II, and in the dim yellow glow he played sometimes until nearly midnight. On the court he became more serious, the lopsided grin that he often wore now replaced by a look of fierce concentration; a great deal seemed to be riding on this. It was as though in playing basketball he might eventually discover someone other than a friendly, gawky kid with a runny nose, might someday come to feel worthy of his size.

Marty Force, however, was good to his word—Eddie never played in a game. He would participate in the pregame warm-up drills, and some people in the crowd would point at him because of his unusual shape and the unorthodox way he ran, almost directly vertical, his legs barely seeming to bend; then a teammate would pass him the ball and he would make a move to the basket, dribbling the ball too high, above his waist, and the coach had been right about this, too, for he would hear laughter coming from the crowd. (At some point he had hit on the idea of tying a handkerchief to a belt loop of his basketball shorts, so that he might blow his nose if he needed to during the game; the dangling handkerchief made him stand out even more, but there was nothing to be done about that.) When the game began he would return to the bench with his warm-up jacket still on, the tallest of anyone sitting there, and cheer on the starting five, especially Irwin Dambrot, the star of the team, who everyone knew was going to City College to play basketball for Nat Holman.

Irwin was, in certain respects, Eddie's opposite. He was boyishly handsome, with light brown hair and ruddy cheeks and full, sensuous

lips; he was tall too, nearly six foot four, but he was graceful, not un-
gainly, and had a strapping athletic build that reminded people of Li'l
Abner. The other kids would often remark, in some admiration, that
Irwin didn't look Jewish; jokingly they referred to him (the son of a poor
cabdriver who had fled Poland to escape pogroms) as "a red-blooded
American boy." In a school of some five thousand students, Irwin Dambrot was the nearest thing Taft had to a campus hero—good-looking
and smart (he hoped to be a dentist someday) and, everyone agreed,
very nice and not at all stuck-up in the way you might expect him to be.
The adjective always used to describe him on the basketball court was
smooth; he appeared less to run than to glide, barely even breaking a
sweat. He was left-handed, which most defenders found more difficult to
guard, his best shot a running one-handed push that he took from the
left side of the court. None of his moves were especially spectacular, but
when the game was over he almost always turned out to be the high
scorer; in the 1945–46 season, his final one at Taft, he broke the school's
single-season scoring record. All that year Eddie Roman sat on the
bench, rooting for Dambrot and his teammates—until the last home
game of the season, when, with only a few minutes remaining on the
clock, the coach stood up and pointed at him.

Not long after entering the game, Eddie received a long pass up the
right-hand side of the court and started dribbling toward the basket.
One of the other team's faster players, who had surely noticed Eddie's
high dribble and anticipated making a steal, came racing after him.
Sensing the pressure from behind, Eddie stopped dribbling upcourt and
veered toward the sideline, letting the defender go flying by, almost like
a matador sidestepping a charging bull; with one fluid motion he
gripped the ball and, planting his left foot, made a reverse turn, so that
he was now facing the basket, and unexpectedly lofted up a one-handed
shot from about twenty feet away. "People held their breath," recalls
Justin Kodner, a Taft student who was in the crowd that day. "Nobody
believed he could sink that shot, but it went right through—never even
touched the rim." Kodner was sitting only a few rows from the court,
and he still vividly remembers how Eddie was smiling as he turned and
took the shot, as though he had already envisioned the whole sequence
and knew how it would turn out. "The gym went crazy," Kodner says.
"From that time on he was everybody's favorite."

• • •

The family's name had been, originally, Romatsky. Eddie's parents, Julius and Sarah, were Jewish immigrants from Lomza, a small city northeast of Warsaw. His father had come to the United States during the First World War, fleeing conscription into the tsar's army, and his mother arrived a few years later. Though both were from Lomza they met in the Bronx, and after marrying they bought a small two-family home with Sarah's older sister Bashke and her husband, taking the downstairs residence, five rooms in which they would raise three sons: Mel, who was born in 1927; Eddie, three years younger than Mel; and Richie, seven years younger than Eddie. Like many of the other Jewish immigrants of the Bronx, Julius and Sarah Roman subscribed to *The Jewish Daily Forward,* the socialist Yiddish newspaper, and belonged to the Workmen's Circle, a Jewish mutual aid society that promoted secular Yiddish culture and left-wing politics. "The values of social justice and equality permeated our home," Richard Roman was later to write, "though these were little discussed." So ingrained were these values that they hardly needed to be; they are perhaps best conveyed by the Yiddish word *menschlichkeit,* which loosely translates as being a humane person: helping others, caring for the common good, taking the side of the powerless rather than the powerful.

Short and stocky with thinning dark hair, Julius was warm and sweet-tempered and exceedingly quiet. Eddie was quiet too, and most of the family's conversations were dominated by Sarah's funny stories and neighborhood gossip. Fifteen years younger than her husband, Sarah was a homemaker who cooked dinner every night and baked challah on Fridays. But she was afflicted by constant anxieties; her youngest son, Richard, describes her as "catastrophic in her thinking," always anticipating that disaster might strike at any moment. In particular, anxiety about money pervaded the household. Julius was a house painter, and for many years he had been a member of the local painters' union, earning a steady wage painting schools and bridges. Over time, however, he came to believe that the union's leadership was bigoted and the hiring system organized so that Jews would not get picked for the best jobs. Finally he had decided to leave the union and become self-employed, and though he had done well for a while, eventually he suffered some serious financial setbacks. By the time Eddie was in high school, Julius was often in ill health and out of work. He spent much of his time in those days puttering around the house, painting and re-painting; a cousin recalls that the family's furniture had been painted so often it seemed to have lost its original shape.

After his single appearance on the court as a sophomore, Eddie contin-ued to practice, and by the fall of his junior year he was a starting mem-ber of the Taft basketball team. The team's regular coach, Bernie Schiffer, had returned from a stint in the Navy, and patiently he worked with Eddie on his center play, showing him how to pass the ball out if he didn't have a shot, how to move his feet so that the defense couldn't double-team him, how to use his size to box out his man for rebounds. Though he was still slow and awkward, and thus prone to committing too many defensive fouls, on offense Eddie had developed into an almost unstoppable force. As a junior he broke Irwin Dambrot's single-season Taft scoring record, earning 306 points as the Presidents won all four-teen of their games.

In his senior year Eddie played even better, scoring 336 points, and at the end of the season he was named All-City and started at center for the Manhattan-Bronx team against the Brooklyn-Queens squad in a game held at Madison Square Garden. At Taft's graduation that spring he was awarded the Spiro Trophy for scholarship and athletics, previ-ously won by Irwin Dambrot. Only two years earlier he had been laughed at when he tried to dribble during pregame warm-ups; now he was, by general acclaim, one of the best high school players in the city.

All at once almost anything in basketball seemed possible, and at the dinner table, talk began to arise that after college Eddie might sign with one of the teams in the American Athletic Union. Before the found-ing of the National Basketball Association, the AAU was one of the most prestigious basketball leagues in the country. Its teams were sponsored by corporations such as Goodyear and Caterpillar, and they provided training and jobs for their players; his parents were sure that with Ed-die's intelligence he would surely advance, maybe even become a com-pany executive. Basketball was no longer simply a means for Eddie to conquer his own self-consciousness; suddenly it seemed to offer a pathway to family mobility. "There was a notion," his brother Richard re-calls, "that if Eddie made it, we'd all make it."

Bobby Sand had been following Eddie's progress at Taft and was more interested in him than in any other prospect he had seen; he believed Eddie had the capacity to become the best shooting center in the coun-try. Taft coach Bernie Schiffer, though, had played for Nat Holman at City College and didn't like him; he counseled Eddie that he would be better off elsewhere, saying, "Please do me a favor—don't go there." New York University offered him a full scholarship, as did Columbia Uni-versity. Other colleges made even better offers. The University of New Mexico, for instance, offered scholarships to the entire Taft starting five, but only if Eddie would agree to go—and Eddie was adamant about not moving to Albuquerque.

The University of Cincinnati was then an emerging basketball power; Eddie had played basketball in the Catskills that summer with two members of the team, and through one of them Cincinnati submit-ted its offer. Not only would the university give Eddie a four-year schol-arship, it would also give a two-year scholarship to his brother Mel, who was applying to master's programs in psychology. In addition to free tuition, the school would provide Eddie with fifty dollars a month in spending money, a job, a rent-free apartment, free textbooks, and free use of a car. Mel urged Eddie to accept the offer; his parents, too, felt that this was an exceptional opportunity, for his brother as well as for him. Eddie wanted to do the right thing, and in September 1948 he and Mel moved to Cincinnati.

Almost immediately the brothers regretted the decision. Away at school, Eddie found that he was homesick for almost everything—his family and friends, deli food, the subway—and, he reported back to a friend, in Cincinnati all of the radio stations played country music. Mel, too, had left a girlfriend back in New York, and he missed her more than he had expected to. Before the week was out, Eddie went to see the Cin-cinnati basketball coach and told him he was sorry, but he had made a mistake, and soon the Roman brothers were back in the Bronx.

For days his mother was inconsolable, wailing that Eddie had thrown away a golden opportunity, that an offer like this one would not come again. By that time NYU had given his scholarship to another player; Columbia's deadline, too, had passed, and the college official with whom he spoke suggested that he try again next year. Later that month Bobby Sand got back in touch with Eddie. He told him that Floyd Layne and Ed Warner, teammates from the Manhattan-Bronx All-Stars, were coming to City, where they would join his old Taft teammate Irwin Dambrot. Moreover, Bobby said, the athletic department was willing to provide Eddie with a student job, at which he would make anywhere from twelve to fifteen dollars a week. One of the school's registrars would also help Mel get into a master's program. And there was one more thing.

Nat Holman, he said, had authorized him to make this offer: If Eddie came to City College, they would get his father a job.

In his first semester at City, between schoolwork and basketball, Eddie was busier than he had ever been. He was up late almost every night

doing homework; sometimes, when the subway wasn't too crowded, he studied on the IND train heading home after practice, uncomfortably shifting his bulk on the narrow wicker seats, squinting down at the pages in the dim fluorescent light. In his first semester he received straight B's, other than a C in algebra, which was a surprise and caused him to work even harder, and the next semester he brought his math grade all the way up to an A. He earned A's in English literature and American economic history as well; he

Eddie Roman as a member of the City College Beavers.
Larry Gralla

had his eye on making the dean's list and perhaps, down the road, even Phi Beta Kappa.

Sometime during that second semester Eddie was called in to see the head of the athletic program, Sam Winograd, in his office in Lewisohn Stadium. A sturdily built man in his midthirties who dressed in tweed sports jackets and bow ties, Winograd had a booming voice and an authoritative manner. Nat Holman was already in the office when Eddie arrived, as well as a clerical worker named Tom Reilly; Winograd explained that they were going to talk about his student employment.

As part of his aid deal Eddie had been assigned to the athletic equipment room, a job they gave to many of the school's athletes. Winograd asked Reilly to take out Eddie's time cards, which would show that he had not worked the hours he was supposed to. Eddie was actually entitled to only eight hours per week of pay, Winograd said, rather than the fifteen that had been promised. He went on for a while longer, explaining something about thirty-minute intervals, but Eddie was barely hearing. As he would later recount about that meeting: "Meanwhile I was working more hours than anyone and he started giving me all kinds of bullshit, and then he cut down my payments, and where's the job they promised my father?"

That job had never materialized. His father was not finding much work and was home a lot those days. (The house itself had become a source of financial anxiety: His parents had bought it in 1925 for $13,000, with a $7,000 mortgage; nearly a quarter of a century later, it had been assessed at a value of only $8,500.) Once after a scrimmage Eddie had gathered his courage and walked over to Nat Holman. "Nat," he said, "you promised my father a job."

"What are you talking about?" said Holman. "I never promised your father a job."

Nearly a year into his college career, Eddie had come to understand how the athletic department worked: He knew that Bobby Sand could never have made that offer without having been authorized by Nat Holman (and, knowing Bobby's character, would not have claimed he had), and Holman in turn must have discussed the matter with Winograd.

Eddie persisted; Bobby, he said, had told him that if he came to play basketball at City College, they would get his father a job.

"I know nothing about that," Holman replied. Waving his hand dismissively in Sand's direction, he said, "Go ask the man who promised you."

Now, walking out of Winograd's office, Eddie felt that he had been ambushed; he left in a daze, trudging up the steps and onto Convent Avenue. Why, he wondered, were Winograd and Holman so strict with him when the equipment room was clearly a make-work job for the athletic department, and he was showing up more than any of the others were? The loss of those hours meant a great deal. The family's financial situation had grown so dire that the following year Eddie would apply for and receive a Tremain Scholarship, an award of fifty dollars per semester for students who had high averages but whose college careers were in financial jeopardy. Winograd, Eddie thought, had broken his promises and still tried to take the high ground—when everyone around the equipment room had heard the rumors about Sam's underhanded deals, how he bought athletic equipment at higher prices than other schools did, and somehow his friend who owned a sporting goods store always seemed to win the bids. All that day in class Eddie could feel his anger building, and at practice that afternoon he pulled Sand aside and told him he wanted to quit the team.

Bobby tried to calm Eddie down, urging him to keep the long view in mind, but nothing he said could mollify him, and when Eddie got home that night the phone rang and it was Holman on the line. He spoke to Eddie for several minutes, reminding him of the value of a City College education, the contacts that could be made in all fields of business. "The only thing that counts," Nat told him, "is how much money you have in your safe deposit box."

By then, though, Eddie had already talked himself out of quitting. His brother had been placed in a master's program at City and he didn't want to jeopardize that; nor, with a semester already under his belt, did he have the heart to tell his parents, who were already so fretful, that he was leaving college again. So he kept quiet, put in his reduced hours in the equipment office, and stayed with the team, and that season he scored 310 points, more than any other freshman in the history of the school. The next year, as his first varsity season began, the souvenir program included a smiling picture of him alongside the observation that he "may be the answer to the College's dreams for a big man."

CHAPTER 4

As the fall semester of 1949 got under way, the City College campus was the usual bustle of activity. The school's theater workshop began rehearsals for a production of *On the Town*, the recently staged Broadway musical about three sailors carousing through New York on shore leave. In Main Hall every Thursday afternoon—Thursdays from 12:00 to 2:00 were designated "club hours"—one could find archery, table tennis, and square dancing; there were meetings of the Camera Club and the Chess Club and the Meteorology Society, and trading sessions for members of the Stamp Club. The Young Liberals Club sponsored coed hayrides up the Hudson River, and they also organized a campus rally on behalf of Newbold Morris, mayoral candidate for both the Republican and Liberal parties; many of the college's students, though, preferred another candidate, East Harlem's radical congressman Vito Marcantonio, running atop the American Labor Party ticket. At a campaign rally attended by eighteen thousand supporters in Madison Square Garden, Marcantonio denounced "the jungle law of atomic diplomacy" that he claimed had led to the persecution of eleven Communists recently convicted of subversion in a trial held at the federal courthouse downtown. "To hell with Wall Street and to hell with the politicians!" he cried. *"Viva il popolo della citta di New York!"*

The country had begun to descend into what seemed a permanent state of armed hostility, a "cold war"—the financier and presidential adviser Bernard Baruch, himself a City College graduate, had coined the phrase. In August the Soviet Union had exploded its own atomic bomb, with the help—it was whispered—of spies in the United States. The chances of atomic annihilation, once the province only of comic books and science fiction, were now regularly weighed and analyzed in the newspapers. In New York, military experts, concerned that a Soviet attack would disable communications systems, began to consider the possibility of training pigeons to carry important messages; Good Humor trucks, with their built-in refrigeration systems, were designated to deliver blood to hospitals in the event of an attack.

There were, everywhere, theories of plots and conspiracies, rumors of impending witch hunts; no one could tell for sure what was real and what was only political paranoia, or whether there was any longer much of a difference. Nineteen forty-nine was the year when the House Un-American Activities Committee began demanding lists of textbooks from colleges and high schools; when the University of California imposed a loyalty oath for its faculty members; when, closer to home, New York's Feinberg Law placed a "security officer" in each school district, whose job was to file an annual report on the political beliefs of every teacher. In 1953 the editors of *Microcosm*, the City College yearbook, recalled 1949, the year they had entered the school: "Perhaps we were only reflecting the temper of a disturbed and perplexed world. But as we look back now we see that this year began at the College the period of the great silence, the silence of conformity—or seeming conformity."

In the Main Gym, Nat Holman was pleased by the progress the team was making. They practiced for two hours every afternoon after classes, Holman calling out instructions, blowing his whistle to freeze the action whenever he saw something he didn't like. He was imperious in his manner; if a player talked while he was speaking, the coach would stop and glare at him. "I'm teaching," he would say. "Do you speak when your philosophy professor is teaching?"

Holman was a perfectionist, and he would repeat a move again and again until he was satisfied that the team understood. Sometimes during a scrimmage he would stop the action to demand of a player why he hadn't changed direction, and then of another why he had slowed down, and of another why he hadn't set a screen or rolled to the basket; eventually the players would realize, in astonishment, that Holman could see all ten of them on the court at once. Day after day he revealed subtleties of the game that had previously been hidden; even young men who had grown up with a basketball in their hands began to find that they were speeding up their ball handling, that their footwork was surer, that they knew, at any given moment, where their teammates were on the court. Again and again Holman blew the whistle and then strode over to snatch the ball from the offending player. "Look at me," he would say, demonstrating exactly what he wanted. "I take the pass, and I pivot." Sternly he'd watch the player repeat the move, his gray eyes as hard as chips of marble; then, satisfied that the lesson had been absorbed, he'd clap his hands to resume play.

Holman was, by his own account, "very exacting." He explained once to an interviewer: "I'm not running a popularity contest. Your teacher in mathematics doesn't care whether you like him, he wants that job done. I am no different."

Holman often compared himself to a professor, but in fact he was a good deal more and less than that. Over the course of a college career a basketball player might have several dozen professors, but he will have only a single varsity coach, with no possibility of obtaining a different one other than by leaving the school. For those young men who were good enough to make the City College team, success in basketball, for which they received no college credit, actually meant far more than a good grade in mathematics or geology or public speaking. From school-yard to school gym and now to Madison Square Garden, it was basketball that had distinguished them, allowed them to excel in public view, and, for a few, offered the prospect of someday earning a livelihood. But for each of the players, everything now hinged on the head coach's valuing the particular set of skills he brought to the team; the players were utterly dependent on the coach, vulnerable to his insights or his whims, and they thought about him—and wondered what *he* thought about *them*—far more than they did any of their actual professors. He existed, for them, in a position of both familiarity and great remove. Unlike a typical professor, Nat Holman never held office hours (many players completed four years of college without ever having seen the inside of his office), and he granted himself a discretion that no other City College professor would have dared, which was the right to lambaste his students even in front of outsiders, to swear at them and call them names.

Though Nat Holman's accent was Upper East Side, his upbringing was Lower East Side, and as he became angry, his diction traveled steadily downtown, back to his origins. "He swore like a sailor," one of his players would later remark; said another, "He was a street man and he used street language, and he didn't care who heard him"; a third simply shrugged and said, "He knew all the words." Even Irwin Dambrot, one of his favorite players, had not escaped his wrath. Once early in his career Dambrot had made a mistake in practice, and Holman immediately halted play. "Dambrot," he barked, "how tall are you?"

"Six foot four, sir."

"Six four? I didn't know shit could be piled that high."

His players respected his knowledge of the game, but they also regarded him as arrogant and aloof; it was distressing, but somehow fitting, that Holman, who seemed to care mostly for himself, often did not remember their names. "If he remembered the guy's name it was wonderful," says Morty Schwartz, one of the team's assistant managers. "You always had the sense that he favored certain ballplayers, and the name he remembered was the player he favored at that time." For two years he called Floyd Layne "Lloyd," and Eddie Roman was "Big Boy." Once during a game, frustrated by a player's mistakes, Holman turned angrily to a reserve player named Norm Mager and said: "Get in there and replace that stupid son of a bitch." Mager leaped up and ran around the court to the scorer's table to check in, then considered for a moment and ran back to the City College bench. "Nat," he asked, "which stupid son of a bitch do you mean?"

The first game of the season, on November 26 against Queens College, was one of only two all year that would be held in the campus gym. Outside Wingate Hall, Raymond the Bagel Man stood at his pushcart hawking his pragels: "They're homogenized!" he cried to passersby. "Lavenderized! Beaverized!" His breath steamed and rose in the frigid night air. A stretch of very cold weather had settled over the city, causing apartment radiators to cough and wheeze and in the mornings coating windows with frost. Pulling their overcoats tighter and turning their collars up against the chill, the students streamed across the City College quadrangle. Together they passed beneath the merrymaking grotesques who cavorted above the entrance to Wingate Hall, then climbed the wooden stairway with the green tile wainscoting on the walls and, handing over their tickets at the entrance to the Main Gym, filed their way along the rows of folding chairs that had been set up on the banked running oval that hung above the basketball court, the rows spaced so tightly that when the spectators sat down, their knees pressed into the backs of the people sitting in front of them. The gym's seating capacity was only 1,100, but *The Campus* estimated that 2,500 spectators were on hand that night, in large part to watch the sophomores, about whom they had heard so much, play their first game on the varsity team.

The darkness outside had turned the gym's tall Gothic windows into mirrors, each one reflecting sections of the steel latticework that buttressed the vaulted ceiling. A kind of electrical hum coursed through the air, as though the switch had been flipped on a great dynamo, as the players ran up the stairs from the locker room and burst onto the court in their glossy satin warm-up jackets and the white uniforms with the lavender trim, the letters *CCNY* sewn in a gentle arc across the front. Clusters of fans stood and launched into a rendition of the school song, "Lavender" (*Sturdy sons of City College / Trusty hearts and mighty hands / Rally where our streaming banner / With its dauntless emblem stands . . .*), while the players on both sides went through their warm-up routines, tossing up set shots and free throws and feeding passes for layups. Then the horn sounded and the gym grew still but for the referee bouncing the ball at midcourt, and Eddie Roman and his counterpart from Queens shook hands and faced off for the center toss. The referee blew his whistle, and the season was under way.

Later on, what everyone would remember most clearly is how Eddie seemed to be everywhere on the court that night, knocking down long set shots and making tip-ins under the offensive basket; he was slow and couldn't jump, everyone in the gym could see that right away, but the fans nudged one another in appreciation each time he maneuvered his big body into position to grab a rebound, each time he faked his defender to create space for a perfect pass to a cutting teammate. Upstairs the students clapped and whooped and stamped their feet in rhythm whenever the Beavers had the ball, the upstairs track shaking unnervingly from the vibrations. ("It was so loud in there," reserve player Ron Nadell would wryly observe, "that you could hardly hear Nat Holman curse.") Before the first half was over, Holman recognized that victory was not in doubt and began sending in wave after wave of platoons, everyone getting a chance to play in front of the home crowd.

The forty minutes of regulation time seemed to pass in a blur, and when the referee blew the final whistle the score was 91 to 45. The sophomores, everyone agreed, were as good as advertised. "In theatrical circles," wrote Marvin Kalb (the legendary journalist was then a sportswriter for *The Campus*), "they'll tell you that rave notices are one thing; substantiating these notices with solid action is another. . . . Unlike many Broadway shows, however, these notices haven't fallen flat."

The Beavers, though, were only now heading to the main stage; their next game, the following Saturday, would be in Madison Square Garden.

That Saturday night the crowd poured up from the ground in waves: A slight trembling of the earth and a screech and a gust of warm air through the subway grates, and a moment later another surge of people emerged onto the dimly lit side street, streaming toward the building on the avenue. Madison Square Garden was a massive buff-colored brick box that sat between Eighth and Ninth avenues and Forty-Ninth and Fiftieth streets, its exterior almost entirely devoid of ornamentation, looking as much warehouse or automobile showroom as sporting arena. Only a block removed from the dazzling lights of Broadway's theater district, here the single suggestion of glamour was the undulating Art Deco marquee that canopied the sidewalk at the Eighth Avenue entrance, its two glowing white sides like lined paper beneath the black capital letters, hung by a worker on a ladder, that announced the evening's competitors in the manner of a heavyweight prize fight: TONITE / BASKETBALL / CCNY V/S LAFAYETTE. A palpable sense of excitement and jittery anticipation hung in the air (sharpened, for many, by the prospect of money lost or won), and overhead, above the hum of laughter and loud voices, the announcer on the public address system kept repeating "Standing room only," which meant a full house again, more than eighteen thousand, while low but insistent came the call of the scalpers to all who passed by, *tickets tickets tickets;* on occasion the scalpers were joined by some of the players themselves, coats thrown on over warm-up suits, who had long ago discovered that the pair of complimentary tickets they received for each game might bring, depending on the quality of the opponent, five dollars or more, better than face value.

Some of the fans passed through the main entrance, holding out their tickets to the takers like a bouquet; others stood waiting for tardy companions to the left of the entrance, leaning against the plate-glass window of Adam Hats, smoking cigarettes and checking their watches and maybe wondering if there was time to grab a frank before the game. On the opposite side of the entrance was Nedick's, the legendary hot dog stand, staffed by a row of countermen in aprons and soda-jerk paper hats doing their minuet of serving and clearing and wiping in the narrow space behind the counter, where customers still in coats and hats

Crowds streaming out of Madison Square Garden after a sporting event in the 1940s.
Ralph Morse/Getty Images

laid down a dime for a sizzling grilled frank in a butter-toasted split-top bun and a nickel for a World Famous Orange Drink, poured in a conical paper cup nestled inside a shiny metal holder, the coins swept up fast and, with a couple of sharp taps and a ding as from a typewriter bell, tossed into the drawer of the cash register. (Nedick's sponsored all the basketball games, and the radio announcer, Marty Glickman, had begun incorporating the product into his game calls: "It's good!" he would cry after a basket was scored. "Like Nedick's!") Leaning on the counter they ate, and wondered when the mayor was finally going to marry his fashion-model girlfriend, and made plans for drinks later at Jack Dempsey's or the Brass Rail, and reported the latest fluctuations of the point spread. *It's nine points on City*, someone might say, and another might shake his head and mutter simply *Not tonight*, and inside the arena, just past the front lobby, men sat at a long bank of wooden telephone booths and called in their last bets before the start of the game.

In 1939 an essayist for the Works Progress Administration observed, "Nowadays, if New York has a heart, it might be the Garden. Almost everyone goes there, for one purpose or another." Five million spectators a year passed through the turnstiles of Madison Square Garden. The biggest draws on the calendar were the major sporting events, boxing and basketball and hockey, and each spring Barnum's circus raised the big top for its dancing elephants and leaping tigers and sad-faced clown Emmett Kelly, in crumpled hat and ragged suit, sweeping up the spotlight on the floor to the delight of laughing children; but the course of the year also brought ice shows and pro wrestling and the Roller Derby, and rodeos and track-and-field meets and six-day bicycle races, not to mention charity benefits and political rallies, and in the Exposition Hall downstairs, shows displaying pedigreed dogs and cats and poultry.

For basketball games, teams of workmen lugged 104 sections of hardwood flooring into the arena and clicked them into place like immense jigsaw puzzle pieces, creating a playing surface exactly one hundred feet long and fifty-seven feet wide, clear-grain white pine covered with two coats of Hillyard's Star Gym Finish. To accommodate the sight lines of spectators at both ends of the arena, the Garden had installed glass backboards, an innovation that for many years visiting teams had never seen before and that required a great deal of practice to get used to. For basketball games the Garden also used an unusual set of double clocks to indicate the time remaining in the half, one clock for the minutes and the other for the seconds, though by the start of the second game of a doubleheader the clocks, hanging from the rafters of the arena, were usually obscured by a thick bluish haze of cigar and cigarette smoke. The smoke was a regular and entirely predictable aspect of the Garden experience—so much so that one prominent head coach, Frank Keaney of Rhode Island State, would light smudge pots in the college gym during practices to prepare his teams for playing there.

The New York Knickerbockers of the Basketball Association of America also used the Garden as their home court, beginning in 1946 (the National Basketball Association was not formed until 1949); on average, though, they drew fewer than twelve thousand fans per game, and even that meager attendance had been pumped up by pairing Knicks games with games of the local Knickerbocker Industrial League—in which the team from Gimbels department store, for instance, might compete against its rival Abraham & Straus. In the 1945–46 season, by contrast, Madison Square Garden hosted twenty-nine college basketball dates that brought an average attendance of 18,196.

The Garden's connection to the college game dated to the winter of 1931, when New York mayor Jimmy Walker asked a group of local sportswriters to organize a college basketball tripleheader to raise money for the city's unemployment relief fund. The event proved to be an astonishing success—more than sixteen thousand fans attended, contributing, at the very depths of the Great Depression, a sum of $20,000—and it would be repeated over the next two years, with similar results.

No one was more impressed with the potential of college basketball in New York than a young writer for the *New York World-Telegram;* his name was Edward Irish, but everyone knew him as Ned. Ned Irish was moody, driven, ambitious, always in search of greater business opportunities, and as he watched those benefit games he recognized the passion that New Yorkers held for basketball, understood that countless thousands of the city's residents had grown up with the game and cared about it deeply, and furthermore that a ready-made spectator base existed among the local colleges' students and alumni. In 1934, at the age of twenty-nine, he quit his newspaper job and went to work for Madison Square Garden, arranging college basketball doubleheaders. By the end of the 1934–35 season he had organized a slate of eight doubleheaders, in which he pitted local college teams against teams from around the country. Irish was, in his way, a kind of visionary, the first person to see college basketball as a truly national sport. Up to that point, schools rarely played opponents beyond a radius of about two hundred miles, owing to the expense and hardship of extended travel; but now the Garden, flush with the funds provided by its huge customer base, could cover the costs of transportation, as well as hotel stays in New York City, and would give the colleges a share of the gate receipts besides.

Madison Square Garden quickly became the most desirable place for any college to play: "the Mecca of college basketball," as it was regularly called in the sports pages. In 1938 the Metropolitan Basketball Writers' Association founded the National Invitation Tournament, a six-team competition (in 1941 it would be expanded to eight teams, and in 1949 to twelve) featuring the best teams from all over the country, with the aim of crowning a national champion. The NIT proved such an immediate success that the very next year the National Collegiate Athletic Association created its own eight-team postseason tournament, with one team selected from each of eight geographic districts. The games were played in venues around the country rather than in New York, which emphasized the NCAA's status as a national organization but also drew far smaller crowds. The first NCAA championship game, held in 1939 at the Northwestern University gymnasium in Evanston, Illinois, was played before a crowd of only five thousand; three years later, in the larger Municipal Auditorium of Kansas City, the game was still attracting no more than six thousand fans. Finally, in 1943, conceding the point, the NCAA moved its championship game to Madison Square Garden. New York City, already the national center of industries including radio, publishing, finance, and clothing, was now also, indisputably, the capital of college basketball.

As for Ned Irish, when he left journalism to become a college basketball promoter in 1934, he had been receiving a weekly salary of $48.60; by the close of the following decade he was earning $150,000 a year and lived in a large apartment on Park Avenue. He was, as in the title of a *Saturday Evening Post* profile, "basketball's big wheel," far more powerful than anyone else connected with the sport. Irish himself insisted that he was merely a booking agent rather than, as he was often called, a "czar," though as he admitted once to a reporter: "I don't care what they say about me as long as they buy my tickets."

The crowd for the Lafayette game numbered 18,393, including several hundred standing-room-only tickets; Madison Square Garden provided 17,400 seats for basketball, which meant that Ned Irish had achieved 106 percent of seating capacity for the doubleheader, or, in the description of *The Saturday Evening Post*, "all that the walls and the equally inflexible fire department allowed." (In the Garden's afternoon game that day, the Knicks had beaten the Baltimore Bullets before only 8,153 fans.) It was, by and large, a formally dressed crowd, as if for the theater, many of the women wearing hats, the men in suits and ties, though upstairs, in the far reaches of the arena, many more, younger in age, wore sweaters. By contract Madison Square Garden had released a bloc of tickets to City College, which were sold for fifty cents apiece; the students sat in the second balcony, up five flights of stairs—the worst seats in the house.

A row of sportswriters sat at a long table courtside, while twenty feet above center court, on a platform at the front of the mezzanine, Marty Glickman would broadcast the game for radio station WMGM. Glickman's voice, with its slight New York edge, had the depth and authority of a newsreel announcer (and indeed for many years he narrated newsreels for Paramount), but in broadcasting basketball he also brought the expressive range of an actor in a radio drama: the ease in his delivery as the ball was dribbled upcourt; the rapid-fire staccato of a give-and-go play; the momentary hush after a shot was released, broken by an explosive *Good!* or *No good!* or his trademark call when a shot went straight through the hoop—*Swish!* That word was a delightful onomatopoeia, perfectly describing the sound of a ball as it nestled into the net; a few years earlier he had heard a couple of Knick players say it while shooting around before a game, and now it was already being imitated by kids in schoolyards all over the city.

Glickman went on the air at 8:30 for the second game of the doubleheader, the featured game; he welcomed his listeners and set the starting lineups as the two teams went through their pregame warm-ups. The Lafayette Leopards of Easton, Pennsylvania, were a formidable foe, having won twenty games the year before and lost only nine. Nat Holman had decided that City's starting five that night would be Eddie Roman at center, Irwin Dambrot and Ed Warner at forward, and Al Roth at guard alongside the senior Mike Wittlin, and after the warm-ups were over and the players had returned to the bench for final instructions, those were the five who ran back onto the court to the cheers of the crowd, taking a few deep breaths and jumping in place to keep their legs limber and burn off any remaining nerves. The referee, Lou Eisenstein, blew his whistle and the game began.

Early on the score was close, but midway through the period Roman went on a hot streak, making three consecutive baskets, and by halftime the Beavers led 36 to 22. In the opening minutes of the second half, City put together two separate seven-point spurts, and after that, noted Everett Morris in the *New York Herald Tribune*, "it was simply a matter of how high the Beavers would run up the score." City College was playing fast, relentless basketball, sprinting up the court after a defensive rebound; it was forty minutes of furious action, and those sitting behind him in the mezzanine could hear Glickman calling the game in his distinctive rat-a-tat: "Rebound-up-no-good, another-rebound-up-no-good, Roman clears the boards. Here comes City on a fast break, Warner from the top of the key . . . *swish!*"

Once again Eddie Roman seemed to be everywhere, grabbing rebounds on both ends of the court, feeding teammates perfectly timed passes out of the pivot; three times he scored as a result of designed inbounds plays, and once, most thrilling for everyone, Eddie actually led the fast break, putting in a layup ahead of his teammates racing behind him. "City College goal by Roman," intoned the Garden's public address announcer, Barclay Cooke, and the big crowd roared; from the end balcony Charles Bernstein let loose a bugle call. Normally the calls were led by his son Al, a CCNY graduate—for the past two seasons Al Bernstein had brought his bugle to every City basketball game—but for this particular game Al was away on business, and so Charles, who had been an Army bugler during the First World War and taught his son how to play, stepped into the breach, and at key moments of the game he stood up to unleash what one reporter called "the ear-busting command," six notes that prompted hundreds of fans to shout in response: *"Charge!"*

The City College cheerleaders watched the game kneeling in front of the press table, and whenever a time-out was called they would race onto the court—the men in black pants and the women in pleated black taffeta skirts, all of them wearing white sweaters on which the letters *CCNY* clasped a lavender megaphone—and they would leap and wave their arms in unison and yell up to the students in the far balcony, leading them in the "Allagaroo," the college's unique cheer:

> *Allagaroo garoo gara,*
> *Allagaroo garoo gara,*
> *Ee-yah ee-yah, sis boom bah,*
> *Team! Team! Team!**

The final score was 76 to 44. In their first two games of the season the City College Beavers had won by a combined total of seventy-eight points.

As the happy crowd filed out of the arena, Louis Effrat of *The New York Times* sat at the press table and typed out his account of the game. "All the glowing reports of superlative court strength at C.C.N.Y. were proved true last night at Madison Square Garden," he began. Effrat had been covering the major team sports for the *Times* for more than two decades; he was not easily impressed, but he concluded his description of the game with a burst of enthusiasm rare to find in the news columns of his paper's sports section. "They do things, these Beavers," he wrote. "They do them knowingly and they do them well. So well, in fact, that at times last night it became difficult to follow their progress. There is drive in the current edition of the Beavers and more is going to be heard from Roman, Roth, Warner and Layne. Yes, it is true what they have been saying about C.C.N.Y. The Lavender is loaded."

---

* No one knew the exact origin of the strange word *allagaroo*, beyond the fact that the cheer had been composed by a member of the graduating class of 1911. Wags around the school liked to say that an allagaroo came from mating an alligator with a kangaroo; a more syntactical theory held that it was a corruption of the French *allez guerre*, meaning roughly "on to the war." The City College athletic booster group was called, inevitably, the Allagarooters.

CHAPTER 5

Eddie Roman's best friend on the team was Floyd Layne. Floyd was also from the Bronx, and the two of them had been playing basketball together since high school, when they were part of a touring club called the Bronx Wildcats. The team had been formed by guys who played in the community center of the Bronx House, a settlement house of long standing; it was made up of black kids like Floyd and Jewish kids like Eddie, and in acknowledgment of that fact, one of the players had designed the team's insignia: a cross inside a Star of David.

At six foot three and 170 pounds, Floyd was rangy and loose-limbed, and playing ball he seemed always to be alert and in motion; on defense his arms were constantly windmilling, his hands darting out to slap the ball loose. He also liked to make gruesome faces while playing defense—a tactic that was apparently intended to intimidate the man he was guarding, but more often had the effect of cracking up his teammates on the bench. He was an especially tenacious defender, the sort of player about whom fans would say admiringly that he started guarding his man in the locker room. Indeed, he prided himself on his defense rather than his offense, which spoke to a certain sense of modesty since it was an attribute that would never show up in a box score but was essential to the success of the team. Eddie envied Floyd his grace, his speed, the fluidity of his motion as he drove to the basket; while he himself was awkward and herky-jerky, with elbows that seemed to fly out of their own accord and too often got him in foul trouble, Floyd seemed always in control of himself on the court. He played with a kind of—there was no other word for it—dignity. His game was fundamentally sound, from the stance he assumed on defense (resting lightly on the balls of his feet, one arm up to prevent a shot or pass) to his two-handed set shot, which he finished with his hands together above his head like a man about to dive into a pool.

Floyd's mother, Lina Griffith Layne, had come from Barbados at the age of twenty seeking better economic opportunities; she worked as a domestic for wealthier families in Manhattan and the West Bronx and dreamed that her son would someday go into a profession. She and Floyd's father, Arthur, had separated when Floyd was eight years old, at which point Lina and her son moved from Brooklyn to an apartment in the East Bronx and Arthur ceased to be much of a presence in Floyd's life. Lina called Floyd "Bunty," a name of endearment common in Barbados. She made dinner for them almost every night on her return from work, often Bajan specialties like rice and peas and salt cod cakes, or flying fish that she bought in the Caribbean groceries on Belmont Avenue and served with a dish called *cou cou*, made from cornmeal and okra. Together they sat at the little kitchen table and said grace before meals, and likewise she made sure that Floyd said his prayers before bed at night, and every Sunday morning she dressed him up in his suit and tie and took him to St. Augustine Presbyterian Church just down Prospect Avenue to listen to the Reverend Edler Hawkins's powerful civil rights sermons. She also enrolled him in the Cub Scout troop that met weekly in the church's social hall, and he remained with the group all through the Boy Scouts, trading in the blue uniform for a khaki one. Like many of the other mothers in the neighborhood she spent what little extra money she had on piano lessons for her son, both to expose him to the beauty of music and because she hoped that the practicing would build a sense of discipline in him, keep him focused and out of mischief. Lina stressed the importance of education, and on Saturdays when Floyd pushed aside the plants hanging in the window to look for friends in the nearby playground she would remind him that he was not going outside until he had finished his schoolwork. In his younger years she was also not averse to giving him a little slap on the behind or the back of the head if she felt he wasn't listening to her. "If you don't hear," she would tell him, "you will feel."

Those piano lessons did in fact foster a love of music in Floyd, and when he was a teenager he took up the saxophone. At Benjamin Franklin High School in East Harlem he joined the jazz band (among the other players was the future saxophone luminary Sonny Rollins), and on a weekend night Floyd might wander with some friends over to Club 845, just a few blocks from home under the Prospect Avenue elevated station, sitting in a leatherette booth in the little smoky room where the musician in the beret and dark glasses on the bandstand that night might be Dizzy Gillespie or Thelonious Monk; or to one of the Latin clubs like the Tropicana on Westchester Avenue, where bandleaders like Machito and Tito Rodriguez merged Cuban dance rhythms with sinuous bebop melodies to create a kind of music no one had ever heard before.

In his senior year at Benjamin Franklin, Floyd was named the captain of the basketball team, leading the Benjays to a 15–1 season record and the finals of the citywide championship; he was named All-City, playing in the Herald Tribune Fresh Air Fund benefit at Madison Square Garden, where his teammates on the Manhattan-Bronx team included Ed Warner of DeWitt Clinton High School and Eddie Roman of Taft. By that time the three of them were regularly playing pickup games on the weekends; most often they played in the schoolyards of the Bronx, the games three-on-three with the winners taking on the next team in line, the three of them so good together that sometimes they could hold the court for hours at a time. Afterward they would head back to Floyd's apartment, dribbling the ball between them as they walked, watching for the crazy bounces on the Belgian blocks of Prospect Avenue. Lina would bring out covered dishes that held leftover gumbo or flying fish pie, or she might fry up some eggs with chopped onion and sweet peppers—she always marveled at Eddie Roman's prodigious appetite— and as time went on she was increasingly happy to see them, reveling in the pleasure and relief she felt in watching Bunty laugh and joke with two reliable friends around the kitchen table. "These are my two Eddies," she would say, gathering them up in her arms. "These are my other sons."

On afternoons before Saturday night games, the Beavers would check in to the Paramount Hotel on West Forty-Sixth Street and stay there until it was time to walk to the Garden. It was not unheard of for white and black players to room together, and Eddie would have been happy to room with Floyd, but Floyd was rooming with Ed Warner, and so Eddie roomed instead with the other sophomore member of the starting five, Al Roth.

Al was known to everyone as Fats, a nickname that had persisted since junior high, though by this time he had grown to six foot four and was muscular and not fat at all. He was a tough, aggressive player and had an unusual habit of spinning the basketball in his hands as he surveyed the court to set up a play, utterly poised, like a gunman twirling his pistol before a fight. The profile of him in the souvenir program for the Queens game referred to his "dual loves: basketball and women," and an article in *The Campus* had modified the assessment slightly, saying that basketball was his second love *after* women, and informing readers that "Al has an address book with more pertinent dope on women than the latest medical journal." He bought his clothing at the Ed Richelson men's shop in Brooklyn, tweed overcoats that he wore with the collar turned up and blue blazers with button-down oxford shirts and striped rep ties, Ivy League all the way down to his argyle socks and loafers; he had been raised in an Orthodox Jewish home (his first language was Yiddish), and he liked to joke that in the next life he wanted to come back as a WASP.

His father, Sol, an immigrant from Poland, owned a seltzer delivery business; every morning he left the family's apartment at five o'clock and usually would be away working his routes until late at night. Over time Sol had been able to put together enough money to buy a bit of property with his brothers, a few buildings in Brooklyn and Queens. Al resented his father's absences, the fact that even now he was still schlepping heavy wooden cases up and down flights of stairs; he could never understand why his father still wanted to be a seltzer man when he owned real estate. His own ambition was to land a well-paying job in a solid American profession like life insurance, maybe someday leave the city for the suburbs; he didn't want to be, as he put it, "a basketball bum," didn't want the game to be his prime goal in life. Fats seemed to have money on his mind a lot, and talking with him in their shared room at the Paramount Hotel, Eddie Roman couldn't help but notice that these days the subject seemed often to be tied up with gambling.

• • •

Gambling had long been widespread in Madison Square Garden, so much so that Ned Irish felt obliged to insert an "important notice" into the program for all college basketball games: "Betting or Soliciting Bets Is Prohibited in Madison Sq. Garden." As far back as January 1935—no more than a month after Irish promoted his first college basketball doubleheader—the *New York Herald Tribune* was already reporting: "Basketball . . . has been adopted by those unerring feelers of the public pulse, the betting commissioners." By 1950 as much as $300,000 was routinely being wagered on Madison Square Garden college basketball games. "You could place a bet in any corner of the Garden," says Bernard Laterman, who played CCNY freshman basketball during the 1949–50 season. (A *Newsweek* reporter, in fact, suggested that pari-mutuel machines should be installed in the Garden to handle betting, as was done at racetracks.)

Almost everyone who regularly attended Garden games in that era can recall incidents when, in the closing seconds of a game, fans would stand screaming at a player as he attempted a pair of free throws with his team ahead by, say, nine points; such behavior would seem unaccountable when victory was assured, but in fact the free throws were vitally important, because if the point spread had favored that team to win by eight points, then those two shots could determine the outcome—the difference between a bet won and a bet lost. "There was booing and catcalling that had little to do with the winning and losing, but a lot to do with the point spread of the game," said Marty Glickman. In a 1944 article on basketball in Madison Square Garden, *Newsweek* cited a game in which NYU was favored over the University of Rochester by fourteen points; near the end of the game, when NYU led by thirteen, "an organized chant welled from bettors . . . 'Shoot! Shoot!' " They were rooting hard, to be sure, but for these spectators, victory didn't mean winning the game; it meant beating the spread.

According to most accounts, the point spread—or, as one veteran book-maker described it, "the greatest invention since the zipper"—was first devised in the 1930s by a securities analyst and aspiring bookmaker from Chicago by the name of Charles K. McNeil; it would make him, in the estimation of *Sports Illustrated,* "one of the most influential figures in the history of American sport."

The bookmakers of the time traditionally employed a system of 6–5 wagering, in which the gambler puts up six dollars for the chance of winning five. In its most simplified form, we might imagine that two bettors who support opposing teams in a particular game have each wagered six dollars; when the game is over, the bettor who has won gets eleven dollars (his original six plus five in winnings), the bettor who loses gets nothing, and the bookmaker retains the remaining dollar as his "vigorish": his service fee, or, to think of it another way, his broker's commission. For the bookmaker, then, the ideal situation is to have the same amount of money wagered on both sides of the bet. That way, the money to be paid out will be the same regardless of the outcome of the game, and the bookie will be guaranteed his percentage. The problem is that two teams are rarely evenly matched; almost always one team would seem more likely to win the game, and thus will receive most of the gamblers' betting money. If the stronger team wins, the bookmakers will have to pay out of their own pockets, because not enough money has been bet on the losing team to cover the amount that must be distributed in winnings.

Thus bookmakers had always looked for a method to bring the total bet on each side into balance, and for a long time the way they did so was by a system of odds. The stronger team might be judged, say, a 3-to-1 favorite to win the game; in this case, a gambler putting down money on the underdog would be less likely to win than if he bet on the favorite, but might be enticed by the prospect of winning three times the initial investment, whereas a bettor on the favorite would receive only his original wager plus one-third. Still, even very high odds could not ensure that bettors would put down money on the underdog when that team had no realistic chance of victory; the bookmaker still faced the age-old problem of equalizing his bets, and moreover, he also exposed himself to financial crisis, or even ruin, in the event that several underdogs managed to win in a brief period, forcing him to pay out more in winnings than he had on hand.

Charles K. McNeil's innovation was to replace the *odds* that a team was likely to win the game with the *number of points* by which it would win. A bettor who placed money on the winning team would collect only if that team won by a margin greater than the listed point spread; on the other hand, a bet could be won even on the losing team if that team managed to keep the final score closer than the spread. The ingenuity of McNeil's point spread system thus lay in its capacity to turn each game, no matter how seemingly lopsided, into an even proposition. Few bettors, for instance, would place their money on Brooklyn College in a basketball game against City College, even at very high odds, but a good portion of them might if the point spread was large enough. If the point spread was listed at, say, thirteen points, a gambler who bet on City College would win his bet only if City won by fourteen points or more; conversely, a gambler who bet on Brooklyn College would win even if Brooklyn lost the game by as much as twelve. (The point spreads were easily available to anyone who cared to know them: Nearly all of the city's newspapers published them.)

For bookmakers, then, it was critically important to determine the appropriate point spread for each game. In the 1940s, that job fell to one person: Leo Hirschfield, the so-called Wizard of Odds. Hirschfield was the owner of Athletic Publications, which occupied the entire floor of an office building in downtown Minneapolis. With a staff of ten handicappers, Athletic Publications produced booklets with names like *Gridiron Weekly* and *Weekly Basketball Record* that were subscribed to by more than eight thousand bookmakers. Hirschfield's syndicate provided relevant information as well as point spreads for nearly all of the significant upcoming football and college basketball games played throughout the United States—the authoritative judgments known collectively as "the Minneapolis line."

In its ceaseless quest for the most up-to-date knowledge, Athletic Publications subscribed to daily newspapers throughout the country, and, perhaps even more usefully, to the student newspapers for every college that maintained a big-time sports program. Hirschfield's handicappers scoured the papers for all of the latest information on player injuries and illnesses, hot and cold streaks, or any other factor that might influence the outcome of a game; it was widely believed (though denied by Hirschfield himself) that Athletic Publications employed a network of student "correspondents" on major college campuses who kept a watchful eye on the local sports teams, ready to report back if a star player seemed to be spending an unusual amount of time in the trainer's room, or had just had a fight with his girlfriend and might perhaps be distracted or demoralized for the next game. "If Joe Zilch, the star at Siwash, falls down the cellar stairs in the privacy of his home and injures his little toe," marveled the *New York Times* sports columnist Arthur Daley, "the syndicate knows about it before he has picked himself up off the floor."

Nor was it just bookmakers who subscribed to Hirschfield's publications. Many gamblers read them as well; after all, it was in their interest to accumulate as much information as possible, learning all they could about the teams to provide themselves with an edge in their betting. That was a reasonable and expected part of the system; however, there were always a few gamblers who wanted to go beyond the mere accumulation of information and actually influence the game itself, by paying players to guarantee a particular outcome, and in so doing, taking what was a nominally illegal activity and turning it into a deeply felonious one.

These men were not just gamblers but fixers, and for them, too, the point spread was a boon. For in basketball's past, gamblers who sought to fix a game had had to persuade players to lose a game they were favored to win. Now all it took was to persuade them to reduce the margin of victory below the point spread—to still win the game, but just by not as much. As the veteran sportswriter Stanley Woodward noted: "If you sidle up to a boy and suggest that he do his best to throw Saturday night's game to the opposition, he may very well take a poke at you—even if he is not an Eagle Scout. But if you carefully guide the conversation around to where you can suggest that he might rake in a nice bundle of cash for himself merely by regulating the point spread in the final score—without changing the actual result of the game in any way—he is much more likely to let himself be sold." An athlete whose long-honed competitive nature would recoil at the prospect of intentionally losing a game might have less resistance to creating a smaller margin of victory. What was the difference, really (so he might rationalize), if you won a game by twelve points or won it by nine? And so, in the years after World War II, a new term of art entered the American lexicon: *shaving points.*

A basketball player who took money to shave points could still contribute to his team's victory. All it took, in the midst of his regular effort, was to miss a shot on purpose now and again, or perhaps throw away a couple of passes, and much of the time the lapse could be far less dramatic than that. A player might simply take the wrong position under the boards for a rebound; or fail to fight through a screen, leaving an opponent open for a shot; or pass to a teammate a moment too early, before he was ready to receive the pass, or a moment too late, when he was no longer unguarded. They were small errors, subtle, and, amid the continuous flow of a fast-paced basketball game, almost undetectable, for they were no different from the mistakes that occurred, honestly and routinely, in the normal course of competition.

In January 1945 a team of New York City police detectives was staking out the home of a man named Harry Rosen, who had been arrested for trafficking in stolen goods. The detectives noticed two young men loitering around Rosen's house, apparently waiting for him to arrive, and took them into custody. The two turned out to be Brooklyn College students, and though they had nothing to do with the stolen goods, they panicked under questioning and admitted that they and three other teammates had accepted money from Rosen to dump a game against the University of Akron. None of the players ever faced criminal charges; all expressed their guilt and remorse, but also made it clear that they were not alone in their misconduct. "I don't see why this should happen to Brooklyn College," said one of them. "Every college in the city is doing it."

In December of that same year, City College's star forward, Paul Schmones, confided to Bobby Sand that he had been approached by another member of the team, Leonard Hassman, with a bribe offer from a gambler: They would receive $1,000 apiece if they shaved points in an upcoming game against Holy Cross. Sand told Schmones that he should report the offer to Nat Holman immediately. Schmones did so, and Holman in turn brought him to see Dr. Frank S. Lloyd, the chairman of the department. After some discussion, during which Schmones expressed his anxiety about possible retribution by gamblers, the decision was made to keep the matter private. City College played the game without incident, and afterward Hassman was quietly dropped from the basketball team, purportedly for not maintaining his academic standing.

Though rumors of basketball fixes persisted, nothing more definite surfaced until January 1949, when Manhattan district attorney Frank S. Hogan announced the arrests of four gamblers for attempting to fix a game between Manhattan College and George Washington University. The rumblings were growing louder, and by the fall of 1949, Holman had begun to address them publicly. On December 6, as the featured speaker at a banquet held by the Union College athletic department in Schenectady, New York, he told the assembled guests that basketball was being demoralized by gambling. "Big-money wagers," he warned, "are going to ruin the game."

The following day, City College was to play its third game of the season, against Southern Methodist University. The Beavers were favored to win by thirteen points. Al Roth told Eddie Roman that Norm Mager had something he wanted to discuss with him.

CHAPTER 6

Norm Mager stood six foot five but weighed only 170 pounds, and he had long arms and coat-hanger shoulders; with his arms extended he resembled nothing so much as a draftsman's T-square. Before entering City College he had served for two and a half years in the Army Air Forces; now, at the age of twenty-three, he was the oldest member of the team and exuded a powerful sense of worldliness. Mager (pronounced "major") had a devilish grin and the romantic, deep-set eyes of a crooner. He smoked cigarettes, a pack a day; he also "spewed profanity" (as one of his teammates described it), owned a convertible, and—at least as amazing to the other players—had a girlfriend who was a fashion model. He was a natural leader, energetic and gregarious and self-confident; after hitting a long shot in practice he might turn to a teammate and say with a grin and a shrug, "What did you expect? When you're good, you're good."

Mager's father, David, was a tough, demanding man who rarely expressed warmth to his children. He had immigrated from Austria with no money at all, but little by little he had managed to establish a building maintenance business; though Norm was majoring in accounting, David was not pleased by the idea of his oldest son running around in shorts playing a boy's game. "Do something real," he would scold. "Get a real job." Norm, for his part, was growing increasingly tired of being told what to do, especially after having spent more than two years taking orders on an Army base. It made for a poor fit with a coach like Nat

Holman—another tough, demanding man, who at a coaches' luncheon a few years earlier had declared, "There's a right way and a wrong way to play this game and I insist my way is right."

As time went on, Mager had come to resent the conditions under which the City College Beavers played their games. He would complain to friends about the indignity, on road trips, of rinsing out his socks in the hotel room sink only to come downstairs to see Holman and Sam Winograd eating a steak dinner in the hotel restaurant and sending their suits out to be dry-cleaned. He didn't like how the players were occasionally granted the opportunity to run copy to the wire room for the sportswriters at courtside and get them Cokes when they were thirsty, in return for a three-dollar payment. He felt the players were being treated like kids when they were clearly performing at an adult level (indeed, Holman often brought in professional teams to scrimmage against them), and he bristled at Holman's mocking refrain whenever the team was playing poorly during a practice: "If you can't play major league basketball, we will schedule Cooper Union."*

To Eddie Roman, Norm Mager made point-shaving seem as natural a part of being on the team as free towels and the chits they got for lunch at the nearby Liberty Restaurant. It had been going on a long time, he said, the procedures passed down from older guys to younger, almost as though they were the rules and rituals of a college secret society. He himself had been brought in a couple of years earlier, as a sophomore, after he came in off the bench and scored several baskets—and in so doing unknowingly blew a fixed game in the Garden against Syracuse. After that, the others realized they had to include him. During that season, Norm claimed, there were nights when as many as four players on the court at once were doing business.

Eddie could see that the guys from Brooklyn, Norm Mager and Fats Roth, had grown up differently than he had in the Bronx, with a sense of anticipation that Fats described as a kind of birthright: In the schoolyards of Brooklyn, you would play against college kids who were already doing it and made no secret of it, and you knew that someday you'd be going to college and it would be your turn. Fats was eager to get

* Cooper Union is a college in downtown New York City; though it offers degrees in various fields, it is most commonly thought of as an art school.

started. He had been working summers since he was thirteen, first as a runner for a brokerage firm in the city and then as a waiter in the Catskills, and his earnings always went back to his family. He was nineteen years old now, and after all this time he still, like a kid, had no cash in his pocket; if he wanted to buy a new suit or a pair of shoes, he had to ask his father for the money. While Normie's voice took on a bluff, hard-boiled tone when he discussed this, Fats could be condescending, even at the momentary indecision of a teammate. It came across without words, in the twist of a lip, a dismissive look in his eyes like a shade pulled down over a window, his whole demeanor conveying the message that this was just the way things worked in the city, this was the real game, and you were naïve and foolish to imagine otherwise.

Norm explained that they were being offered $4,500 for the Southern Methodist game. City College was favored by thirteen points, a margin that provided plenty of room to maneuver. They weren't being asked to lose—all they needed to do was come in under the point spread. The money would be handed over by someone from Brooklyn; Norm called him Eli Kaye, although this seemed not to be his real name. He would always remain to Eddie Roman a shadowy figure; later, Eddie would see photographs in the newspaper of a thick-necked guy with heavy-lidded eyes and a hard, penetrating stare. Kaye had been a welder in the Navy Yard during the war but by trade he was a bookie, from a family of bookies; of late he had branched out, and now he was the front man for a gambling syndicate that reached all the way into the South and Midwest. There would be $1,000 apiece for Norm, Fats, Irwin Dambrot, and Eddie if he wanted it, and $500 for Herb Cohen because he was a sub. Those were the guys Kaye had wanted; they were the ones he felt he could trust.

Herbie's participation Eddie understood—he was Fats's old friend from Erasmus Hall High School in Brooklyn—but it was a surprise to learn that Irwin, his former Taft teammate, was in as well. Irwin was now a married man (he had married his high school sweetheart, Pearl, over the summer) and was planning to attend dental school after graduation. As a college senior, Irwin was much the way Eddie remembered him from high school, still cheerful and easygoing, friendly to everyone but also a bit separate from the other guys; he scored his points and earned his grades and somehow seemed immune to the normal grind of daily life, like that frictionless wheel they had read about in physics class, gliding smoothly on forever with no loss of energy. For his part, Eddie was dizzied by the prospect of a thousand dollars, at a time when he was planning to apply for a City College scholarship worth fifty dollars for a semester. Imagining it, he recalled the nights when he would do his schoolwork in the dining room while his mother sat at the kitchen table fretting about bills. She was plagued by an immigrant's anxiety that something terrible and irreversible was going to descend on them at any moment, and though her fears seemed to stem from a childhood riven by wars and pogroms and deportations, as she got older and further away from her youth they grew only worse, increasingly keeping her cooped up inside the little house that was slowly but steadily losing its value.

Eddie himself was away from home so much, off to the subway early in the morning for classes and often not getting back from practice until nearly eight o'clock. *What do you owe the school?* Norm kept asking, reminding him of all the hours they put in for the team, all the money they made for the athletic department, the way Nat blamed the players when they lost and took the credit when they won, how little interest he took in them as people, never inquiring about their classes or their families, barely even giving them the respect to call them by their names. Listening to Norm talk, Eddie began to suspect that for him the money was secondary: He hated Nat so much he would have dumped for nothing.

It was a sure thing, Norm told him. They would win the game for City College and pocket some money besides; Eli Kaye's people would bet on SMU to cover the points—to end up no more than thirteen points behind—and would collect on their bets. Nobody was going to lose on the deal except maybe some bookies, and what were they going to do, call the cops?

The conversations were accompanied by surreptitious glances that only reinforced the impression of exclusivity. Eddie couldn't help but feel flattered that the most popular guys on the team were reaching out to him, asking him, in a sense, to join their club; Normie and Fats exuded confidence, and if Irwin was involved it was probably all right. In the evenings after practice Eddie would walk down 170th Street from the Grand Concourse back home, hunched against the December cold in his big overcoat. At this hour the smells of cooking came from everywhere and nowhere; his mother would have dinner waiting for him, one of her weekday American meals, maybe a couple of lamb chops with canned spinach, or spaghetti with tomato sauce, and a Jell-O mold for dessert. He passed his old haunts, Rappaport's candy store, the Sugar Bowl, Pete's pool hall, where the bookmakers always congregated in the back. Listening to Norm and Fats talk so matter-of-factly about the corruption inside the Garden, Eddie couldn't help but recall his father's denunciations of the painters' union, how he railed at the cronyism, the favoritism in hiring. Julius was mild-mannered and spoke very little, but when he did, municipal corruption was one of his regular themes. Each night returning home Eddie hoped that his father had found some work, that the house, when he entered, wouldn't smell of fresh paint. Someday, he figured, when everything had quieted down, he could give the money to his mother.

So it would be Normie, Fats, Irwin, Herbie, and Eddie: the guys Eli Kaye wanted, the ones he felt he could trust.

Floyd Layne had been friends with his teammate Ed Warner since they were fifteen years old and played together on the Harlem YMCA Juniors. Back then, Ed's father had been a regular presence at all the Juniors games. Born in Antigua in the West Indies, Charles Warner was known around town as Pops, a nickname that Ed would later take as his own; at least nominally, Pops worked in a laundry, but everyone knew that his main business was running numbers. The numbers racket—also known as the "policy"—had been invented in the 1920s by an immigrant from the Virgin Islands; by the 1940s it had become Harlem's biggest and most important industry (a reported 75 percent of residents played the numbers), so enmeshed in the life of the community that it was scarcely seen as illegal. As a kid Ed sometimes helped his father on his route, accompanying him into the local bars and barbershops and beauty parlors, collecting money, handing out slips, jotting down the picks in a little notebook for five o'clock, when the winning number would be announced.

Ed could no longer remember his mother's face; she had died of pneumonia when he was only five years old. The next year Mayor La Guardia's commission found medical care in Harlem to be "dangerously inadequate," with one square block—bounded by Lenox and Seventh avenues and 142nd and 143rd streets—known as the Lung Block because of its astonishingly high incidence of respiratory diseases. That was Harlem: where no new hospital or school had been built in years, despite a quadrupling of the population (and the refusal of Manhattan's private hospitals to accept black patients); where rents were higher than those for comparable apartments downtown because racial covenants, formal and informal, prevented blacks from living almost anywhere else, thus creating an excess of demand for limited supply; where too often in those apartments roaches would scatter like shotgun pellets when a kitchen or bathroom light was turned on, and holes in the wall were stuffed with steel wool in desperate efforts to keep out the rats; where no white-owned business would hire a black person other than as a porter or cleaning woman; where the sidewalk stands were filled with windfall fruit and bruised and discolored vegetables rejected by grocers farther downtown.

Ed Warner had grown up playing cops and robbers in garbage-strewn lots, imagining jagged shards of concrete into guns and taking cover behind burned-out cars and rusted iceboxes dumped there by indifferent landlords. He first picked up a basketball at the age of ten, at the Colonel Young playground at 145th and Lenox; two years later he wasn't even good enough to make the YMCA Midget team, but he kept at it, and by the time he was fifteen he was the star of the Y Juniors. During those years he was an altar boy and sang in the choir at St. Philip's Episcopalian church on 133rd Street; he also made a little money doing odd jobs for a dentist in the neighborhood, and he was enough of a known presence that some of the white store owners felt comfortable leaving him behind the counter while they ran out for lunch or a pack of cigarettes.

Ed's friends recognized that over time he had developed a kind of split personality: He was warm and deeply loyal to those he cared about but tough and aggressive to those he perceived as a threat; when he felt comfortable in a situation he was easygoing and quick to laugh, but he would stand stone-faced and nearly silent around those he didn't know or trust, particularly white people and figures of authority (who regularly used the word "sullen" to describe him). He was a would-be numbers runner who attended church regularly; he freely dispensed advice to the younger kids of the neighborhood and often urged them to stay in school, but he himself cared little for education and was drawn to the flash and excitement of the racket life, as his father had been before him.

By the time he entered Frederick Douglass Junior High School, Ed had joined the Sabers, one of the largest street gangs in Harlem—though he wasn't one of the more hard-core members, one of the kids who fashioned zip guns on the sly in Mr. Anthony's shop class, grinding out pieces of wood and fitting them with lengths of pipe and heavy rubber bands to fire a single .22-caliber bullet. There were dozens of gangs in Harlem; they had names like doo-wop groups—the Comets, the Chancellors, the Barons, the Buccaneers, the Socialistic Dukes—each with its own particular rituals of initiation and promotion, each one jealously guarding its own little patch of territory. In 1945, Ed and a few of his friends got into a rumble with members of the Nomads, an incident that turned more serious when a patrolman who broke up the fight discovered that one of the Sabers was carrying a pistol. Ed was arrested and brought into Children's Court as a juvenile delinquent, where he was found guilty of fighting and released on probation—a conviction that would remain on his record, to be used against him if he were ever arrested again.

The following year, Ed's father died under mysterious circumstances, discovered at the bottom of an elevator shaft in a building on 125th Street. Distraught over the loss, Ed wanted to quit basketball, but many of his friends, Floyd Layne among them, persuaded him to stick with the game, which they already understood offered his best chance of advancement—the possibility of someday joining the Harlem Globetrotters or one of the other touring teams, and beyond that, landing a coaching job with some social service agency or the city. And, in any case, time spent playing basketball was time that couldn't be spent shooting craps under a lamppost in St. Nicholas Park, or getting in deeper with the Sabers, who were then entering into a gang war with the Slicksters that would culminate in a series of shootings and stabbings throughout Harlem and the Bronx.

Even when his father was alive Ed hadn't lived with him; he had been shuttled around Harlem, taken in by a succession of female relatives, aunts and great-aunts and grandmothers, who cared for him as long as they were able to. By the time he began attending City College he was living with his great-aunt Anna Johnson and her daughter Dolly in a small apartment on the second floor of a five-story tenement on 135th Street between Fifth and Lenox avenues; his great-aunt didn't understand or appreciate his attachment to basketball, and the two of them often got into arguments, so he spent as much time as he could outside the house. Ed was tall, standing a shade under six foot three, and he had grown a mustache as soon as he was able to; he would stride down the sidewalk as his late father had before him, wearing pegged pants and an open-collared knit shirt that displayed his musculature, and in the colder months a raglan overcoat and a fedora with one brim bent down to a rakish angle (as he became better known as a basketball player, some of the local gamblers had started passing the hat to get him new clothes), on his way to a movie at the Franklin or the RKO Alhambra, or to Snookie's Sugar Bowl to hang out with his basketball buddies, or maybe to a party in a basement or at the Sportsman's Club or the clubhouse of the Vulcan Society, the Negro firefighters' association. Someone would be playing Duke Ellington or Count Basie records on a hi-fi set, and there would be bottles of rum uncapped on a table with paper cups and bags of ice, men and women talking and flirting on couches and hard-backed chairs, the music and smoke and alcohol blending together to create a kind of happiness spell, and Ed would often join in the dancing, sliding smoothly from woman to woman, laughing and swinging them around the room in his arms. On the way home, dreading what would likely be another quarrel, he might stop into one of the taverns where the rows of bottles were lit up like torch singers above the counter, and if someone on a stool recognized him they might talk for a while about the previous game or the upcoming one.

City College, everyone seemed to know, had four black players this year, which was the most they had ever had. One of them, Joe Galiber, was a team cocaptain; maybe someday Ed himself would be captain, as he had been in junior high and high school. He had been playing basketball for half his life; those moves that had felt so frustratingly clumsy on the Colonel Young playground were now, under the spotlights of Madison Square Garden, fluid and strong. He was doing things with the ball that no one had ever seen before, his hands twisting one way while his head moved the other, all feints and delays, spinning shots off the backboard, improvising sequences on the fly like the saxophone players he sometimes heard down the street at Small's Paradise. The games, after all, had never been the problem. Despite Floyd's encouragement he couldn't seem to get a handle on his schoolwork, had no interest in the student tutors Bobby Sand sent his way. He had barely made it out of junior high but got moved on to a good high school; he had barely graduated, but lots of colleges had offered him scholarships. Somehow or other he always managed to get by.

By his sophomore year, stories were already circulating around City College about Ed Warner's phenomenal physical gifts. There had been that time, for instance, outside of German class. Lots of basketball players took German at City College, since it was widely understood that certain teachers in the department would not issue failing grades to members of the basketball team. The hallway outside the classroom had a high ceiling, and several basketball players had each bet a quarter and were jumping to see if anyone could touch it. None of them, though, had been able to collect the money. Coming out of class, Ed saw what was going on; he put his books down, steadied himself, and leaped.

For a long time afterward the assembled basketball players just stood in the hallway and gazed in wonder at the palm print Ed Warner had put on the ceiling.

Ed had large hands and very long arms (Irwin Dambrot once noted to a reporter in astonishment that Warner wore a 39-inch sleeve), and he was far more muscular than anyone else on the team. "He was built like an Adonis," says one of his teammates, recalling how Ed would walk naked around the locker room, "and he wasn't embarrassed to show you." Much about Ed was different from the other players, like the fact that he put on cologne before games because he believed he played better when he smelled good. More significant, Ed was the only orphan on the team, with a personal background far different from even the other black players'. Joe Galiber's father, for instance, worked for the post office; Floyd Layne's father was the superintendent of an apartment building; Leroy Watkins's father was a construction worker. Ed was also the only player who lived in Harlem, and while Al Roth liked to affect a tough gangster air, Ed had actually been a gangster; alone among them, he had an arrest record.

Ed had long seen gamblers hanging around the edges of his teams. He wore flashy clothes and no one knew where he had gotten the money to pay for them. And from the beginning of his sophomore season it was clear that he and Eddie Roman were the team's most reliable scorers. Warner would seemingly have been a prime candidate to involve in the point-shaving scheme in the game against Southern Methodist University, but he wasn't. Neither he nor Floyd Layne, the two black players among the starting five, was among the guys Eli Kaye trusted.

Nearly 17,000 fans were on hand at Madison Square Garden to watch City College take on the Mustangs of Southern Methodist University. Dressed in their white uniforms with the black and lavender trim, the City College players went through their warm-ups, many of them almost silent, lost in thought. Eddie Roman always felt nervous before a game, but this nervousness felt different, sharper; Norm Mager was an old hand at this, but Eddie couldn't help but wonder how the others would respond, or how he would.

The pace of the game was furious right from the opening tip-off, the ball moving up and back, up and back, and on City's end of the court Irwin Dambrot kept shooting, almost frantically, like someone who cannot stop talking when nervous. He took ten shots in the first seventeen minutes of the game, from all over the court, and made six of them, an unlikely offensive barrage in an era of college basketball when a .350 shooting percentage was considered exceptional. Dambrot had always been an aggressive shooter, so much so that the other players sometimes joked about it: With most basketball players, they would say, it was the legs that wore out first, but with Irwin it would be the arms. Now, though, that joke didn't seem quite so funny, and Eddie could almost imagine Normie Mager staring daggers at Irwin from the bench—thirteen points was a plenty big margin, but there was no need to make things more difficult than necessary.

Despite Dambrot's offensive outburst, Southern Methodist managed to stay with City, matching them almost shot for shot in a first half in which the Beavers made seventeen out of thirty-eight shots, a .447 percentage. At the half CCNY led by seven points, 35 to 28. Wrote the reporter from the *Observation Post*, "It was unquestionably the finest single period of court play seen in the Garden this year."

In the second half, though, as that same reporter would note, "the Beavers seemed to become plagued with a continual inability to score." At one point they somehow missed baskets on three consecutive fast break opportunities. Irwin Dambrot's outside shot seemed unaccountably to have deserted him; after scoring twelve points in the first half, in the second half he scored only two. For his part Eddie Roman found, to his horror, that he was missing shots even when he didn't want to; he was playing with one eye on the scoreboard, worrying and calculating rather than simply observing and reacting, and the constant flow of thought interfered with the smooth, effortless motion he had worked so hard to establish, his shooting now as labored as walking when you suddenly become conscious of the motion of your legs.

Midway through the second half SMU had pulled to within four points, 41 to 37. That was when Floyd Layne and Ed Warner took charge of the game. Layne scored on a driving layup to finish a fast break, which he followed with a long set shot. Then Warner made two hook shots on consecutive possessions, one with his right hand and one with his left. He was also dominating the rebounding on both backboards, shutting down the Mustangs and providing his own teammates new scoring opportunities, and as the period dragged on, Eddie Roman couldn't help but feel sick inside, watching Floyd and Ed play their hearts out, and a little bit frantic as well, because now the Beaver lead was inching up toward the thirteen-point spread, and with ninety seconds left Warner maneuvered himself free for a layup that would turn out to be the last basket of the game.

The final buzzer sounded; City College had won by a score of 67 to 53, remaining undefeated for the season, and as the lights came up the Garden crowd stood and cheered, and the students in the upper balcony serenaded the players with "Lavender" as they ran off the court. In the locker room Irwin Dambrot looked ghastly, his normally ruddy cheeks drained of color; he looked as if he was expecting to have his legs broken in a dark alley after the game—or maybe, with Irwin, it would be the arms. The team managers circulated with trays of orange slices and cups of water, and Eddie Roman sat in front of his locker and found, amid the loud talk and laughter swirling around him, that he was almost overcome by shame. He had made just four of fourteen shots, and two of those were easy tap-ins under the basket. He had played the worst game of his life; he had let down his teammates, especially Floyd and Ed, and now he had a secret, one that he knew he could never share with his family and his friends. He had crossed the line and could not go back; this was who he was now—a point shaver—and moreover they had failed even at that, having exceeded the spread by a point. City College had gained a hard-fought, stirring victory, but everything seemed terrible and it was all Eddie could do to smile for the reporters as he edged his way out of the crowded locker room.

Outside the Garden, Eddie found his friend Ron Schechter waiting for him. "Let's get out of here," Eddie said, and the two of them walked down Broadway to the Astor Theater on Forty-Fifth Street, where they caught the late show of the new movie *Battleground,* about a company of American soldiers fighting in Belgium during the Second World War. It was a great picture, full of vividly rendered battle scenes, the best one of all near the end, when the company is facing a devastating German bombardment. The GI played by Van Johnson, up to that point the epitome of American moxie, suddenly loses his nerve and runs away; but then, ashamed of his own cowardice in front of a buddy, he stops running and from his new position launches a counterattack that leads to victory.

That night, while Eddie Roman sat in a Times Square movie theater, Norm Mager was meeting with Eli Kaye. Kaye could not believe that Mager had the chutzpah to ask him for the $4,500 they had been promised. "What are you, crazy?" he said. "How the hell can you ask for the money when you went over the spread? I took a beating and you guys ain't getting a dime."

Mager had to concede that he was right. More to the point, Kaye had unnervingly steely eyes and he drove a big car and it was not clear for whom he was acting as the front man; when talking to him a threat seemed always to linger unspoken in the air, a whiff of violence that clung to him like smoke. By the time they parted, Mager had assured Kaye that the players would make it up to him later in the season.

At the next practice Mager pulled the other guys aside. "You owe them a game now," he said. "I'll tell you when."

The Sunday after the SMU game, Ed Reid, a reporter for *The Brooklyn Daily Eagle*, began an eight-part series on a crime syndicate that he termed the Combine, which had as its chief sources of revenue "the bookmaking and policy rackets." He wrote, "The Combine could not exist in Brooklyn or any other place without the protection of a few crooked politicians and crooked police."

In response to the *Eagle*'s series, Police Commissioner William P. O'Brien—who had been appointed earlier that year by Mayor William O'Dwyer—would say only: "The Department will investigate any allegations made against any member or members of the force." The mayor himself made no comment.

CHAPTER 7

In the fall of 1949 the Democratic mayor of New York City, William O'Dwyer, the one hundredth mayor in the city's history, would seem to have been riding high. On November 8 he had been reelected to a second term, a mandate given by the citizenry of New York for his policies of expansive government ("Government should permeate," he liked to say, "it shouldn't crush") and the patronage jobs that he dispensed at a rate not seen since the glory days of Tammany Hall, the city's venerable Democratic machine. Yet the mayor was deeply troubled. In his relatively brief but highly successful career as a politician, O'Dwyer had been driven by two conflicting forces: ambition and fear. Though he had long dreamed of occupying the city's highest office, he had more than once tried to give it up when it was within his grasp, as if, historian Robert Caro observed, he was "desperately afraid of what the spotlight in which a mayor must walk might reveal when it shone on those shadowy places in his past."

On the very day in 1945 that O'Dwyer received the Democratic nomination for mayor of New York, he had pleaded with party leaders to name him to a judgeship—for, by an arcane provision of New York electoral law, that was the only way the winner of a primary election could refuse the nomination. That request had gone unfulfilled; O'Dwyer won the mayoral election decisively and served out a successful first term.

Now, less than three weeks after his reelection and at the apex of his political power, he began to complain of dizziness and palpitations of the heart. On November 28, 1949, he checked in to Bellevue Hospital; there, in his hospital room, having not yet been sworn in for a second term, he wrote out and signed his letter of resignation.

William O'Dwyer (Bill-O, as he was known to his friends, and he had friends in every part of the city) was fifty-nine years old, still a hand-some man, with broad shoulders and a ruddy face and a thatch of gray-ing hair that set off the thick black eyebrows that were his most distinctive feature—other than his voice, which was exceptionally fine, deep and resonant and with just a trace of an Irish lilt. O'Dwyer's was a classic New York success story. An immigrant from County Mayo, one of eleven children born to a pair of village schoolteachers, at the age of twenty he had arrived in the city with twenty-five dollars in his pocket and no clothes but the suit on his back. Eventually he found work as a plasterer's helper; years later, as mayor, O'Dwyer would stand on the steps of City Hall and, gesturing up at the Woolworth Building towering across the street, say proudly, "It was with these hands that I helped erect that building. And so, for all time, I have left my mark on the city."

He had always loved books (he quoted lavishly from Dante, Yeats, and Byron) and during his time in the construction trade he read West-ern novels to his fellow hod carriers on their lunch breaks; the other men, grateful for the diversion, didn't realize that he was working on his pronunciation, trying to lose his thick brogue, which he understood was going to be an impediment to his success—he just didn't yet know in what. After several years in construction he took a job as a bartender at the Vanderbilt Hotel, where he spent endless hours watching the cus-tomers, the wealthy and well-dressed whom he thought of as "the dainty people," trying to figure out how to act like one of them; more important, while working at the Vanderbilt he fell in love with one of the hotel's switchboard operators, Catherine Lenihan*—Kitty, she was called—who believed in him and gave him confidence when he had lit-tle, who persuaded him to take the civil service examination and be-come a policeman. Later, with Kitty's encouragement, he enrolled in

* The two met when O'Dwyer mistakenly handed her a Canadian dime to pay for a phone call; she carried that dime in her purse for the rest of her life.

evening law school at Fordham University; in 1925 he passed the bar exam and went into private practice as a defense attorney.

In late 1932, Acting Mayor Joseph V. McKee appointed him magistrate; it was the lowest tier of judgeship but a platform from which a political career might be launched, and in those years O'Dwyer passed many evenings in Brooklyn's fraternal lodges and the banquet rooms of the political clubhouses. Even then, Bill-O knew how to win over a crowd, with his swept-back hair and the expansive gestures of a Broadway idol, opening his arms wide as he spoke of how as a young man from a small Irish town he had fallen in love with the great hectic city of New York, where people from the four quarters of the earth lived together in peace and harmony—but how he also knew they could do better still, and he clasped his hands prayerfully to his chest as he called on the city to build better schools and playgrounds for its children, to clear slum housing and build new hospitals, his rich voice lowering in sorrow as he spoke of "the needy sick, those helpless ones." No one could doubt O'Dwyer's deep concern for the welfare of the poor and weak and newly arrived—they were, he felt, his own people—but it seemed just as clear that he was a man on the move. Among those who recognized the magistrate's political talents was Frank V. Kelly, the Democratic leader of Brooklyn; after first maneuvering O'Dwyer's appointment as a County Court judge, in 1939 Kelly put him forward as the Democratic candidate for district attorney, which in Brooklyn was tantamount to election.

Over the next two years O'Dwyer earned a citywide reputation as a crusading DA, obtaining eighty-seven murder convictions, including death sentences for seven members of Murder, Inc., Brooklyn's ruthless gang of killers for hire, and in 1941 he ran as the Democratic candidate against Fiorello H. La Guardia—a feisty Republican progressive and one of the most popular mayors in the city's history. Though O'Dwyer lost that race he kept the margin of victory to only six percentage points; it was clear to all observers that his political future in the city was still bright, and that he could very well return City Hall to the Democrats if he were to face an opponent less formidable than La Guardia.

When the Second World War broke out, O'Dwyer enlisted and was sent to Wright Field in Dayton, Ohio, eventually rising to the rank of brigadier general. In December 1942 he took time out from his military duties to travel to New York for a small cocktail party hosted by Frank Costello, the most powerful of the city's underworld bosses, at his penthouse in the Majestic Apartments on Central Park West. Costello was a former bootlegger turned gambling czar who had now expanded his empire into legitimate businesses including oil and real estate, whose friendships with political officials and ability to dispense favors had earned him the respectful sobriquet "the Prime Minister." He was a potent political force in the local Democratic Party, and Manhattan district leaders were regularly seen with him at the city's most high-profile restaurants and nightclubs. "I know the leaders, know them well, and maybe they got a little confidence in me," he said modestly. In 1949, Manhattan borough president Hugo Rogers summed up the situation concisely: "If Frank Costello wanted me," he said, "he would send for me."

Some of those who knew about the penthouse meeting between the general and the mob boss would later say that it had been arranged in hopes of obtaining Costello's support for O'Dwyer's next mayoral campaign; O'Dwyer himself claimed that they had discussed only Army business, but he could never explain why, if that were the case, several Tammany leaders and political contributors were also in attendance that evening.

Fiorello La Guardia chose not to run for a fourth term in 1945, and this time William O'Dwyer received 57 percent of the vote and became the mayor of the City of New York. On New Year's Day 1946 he was inaugurated in a festive ceremony at City Hall, joining with the Police Glee Club to sing

William O'Dwyer in 1945, having just received the news that he had been elected mayor of New York.
Associated Press

"It's a Great Day for the Irish." In his inaugural address the new mayor struck a forward-looking note, speaking of the great responsibilities he felt in leading the city, the need to address problems left unattended during four years of war. After the swearing-in of his cabinet members, he was escorted to his new office as the glee club sang "For He's a Jolly Good Fellow."

Yet even as the city's highest officeholder, Bill-O could not escape the rumors that he was operating in the service of forces more powerful than himself. Much of the gossip swirled around his closest aide, a shadowy figure named James J. Moran, who, it was whispered, ran the city from his office on the eleventh floor of the Municipal Building. One City Hall observer would later write that Moran "acted as though he owned O'Dwyer"; some who heard the two in conversation would say that they were never quite sure who was giving orders to whom.

Jim Moran was a colossus of a man, a tough, hulking redhead with a lantern jaw and hands like slabs of beef; he had a pink complexion, hooded eyes, and a deep crease on each side of his face that ran from his nose to his mouth, giving him the cobbled-together, slightly mechanical look of a ventriloquist's dummy. Born into an Irish immigrant family in a rough section of Brooklyn, Moran had started out on the waterfront as a checker of cargo, but like O'Dwyer he studied at night and eventually took the civil service exam and became a legal stenographer and court attendant, a huge man in an ill-fitting uniform who was always available to do a favor for the attorneys and political functionaries who used the courthouse as their base of operations. Judge O'Dwyer, the newly appointed magistrate, seemed to appreciate how easily Moran moved through the world of the courthouse, trading favors and pulling strings, and he hired him as a special attendant. When O'Dwyer became the district attorney of Brooklyn he made Moran his chief of staff. By then Big Jim Moran was already understood to be the man to see if you needed something from Bill-O; he was, in the description of one observer, "as close to O'Dwyer as his shirt."

As mayor, O'Dwyer appointed Moran first deputy fire commissioner, a position from which he could set into motion an audacious form of shakedown. The city's building regulations required that oil burners and storage tanks pass inspection by a fire marshal before any new construction could be completed; shortly after taking office, Moran called in his senior-level inspection personnel and instructed them that in the future no oil burner permit would be issued until a private fee had been paid to the inspector. Moran provided a sliding scale of rates, from five dollars for a small one-family house all the way up to five hundred dollars for a factory or warehouse. This fee was to be paid whether or not the inspector found a violation; nor, if one actually was found, did Moran care if it was ever corrected. In issuing a permit the critical factor was simply that the inspector had received his payment—a portion of which, of course, was to find its way back to Jim Moran. Withholding an oil burner permit could hold up construction for weeks or months, a price that no developer was willing to pay; it was far cheaper and easier simply to fulfill the transaction, to hand over the bribe and receive the necessary permit, no questions asked. Nor would a developer who desired ever to build again in New York City see any gain in challenging a directive that, it would have been made clear, came straight from the mayor's closest political adviser.

In 1949 the Republican mayoral candidate, Newbold Morris, had tried to make an issue of William O'Dwyer's ties to party bosses and organized crime. Morris denounced O'Dwyer as "the mob's man in City Hall," releasing a list of 124 alleged bookmaking sites in the borough of Brooklyn alone. A descendant of an aristocratic family who had attended Groton and Yale, Morris could gain little traction with his charges, and for his part O'Dwyer did not deign to respond to them, saying simply, "There are more serious things for police to do than hunt bookmakers."

O'Dwyer's own campaign proclaimed that he was "Courageous, Reliable, Experienced," those descriptives emblazoned alongside his smiling face on posters displayed all over town, and the incumbent seemed to be everywhere that fall, his Cadillac limousine screaming through the avenues as a motorcycle cop ahead cleared traffic, up the East River Drive from his home at Gracie Mansion to a campaign stop where the mayor would recount the illustrious history of the city: Reminding the audience of how in earlier days George Washington had commanded from Belview Mansion, on the very spot where Gracie Mansion now stood, and Alexander Hamilton had led rebel troops up a cow path called Broadway, noble forebears who had conquered the seemingly un-conquerable, he clenched his fists and extended his arms, and before long his listeners were accompanying Lewis and Clark on their trek through the Northwest. "Over river and hill and plain and mountain," he intoned, "under the winter's blast and the summer sun"—and when that excursion was completed, Bill-O had somehow come back around again to New York, describing the 58 new schools, 42,000 units of pub-lic housing, 760 new subway cars, and 2,000 new buses he had pro-vided for the city during his four years as mayor, and the money for municipal hospitals, and the swift and efficient snow removal during the blizzard of '47.

His hair was grayer now, and shadows darkened under his eyes, but his posture was still ramrod straight, as if to remind his audience of his service in the Army during the war, and indeed, some of his supporters addressed him as "General." His demeanor was commanding but unpre-tentious as he stood on the dais wearing one of the double-breasted suits that even now, as mayor, he bought off the rack (often smartened by a carnation in his lapel), with a loud patterned tie and the same style of comfortable thick-soled black oxfords that he had worn when he walked a beat on the streets of Brooklyn. What always came strongly across to his listeners was that unlike so many would-be reformers, he seemed genuinely to love this city and to know it inside and out, and those in the audience couldn't help but recall, too, that the mayor's heart had been broken when his wife passed away during his first year in office; that trag-edy seemed to make his attention to their concerns even more affecting, and when his speech was over they invariably gathered around him—he was never one to deflect physical affection—patting his shoulder and clutching his arm as they pumped his hand, and then he murmured his apologies for his crowded schedule and he ducked out a side door and was back in his Cadillac heading somewhere else.

After many years of ill health, Kitty had succumbed to Parkinson's dis-ease in 1946. Her brief stay in Gracie Mansion had been filled with hardship and sadness, and her death, after thirty years of marriage, was the great sorrow of O'Dwyer's life; even six months later he still broke down when he spoke in public of "Mrs. O'Dwyer." He spent two years filling up his evenings with social and civic events, but in 1948 he met a fashion model from Dallas named Sloan Simpson and had soon taken up with her, the two of them regularly photographed attending a Broadway show or walking hand in hand in the park. When the mayor was going to marry Miss Simpson had become a preoccupation of the city's papers, but she was twenty-seven years his junior and, as he would later write, "misgivings about a May-December marriage continued to haunt me."

On the evening of November 28, 1949, he was almost overcome with dizziness, and he instructed his secretary to have his physician meet him at Gracie Mansion. When the doctor arrived he found O'Dwyer weak and trembling, barely coherent; he was sped by ambulance to Bellevue Hospital, where upon examination he was diagnosed as suffering from "almost complete nervous and physical exhaustion" compounded by "very definite heart strain." The mayor was checked in to a three-room hospital suite, and over the following week he undertook a regimen of near-complete rest. He was often under mild sedation, but as the days went by he became increasingly depressed; finally, on Sunday afternoon, December 4, he resolved that he could no longer endure the burdens of the job, and he wrote out a letter of resignation for his secretary to type up. That afternoon he called James Moran and informed him that he had resigned as mayor; Moran told O'Dwyer to calm down and do nothing more until he got there.

Sometime around five o'clock Moran, red-faced with anger, stormed in as O'Dwyer lay in his hospital bed. Back and forth he stomped, his massive body seeming to fill up the entire room, pausing only to pound his fist on the dresser as he shouted at the mayor that he could not resign, *would* not resign, without first taking care of him, that he needed to be rewarded for his years of service. O'Dwyer shouted back that he very well could resign, no one could stop the mayor from resigning, and with a flourish he pulled out the resignation letter, typed and signed, from a drawer in the bedside table and brandished it at Moran. In a burst of fury Moran snatched the letter away and, taking a book of matches from his pocket, lit the paper and let it burn for a moment before dropping it into a metal wastepaper basket.

Sitting in an adjoining room, the mayor's bodyguard, Detective Joseph Boyle, suddenly heard a startling cry: "It's on fire!"

The resignation letter had ignited the other papers in the wastebasket and the room was quickly filling with smoke. Boyle rushed in and managed to extinguish the flames, but by then the smoke had gotten into the ventilation system, and in the corridor one of the nurses noticed it and called the hospital switchboard. In a matter of minutes, twenty New York City firemen arrayed in helmets, rubber coats, and boots were tromping through the corridors looking for the source of the smoke.

At the entrance to the mayor's suite they were met by Detective Joseph Boyle. "What's the trouble?" he asked.

"Smoke in the corridor," said the battalion chief. "Any fire in here?"

"Nah," the detective replied; he explained that he had been making toast in the suite's kitchen when the phone rang, and since the mayor was asleep he ran to get the phone, and as he did he accidentally dropped a dish towel on the toaster and the end of it got burned a little. But everything was okay now, he assured the chief, so there was no need to investigate further. "Besides," he added, "the mayor's sound asleep in that room. We don't want to wake him up."

The firemen duly retreated, and the next day the city's papers carried an amusing item about the little fire that had been caused by the spark from the dish towel.

"The mayor," reported the Associated Press, "slept through it all."

Mayor O'Dwyer checked out of the hospital a few days later and flew down to Florida for a long vacation. While there he held a press conference to announce that he was getting married, and in the coming days the city's news pages were dominated by speculation about the details of the wedding, to be held December 20 in a Catholic church in the small Florida town of Stuart.

The sports pages, meanwhile, were full of stories about the surprising City College basketball team, which had now compiled six victories against only one defeat. On December 27, City was scheduled to play against the Bruins of UCLA. That afternoon Norm Mager passed the word: This was the game they owed the gamblers.

CHAPTER 8

It had been nineteen days since the ill-fated game against Southern Methodist, and Irwin Dambrot had been, as he described it, in "a living hell." All that time, waiting for Norm Mager to give the word about the next game they owed the gamblers, his mind had been occupied by the same grim thoughts: *When will Normie tell me? Will they kill me if I don't deliver?* A sense of dread hovered above him, ugly and frightening, like the grotesques who watched over the entrance to the college gym, until the afternoon of December 27, when Mager sidled up to him and murmured, "This is it." City was favored by nine points; the deal was the same as it had been against Southern Methodist—they could still win the game, as long as they came in under the spread. The news, having finally arrived, brought both dread and relief.

It was, Irwin felt, his own weakness that had brought him to this point. Years later, when he was finally able to talk about his decision, he said simply, "I wanted the guys to like me." Even though he was the cocaptain of the team, he had never been one to hang around with the other guys outside the Garden after a game, basking in the praise of the crowd, just schmoozing, laughingly recalling this play or that one, until eventually someone would look at his watch and ask, "Who's got a lift? Anyone going back to the Bronx?" and things would start breaking up. He found that he never quite knew what to say, and besides, his wife, Pearl, and his parents were always there to take him back home. "His ambition in life," the sports columnist Jerry Izenberg would observe about Dambrot, "was to be a guy who hung out on the corner. But he had nobody to hang with."

Eddie Roman, who had spent more nights than he could count hanging out on Bronx street corners, had agreed to participate in the scheme in part because Irwin was doing it: Irwin, who had been the king of their high school, with a good-looking steady girlfriend and the cheerleaders calling his name; who lived, more than anyone he had ever met, inside a nimbus of glory; who seemed never to have made a wrong move on the court or off; who had the smoothest push shot anyone had ever seen; and who, arriving at City College, was immediately hailed by Nat Holman as "potentially the greatest ballplayer I've ever coached." Eddie hadn't told Irwin that, though. The two didn't speak of point-shaving to each other, not then and never after.

Madison Square Garden was full the night of December 27: a sellout crowd even on a Tuesday night during the Christmas season, everyone excited to see how City's young players would fare against UCLA, one of the premier West Coast teams. Just that week Marty Glickman, the WMGM radio announcer, had told *The Campus*'s Marvin Kalb, "Those City College sophs are really something. This Roman and Layne, and the rest of them—boy, they're really something to watch."

City College was favored by nine points, but UCLA had a very good team led by a talented coach—still young enough to be called "Johnny" Wooden—who was in the second year of what would become one of the most storied careers in college basketball. At the end of the first half City led by two, 32 to 30, but as the second half got under way, the Bruins reeled off fifteen points in five minutes. UCLA was well drilled and well conditioned, and the Beavers, wrote the *Post*'s Milton Gross, "committed more wild throws than Yogi Berra will make in a lifetime of baseball." Before long UCLA had amassed a sizable lead, 45 to 36, and City College was never able to catch up. The final score was 60 to 53. After his ill-advised offensive outburst against SMU, this time Irwin was taking no chances: He attempted only four shots in the entire game, missing three of them. Eddie, too, had played poorly despite scoring twenty-two points, and he was upset that the Beavers had lost; still,

UCLA had more than covered the nine-point spread, so at least now they no longer owed the gamblers a game.

With the team having lost twice now in eight games, many City fans began to suspect that their enthusiasm about the talented sophomores had been premature and that this season would end much as the others had, in discouragement and defeat. "Hope," sportswriter Ben Gould noted in *The Brooklyn Daily Eagle*, "based on a consistent flow of brilliant prospects, springs eternal in City College's basketball bosom— but somewhere along the line something invariably misfires, and the Beavers usually wind up as an also-ran." Like another beloved but seemingly luckless New York team, the Brooklyn Dodgers, City College regularly produced a team just good enough to break the hearts of their fans, a scrambling, scrappy team, talented and exciting and yet never able to win a championship. Whatever hopes for success might be harbored by the City College fan base were thus tempered by a certain historical awareness, the recognition that the thaw of March days would bring misfortune for the Beavers as the frost of October nights did for the Dodgers: the law, seemingly as ineluctable as Newton's Third, that every early triumph is offset by late disappointment.

Making things worse for CCNY fans, each of the city's other top basketball programs owned not just one but two national championships: Long Island University had won the NIT in 1939 and again in 1941, while St. John's University had won the NIT two years running, in 1943 and 1944. This year St. John's looked as if it might be poised to make a run at another title: The Redmen had won their first twelve games, and the latest Associated Press poll had ranked them the best college team in the nation.

LIU, for its part, was ranked fourth, its team stocked with gifted players that head coach Clair Bee had discovered in his "cattle calls"— twice-a-year tryouts in which a couple of hundred young men, each with a number pinned to his back, competed in a grueling competition to win free admission to the college. Day after day the players worked out in front of Bee and his assistant coach, the group being steadily winnowed down, like unknown young actors called back again and again to audition for a choice role on Broadway, the level of tension and desire continuing to build until only the most promising prospects remained to play a real game on the final day: a game, in its way, more significant than any other these young men would ever play, after which just one or two might be deemed good enough to be offered a scholarship to LIU.

Long Island University was, like City College, a subway school, providing no dormitories for its students—except, that is, for the basketball players, who, in addition to their scholarships, were given private rooms off campus. The players were likewise provided free meals and books and easy make-work jobs, such as checking to see that the lights were off in the gym, in addition to a variety of other perks, including an all-expenses-paid preseason "training trip"—one year it was to Puerto Rico—led by Clair Bee himself.

In the era of postwar affluence, college basketball had become truly big time, the crowds larger than ever, money pouring into the game as never before. Booster groups footed the bill for the construction of basketball arenas far larger than the fieldhouses of an earlier era; alumni funds swelled the budgets of athletic departments, paying for new training facilities, higher coaches' salaries, the ever-intensifying recruitment of players. At the University of Oklahoma, an alumni group called the Touchdown Club (comprising mostly millionaires from the oil and cattle industries) paid for 140 athletic scholarships a year; at the University of Kentucky, head coach Adolph Rupp was able to offer each of his fifteen varsity basketball players a scholarship package that included tuition, room, board, books, and ten dollars a month in spending money—which was itself generously supplemented by the cash that was often slipped to the school's athletes by friendly alumni and other supporters of the athletic program. All the merchants of downtown Lexington, it sometimes seemed, wanted to show their appreciation for the unparalleled success of their Wildcats. Gifts came from jewelers, liquor distributors, clothing merchants. Like visiting royalty, a Kentucky basketball star was treated to meals wherever he went; men who had attended the college and subsequently grew rich in horses, land, tobacco, would shake his hand after games, leaving twenty-dollar bills in his palm. Often the money came not from college boosters but from local gamblers. "If a man won some money betting on [his] talent," noted one reporter, "it seemed almost right for the kid to get part of it."

• • •

City College's first game of the new year, on January 3, 1950, was against St. John's University. City versus St. John's was always the most highly anticipated regular season game of the year, and outside Madison Square Garden $2.50 tickets were going for $4.50 and $4.50 seats for $10. The voice on the loudspeaker kept repeating that all available tickets had been sold, which meant that more than eighteen thousand fans would be in the arena that night, and untold more would-be patrons, realizing that they weren't going to get in, eventually gave up and drifted away down to one of the Times Square movie houses, or over to Rockefeller Center to see about tickets for the ice show, or just across the street to stand at the bar of Jack Dempsey's restaurant and raise a glass of Dempsey's Special Label Whiskey ("The Whiskey with a Punch!") and marvel at the crowds still milling around outside the Garden. "Thousands more just stood on the sidewalks," Tommy Holmes reported the next day in *The Brooklyn Daily Eagle,* "hoping for a miracle, I guess."

Inside the arena, a spotlight filtered through the blue haze of cigarette smoke to illuminate the polished hardwood court. The anticipatory rumble that filled the vast space grew to a roar when the City College starting five trotted onto the court in their white uniforms with the lavender trim, and then again for the St. John's squad in their uniforms of brilliant red. Originally the team had been known simply as the Johnnies, but in the 1920s a newspaper reporter had dubbed them the Redmen, after the color of their uniforms, and the nickname had stuck. Over time, though, the name had taken on an American Indian connotation, a connection further emphasized by the team mascot, Chief Blackjack, a full-sized wooden Indian that had been lifted from the front of a cigar store by two members of the class of 1932. Since that time, Chief Blackjack had been carted to all team games, "having been granted," according to one of the students who had taken him, "a lifetime lease on the St. John's Reservation."

As the game got under way, both teams seemed tentative with each other, like boxers throwing only jabs in the early rounds, feeling for the opponent's weak spots. City College missed its first nine shots and St. John's edged out to an early 5–0 lead, but at the five-minute mark, guard Mike Wittlin hit an outside shot to get City on the scoreboard, and that seemed to energize the Beavers: Little by little their offense began to click. By the midway point of the half they were working the weave to perfection, whirling and feinting and reversing direction, the passes so fast and precise that one observer commented that it looked as if the ball was being controlled by a puppeteer's strings. Before long City College had pulled ahead, and in the upper balcony the City fans cried "Charge!" to Al Bernstein's bugle calls and joyfully shouted out their Allagaroos, and in response the St. John's rooters let loose a series of "war whoops": an uproarious competition that one reporter termed "the battle of the bellows."

At the end of the first half, City College led 27 to 18. The halftime buzzer sounded and the teams trotted through the tunnel into the locker room and the house lights came up; in a booth high above the court the organist Gladys Goodding serenaded the fans with standards such as "Shine On, Harvest Moon" and "Sidewalks of New York."* As the organ cheerfully trilled, the fans stood and chatted with those sitting around them, the question in everyone's mind whether the Beavers could keep the momentum going or would fade in the second half as they had against UCLA.

In the locker room Nat Holman had decided to employ an all-sophomore five to start the second half, with Al Roth and Herb Cohen joining Eddie Roman, Ed Warner, and Floyd Layne, and for the first several minutes that approach seemed to work as City College extended its lead to fifteen points, 41 to 26. But then the greater experience of St. John's began to assert itself, and City's offensive machine, which had been functioning so smoothly, began occasionally to hiccup: an errant pass here, a forced shot there, not many but enough for St. John's to pull itself back into the game. Occasionally City College was able to push the lead back up, Roman hitting turnaround jump shots and Warner hook shots from under the basket, but by this time City seemed like a racehorse that had broken to an early lead and was tiring in the homestretch, just willing the finish line to arrive. Newly energized, the St.

---

* Gladys Goodding played the organ for all the college and professional basketball games held at Madison Square Garden, and the hockey games as well, and in the summer months for the baseball games at Ebbets Field. In those days a favorite trivia question in New York was: Who is the only person ever to play for the Knicks, the Rangers, and the Dodgers? The answer, of course, was Gladys Goodding.

John's rooters booed and whistled whenever a City player stepped to the free throw line, and Roth and Irwin Dambrot missed key foul shots. With less than a minute left, City College was holding on to a slim 54–51 lead and St. John's had possession of the ball.

Now a three-point play—a basket plus a foul shot—would send the game into overtime, and as the hand of the seconds clock overhead wound down toward zero, with all the fans in Madison Square Garden on their feet and roaring, St. John's forward Ronnie MacGilvray managed to extricate himself from a cluster of defenders and drive to the basket, and suddenly there it was: Reaching for the ball, Al Roth made contact with MacGilvray, sending him flying just as he lofted up his shot, and the referee under the basket raised his arm to indicate a foul.

The final buzzer sounded even as the basketball was still in the air. All eyes in the arena were focused on that narrow cylinder of space as the ball hit the rim and bounced softly up, rolled around the basket, and then, as if having finally made up its mind, fell out beside the sprawled MacGilvray, who pounded his fists on the hardwood in frustration as the arena erupted and the City College players, triumphant, loped off the court and the students in the upper balcony cheered themselves hoarse; one of the students there described the scene as "mass hysteria," with "yelling, shoulder slapping, and handkerchief waving that was part of the greatest basketball spectacle in a decade." Almost unnoticed amid the excited swirl going on around him, MacGilvray stepped to the line to attempt his two free throws, meaningless now with City ahead by three and the clock having run out (meaningless even to the gamblers in the crowd, as the shots would not affect the point spread, which had favored St. John's by two points). He made the first shot and missed the second, and the final score was City College 54, St. John's 52.

Three days into the new decade, the game seemed to the Beavers and their fans to be a turning point. For the first time this season, City College had defeated a nationally ranked team. The Beavers had demonstrated that they could maintain a lead under the most intense pressure, with eighteen thousand fans roaring and untold thousands more listening on the radio. The team had played with skill and heart, and when the Christmas break was over those students who had been in the Garden that night spoke of the game in wondrous tones, telling their classmates about Warner's speed and Roman's precision, and that heart-stopping moment when MacGilvray's shot rimmed out; and on the City College campus the feeling began to spread that the early excitement about the team had not been entirely unfounded, and that perhaps this year was going to be different after all.

CHAPTER 9

In the heart of downtown Brooklyn, the Hotel St. George boasted 2,632 guest rooms, sixteen banquet rooms, and a saltwater swimming pool that was said to be the largest and most expensive ever built; it offered thirty-odd shops and restaurants, as well as a subway station that exited directly into the hotel, and amid the throngs coming and going on the morning of Monday, January 2, 1950, a doorman would scarcely have given a second glance to the twenty-nine young men who arrived one by one, striding through the marble-clad lobby, past the easy chairs and the rows of potted plants, to the bank of elevators.

They were, to a man, clean-cut and muscular, and they walked with the lithe, careless step of athletes, but they were not athletes; each carried a revolver holstered at his hip, only partially hidden beneath his sport jacket or windbreaker. Taking an elevator to the fourth floor, each of the men located the right suite and knocked on the door—three times, as he had been instructed—and when the door cracked open he murmured a single word, like a password at the barred entrance to a speakeasy: "McDonald."

Miles McDonald, the district attorney for Kings County, had called that morning's meeting, in the wake of a newspaper exposé about which Brooklyn was still buzzing—an eight-part series published in *The Brooklyn Daily Eagle* called "The Truth About Brooklyn's Rackets." "It isn't a pretty story," the *Eagle* had promised its readers in a full-page advertisement, "but it is one that every Brooklynite will want to read."

The series had been born from a chance remark overheard by one of the paper's staff writers, Ed Reid. A robust dark-haired man who wore a pair of horn-rimmed glasses, Reid was thirty-four years old and had been working at the *Eagle* for fifteen years. During that time he had served as a kind of jack-of-all-trades for the paper, his subject matter ranging from an exotic variety of lily cultivated by a Flatbush home-owner to Dodgers star Jackie Robinson's life in and out of baseball. Reid, however, had a particular interest in crime stories, and in September 1949 he stumbled across one while he was drinking a beer after work at a popular Brooklyn restaurant called Joe's.

Occupying a long, low corner building near the courthouse, Joe's was a convivial haven of polished wood and tile and Victorian chande-liers, where businessmen and politicians and priests rubbed shoulders with gangsters at the linen-covered tables in the large dining room in the back. On this evening the front room was alive with the usual hum and clatter, customers laughing and ordering rounds and making brave predictions about what the Dodgers would do to the Yankees in the Se-ries that year if they got the chance. Reid was leaning against the res-taurant's long mahogany bar when his attention was drawn to the conversation of two men nearby drinking martinis. "Jimmy," one of them said, "I hear a new guy has taken over the bookie joints in town. Guy they call Mr. G. They say he was put up in business by three cops after he ran out owing his customers a hundred grand."

The man called Jimmy murmured a noncommittal reply and re-turned to his drink. For Reid, though, that remark was, as he would later characterize it, "the tiny seed" that would eventually grow into a newspaper series that would shake New York to its core and win Reid a raft of journalism awards and *The Brooklyn Daily Eagle* a Pulitzer Prize in Public Service. For the next three months he pursued this single story, interviewing, by his own estimate, "thousands of people," work-ing sometimes twenty hours a day. For a while, seeking to trace the mob's penetration of the Brooklyn waterfront, he loaded crates as a longshoreman. For much of those three months, keeping a close tab on his sources, he visited five bars daily, and, as he would write later, "put on about thirty pounds drinking."

By the beginning of December, though, as the series was slated to run, Reid had not yet discovered the identity of the fabled Mr. G. That week he paid a visit to the office of the Brooklyn district attorney.

A former lifeguard and college football player, Miles McDonald was tall and still lean at forty-three, with silvering hair that always looked freshly barbered; he was a formal dresser who in the office favored dark suits and ties that he clasped to his shirt with a sterling tie bar, and Norfolk jackets even when relaxing at home. By nature he was soft-spoken and cerebral and seemed perpetually to wear a mild, congenial expression, and while some who knew him believed he was more cut out to be a priest than a prosecutor, the law ran in his blood. His father, John, had been chief clerk for the local Surrogate's Court; he was renowned for his probity and independence, and after his death a major thoroughfare called Gravesend Avenue was renamed McDonald Avenue. The name was especially fitting, his neighbors liked to say, because it was the straightest road in all of Brooklyn.

Miles McDonald graduated cum laude from Holy Cross College and ten days later took a job as a law clerk with a firm in Brooklyn; he worked during the day while attending evening classes at Fordham Law School, and he passed the bar exam while still in school. In 1940, after fourteen years in private practice, he was asked to join the district attorney's office. The new position meant a reduction in income, but McDonald's father had always wanted him to be a justice on the state Supreme Court, and this seemed to offer a stepping-stone toward that position. McDonald became an assistant district attorney in the Appeals Bureau. He was, in the characterization of one Brooklyn judge, a "profound" attorney, whose briefs were always thoughtful and precisely argued; in later years, going back over his record, *The Brooklyn Daily Eagle* found that the DA's office had won every single appeal for which McDonald had prepared the brief.

Despite his success, however, Miles McDonald found it to be an awkward fit in an office where criminal prosecutions, or lack of them, often seemed like the continuation of politics by other means. In particular McDonald disliked William O'Dwyer's chief aide, James Moran, the coarse, blustering power broker who decided which cases the office would take on and which it would not, despite having no background in the law. In 1945, when O'Dwyer gave up his position as district attorney to run for mayor, McDonald ran for DA and won with 71 percent of the vote. Local political observers took notice of the fact that neither man mentioned the other while campaigning. "I never liked him from the beginning," O'Dwyer would later tell a friend. Said McDonald, "I didn't want to be in a position of espousing a man who might be wrong."

Above his desk in the district attorney's private office, McDonald had hung a large reproduction of the famous Holbein portrait of St. Thomas More, illustrious author and royal counselor, who had gone to his death rather than submit to illegitimate authority. In Holbein's depiction, More sits swathed in rich coats trimmed with fur and velvet but is himself weary-looking and unshaven, his eyes bordered by dark circles, his expression deeply troubled; the painting seemed to show a man gazing into his own grim future, and the effect on a visitor to the district attorney's office could be disconcerting.

Ed Reid had come to the office because he had known Miles McDonald for many years and he thought McDonald was the only Democratic official in Brooklyn who might be willing to pursue an investigation that, he suspected, would lead across the river to police headquarters, perhaps even as far as City Hall. Reid spoke in clipped, decisive tones, the voice of a newscaster but for a trace of the Brooklyn accent that doesn't acknowledge the letter *r* at the end of a word. "I was having a beer," he said, "and just sort of listening around, you know. I noticed these fellows not far away at the bar. They were talking about betting the horses."

"Anybody you knew?" McDonald asked.

"No, never saw them before, but they said something I think you'll be interested in. They said that you can't do bookmaking anymore unless you're willing to work for a certain Mr. G."

McDonald thought about this for a moment. "They mention his full name?"

"No," Reid said. "Just kept calling him Mr. G, but this Mr. G sounded very big. And Miles, here's the kicker—they say this guy was set up as boss of all the bookie joints in Brooklyn by three of the highest cops in the Police Department."

McDonald had long suspected that certain policemen were shielding bookmakers, but at the same time he knew that his office didn't have the manpower to undertake a full-fledged investigation; he needed a public outcry, something he could use to pressure the city administration into providing the necessary funding. "Ed," he told Reid before he left, "if you can get the people sufficiently aroused so that we can get a big enough appropriation, I'll go after the bookies with everything I've got."

On Sunday, December 11, the *Eagle*'s front page was dominated by an article headlined LUCRATIVE BOROUGH RACKETS FEED VAST CRIME SYNDI-CATE. In this and seven subsequent articles, Ed Reid detailed the elaborate system by which the revenue from bookmaking served to enrich a far-reaching criminal network that he called the Combine.* The leaders of the Combine preferred gambling money above all, for, as they liked to say, it was a "clean dollar," as opposed to the "dirty dollar" of drugs, prostitution, and blackmail; the Combine took a cut of all the sports betting in Brooklyn, and the millions of dollars that had been brought in over the years had helped fund its incursion into legitimate industries (especially trucking and liquor) and its control of the waterfront. The Combine had even found its way into Brooklyn's schools through a network of young bookmakers—they were to be found on every college campus, Reid claimed, in every high school, in most junior high schools, and even some elementary schools—hired to distribute gambling cards to their fellow students, who would bet quarters, dimes, as little as a nickel on a slate of the upcoming weekend's football and basketball games. Just as shocking was the revelation that this criminal organization protected itself from arrest by making weekly payments to New York police officers. According to Reid, Brooklyn was divided into thirty "bookie districts," each one controlled by a major bookmaker for whom hundreds of people worked as lower-level bookies, assistants, runners, and in various other capacities.

Each of the districts paid the police about $7,500 every week in protection money; patrolmen collected cash-filled envelopes from the book-

---

* The leaders of the Combine included figures such as Vito Genovese and Lucky Luciano, whom the public would later come to identify with the Mafia.

makers and brought them back to the local precinct house, where—in a kind of grotesque replication of the criminal enterprise itself—the money was distributed up the chain of command, the specific amount apportioned according to rank. One local bookmaker, identified by Reid only as "Charlie," estimated that nearly eighty cents of every dollar he earned ended up in the pockets of law enforcement. The system was highly coordinated and rigidly enforced by the police; indeed, the major bookmakers had divided Brooklyn into thirty districts precisely because Brooklyn had thirty police precincts. "Look, my friend," Charlie told Reid, "it's not that the bookmakers are so well organized—it's the cops that are organized."

The series "The Truth About Brooklyn's Rackets" exposed for the first time the full dimensions of a netherworld known to few of the *Eagle*'s readers: a frightening place in which mobsters became industrialists, gamblers preyed on children, and cops made alliance with criminals. The response was strong and immediate. On December 13, just two days after the first article appeared, Congressman Emanuel Celler of Brooklyn, chairman of the House Judiciary Committee, was already calling on the FBI to look into the charges made by the *Eagle*, which he admitted sounded "fantastic" but thought were worthy of investigation nonetheless. By the end of the week the president of the Board of Education had launched a probe of gambling activities in the city's schools. The president of the City Council declared that he would introduce a bill in the next session levying heavy fines and jail terms on those found guilty of selling games of chance to minors. It was just the sort of public attention that Miles McDonald had been hoping for, and he appeared before Judge Samuel Leibowitz in County Court to request that the term of the December Kings County grand jury be extended for three months to "investigate the alleged activities of criminals, racketeers, and gamblers in Brooklyn"; on December 22, Judge Leibowitz granted that request. Right away the district attorney's office was flooded with calls and letters from people wanting to give evidence to the grand jury.

McDonald assigned Assistant District Attorney Julius Helfand the task of following up on the new leads; meanwhile he was contemplating the possibility of a far more daring operation, one without precedent in New York.

• • •

That week Miles McDonald stayed late in his office, jotting down thoughts on a notepad under the penetrating gaze of St. Thomas More. His suit jacket was off now, shirtsleeves rolled up nearly to the elbow. He smoked one cigarette after another, stubbing them out on the miniature anvil that he kept on his desk as a tribute to his great-grandfather, also named Miles McDonald, who had made his living as a blacksmith.

How far his family had traveled in the past century, from the Brooklyn potato farm on which that long-ago Miles McDonald had grown up to his own four-story brick home in the genteel neighborhood of Park Slope. It was a comfortable life they enjoyed now, and much of that, he understood, was owed to the Democratic Party. His grandfather had been a power among the Democrats of the Tenth Ward, and his father was the longtime right-hand man for the Brooklyn Democratic boss. McDonald considered himself an organization Democrat as well, but he also knew that any investigation of political corruption he might undertake in Brooklyn would be widely viewed as a vendetta against the party, no matter how often he might insist that it was not. What was worse, given the opposition of the local power structure, the investigation would likely fail; his office would spend a lot of the people's money and get nothing in return, and he would be lambasted in the press as an incompetent and vilified in his party as a traitor, and even though he had been overwhelmingly reelected as district attorney, when he next came up for election he would surely be denied the Democratic nomination. Nor, for that matter, would he ever be put up for a seat on the state Supreme Court. Longtime friendships would be lost, and when he returned to private practice there was no telling how many of his former clients would still want him to handle their mortgages or wills, hesitant now about being too closely associated with him. Perhaps he and his wife, Alice, would no longer be able to afford the Catholic schools in which their children were enrolled, the two older ones away in lovely places in Connecticut and Rhode Island. There would be consequences for what he was planning to do, he understood that, and in the silence and solitude of his office he couldn't help but admit that he was frightened.

Still, he reminded himself, a man had to sleep nights; a man had to be able to live with himself.

One afternoon in December 1949, McDonald held one of his special "quarterback" sessions, the meetings that he called whenever an important decision had to be made. He sat down in his office with three of his assistant district attorneys; his chief clerk, William Kelly; and a county detective by the name of William Dahut. McDonald had chosen those five because they were tough, experienced investigators in whom he had complete trust. He told them that he wanted to launch an investigation that would expose the alliances between bookmakers and the police, and, if necessary, their political patrons as well. He said, "As you know, we've got to have extra men to undertake this investigation. The staff we have at present is completely taken up with routine duties. For a job of this kind I'm guessing we need twenty or thirty, perhaps forty more detectives or policemen."

Bill Kelly suggested that those additional men could be requisitioned from the Police Department; it might be tricky getting them reassigned, but he thought it could be done.

"Sure, but then how do we know what we're getting?" replied McDonald. "We know there are a great many cops in the department who are on the take. How do we know we wouldn't be given those very cops, or other cops who are connected with them?"

"That's right," said Bill Dahut. "But where else can we get men?"

"Well," McDonald said slowly, "I've been thinking that maybe we ought to take men right out of the Police Academy—get a bunch of rookies."

"Rookies?" cried one of the assistants. "Miles, you'll have enough trouble if you use experienced cops. But rookies! It'll be months before they even figure out what they're doing."

"That's a chance we'll have to take. I don't expect they'll pull off miracles. But gentlemen, I want to remind you that not one of these kids has ever been on the take."

"But Miles, these kids don't know anything yet. They don't even know how to direct traffic."

"I'm not going to ask them to direct traffic," said McDonald. "I'm just going to ask them to go to college."

• • •

Miles McDonald put in a request to Police Commissioner William P. O'Brien for a special forty-man squad, to be drawn from the department's graduating class of three hundred probationary policemen. The purpose of the squad was to infiltrate Brooklyn's colleges, to investigate the charges of student bookmaking made in *The Brooklyn Daily Eagle*. It seemed a reasonable enough proposal, given the wide publicity the series had already gotten and the political pressure that was being applied to investigate gambling in the schools. McDonald had not told the Police Department, though, that once he had those young policemen, he intended, as he put it, to "branch out": "We're going to catch bookies in Brooklyn," he assured his investigators, "whether they went to college or not." No longer would bookies be arrested and quickly released, as had always been done before. Instead, his men would make it clear that the charges would be prosecuted as fully as the laws would allow; this, McDonald hoped, would squeeze the lower-level bookies into identifying the bookmakers for whom they worked, and if possible, the policemen to whom they paid protection money. He and his men would just keep adding links to the chain, slowly and patiently, following it as high as it would go. Eventually, if they did their jobs right, they might even reach Mr. G.

After several days the word came back from the Police Department that the request had been granted—not for forty men, though, but twenty-nine. Having received the department's approval, McDonald dispatched Chief Inspector William Dahut and Assistant District Attorney Julius Helfand to the Police Academy in Manhattan. Dahut and Helfand both worked in the office's Homicide and Rackets Division. Over the past five years Dahut had gathered evidence for many of the division's most important cases, and he understood undercover work, having run counterespionage operations among longshoremen on the Brooklyn docks during World War II. Helfand was a veteran prosecutor who had earned his reputation putting away the hired killers of Murder, Inc.; McDonald considered him especially useful for this assignment, for as he once said, Helfand could "spot a liar faster than any other man I have ever met."

For days the two men occupied a classroom in the Police Academy, a former schoolhouse in a desolate section of the Lower West Side, inter-

Brooklyn district attorney Miles McDonald with his staff. McDonald is in the dark suit in the background; Assistant District Attorney Julius Helfand, with striped tie and rolled-up shirtsleeves, is in the center. Lisa Larsen/Getty Images

viewing every one of the 290 members of that year's graduating class. Each recruit's background was carefully scrutinized; anyone with a family member on the police force was automatically rejected. Finally Dahut and Helfand had found twenty-nine men whom they believed were up to the job. Those selected were given no indication of what they were being asked to do; all they knew was that they had been chosen for a special assignment, and that on Monday morning, January 2, 1950, they should report to the fourth floor of the Hotel St. George to receive their instructions.

It was Bill Dahut who met them at the door and, upon receiving the code word "McDonald," ushered them into the suite. When all of the recruits had arrived, Julius Helfand rose to address them. He was forty-six but looked older, a short, beefy man once described by a journalist as having "gray hair combed straight back from a high forehead, sharp brown eyes, and a nose like the blade of bayonet." He took a pack of cigarettes from his suit jacket and lit one, and as the smoke curled up around his face he squinted at the recruits like a jeweler assessing the quality of a stone.

"You know what you guys are?" he said at last. "You're a pack of rats. Rats and sneaks and stool pigeons. You'd sell your best friend out for a dime and turn in your mother for a quarter. You're the scum of the city and you got this job because of it."

The words crackled through the room like electricity, and the effect on the recruits was immediate: backs straightened, jaws clenched, legs began twitching in anger. Helfand's voice softened a bit. "Wait a minute, fellas," he said. "That's not my opinion of you. But it will be the opinion of others. I just figured I'd let you know in advance. I want you to know before you take the job we're going to offer you that you're going to be considered by every other cop in the department as something a thousand times worse than the lowest stoolie."

He continued, "You're policemen, and frankly, you don't know much about police work yet. But you have what we need and that's why we picked you. You have one big thing in your favor—you haven't learned the motto of a lot of lazy cops: 'One hand washes the other.' That means, of course, 'You do me a favor and I'll do one for you.' Well, that's not the attitude we want for the job we have to do. We want men who will be swerved by nothing, neither friendship nor sympathy nor money. That's why I think you're going to be called rats. That's why you're going to get it from some of the old-time cops. You men had better get used to the names I just tossed at you, because you're going to hear them all the time. You were selected for a special job. It's one no policeman has ever tackled before—especially no young policeman. The job is so special that not even your commanders know what you're going to do. We didn't tell them."

As he spoke, Helfand paced slowly up and back in the aisle, scanning the faces looking up at him. He said, "What I tell you now must remain in this room, a secret until we complete what we're setting out to do. And this is it: You men are going to investigate your own department and the men in it. You are going to check on cops who might have become your buddies, but who will never talk to you again from now on. You are going to ferret out and expose any member of the department who has violated his oath of office and is playing ball with gangsters, bookies, or crooked politicians. You're going to expose them all, and it's going to be a tough, dirty job."

The room was utterly silent, all attention rapt on Julius Helfand. "Before I go any further," he said, "I want to tell you that if you don't like this idea, this is the time to walk out. If you have any doubts, just leave now and forget the whole thing." He paused again to take a last drag on his cigarette; then he blew out the smoke and ground out the stub in a nearby ashtray. He looked around the room. Not a man moved.

Helfand smiled. "Okay," he said. "This is it."

CHAPTER 10

That January, as Miles McDonald's twenty-nine police recruits began to infiltrate five Brooklyn colleges, City College closed for its midwinter break. In the pale afternoon sun, the heavy stones of the buildings seemed almost to contract in the cold, the whimsical little men along the trim looking to have been frozen in their contortions, with icicles hanging from beards and whitecaps of frost covering fingers and toes. The central quadrangle, normally bustling, was now often deserted but for the occasional staff person going about his rounds or a student hurrying to the library to finish an overdue course paper; the basketball team, though, was on campus daily for afternoon practice sessions in the Main Gym.

Watching the players work out, assistant coach Bobby Sand was feeling hopeful. From the first game of the year the Beavers had shown themselves to be a powerful fast-break team, but Bobby was even more impressed with their half-court play, how crisply they kept the ball moving, always focused, hitting the open man. With this team he sometimes found himself admiring as much as coaching. He took great pleasure, for instance, in watching Eddie Roman pass, noting how Eddie delivered the ball so that his teammate would be in the best possible position to make an offensive move; Irwin Dambrot, who in the past had always looked to shoot, was now feeding off and rebounding and playing tough defense. Even Nat Holman increasingly expressed satisfaction with the quality of the team's play.

In a City College publicity photograph, head coach Nat Holman diagrams a play for members of the City College Beavers. Front row, left to right: *Norm Mager, Joe Galiber, Irwin Dambrot, Mike Wittlin, Ed Roman.* Back row, left to right: *Ed Warner, Al Roth, Seymour Levy, Herb Cohen.* Larry Gralla

Among themselves some of the City players said that Holman was a "gym coach" rather than a "game coach," a master of tactics but with little sense of overall strategy. He was a marvel in practices, but during games he tended to lapse into a kind of tunnel vision—overly focused on technical mistakes, fuming about a missed pass or a careless foul— and in the process lost track of the flow of the game. Sometimes this led to basic coaching errors, like trying to send in a player who had already fouled out of the game, and he depended on his assistant coach to handle substitutions and make many of the other in-game decisions, though of course he didn't like people to know that. When magazines such as *Scholastic Coach* and *Sport* asked Bobby to write articles on basketball strategy, Nat refused to allow it; he did not think it appropriate for an assistant coach to publish anything under his own name. "I'm the big shot here," Holman once told him. "Lou Little at Columbia doesn't let his staff write articles, so why should I?"

Bobby never confronted Nat about this; nor did he mention the head coaching offers that had begun to come his way from colleges around the country, schools like Pepperdine and Penn State, which he invariably turned down because he knew that his wife, Sylvia, was not willing to leave New York. Though word had begun to get around that this was the best City College team in years, few people knew who had worked the hardest to assemble it—who, for instance, had taken an advance on his own salary so he could lend Floyd Layne forty dollars to register for college—any more than they knew who, during the games, was suggesting most of the substitutions and time-outs. Sand himself did not feel obliged to publicize that information. A profile in *The Campus* had noted that Sand's "endless drive in talking to ballplayers, his warm understanding of personal problems, have endeared him to his players," as did his "appreciation for the problems of individuals"—a quality, the writer did not fail to point out, that was otherwise lacking in the upper echelons of the athletic office: "If he perhaps lacks the huckster 'me-me-me' spirit, that is something decidedly in his favor."

At the end of January, near the end of the midwinter break, the Beavers went on the road. First they traveled by train to Allentown, Pennsylvania, where they overwhelmed the Muhlenberg Mules by a score of 95 to 76; Eddie Roman scored twenty-seven points, the most for any City College player that season, despite having spent the afternoon in bed at the hotel with stomach flu. The next ten days brought three more victories, against Boston College, Princeton University, and St. Francis College, but the trip ended with a long, cold train ride to Buffalo, after which the Beavers lost 53 to 49 to Canisius College. Given the loss, Eddie could take but scant consolation in knowing that with his fifteen points he had broken Irwin Dambrot's CCNY single-season scoring record of 276 points (breaking his scoring record in college just as he had in high school), and had done so in only sixteen games, whereas Irwin had needed twenty-five. The midseason road trip had begun with hope and ended with disappointment, and it was a relief to return to City College, where registration for the spring semester was under way in the Great Hall.

The architectural jewel of the CCNY campus, the Great Hall would not seem out of place in one of the medieval colleges of Oxford or Cambridge.

Buttressed by huge timbers, the ceiling rises sixty-three feet above the limestone floor, the cavernous space ringed by Gothic arches, stained-glass windows thirty feet high, and twin processions of colorful banners from all of the world's great universities. Almost singularly at City College, where ceiling lights regularly flickered and steam pipes banged and dripped and nearly every square foot of space was put to some productive use, the Great Hall had managed to retain much of its original grandeur, in large part because it was spared from the workaday routines of a busy, overcrowded school—except, that is, for the first week of each new semester, when undergraduates were required to register for classes. Then blackboards were carted in and folding tables set up on the stage, and a churning mass of students filled the vast space and overflowed out the rear doors, piling the edges of the room with coats and bags. It was a routine and entirely predictable mob scene, described by *The Campus* as "City College's answer to the Grand Guignol."

The registration process invariably took at least two hours for a student to complete, except for those who had been granted the right to early registration; each year that included the entire varsity basketball team. In February 1950, when registration began for the spring semester, Eddie Roman did as he had been told—go to the front of the line and mention the name Hy Gold—and he was escorted out of the clamorous Great Hall and into the office of a registrar's assistant named Hyman Gold who served as the liaison between the registrar's office and the athletic program. Before he met with a member of the team to help him arrange a course schedule, Gold often took the liberty of registering the player with a class in the German department, where to all indications failure was not an option (Ed Warner, for instance, was about to embark on his fourth consecutive semester of German, having previously received a C and two D's), or in the personal finance course taught by a professor in the economics department who was a prominent supporter of the basketball team. Despite Eddie's solid B average, Gold had also set him up with the personal finance course; beyond this, though, Eddie would be carrying a serious academic load, comprising two economics courses plus courses in sociology, European history, art history, public speaking, and psychology, the subject that he was now considering for his major. The previous semester Eddie had earned an A in chemistry; he had loved the subject and planned to major in it, but Gold informed him that this would be impossible: City College's chemistry courses held their lab sessions in the afternoon, and a chem major would require late arrival to far too many practices. Reluctantly Eddie had agreed to switch his major so that he could keep up with basketball.

That same week, the first of the semester, Norm Mager took Eddie aside and told him that he had set up a deal to shave points in the next game at the Garden, against Niagara University. The betting line had the Beavers to win by eleven points, a solid margin; all they needed to do was come in under the point spread and it would be another thousand dollars for each of them. Discussing this, Normie looked terrible, pale and drawn and jittery—he had been having trouble with Eli Kaye, he admitted. Kaye had followed him home once after a game, pulling up alongside him in his car and giving him that dead-fish stare. He had started calling Norm's house at all hours, too, eager to fix another game. Fats Roth was in, and Herb Cohen too, and Norm was clearly counting on him as well—Eddie, after all, had been the team's leading scorer in ten of the previous eleven games—and Norm assured him that this would be the last shaved game of the season. An extra thousand dollars would have been a godsend for his family, but this time Eddie gathered up his nerve and told him no.

"I've had enough," he said firmly; if Normie and the others wanted to keep doing business there was nothing he could do about it, but as far as he was concerned he was out.

It was no great surprise to hear that Fats and Herbie had agreed to work the Niagara game. The two had been friends since high school; like Roth, Cohen was enrolled in the business program at City's downtown campus, and he, too, maintained a resolutely entrepreneurial view of the role of the big-time college basketball player at Madison Square Garden. "I would look up and the stadium was always full, eighteen thousand," he was later to recall. "And I would think to myself, 'Every one of those people paid to get in tonight.' And where did that money go? Not to me—I was getting maybe five bucks from selling my tickets."

Near the beginning of the season *The New York Times* had run a story about a letter sent by the vice president of Local 802 of the American Federation of Musicians to six New York colleges, City College among them, notifying them that in the future the union would ban the appearance of student bands at Madison Square Garden college basketball games. In his letter Samuel Suber wrote, "It is our understanding that the universities lease the use of the Garden on a percentage basis, and, therefore, it is in a real sense a business venture for profit," and as such the colleges "should hire professional musicians at regular union rates" rather than rely on unpaid student labor. The employment of amateur musicians at Madison Square Garden was an issue important enough to reach the front page of *The New York Times;* left unaddressed, however, was the status of the college students whom the fans had actually paid money to see—not the band members but the basketball players themselves.

Though basketball players, unlike musicians, did not have a union representing their interests, no one could deny the highly professionalized atmosphere in which college games were played at Madison Square Garden. The college players used the very same facilities as the professionals; the referees and official scorers and even the organist were the same; the games were broadcast by the same announcers over the same radio stations and were reported in the same newspaper sports sections, in which the Garden had likewise placed advertisements for the games. If the teams' names were to be removed from the uniforms and the scoreboard, any stranger introduced to a basketball game at the Garden would have had little way of telling whether the game being played was amateur or professional. Indeed, noting the afternoon start time, the half-filled arena, the opening game featuring department store employees, the stranger would reasonably have supposed that the professional game was being played by the amateurs.

The promoter Ned Irish, of course, had become wealthy as a result of college basketball, but he was by no means the only one who profited from it. On a college basketball night, other than the fans who had paid to get in, nearly every individual inside Madison Square Garden was in some way deriving income from the games. The coaches, the referees, the ushers, the ticket takers, the food vendors, and countless more Garden employees—not to mention the colleges' own athletic departments— all owed their income, at least in part, to the enormous profits that were generated by the desire of many thousands of New Yorkers to watch high-quality college basketball. The only ones not reaping a share of those profits, reasoned Herb Cohen, were the players themselves: the very ones whose talent made all the rest of it possible.*

As it turned out, Irwin Dambrot had also said no to Norm Mager. Thus the two Bronx kids were now out, while the three Brooklynites remained.

Niagara broke out fast, taking a 16–4 lead, but City managed twice to cut the lead to four points and at halftime trailed by only two, 35 to 33, after Dambrot hit two shots in the final fifteen seconds of the half. Still, it was clear that City College was not playing well that night. Where in earlier games the Beavers had moved the ball with speed and precision, now they held it aimlessly or passed it to no effect; where they had attacked the basket, now they settled for the outside shot; where they had shifted and stayed alert and communicated well on defense, now they defended sluggishly and got beat jumping for rebounds and diving after loose balls. Collectively, Mager, Roth, and Cohen shot three for thirteen. Watching them fumble passes and send up halfhearted shots, Eddie experienced a new and unsettling sensation: that he was competing not only against his opponents, but against members of his own team as well. With each shot that clanked off the rim he became even more aware that he also appeared to be shaving points, and that only caused him to press even harder to prove it wasn't so, sending up another wild shot, like a card player who keeps pushing a cold streak, each time believing that *this* hand will be the one that changes his luck, but which ends up putting him only deeper in the hole.

As the final minutes ticked down and the Purple Eagles began to freeze the ball to protect their lead, Eddie felt almost blind with frustration and disgust. He was angry at himself for not having played a stronger game, and bitter at his teammates because they had taken the money, and at least a little jealous because he had not, and ashamed,

---

* The sportswriter Jerry Izenberg indicates that Herb Cohen had another motivation as well for shaving points. Izenberg recalls Cohen saying of Nat Holman, "I hated that motherfucker. I would have done anything, I didn't care. I spent the money on clothes. I earned it, I spent it, that's all, fuck them."

too, because now he had another secret, one that he had not asked for and was loath to carry. With twenty-three points, Eddie was again the team's leading scorer, but over the course of the game he had taken thirty-three shots and made only nine of them. Irwin seemed as rattled as he was, for other than the two baskets at the end of the first half he had missed all twelve of his shots. The two of them, Roman and Dambrot, were clean, and yet they had played every bit as poorly as those who weren't. It was as though the deceit were a virus that floated through the air, seeking weakness, reinfecting all those who had ever been exposed to it.

That week in the student newspaper the *Observation Post,* staff writer Dick Kaplan wrote a column called "The Case of the Expanded Hatbands," in which he argued that some members of the basketball team seemed to have grown swelled heads—as if they had spent too much time reading their own press clippings. "Somewhere along the line," he wrote, "the boys seem to have gotten the idea that they're the greatest thing since Captain Video, and have lost that lean and hungry look."

Later that week Kaplan was having lunch in the City College cafeteria. Located in the basement of the Main Building, the room was a loud, crowded, bustling place, the air heavy with the smells of pot roast and pipe smoke. A number of the tables tended to be occupied by particular social groups: a table for the editors of the school papers, a table for theater people, a table for folk singers and other bohemians, a table for African American students who liked to play whist while they ate. There was also one table where the college's athletes and their friends ate lunch. Kaplan was close with several members of the basketball team, and this afternoon he had sat down at that table. Sitting at the other end, with his books and lunch tray, was Eddie Roman. Somehow Kaplan began to get the sense that Eddie wanted to tell him something but didn't want to say anything out loud, with other people around. He watched as Eddie tore a piece of paper from a notebook and wrote something on it, then passed it down the table to him. On the paper was a single line:

How much easier it is to be critical than to be correct. —Disraeli.

Pulling out a pen, Kaplan wrote beneath that line: *Something is rot-*

ten in the state of Denmark. —Shakespeare. Without a word he passed the paper back down the table.

Eddie read what Kaplan had written there; he nodded and shrugged and scrawled another line, then stood to go.

He had written, *Would they ever have this discourse in Kentucky?*

Kaplan watched Eddie pick up his tray and leave.

By the end of February, three teams had received bids to the National Invitation Tournament: Duquesne University of Pittsburgh; Bradley University of Peoria, Illinois; and St. John's. Kentucky, Western Kentucky, North Carolina State, La Salle, and Arizona seemed certain to fill five of the remaining nine slots, as did the previous year's NIT champion, San Francisco. Two more slots would probably go to the upstate powers Syracuse and Niagara, and Long Island University's record of 19 and 4 was likely strong enough to earn it a tournament bid. That left only a single available slot.

The NIT often reserved a spot for the winner of the so-called Subway Conference—the team that had the best record against the other teams from New York. The Beavers were 4 and 0 in Subway Conference games, with two remaining, the first one against Manhattan College on Thursday, March 2. The remaining NIT invitations were to be sent out shortly after the Manhattan game; if the Beavers could beat Manhattan at the Garden, they would be, in the description of the *Observation Post,* "the holder of the unofficial New York diadem," and there was at least a chance the NIT selection committee would decide to reserve a slot for the hometown champion.

This year, for the very first time, the National Invitation Tournament had expanded its field from eight teams to twelve. On that twelfth slot the City College Beavers would hang their hopes.

A sense of nervous anticipation coursed through the Madison Square Garden crowd that night as the players conducted their pregame shoot-around, the City College Beavers in their white uniforms, the Manhattan Jaspers in bright kelly green trimmed with white. As play got under way the Beavers fell behind 16 to 15, then scored nine consecutive points and didn't relinquish the lead for the rest of the half. By the mid-point of the second half they had stretched their lead to double digits for the first time, 48 to 38—but that was when, as Sid Friedlander would report in the *New York Post*, "the going began to get a bit up-hillish."

Manhattan's two best players, Jack Byrnes and Hank Poppe, were both seniors; this was the last game of their college careers and they were not willing to go down without a fight. Fed perfectly by Byrnes's dead-eye passing, Poppe hit three consecutive set shots; forward Byron Igoe added four free throws, center Mike Joyce made a layup, and the game was now tied at 50. Thus began, according to another newspaper account, the "nail-biting session." For more than a minute neither team could manage a point; then, with 3:35 remaining in the game, Irwin Dambrot was fouled while shooting and he went to the line and sank his two free throws to break the deadlock. Igoe was fouled and made another free throw to bring the Jaspers within one; the Beavers brought the ball back downcourt and patiently worked it around until Al Roth broke free to hit a jump shot to put City back up by three. Joyce quickly retaliated with a jump shot of his own, though, and the lead was again but a single point. Driving between a phalanx of Jaspers to the basket, Ed Warner was fouled as he made a layup; he converted the penalty shot for a three-point play that put the Beavers ahead 57 to 53. On the next possession a missed shot by Manhattan led to a City College three-on-one fast break, but Roth, leading the charge, made a bad pass and Poppe stepped in to intercept it; he tossed the ball the other way to Joyce for an easy layup, and instead of having a six-point lead, City led by only two, 57 to 55.

By this point Madison Square Garden had descended into a state characterized by the *Herald Tribune* as "hysteria." The CCNY students in the upper deck were especially aware that the team's season might well hinge on the outcome of the next two minutes, and with a growing sense of alarm they implored their team to shoot, or not to shoot, and to protect the ball, while Manhattan's fans chanted "Green and white, fight, fight, fight!" Amid the roar Nat Holman stood shouting instructions to his players to freeze the ball; having brought the ball over the midcourt line the Beavers went into a weave, the players moving in both directions around the perimeter of the court while the Jaspers swarmed whichever man had the ball, a river of green rushing this way and that, until in desperation, with forty-five seconds remaining on the clock, Jack Byrnes intentionally fouled Irwin Dambrot. To the City fans' consternation, however, Dambrot missed the free throw, and over the next thirty seconds the Jaspers sent up a barrage of shots, four in all; each missed the mark, but each time, one of the Manhattan players underneath the basket managed to tap the ball back outside, away from City's control, until finally a Manhattan shot was blocked out of bounds and with ten seconds remaining the Jaspers called time out to set up the inbounds pass. When play resumed, the pass went in to Mike Joyce, at six foot seven the tallest man on the floor, who caught the ball with his back to the hoop, pivoted, and tossed up a shot that apparently went in to tie the score and send the game into overtime—except that it didn't. The ball settled halfway into the basket and then, unaccountably, bounced back out; after another scramble Hank Poppe launched a set shot from the corner, but by that point the final buzzer had already sounded and the game was over.

Those in the crowd filed slowly down the Garden's steep exit ramps shaking their heads and still not quite believing what they had seen; as the *Post*'s Sid Friedlander would write in his game account, "It was the hand of fate that spilled the ball out of the basket." For City fans, Joyce's unsuccessful turnaround couldn't help but conjure up memories of Ronnie MacGilvray's unsuccessful layup at the end of the St. John's game: If either of those two shots had gone in, the Beavers would likely not even be in consideration for a postseason tournament berth.

City College's season record stood now at 16 and 5; the team was undefeated in the Subway Conference, and with the final game against New York University not scheduled until the following week there was nothing left for the players to do but go to class and attend practices and nervously await the announcement of the final NIT invitations.

It was Thursday, March 2, 1950. That day, in Brooklyn, District Attorney Miles McDonald announced the first three arrests in his office's investigation of sports bookmaking at local colleges.

CHAPTER 11

At a secret meeting convened with the deans of four local colleges, Miles McDonald and his assistant Julius Helfand had made arrangements for their squad of twenty-nine rookie policemen to enroll in classes at Brooklyn College, Brooklyn Law School, Pratt Institute, and Long Island University. They would be going undercover, posing as college students to try to identify the student bookmakers that Ed Reid of *The Brooklyn Daily Eagle* had alleged were doing business on every local campus—to learn as much as they could about the bookmaking operation, including, if possible, the identities of any policemen who were receiving bribe money in exchange for protection.

Most of the recruits who had been chosen for the squad were white, but a few were black; some had crew cuts, while others wore their hair longer, slicking it with Brylcreem or Vitalis; some wore glasses, which gave them a more scholarly mien. All of them, however, were unavoidably aware of the strangeness, not to mention the precariousness, of the assignment they had taken on. Only three weeks earlier they had graduated from the Police Academy, Police Commissioner William P. O'Brien himself welcoming them into the ranks. The commissioner stood before them as a classic tough cop in a double-breasted suit, with icy blue eyes and a ruddy, pockmarked face, white hair combed straight back, talking out of the side of his mouth as if it held an invisible cigar. "You didn't need to know anyone to get this job," he told them, "and you won't need to know anyone to go up. Just keep studying to prepare yourself and keep your record clean."

Now, when they had only just received their probationary assignment to a precinct house, they were instead working plainclothes, trading in the peaked patrolman's cap and crisp navy uniform with the numbered silver badge, the handcuffs and the billy club, the holstered .38 and the bullets in the belt, for an undergraduate wardrobe of cardigans and corduroys. They well understood that if the bribery was really as widespread as the *Eagle* had suggested, this was an arrangement on which many of their fellow officers had come to depend, and those who were involved would not take kindly to any threat to their livelihood posed by upstart rookies making barely $3,000 a year, with no personal stake yet in the system; they would be challenging the normal way of doing things, and though at the moment only a few senior commanders knew who they were, once their identities came to be known around the station houses—as seemed inevitable—they would be exposing themselves to a future of ostracism and, likely, retribution of a sort they were not experienced enough even to imagine. In the squad's headquarters the young policemen, still mostly strangers to one another, exchanged the shrugs and wry smiles they might have seen in the movies, on commandos who had volunteered for an apparent suicide mission. *This is a hell of a way,* one of them was heard to say, *to start a police career.*

Only days after forming the new investigative squad, Miles McDonald received an unexpected visitor: Chief Inspector August Flath, the top aide to Police Commissioner O'Brien. Flath was fifty-two years old, with a Roman nose and dramatically arched eyebrows, as if he were perpetually suspicious of what was being said. Though he was not an especially large man, Flath was trim and vigorous and cut an imposing figure in his chief inspector's uniform, his cap a sea of gold braid, a line of gold stars on each shoulder, and the widest possible gold stripe running down the side of his trousers. He seemed as much Army general as police inspector, and he spoke with all the authority and expectation of consent that the rank conferred. He told McDonald that the New York Police Department would like to provide the district attorney with a lieutenant to supervise his gambling investigation. Those twenty-nine rookies of his, after all, were merely on loan from the department; they were still policemen, and as policemen the commissioner expected that they would serve under a representative of the department's own choosing.

McDonald gazed at Chief Inspector Flath for a moment, considering his response. He knew that this demand had not been initiated by Flath himself; it had surely come from Commissioner O'Brien, who in turn had likely consulted with his immediate superior, Mayor O'Dwyer. McDonald and his assistant Julius Helfand had often spoken of their suspicions that a kind of palace guard existed at the highest levels of the New York Police Department, its goal to thwart outside efforts at reform; now, with Flath's visit, McDonald felt that he was being given a glimpse into the future, one in which that palace guard would seek to obstruct his investigation at every turn. Through its designated lieutenant, he understood, the department would try to limit the work of the squad or direct it into pre-approved channels, and all the while the lieutenant would be providing a ceaseless flow of information back to the police brass.

"No," McDonald replied. "Absolutely not." His investigators, he insisted, would report to no member of the Police Department; he did not want to risk the possibility of leaks to other policemen. And besides, he added, "A prosecutor must have independence of action or his hands are tied."

McDonald had chosen those words carefully: for they were the very ones that Brooklyn district attorney William O'Dwyer had spoken to Mayor Fiorello La Guardia when La Guardia demanded that O'Dwyer file regular reports about his investigation of Murder, Inc. Though he was speaking to the chief inspector, McDonald felt confident that what he had said would soon be repeated to the mayor himself.

Meanwhile the work of the new investigative squad was getting under way. Six of the rookies had been assigned to investigate possible book-making at Long Island University, one of them a patrolman by the name of Anthony Russo. Russo was twenty-three years old but he looked barely eighteen, as he was short and slight, with a wispy mustache that gave an impression of youth rather than maturity. Much like any other student he attended class during the day and gave over much of his evenings to homework. It was a grind for him, as his courses at the Police

Academy—with titles like "Juvenile Delinquency and Crime Preven-
tion" and "Local Law, Administrative Code"—had given him little preparation for the study of philosophy and art history. Scrupulously he
worked to maintain his cover, not even daring to nod to a fellow officer
if he happened to pass one in a corridor. For several weeks he did his best
to strike up conversations with his fellow students, but each time he was
frustrated to find the talk turning to Horatian odes or the prospects for
the new United Nations; not one of the students expressed any interest
in gambling. Each night Russo prepared his report for Inspector William Dahut, and each night it provided nothing of substance. He was
discouraged, but he persisted, and one afternoon he decided to eat lunch
at a nearby luncheonette called Jiggs' Smoke Shop.

The shop was run by a man named Samuel Jacobs—the eponymous
"Jiggs"—tall and gaunt, with thinning black hair plastered flat to his
head. His was a typical luncheonette, sparely furnished, the walls fes-
tooned with signs for Coca-Cola and Doublemint gum, with one counter at the front and another that ran all the way to the back of the shop.
The counterman, Joseph Sacco, was in truth no older than the college
students he was serving; he was a friendly, energetic presence, eager to
earn his forty dollars a week plus tips.

For several days Russo ate lunch at the Jiggs' counter and saw nothing out of the ordinary. One afternoon, though, taking a stool at the
back counter, he said hello to Joseph Sacco and ordered his regular
lunch, a tuna fish sandwich and a Coke. Sitting next to him he noticed
a couple of college students studying some newsprint laid out on the
counter: a scratch sheet—the daily publication that provided a bettor
with the necessary information for the upcoming races, from odds to
horses and jockeys and expected weather conditions. One of the students scribbled some notations on a slip of paper, then each pulled out a
dollar bill and the student rolled the two dollars into the paper. When
Sacco returned with their sodas, the student casually passed the rolled
slip to him; Sacco walked to the back of the luncheonette and handed it
to Samuel Jacobs, who pocketed the slip containing the money.

Russo decided to skip his next class; after finishing his sandwich he
ordered a chocolate fudge sundae, and as he ate the ice cream he
watched the crowd coming in and out. He counted seven more bets,
each transaction proceeding just as the first one had, bettor to Sacco to

Jacobs. For the first time since he left the Police Academy, Anthony Russo felt like a cop.

That evening Russo was pleased to deliver a report to Inspector Dahut that at last contained potentially valuable information. Dahut in turn brought the report to Assistant District Attorney Julius Helfand, and they decided that all six of the rookies assigned to Long Island University should now concentrate on Jiggs' Smoke Shop, spending as much time there as they could without drawing attention to themselves.

The next afternoon, Russo, sitting at the back of the lunch counter, quietly asked Joseph Sacco if he'd handle a bet for him. "Nah," Sacco said with a shrug. "How do I know you ain't a cop?"

"Me?" asked Russo in a surprised tone. "Hell, I'm too small to be a cop."

Sacco looked Russo over for a moment, taking in the slender frame, the undergrown mustache. He laughed. "Yeah. Christ, yes. You're much too small to be a cop." He held out his hand and Russo gave him a dollar bill rolled into a slip of paper on which he had marked a one-dollar bet on a horse named Red and Green to win in the seventh race at Hialeah.

As it happened, Red and Green won that race, paying $7.20 on a two-dollar bet, and the next day Russo collected his $3.60. He made another bet at lunch that day ("I want to give the bookie a chance to get even," he joked), and for each of the next several days he placed a bet with Sacco. Scattered about the luncheonette, coming and going at various times of day, the other members of the investigative squad were surreptitiously watching the crowd. It wasn't long before they had taken notice of a middle-aged man—he was referred to simply as J.G.—who arrived each morning and settled into a table at the back. Before long Samuel Jacobs would join him and the two would sit together with a pile of paper slips, going over accounts. Eventually, their business concluded, Jacobs would hand over some cash and J.G. would stuff it into his pocket and leave.

Inspector Dahut ordered a member of the squad to tail J.G. and see what could be found out about him. His real name, it turned out, was Joseph Gross, and he was a runner for what appeared to be a significant bookmaking operation; each day Gross made his rounds, as regular as a postman, stopping briefly in to luncheonettes, candy stores, poolrooms, repair shops, collecting the day's bets and tallying them in his little account book. It wasn't long before District Attorney Miles McDonald had all the evidence he needed to arrest Sacco, Jacobs, and Gross on bookmaking charges. At a meeting in his office, though, McDonald surprised the members of his staff by announcing that he did not plan to arrest the three men; instead, he would ask the Brooklyn grand jury to issue indictments against them.

Typically, anyone arrested in Brooklyn on a bookmaking charge would appear in Gamblers' Court, established a decade earlier to ease overcrowding in Special Sessions Court. After his sensational exposé appeared in *The Brooklyn Daily Eagle* in December, Ed Reid had undertaken an investigation of Gamblers' Court, coming to a startling conclusion: "Bookmakers are immune to jail sentences in Brooklyn." Despite hundreds of arrests, since January 1, 1949, only a single bookmaker had served any time in jail; in every other instance the case was dismissed or the accused paid only a small fine. By indicting the three men on charges of bookmaking and conspiracy to violate gambling laws, McDonald intended to keep them out of the revolving door of Gamblers' Court and give them a proper trial in County Court. This was unprecedented in a gambling case involving two small-time bookies and a runner, but for McDonald, trial and conviction were the necessary first phase of a longer-term plan. He was not interested in exacting serious punishment on the pair from Jiggs' Smoke Shop, Samuel Jacobs and Joseph Sacco (for Sacco, who was only twenty years old, he would seek a suspended sentence), but he suspected that Joseph Gross could be the linchpin. Facing the prospect of a year in jail, Gross might break down and tell investigators what he knew, including the names of the men who ran the syndicate that controlled the borough's bookmaking and the policemen who were paid to protect them.

Julius Helfand's warnings to the rookies about the abuse they should expect from their fellow officers had quickly been borne out. While other policemen did not know precisely what the rookies were investigating, it was generally understood that they were assisting Miles McDonald's probe and thus should be treated as pariahs. Even those policemen who had no dealings with bookmakers and did not need to fear the investigation despised them as stoolies, rats, the lowest kind of cops: those who had broken the unofficial code of silence.

Though they were working for the Brooklyn district attorney, the rookies were still on the payroll of the New York Police Department, and every two weeks they had to return to their assigned precincts to pick up their paychecks. Invariably the desk sergeant would tell them that their checks weren't ready, and for as much as an hour they had to stand around under the contemptuous stares of their fellow policemen, many of whom found a way to bump into them as they passed by. Veterans sidled up to remind them that when the investigation was over they would be assigned back to the station house—"and then we'll take care of you." When the checks finally arrived, obscenities had been scrawled across the envelopes.

At home, the arrival of the mail became a daily source of anxiety; anonymous letters and postcards carried vulgarity and threats. Their phones would ring at all hours, and often when they picked up the receiver there was no one on the other end of the line; the call had been made simply to rattle them, to send the message that someone knew who they were. Sometimes the caller would mutter a threat and then hang up. One time a rookie who lived with his mother answered the phone early in the morning as he was getting ready for work. The voice on the other end told him that if he didn't quit the squad his mother would get her head cracked open someday on the way to the grocery store. When the rookie threatened to have the next call traced, he was reminded that they knew where he lived, and if he traced a call they would burn down his house.

What made the calls especially unnerving was that the rookies had all taken unlisted phone numbers; their home numbers were known only to the district attorney's office and to their commanding officers in the Police Department. Some of the rookies changed their phone numbers, yet night after night the calls still came.

Meanwhile, returns were beginning to come in from the district attorney's investigation. At Brooklyn College, the rookies had uncovered a ring of students—including the star of the basketball team—who distributed weekly betting cards among their fellow students, each card listing twenty-five college basketball games with their point spreads. Most students bet little more than a quarter on a card, but these betting cards were so popular on campus that the ring was averaging $5,000 in bets per week. Inspector Dahut ordered a tail to be placed on the basketball player, Michael Di Tomasso; ultimately this led investigators to a candy store in Greenwich Village, where Di Tomasso handed over the betting money to a twenty-one-year-old former boxer and petty criminal named Vincent Gigante. Gigante was subsequently indicted, with two other defendants, on a charge of conspiracy to commit bookmaking.*

The Brooklyn grand jury had also issued indictments against the three men connected to Jiggs' Smoke Shop, and though Joseph Gross continued to deny that he worked for bookmakers, McDonald was confident that eventually he would begin to talk.

The groundwork was being put in place for a large-scale investigation of bookmaking and police corruption. Still, despite the progress, Miles McDonald had not yet been able to ascertain the identity of the fabled Mr. G, the man who allegedly controlled all of Brooklyn's bookmaking operations and had been installed in his position by high-ranking police officials.

One afternoon the phone rang in his office; ever since he extended the term of the grand jury to focus on bookmaking, he had been receiving several anonymous tips a day, and he had instructed his secretary to pass along all of those calls. He picked up the phone. "District Attorney McDonald," he said.

"Listen, McDonald," growled the voice on the other end of the line. "I got something to tell you."

"Yes?"

"McDonald," the caller went on, "you're some jerk. You got the wrong Gross."

"What do you mean?" McDonald asked. "Is there another one?"

The caller, though, said nothing more; McDonald heard only a short, scornful laugh, and then there was a click and a steady buzzing in his ear.

---

* In 1981, Vincent ("Chin") Gigante would become head of the Genovese crime family, a position he held until his death in 2005.

CHAPTER 12

The Madison Square Garden locker room had, in fact, no lockers— just hooks on the wall on which players hung their street clothes while changing into their uniforms. As they undressed, the City College players handed their valuables to the team manager, Al Ragusa, who stuffed them into a large bag for safekeeping. The team's equipment managers were filling water jugs and folding and stacking towels while, at the back of the room, the trainer was taping ankles. Some of the players began their stretching routines; others sat tightening and retightening laces. The room smelled of liniment and sweat and the sliced oranges that were always handed out during halftime; that was, for each of them, a familiar smell, and they could feel the tightness rising now inside them, the clutch in the belly, the slight weakness in the legs: This was the opening round of the National Invitation Tournament, for almost all of them the first postseason game of their career.

The announcement had come only five days earlier: Along with Arizona and Niagara, City College would be one of the last three teams selected for that year's National Invitation Tournament. The Beavers had closed out the 1949–50 season with a victory over New York University, giving them an impressive final record of 17 wins and 5 losses and the Subway Conference title. Still, even their most fervent fans didn't think they had much of a chance. All but one of the other eleven teams in the tournament had won at least twenty games. Other than St. John's, City had not defeated any team of note and had lost to UCLA and

Niagara, both of which were in the tournament. The teams in the NIT included those ranked first, third, sixth, eighth, ninth, and tenth in the Associated Press national poll; City College, in contrast, had ended the season tied for twenty-seventh place. And in the first round the Beavers would have to face the Dons of the University of San Francisco, the defending NIT champion.

The opening game of the afternoon, between Western Kentucky and Niagara, was already going on, and beyond the walls of the locker room the players could hear the rise and fall of the crowd, a deep sound like the ocean or the rumble of a distant subway. Every once in a while a man with a cigar in his mouth stuck his head into the room to announce the score of the game and how much time was left on the clock, and eventually there was a great wave of sound from the crowd, and the attendant came in to tell them it was time to go. The team's two captains rallied them into a huddle for a team handshake, Joe Galiber's black hand clasped with Irwin Dambrot's white one, and then together they ran through the tunnel and out into the sudden vastness of the arena.

On the City College sideline Eddie Roman could feel the smooth, almost slick leather surface of the basketball in his hands. As if before the start of a Broadway show, the house lights had been brought down, and in the arena all around him hundreds of orange dots bobbed like swarms of fireflies: the burning tips of cigarettes. Suddenly he was caught in a blinding light, and Barclay Cooke's voice rumbled over the public address system: *And for City College, Ed Roman*—his name, he was the first to be called— and without thinking he dribbled onto the court from the sideline as he had been instructed to do, unable to see anything in the darkness beyond the moving beam of the spotlight. He had never felt comfortable dribbling, and certainly not when the attention of the crowd was focused on him and he could see only a few feet in front of his face, but he managed to dribble out to center court and then turn and roll the ball back to the bench; then, thankfully, the spotlight left him and returned to the sideline, picking up Irwin Dambrot, who dribbled smoothly out to center court next to Eddie, rolled the ball back, and waited to greet Ed Warner. For a moment it was just Eddie and Irwin standing in the darkness at center court, the two former Taft Presidents basking in the cheers of the crowd.

Eddie was wearing his satin practice jacket but his legs were bare and he jumped up and down a bit to stay warm and keep his nerves at bay. He was as fit as he had ever been, 218 pounds, a number he hadn't seen on the scale since high school. The previous summer he had worked as a waiter at Scaroon Manor in the Adirondacks, where the waitstaff got three all-you-can eat meals every day, and Eddie was legendary for all he could eat; there was a world of delicious food available to him, spaghetti and steak and roast chicken and chocolate pudding, not to mention dishes he had never seen before, like Welsh rarebit and baked Alaska and these little cakes called petits fours, and he had figured that between the hotel work and the basketball at night he could eat whatever he wanted. That was a mistake: He had come back to school even heavier than usual, but he had worked hard and lost more than thirty pounds and played himself back into shape. Now he felt strong and ready, and after all that had happened he was thrilled to be in the NIT—just playing, free now of the weight of business. He and Irwin had put the kibosh on Norm Mager earlier that day: Normie had called a meeting with Fats and Irwin and Eddie and told them that Eli Kaye had gotten back in touch, wanting to do business on the San Francisco game. He was willing to double the pot, two thousand for each of them. Irwin, for his part, looked stricken at the idea, and Eddie knew he must have looked the same. *No*, they said. *Not now. We've come too far.* Normie told Kaye sorry, they couldn't do it.

Ed Warner dribbled up beside Irwin, and then came Floyd and Fats, and the crowd cheered and the house lights came back up; the two teams' starting fives pulled off their practice jackets and huddled near the sideline for some final instructions from their coaches. The officials called time and the players trotted back out onto the floor, the Beavers in their white uniforms and the Dons in green trimmed with gold, everyone on both sides wearing black high-top sneakers. Each player shook hands with his counterpart from the other team, and then, as if by direction, the crowd grew silent for the center jump.

The first play was classic City College ball movement: Eddie Roman tipped the ball up and Ed Warner grabbed it near midcourt; he dribbled it ahead a couple of times, a kind of sounding, probing the defense, then passed off to Irwin Dambrot, who dribbled toward the right sideline and passed back to Floyd Layne near the top of the keyhole, who noticed

Roman breaking free in the right-hand corner and fired him a pass; Eddie turned and sent up a one-handed jump shot, the ball settling straight into the net for the first two points. The game was not yet fifteen seconds old. Over the next several minutes the Beavers built an early lead: Layne connected for a pair of baskets, swooping across the lane for a scoop shot and a layup; Dambrot made a couple of left-handed jump shots with that distinctive shooting form of his, left knee raised as though he were about to board a streetcar.

On defense the Beavers had been well schooled by Bobby Sand, and the Dons were surprised to find the City defenders anticipating their moves, switching men easily, poking the ball away or moving into position to block off a path to the basket. Earlier that season Bobby had seen St. John's defeat San Francisco with a sagging zone defense, and now City College adopted it as well, clogging up the inside and forcing the Dons to toss up long set shots that thudded harmlessly off the backboard or clanged off the rim. The pace slowed, and after the first few minutes neither team seemed able to generate any offensive rhythm, but still City's lead crept steadily upward, and at halftime the Beavers headed into the locker room ahead 32 to 19.

As play began for the second half, Eddie Roman again jumped at center, but then Ed Warner moved into the pivot position and began to dominate the area under the basket, twirling and feinting and shooting with either hand, putting on, in the description of Everett B. Morris of the *Herald Tribune*, "an exhibition of fakery and dexterity . . . a blood-tingling performance." In the first fifty seconds of the half he scored three straight baskets, on a hook shot, a tip-in of his own missed shot, and a layup. The layup, which came at the end of one of the team's few fast breaks, served as a kind of exclamation point, bringing the crowd to its feet, extending the lead to nineteen points and seeming to eradicate any possibility of a San Francisco comeback. After ten minutes City College had stretched the lead to 22 and Nat Holman began sending his reserves in, not just the usual substitutes but all twelve players down to the end of the bench, everyone getting some tournament court time.* The final score was 65 to 46.

* The regular-season squad of fifteen players had been trimmed to twelve for the post-season.

In the lobby after the game the crowd moved slowly past the Kelleher Memorial Trophy that was on display there all week, gleaming silver with the words NATIONAL INTERCOLLEGIATE INVITATION BASKETBALL TOURNAMENT engraved on it. They talked about Warner's spin moves and Roman's rebounding and Dambrot's tough defense, their voices merging into a hum that filled the large space, unfocused but still powerful, like the sound of a great orchestra tuning up. It had been a scrappy, inelegant sort of game. To beat the reigning champs the Beavers had jettisoned the centerpiece of their offense, the fast break; they had played with discipline and intelligence, and they had shown that they belonged in the tournament, despite what the national rankings might say. City College had now moved into the quarterfinal round of the National Invitation Tournament and would be playing its next game in just two days, and the team's fans looked forward to that with excitement and anticipation and also a sense of dread: for the next game was against the University of Kentucky.

The Kentucky Wildcats were to college basketball what the New York Yankees were to Major League Baseball: the glamour team, the premier program in the sport, the perennial favorite to win a championship. The university was then putting the finishing touches on a new campus field house for the basketball team; it cost four million dollars and had a seating capacity of twelve thousand, which made it larger than almost any public arena in the country. Over the previous six seasons Kentucky had won six straight Southeastern Conference championships, two NCAA championships, and an NIT championship, and had been selected for at least one of the national tournaments every single year. In the 1948–49 season three members of Kentucky's starting five were named All-American, the only time three All-Americans had ever played on a single team. The starting five had been selected for the 1948 U.S. Olympic basketball team, which earned the gold medal; after graduation an NBA franchise had been created expressly for them, named, in honor of their international triumph, the Indianapolis Olympians. Adolph Rupp himself was the most successful coach in college basketball, an accomplishment for which he had a ready explanation. "The secret of my success is easy," he would tell anyone who asked. "It's good coaching."

In 1950, Adolph Rupp was forty-eight years old and had been the head coach of the Kentucky Wildcats for twenty years. He was an instantly recognizable figure on the Kentucky bench: a burly man in a brown suit waving his arms constantly, squirming in anger and frustration. Once, in his early years as a high school coach, Rupp wore a new blue suit to a game and his team got shellacked; since that time he had worn a brown suit, brown tie, brown socks, and brown shoes in every single game he coached. To wear the same color outfit; to sit in the same seat on the team bus; to eat the same pregame meal of bacon and eggs year upon year: All of this he was willing to do even if it offered only the slimmest, least likely prospect of an advantage. It was of a piece with Rupp's utterly single-minded devotion to winning, for which he was willing to sacrifice much else. His assistant coach, Harry Lancaster, who knew him as well as anyone, wrote in a memoir that as far as he could tell, Rupp had never had a close friend, nor apparently ever wanted one. Many people, on the other hand, strongly disliked him. "I know I have plenty of enemies," Rupp once acknowledged, "but I'd rather be the most hated winning coach in the country than the most popular losing one."

Sometimes after a defeat Rupp would order his players to keep their uniforms on; then, after the arena had emptied out, he would send them back onto the floor for another practice, to correct the mistakes that he

University of Kentucky head coach Adolph Rupp. Associated Press

had observed during the game. A basketball was not a toy, he would admonish them again and again; it was a tool, and the purpose of that tool was to win basketball games. "You are all now in business for yourselves," he advised freshman players in their first practice. "You have been hired to do a job. You will do that job or be fired and we'll get someone who does do the job."

Adolph Rupp believed that basketball games were won and lost in the practice gym, much as the battle of Waterloo was said to have been won on the playing fields of Eton. His sessions were highly regimented and discipline was sternly enforced, and the analogy offered by all who had gone through them was boot camp. Rupp and Lancaster always wore starched khaki shirts and pants to practice; the effect was so Army, two Kentucky players would later recall, that you could almost see the sergeant's stripes on the arms. "He made the rules and we obeyed them," said another player. "There was no joking, no laughing, no singing, no whistling, no horseplay, no breaks in practice, and certainly no questioning his rules." One reporter attended a Wildcats practice and said later that it reminded him of nothing so much as a forced march. "On and on it goes," he wrote, "silent, efficient, implacable; basketball at Kentucky is like rolling a boulder uphill."

As Nat Holman was etched in the popular imagination as Mr. Basketball, in Kentucky Adolph Rupp's honorific was the Baron of the Bluegrass, often shortened simply to the Baron. What a basketball star was to the University of Kentucky campus, Rupp was to Lexington as a whole. He owned a pair of farms on which he raised tobacco and Hereford cattle; he also owned an insurance business and held a substantial piece of a large tobacco warehousing corporation. His name was perennially bandied about as a candidate for statewide public office, for which his popularity, everyone agreed, would make him a shoo-in. When he wanted to be, Rupp was convivial, a raconteur with an earthy sense of humor; from the beginning of his time in Lexington he cultivated friendships with reporters and community leaders, hosting chili dinners in the modest brick house he shared with his wife and son. Albert "Happy" Chandler, the former governor of Kentucky and leader of the segregationist "Dixiecrat" movement in the state, would come visit, as did other local politicians seeking favors and advice.

In the 1940s, Lexington, Kentucky, was a deeply segregated city: African Americans could not eat in white-owned restaurants, nor sleep in white-owned hotels; St. Joseph Hospital maintained a "colored ward"; the Greyhound bus terminal had twin waiting rooms, one reserved for white passengers, one for black. One of the city's newspapers, the *Leader*, even included a separate section for funeral notices and organizational announcements entitled "Colored Notes." Discrimination in housing restricted black residents to certain sections of Lexington, mainly the least desirable; the city's children, white and black, played in separate parks, and when they were thirsty they drank from separate water fountains.

The city's schools, too, were segregated, and that included the University of Kentucky. The state's Day Law, enacted in 1904, mandated a policy of strict educational segregation, prohibiting Kentucky schools from "teaching students of different races in the same room." By the 1940s white students in Kentucky could choose from among five public and fifteen private colleges, while black students had only one public and one private college, neither of which offered graduate study. Finally, in 1948, in response to intensifying public pressure, the University of Kentucky established a partnership with Kentucky State College for Negroes in nearby Frankfort. Under the partnership, black graduate students would attend classes at the University of Kentucky but be formally enrolled at Kentucky State; however, in deference to the Day Law, the students would be required to use separate classrooms, study in separate library sessions, and eat in a separate dining hall. Only the most meager of resources were allocated to the program, and between 1948 and 1950 no more than eleven students were accepted. In 1949 an African American educator named Lyman Johnson—represented by NAACP attorney Thurgood Marshall—filed a lawsuit demanding entrance to the university, and a federal judge ruled in his favor. For that year's summer session a class of thirty-one African American graduate students entered the University of Kentucky, but not without resistance: During the summer seven crosses were burned on the campus, and death threats against Lyman Johnson were broadcast on a Kentucky radio station.

Still, despite the attempts at intimidation, African Americans continued to pursue graduate studies at the university; not until 1954, however, and the Supreme Court's landmark *Brown v. Board of Education* decision, were black undergraduates permitted to register for classes. In the 1949–50 season, then, Adolph Rupp could not have included black players on the Kentucky Wildcats, since there were no black students in the college from whom to choose; nor would he have felt free to send his team of scouts to recruit black high school players. To do so would have required challenging the laws of his state, not to mention the all-white policy of the Southeastern Conference, the athletic conference to which the University of Kentucky belonged, and in truth Rupp had shown not the slightest inclination to integrate his team.* He had not allowed the Wildcats to take the floor against a team with any black players until after the Second World War, when the integration of several top-flight Northern teams meant that maintaining the policy would effectively bar Kentucky from participation in the major postseason tournaments. This was only during road games, however; by 1950 no black player had yet appeared on Kentucky's home court. "I remember walking through the arena in Lexington with Adolph Rupp when we went there to play Kentucky," the longtime DePaul coach Ray Meyer wrote in his autobiography. "He put his arm around me and said, 'See, Ray, there are no blacks in here. If you bring black players we can't play anymore.' "

Nor had Rupp himself been especially secretive about his racial views. Once, for instance, when Kentucky was scheduled to play at Madison Square Garden, he was talking with some New York sports-writers and the conversation turned to the emergence of black players in the college game. "The Lord never meant for a white boy to play with a colored boy," Rupp theologized, "else he wouldn't have painted them different colors."

On Tuesday, March 14, 1950, the Beavers of City College would play the Kentucky Wildcats, the team that in much of the country had become doubly iconic, for its excellence on the basketball court and as a symbol of racial segregation. This was the team, after all, that had helped bring home a gold medal for the United States in the Olympic Games, the team that had won three national tournaments in the previous four years, the team that would soon have an arena two-thirds the size of Madison Square Garden for its own use. It was also a team representing a college that among its 9,779 undergraduates had not a single black student, on

---

* The University of Kentucky would not bring on its first black varsity basketball player, Tom Payne, until the 1970–71 season—sixteen years after black undergraduate students began attending the university. The neighboring teams of Western Kentucky University and the University of Louisville had been integrated since 1963.

a campus that had desegregated only under court order and that the previous summer had been the site of numerous cross burnings, in a city where racial segregation was widespread and the most revered monuments were to heroes of the Confederacy.

Now Adolph Rupp and his Wildcats were coming to New York to play a team in which every player—every single one—was either black or Jewish, and whose head coach and assistant coach were Jewish as well. It was a team whose cocaptains were an African American and a Jew, one of whom, Joe Galiber, was also a member of the Congress of Racial Equality and the Young Progressives of America. The team represented a college that for decades had been seen as perhaps the most left-wing in the country. Every one of the college's students lived in New York, a city that, for all its ethnic tensions and divisions, had long taken pride in its distinction as the most diverse place on earth, where more than one-quarter of the residents were foreign-born immigrants (the mayor himself among them), with some sixty nationalities represented among its people, having more Jews than Israel, more Irish than Dublin, nearly as many Italians as Rome and Puerto Ricans as San Juan: It was where the whole world lived, the daily embodiment of the modern glass-and-marble UN building that was then rising on the city's East River.

In the days before the Kentucky game a rumor swept through the campus that Adolph Rupp was publicly disparaging the City College Beavers as a team unworthy of his own and that he had described them as "a team of niggers and Jews." No evidence was ever produced for this charge, but to those at City College it seemed perfectly characteristic and utterly believable—and served only to reinforce the notion that the upcoming game was not just against Kentucky, the elite team of the old South, but against the idea of segregation itself. Marvin Kalb, a sports reporter for the student newspaper *The Campus*, would write years later, "The buildup to the game, at least among City College students, was electric with tension and anxiety. My editor called it a 'culture war'—not a basketball game but a collision of fundamental values." Tickets to the Kentucky game were the most precious commodity that anyone just then could imagine, and on a lively, crowded campus renowned for its freewheeling talk there was in those days but one stream of conversation, and only one hour that occupied everyone's mind: nine o'clock Tuesday night.

CHAPTER 13

That night the crowds streamed again to the Garden, a strong tide surging up and down the avenues, filling the sidewalks and flowing into the street. Along the older sections of the West Side the night sky was punctuated by honeycombs of lighted windows in the warehouses and office buildings; around a corner the darkness abruptly gave way to the lurid blues and oranges of Times Square, neon signs piled atop one another hawking beer and soda and candy bars, the messages endlessly scrolling and unscrolling, and every four seconds the smiling man on the Camel billboard exhaled another perfectly formed smoke ring. The colors from overhead puddled and slid over the shiny roofs and segmented windshields of the red-and-yellow taxicabs as they glided down the avenue, and some stepped out of the crowd to hail a cab; those shuffling along the crowded sidewalks passed the ramshackle hole-in-the-wall enterprises tucked amid the neon and the chrome, the dance halls and fleabag hotels and While-U-Wait photo galleries with their headless cutouts of strongmen and Indian queens, and on many of the corners a green wooden newsstand with magazines hanging daintily from clips like wash on a line.

On Eighth Avenue the people spilled out of the saloons, from Downey's on Forty-Fifth all the way up to Gilhooley's on Fifty-First, the sense of coiled anticipation growing stronger with each successive block, until in front of Madison Square Garden the streams converged, the crowd milling excitedly under the illuminated marquee as it did in the minutes before the curtain rose on a hit Broadway show. They were the biggest show in town now, those City College Beavers, bigger than *Gentlemen Prefer Blondes* or *Mister Roberts* or *Death of a Salesman*, bigger even than Mary Martin and Ezio Pinza in *South Pacific*, the show Adolph Rupp had taken his players to see that weekend. In his earlier days as a coach, when Rupp brought his team to New York he had allowed the players considerable liberty to attend nightclubs and the like, and over time he came to suspect that "our boys left a lot of their basketball out on the streets of the city." These days he kept a much tighter rein; he and his assistant coach Harry Lancaster and their wives would chaperone the players for a steak dinner and a Broadway show, and that would be sufficient. He would have a daily schedule mimeographed and distributed to each member of the club, giving practice times, meal times, nap times; on Monday night the team would attend a pair of opening round games at the Garden so the players could have a look at the teams they might face in a later round. He was leaving nothing to chance. The previous year he had come to New York with the idea that his team might accomplish something no team ever had, the so-called Grand Slam—to win the NIT and NCAA tournaments in the same year. He'd believed he had the players to do it, but the Wildcats had unaccountably lost to Loyola of Chicago in the first round and that had been that.

Nor would there be any possibility of a Grand Slam this year, as he had turned down the opportunity to participate in the National Collegiate Athletic Association tournament. NCAA officials had requested a playoff game between Kentucky and North Carolina State to determine the tournament's District 3 entry.* Adolph Rupp objected to that—the Wildcats, he fumed, were ranked third in the Associated Press poll, while NC State was no better than ninth; Kentucky wasn't going to submit to a playoff game to earn an invitation that by rights should already belong to it. The District 3 Selection Committee didn't see things that way: North Carolina State was given the slot without a playoff game.

So this year the Wildcats would have to content themselves with the possibility of another NIT trophy. Much like City College, the Kentucky team was composed primarily of sophomores, and after a few of the early

---

* At that time the NCAA tournament consisted of eight teams, one chosen from each of eight geographic districts across the country.

stumbles that were to be expected of such a young and inexperienced group, the team had found its footing and finished the season by winning fourteen games in a row—including a four-game stretch in which the margins of victory were twenty-seven, twenty, forty, and thirty-five points—and the Metropolitan Basketball Writers Association had named Adolph Rupp coach of the year. Before leaving Lexington for New York, Rupp told reporters, "I think this is the best sophomore basketball team I've ever had. Potentially it's the best team in Kentucky's history."

There was no doubting the game plan that Rupp would bring to postseason play. Rupp disdained the patient, careful style of offense used by many of his Southeastern Conference rivals, embracing a fast, relentlessly aggressive approach that he elevated to something of a patriotic credo. "We like to take chances," he had written in his 1948 book *Rupp's Championship Basketball for Player, Coach and Fan.* "That is the very spirit of aggressive play and is the spirit of modern youth. That is the spirit of our pioneer forefathers. What security did Daniel Boone ask for when he penetrated the wilderness, and what security did our pioneer mothers and fathers have when they carved their homes out of the western plains?"

The Kentucky fast break was a model of precision—the first outlet pass made by the rebounder to a teammate at the top of the keyhole, who passed the ball to another teammate streaking across midcourt, who in turn passed it to another teammate running at the opponent's basket, in perfect position to sink a layup: the length of the court often covered without benefit of a single dribble, in almost the blink of an eye, leaving opponents flat-footed and bewildered about how to respond. Even Kentucky's half-court offense moved very quickly. As soon as the play began, each of the Wildcats understood where every pass would be going, just as he understood where on the court he was supposed to be and what his responsibility was for the success of the play. The Kentucky half-court offense was as carefully organized and precisely balanced as a complex piece of machinery; indeed, it was a style of offense that Rupp liked to refer to as "mechanical." "We do not believe that an offense can be effective if it is left to chance," he wrote. "We have a set of plays off our pivot post offense that are absolutely mechanical in their execution. Everybody on the team knows exactly what we are going to do in our offensive move as soon as we cross the center line."

Of course, even the most rigidly conceived set offense provided a certain measure of flexibility, allowing for variations of a given play, but there was no mistaking the fact that Kentucky's offense was conceived and organized from the top down. A *Saturday Evening Post* article once went so far as to compare it to the "orthodox order of mobile warfare, with those engaged striving to carry out plays dictated by the general staff." It was a system in which everyone, from the head coach down to the lowliest reserve, recognized his specific role; Coach Rupp not only preferred it that way but, as he often indicated, his players did as well. "The boys like to play this kind of game," he declared, "as they all understand what they are supposed to do. In the freedom system, or in that style where boys make their plays as they go along according to their own judgment, it is hard to trace the responsibility for a play's failure to work."

Bobby Sand took a very different view. He was a champion of the spontaneous style of offense (what Rupp preferred to call "the freedom system"), which rarely used plays called in by the coach; instead, the players themselves created the offense during the course of play, in response to the defensive situations that arose. Unlike the set offense, the spontaneous offense emphasized the qualities of versatility, adaptability, and initiative; it was, in a sense, a music born of improvisation rather than composition. To Sand's way of thinking, an offense that relied on preconceived plays ran the risk of becoming predictable. He was convinced that an astute defense could solve the problems the offense presented, like a cryptographer breaking an enemy code, and "once the pattern is diagnosed, the offense may crack with pathetic results."

More than eighteen thousand fans were in Madison Square Garden that Tuesday night, as many as the arena could hold for a basketball game, every seat taken and fans standing several deep along the rail at the top level, nearly eighty feet above the court. A pall of cigar smoke swirled thickly around the upper reaches of the arena, the fans in those sections having a view that *New York Post* columnist Jimmy Cannon once compared to looking out an airplane window through the clouds.

At the front of the mezzanine Marty Glickman leaned into his microphone to once again welcome the WMGM radio audience to "Madison

Square Garden, basketball capital of the world." Nearby sat announcers representing three Kentucky radio stations, who had flown to New York with Adolph Rupp and the team on a chartered plane and at nine o'clock would each begin broadcasting the game back to Lexington. By that time the Wildcats had already taken the court in their royal-blue warm-up suits with the white double stripes running down the arms and legs, and as Coach Rupp stood watching from the bench they launched into their famed pregame warm-up drill, the intricate display of cuts and passes that Holy Cross coach Alvin Julian had called "the finest exhibition of ball handling that I have ever seen." Moving up and back and from sideline to sideline, the players formed shifting blue patterns on the yellow court; big number 77, center Bill Spivey, stood at the foul line with his back to the basket, leading the drill like the conductor of an orchestra, snapping the ball out to a player cutting across the top of the key or, with a casual flip of a wrist, shoveling it back underhanded to a teammate cutting in for a layup. The Wildcats carried themselves with a gunfighter's casual swagger, and in the stands a nineteen-year-old City College student named Hannan Wexler watched with a mixture of awe and dread. Years later he would recall, "The Kentucky warm-up was the closest thing to a Roman legion I had ever seen. The way they moved the ball—it was perfection. It was absolute perfection."

On the other end of the court the Beavers' warm-up looked to be no more organized than a shootaround before a playground pickup game—here and there players tossed up shots, balls knocking into one another, bouncing off at crazy angles, having to be chased down as they rolled out of bounds. "You had anarchy," says Wexler. "You had chaos. You had a bunch of guys freelancing. No fancy drill, nothing to impress you. And I remember some people around me saying, 'We're gonna get killed.'"

When the warm-up had concluded, announcer Barclay Cooke presented the starting lineups, first for the University of Kentucky and then, to a great roar, for City College, a swelling wave of sound that broke momentarily as the name of City's starting center reverberated across the Garden. It was not Eddie Roman, the team's leading scorer—it was Leroy Watkins! The crowd gave a collective gasp and then, noted a reporter, "bedlam broke loose" as Watkins, a popular senior, trotted out to center court to join his teammates, smiling and bowing his head in embarrassment as the cheers rained down; the opportunity to start that night was, he would say later, "the greatest thrill of my college career." Watkins was the team's third-string center; at six foot seven he was the tallest man ever to play for City College, but he had only begun playing basketball in earnest after his discharge from the Army, and despite his height he rarely got into games other than in the closing minutes, when a victory was already assured. In his three years on the varsity Watkins had not started a single game—and now here he was, coming out to play center in the most highly anticipated game in the college's history.

During a practice session earlier in the week Bobby Sand had conducted a "jump-off" among the team's centers, and Leroy Watkins, to Sand's great satisfaction, had won. Sand suggested to Nat Holman that they start Watkins, who stood the best chance of winning the opening tap against the seven-foot-tall Bill Spivey; they could keep Eddie Roman at the scorer's table, Sand pointed out, and send him in at the first stoppage of play. Looking for any advantage he could get against Kentucky, Holman had agreed to the unorthodox approach. Sand may have had another motivation as well—for Watkins, like Floyd Layne and Ed Warner, was black. Playing against the country's most prominent segregated team, City College would thus send out a starting five composed of three African Americans and two Jews; it was the first time in the history of either postseason tournament that a team had started three black players.

The players took their positions around the center-court circle, the Wildcats in white uniforms with blue trim, the Beavers in black trimmed with lavender and white. As referee Jocko Collins prepared for the opening toss, the City College players extended their hands to their Kentucky counterparts. The pregame handshake was a standard ritual, a simple gesture of courtesy and sportsmanship, but this time was very different: This time three of the Wildcats turned away.

It was as though a lightning bolt, brief and unexpected and frightening, had pierced the arena, bringing a burst of intense illumination but leaving a foul smell in its wake. All through Madison Square Garden, fans turned to one another for confirmation, not quite believing what they had seen. It was one thing for Kentucky to maintain an all-white team (indeed, several of New York's top basketball programs, like

NYU and St. John's, had yet to integrate), but to refuse to shake hands with a black opponent was an affront, a kind of racial slur thrown before all of them, in their own home. Inside Madison Square Garden something changed in that moment. The atmosphere suddenly seemed to crackle with excitement and anger; the adjective used by everyone who was there that night, player and fan alike, was *electric*.

Bobby Sand had anticipated that this would happen; just before the game, outside the locker room, he had pulled aside Ed Warner and Floyd Layne. "They're not gonna want to shake hands with you," he told them. "And if you're gonna take that kind of crap from them, don't ever speak to me again—I don't even want to know you. You're gonna go out there and show them that you belong on this court because you've been here all your life. Who the hell are these guys to come in and put you out of a tournament?"

Layne and Warner, old friends from their days in Harlem, nodded. Years later Layne would recall the brief, matter-of-fact conversation that passed between the two of them: "We just said, 'We're gonna go out there and bust their ass.'"

Jocko Collins blew his whistle; he tossed up the ball and the game was on. Bill Spivey controlled the center jump for Kentucky,* tapping the ball across the midcourt line to his teammate Shelby Linville. Linville tried to dribble down the right sideline but his path was immediately cut off by Floyd Layne, and in reversing course Linville lost his footing, managing to pass the ball to a teammate while sprawled on the floor; after a couple of hurried passes, guard Dale Barnstable tossed up a long set shot that bounced off the rim. Ed Warner came down with the rebound and passed the ball ahead to Al Roth, who dribbled across center court, at which point City launched into its weave, the ball moving fluidly from one player to another, five passes in all, until Warner received a pass above the top of the keyhole and then, sensing an opening, sliced toward the basket, leaving a pair of Wildcats in his wake, and from the left side of the lane, using his right hand, flipped up an improbable-looking scoop shot that arced high over the Kentucky defenders and settled into the net for the first points of the game.

---

* Many later accounts suggested that Leroy Watkins won the opening tap, but surviving film of the game shows that that was not the case.

That week in practice the Beavers had worked on cutting off the Kentucky fast break before it could get started, forcing the Wildcats to rely instead on their half-court offense. As he always did in the days before a game, Bobby Sand had taken to the chalkboard in the City College gymnasium, drawing up several of Kentucky's plays, intricate, meticulously timed sequences of passes (represented as dotted lines), dribbles (wavy lines), movement (solid lines), and screens (double slash marks)—showing the City players how, for instance, the Wildcats liked to run a guard around two outside screens to receive a bounce pass from the center for a layup, or how they timed their cuts so that a guard and a forward could simultaneously use the pivot man as an inside screen. The Kentucky system was a powerful precision instrument, and the Wildcat players themselves were too big, too strong, too disciplined to be rattled by a conventional defense. In recruiting players for the Beavers, Sand always looked for two qualities that he believed were not teachable—speed and aggressiveness—and those were the qualities on which they would now have to depend. During practices that week Holman and Sand ran the squads through many of Kentucky's plays, instructing them to be ready at all times to help out a teammate: to attack the offense from unusual angles, to switch assignments quickly and smother the man with the ball, creating as much havoc as possible. By disrupting its timing they might prevent the Kentucky offensive machine from running smoothly, perhaps even force the Wildcats to dispense with set plays and begin improvising—to play the City game, on offense and on defense as well.

"Let them play your game, which they don't want to do," one of City's reserve players, Ron Nadell, remembers Sand saying about the Wildcats. "If you run against this team you're gonna beat them. They don't have the quickness that you guys have. You're gonna shock them." From almost the opening tap City College set a blistering pace. With each rebound the Beavers sped off down the court, the basketball moving as fast as a pinball up the alley and then ricocheting up and back and side to side, from the rebounder who whipped a pass ahead to one of the two wing men, who in turn sent the ball back to the other flank or flipped it over a shoulder to a trailer coming up the center; each time they took the fast break as far as it would go, all the way to the basket if possible. Over the course of the first four and a half minutes, Ed Warner followed that first basket with a put-back of a missed shot by Floyd Layne, which in turn was followed by an Irwin Dambrot push shot on a two-on-one fast break, a Roth running one-hander plus a free throw, another layup by Warner, and two more free throws by Warner and Roth, for thirteen points in all. In that time, Kentucky's only scoring consisted of a single foul shot by Bill Spivey.

In the face of the relentless City College attack the Kentucky team looked slow, confused, overmatched; stunned by the turn of events and anxious to get back into the game, the Wildcats began tossing up shots from twenty-five, even thirty feet from the hoop. The correspondent for the *Lexington Leader* observed that the Wildcats were "visibly shaken by the onslaught" and that they "began to shoot hurriedly—from anywhere—almost any time they got the ball." By the time guard Bobby Watson sank the first Kentucky basket on a long set shot, nearly five minutes had elapsed.

Eddie Roman had struggled with his defense all season. Now he had the most demanding and important defensive assignment of his career: to keep the seven-foot-tall Spivey in check. Spivey had a lethal hook shot and was almost unstoppable when he could get into position under the basket to put back his teammates' missed shots; in one game that season he had scored forty points, the sixth-highest mark in the nation. During practices that week Leroy Watkins, the team's tallest player, had stood in for Spivey, and Holman drilled the squads for hours on defending pivot play, cutting off passing lanes, boxing out, until the players were sure they knew exactly what to do. Now, against Spivey, Roman's energy and concentration seemed never to flag. Although he was half a foot shorter, he used his wide body as a kind of fulcrum to lever Spivey away from the basket—letting distance serve as an extra defender— and all the while he kept his arms up and his feet moving, staying between his man and the man with the ball; if Spivey did receive the ball, other City defenders quickly rotated into the middle to surround him, preventing a shot and knocking the ball away several times. Before long Spivey became frustrated, throwing elbows and being overly aggressive in contending for rebounds, and the officials began to whistle him for personal fouls. He committed his fourth foul less than twelve minutes into the first half (after five fouls a player was ejected from the game), leaving Adolph Rupp no choice but to sit him down. In the first half

Spivey scored just one point—having taken only three shots, all of which he missed.

In the 1950 National Invitation Tournament quarterfinal game at Madison Square Garden, Kentucky center Bill Spivey attempts a hook shot against CCNY defender Eddie Roman. City College teammates Irwin Dambrot (5), Floyd Layne (9), and Ed Warner (8) look on. University of Kentucky Athletics

Few of those watching the game that night could recall another such fearsome, sustained attack. Irwin Dambrot seemed to be everywhere on the court: On three successive possessions he scored on a push shot, stole a pass and hit Eddie Roman for a one-hander in the corner, and then sank another push shot at the end of a fast break. Roman was getting his points, too, in typically unspectacular fashion, a jump shot here, a hook shot there, the point total rising with the steady *clack-clack-clack* of an adding machine. On this night, though, City's offensive star was Ed Warner.

Leading the fast break, slicing effortlessly toward the basket for a layup or a kick-out pass to an open man, leaping high to clear the backboard with one-handed rebounds, Warner seemed to be playing a different game from everyone else. He was not tall but he was strong, and his moves, honed in endless pickup games on the Colonel Young playground on 145th Street, were quick and hard and precise. He was the only member of the City College team who could create shots solely through his own craft—the endless variety of twitches and nods and feints that on the playground was known as "the hipper-dipper stuff"— and at times he seemed to be moving in several directions at once, as though his hands and hips and head were operating independently; then he would abruptly dart left or right for a hook shot—he could shoot equally well with either hand—or slide toward the hoop for a layup. Sometimes, standing underneath the basket, he simply tossed the ball over his head, like a bride with a bouquet, banking it delicately off the backboard and into the net.

On the bench Adolph Rupp reacted visibly to each Kentucky miscue, rearing back in surprise and pain as though he had been struck. From his perch above the court, radio announcer Marty Glickman was doing all he could to keep up with City's rapid ball movement, leaving a moment's hush as the shot arced toward the hoop and shouting "Good, like Nedick's!" on especially dramatic baskets, being sure to make his calls quickly so as not to be drowned out by the roar of the crowd. From the City College sections of the upper balcony came cries of "Charge!" and regular invocations of the Allagaroo. Near the end of the half someone was heard to call, "Pour it on, City!" and soon thousands of others had taken up the cry, "Pour it on, City! Pour it on, City!" while others chanted in counterpoint, "More, more, more! More, more, more!" and stamped their feet in rhythm, the floor vibrating so intensely that some of the fans began to worry that the balcony was going to collapse.

Irwin Dambrot hit a push shot just as the buzzer sounded, and at the end of the first half the score stood at 45 to 20. "The excitement was unbelievable," says City College student Myron Neugeboren. "Everybody in the balcony was just looking at each other in amazement, like they couldn't believe what was happening." What was taking place on the court seemed almost impossible, something conjured in a dream, and some of the City fans didn't want to do anything that might break the spell. "At halftime," remembers another student, Martin Schaum, "we were afraid to leave our seats because we were afraid to jinx the team." Less superstitious fans chatted and laughed as they made their way toward the exits, using the fifteen-minute halftime period as an opportunity to stretch their legs, visit the restroom, maybe brave the crowds at the Nedick's stand for a hot dog and an orange drink. Marvin Kalb heard one fan intoning as he headed toward the lobby, "Though I walk through the aisles in the shadow of the Garden, I shall fear no foe; for Warner art with me. His rebounding and shooting—they comfort me . . ." With that the fan proceeded down the aisle, moving too far away for Kalb to hear the conclusion of the psalm.

Stopping by to chat with Marty Glickman during his halftime recap, one of the Kentucky radio announcers asked, "Do these guys play like this *all* the time?" It was a question the Kentucky players were surely asking themselves as well. "CCNY was an unknown type of team," Bill Spivey would say later. "They hadn't any type of impressive record and we weren't the least bit concerned, and we waltzed right onto the floor thinking all we had to do was show up."

In the second half Spivey finally began hitting some shots, while the Beavers, for their part, slowed the pace, letting time run off the clock. With eleven minutes left in the game the Wildcats had drawn within sixteen points, 54 to 38, causing a tremor of unease to pass through the Garden. "We kept expecting the roof to fall in," recalls Mark Maged, managing editor of *The Campus*. "We always had the sense that Kentucky would regroup and they would kill us." At that point, to the crowd's great joy and relief, the Beavers began attacking the basket again. Dambrot hit two one-handers in a row, Warner drove in for a layup, Norm Mager added a one-hander, Warner made another layup, Leroy Watkins tapped in an offensive rebound, Al Roth sank a jump shot, and then Warner hit a set shot. It was a stunning offensive display: In a span of two and a half minutes, City College reeled off sixteen consecutive points.

Ed Warner was not known for his outside shooting, but this was a night when it seemed everything he tossed up found the basket, culminating in a miraculous forty-foot set shot just before Nat Holman removed him with two minutes remaining. Warner had scored twenty-six points, and as he trotted off the court the crowd cheered and called his name over and over, even as play resumed; after the game Holman would call the ovation "the greatest ever given to a City player."

In the closing minutes someone in the City College section had the idea to launch into a rendition of "My Old Kentucky Home" as a kind of farewell to the visiting Wildcats, and he stood and began singing, "Oh, the sun shines bright on my old Kentucky home," and by the time he came to the chorus much of the upper balcony had joined in. "Most of us knew the words," recalls Jerry Koral, a CCNY freshman of the time, "so it got pretty loud."

> *Weep no more, my lady,*
> *Oh, weep no more today!*
> *We will sing one song*
> *For my old Kentucky home,*
> *For the old Kentucky home far away.*

When the final buzzer sounded, the players on the City College bench stormed onto the court as though they had won the tournament—as though the season had ended right there. They hugged and clapped one another on the back as the fans stood and roared for long minutes, in astonishment as well as euphoria, together producing an immensity of sound that reverberated in their ears long after they had left the Garden. The victory over Kentucky had been the greatest sports triumph in the history of City College, but for those in attendance that Tuesday night it could not help but feel like something greater; it felt, says Mark Maged, "like something of a revolution."

Almost from its inception the mission of City College had been to welcome the poor, talented young people of New York, children of push-cart peddlers and garment workers and washerwomen, grandchildren of peasants and slaves, and help them to move from the margins into the mainstream of American society. This victory seemed of a piece with that: an assertion by Jews and African Americans, historical outsiders, of their right to inclusion; and, in its way, a blow struck against the narrow-mindedness and bigotry that, for many of New York's basketball fans, had come to be personified by Kentucky head coach Adolph Rupp. Years later Marvin Kalb would describe the game: "It was City College's way of saying—forgive me—'Screw you, Adolph Rupp. We are also part of this country. It's not just yours. It's ours too.'"

The final score was City College 89, Kentucky 50. It was the most lopsided defeat in Rupp's career at the University of Kentucky.

After the game the Kentucky locker room was absolutely silent, the players sitting with their heads in their hands. This was the worst loss any of them could remember, and now, with their invitation to the NCAA tournament having been spurned by Coach Rupp, there was nothing left to look forward to but the long flight back to Lexington. Rupp paced before them in his lucky brown suit, wrinkled now from his agonized squirming on the Kentucky bench. "I want to thank you boys," he told them. "You get me selected coach of the year, and then you bring me up here and embarrass the hell out of me."

At the press table a long row of sportswriters sat hunched over portable typewriters clacking out their accounts of the game, searching for superlatives that would adequately describe the performance they had just witnessed. "Those earthquake tremors that seem to be raising your roof today," Sid Friedlander advised the readers of the *New York Post*, "come from one easily located center—City College." In *The New York Times*, Louis Effrat extolled Ed Warner's "amazing shooting," Eddie Roman's "flawless defense," Floyd Layne's "incredibly successful handling of rebounds." Everett B. Morris of the *Herald Tribune* called the game "a team effort of such surpassing excellence that it defies description by normal adjectives."

Playing on City College's unique cheer, the Allagaroo, Morris also alluded to the highly charged tenor of the evening. "You've seen Southern football teams in that emotional state fighting the Civil War all over again on a gridiron," he wrote. "This was something like it in reverse— the sons of Allah Guru carrying on a holy crusade against the South."

In the University of Kentucky student newspaper, the *Kentucky Kernel*, sports columnist Tom Diskin pointed out that few of the college's students had thought the Wildcats would lose even by a single point, much less by thirty-nine; many of the students with whom he spoke after the game remarked that they had never heard of CCNY until the tournament and were hard-pressed to say what the letters stood for. Diskin concluded: "There isn't much left to say about the CCNY 'catastrophe,' as it has been called, except that the upset will be remembered for a long, long time by Kentuckians."

On the day after the game, the Kentucky legislature considered a proposal to lower the state flag on the capitol to half-mast in mourning. Ultimately, the proposal was voted down: As one state senator argued, it would "add insult to injury."

CHAPTER 14

The night after the Kentucky game Nat Holman celebrated the victory by taking the team to see *South Pacific*. The Majestic Theater, where the musical was playing, was one of Broadway's grandest houses, maroon and gold everywhere, with plush velvet seats and a neoclassical ceiling and a seating capacity of eighteen hundred. Just before the house lights dimmed, the public address announcer came on the speakers to introduce Holman and the players to the crowd, and they all stood as the rest of the audience gave them an uproarious ovation. "At that moment," recalls Ron Nadell, "it seemed like we all could have run for president."

On Thursday evening, March 16, City College faced off against Duquesne University in the first of two semifinal games, with the winner to play for the championship on Saturday against the winner of the second game, Bradley versus St. John's. The St. John's game was important for another reason as well: The National Collegiate Athletic Association had reserved its District 2 slot for one of the remaining three teams from the region—City College, Duquesne, or St. John's. Whichever team went furthest in the NIT would also receive an invitation to the NCAA tournament.

City jumped out to an early lead on baskets by Eddie Roman and Irwin Dambrot, and as the game went along the lead grew and dwindled but never disappeared, and the Garden fans (some of whom had reportedly paid scalpers as much as $12.50 for their tickets) mostly remained seated, as though they were still exhausted from the Kentucky game two nights earlier. The Beavers' offense moved smoothly and with scarcely a hitch, an engine firing now on all cylinders, and City College cruised to the win by a score of 62 to 52. Later in the evening the Bradley Braves defeated St. John's 82 to 72, which not only set up the NIT championship game for Saturday night—number one Bradley against number twenty-seven City College—but also eliminated St. John's from consideration for an NCAA slot. City College was now the last team standing from District 2, and the next day it received its invitation to the NCAA tournament.

On Friday, the day before the NIT championship game, Nat Holman persuaded the college administration to excuse his players from classes, explaining that he wanted to keep them together and make sure they got sufficient rest. That afternoon the team checked in to rooms in the Paramount Hotel on West Forty-Sixth Street.

Bobby Sand would have liked to stay in the Paramount as well, to provide an adult presence for the players, but his wife, Sylvia, was ailing at home in Brooklyn and she felt especially vulnerable when he was away. Holman, for his part, was laid up in his apartment on Madison Avenue. He had taken ill almost immediately after the Duquesne game on Thursday night, and by Friday he was running a high fever. His physician made a house call and prescribed a course of aureomycin and strict bed rest; as far as he was concerned, no fifty-three-year-old man with a temperature of 103 degrees had any business attending a basketball game. Holman took a different view: He had been the City College basketball head coach since 1919, this was his first opportunity to win a national title, and he was not about to let a case of the grippe keep him from being there. The doctor agreed to check in on him again the next day and reevaluate the situation.

That night the winds began, knocking down trees and telephone poles across the city and loosening bits of cornice that fell like cannon shot to the street below. By six o'clock Saturday morning, weather stations were measuring gusts of sixty-three miles an hour, near hurricane proportions, though the air remained entirely dry. Pedestrians strained even to cross the street, heads bent as though looking for dropped coins, holding on to loose articles of clothing to keep them from blowing away. Along the edge of the island, the wind churned up white-caps that rocked piers and splintered small boats; even great ocean liners like the *Queen Mary* remained out at sea, unwilling to enter the harbor. The wind would persist throughout the day, howling through the canyoned streets like a never-ending air raid siren.

After a midday strategy session led by Bobby Sand, followed by an early dinner, the players retired to their rooms to rest. The feeling of the game had now drawn close, and as the wind screamed outside the windows each man tried to calm himself and think about what he needed to do. The Bradley Braves were a tough, unusually mature team, with several Army veterans among their top players. Their leading scorer was the All-American forward Paul Unruh, who was six four and exceptionally fast (he held the school record in the 440-yard dash) as well as a lethal left-handed shooter. Their other main scoring threat was the guard Gene Melchiorre; though Melchiorre stood just over five eight, he was as powerfully built as a fullback, and almost alone among small men he preferred to play near the basket, backing his taller defender down into the pivot, where a series of twists and feints would throw the defender off balance and allow Melchiorre to score with a layup or hook shot. All the while he maintained an absolutely deadpan expression, the look of a man engaged in very serious business. Earlier that season, at the end of the first half in a game against Wichita, he had thrown in a shot that was later measured as having traveled 64 feet four inches; it was the only time he had ever been seen to smile on a basketball court.

Eddie Roman would be facing the Bradley center, the six-foot-seven junior Elmer Behnke. Behnke was big but he was awkward; he had worked hard on his coordination that year, even going so far as to enroll in ballet lessons, but Bobby Sand had explained that Behnke was still not confident in his footwork and on defense he wouldn't want to follow Eddie to the outside, away from the comfort of the basket. Those were the deeper waters, Eddie understood; there would be good shots out there; he just had to find them. This was what it had come to, all those winter days shooting by the warmth of a burning trash can, learning the precise push from the shoulder, a light brush from the fingertips creating backspin so the ball would settle around the rim rather than bounce out. He wondered if any of those kids from junior high who had laughed at him when he made five baskets in a row in gym class would be in Madison Square Garden that night watching him play for the championship. He had been coming to the Garden to watch the NIT ever since he was a kid, before he ever dreamed that he might someday be one of those players introduced by name, the blue-tinged spotlight wrapping them like a royal robe. Now other kids would be in the seats watching him, wondering if someday it might be their chance.

Before long they heard Bobby Sand walking up and down the hallway, knocking on doors and telling them it was time to go. (Normally rumpled and tweedy, Bobby was dressed more sharply than usual that night, in a gray three-piece suit; for good luck he had tied his Phi Beta Kappa key to one of the vest buttons.) Carrying their uniforms and sneakers in their gym bags, the players gathered in the hotel lobby and then headed outside. The temperature had dropped into the midtwenties, and the winds had turned the city arctic. Filling their lungs with the frigid air, they turned and walked uptown to Madison Square Garden to face the Bradley Braves of Peoria, Illinois.

"Except for Brooklyn," a *Saturday Evening Post* profile had noted a year earlier, "no community in the United States has been slandered so elaborately as Peoria, Illinois. Generations of comedians have vulgarized Peoria as the home of the rube and the boob. . . . Peoria has become a companion word for 'hayseed,' an all-too-common denominator, a municipal equivalent of the man on the street."

Peoria was a national symbol of dullness and provincial thought (for decades entertainers seeking not to offend had asked, "Will it play in Peoria?") but it was also a vibrant manufacturing center, the home of the Caterpillar tractor company and the Hiram Walker whiskey distillery, the largest in the world. Peoria was a small city of vivid contrasts, of haves and have-nots, many of the haves living in stately homes set high on a bluff above the Illinois River; President Theodore Roosevelt had once described the road along the river as "the world's most beautiful drive," a phrase so often and proudly repeated that it got turned into the call letters for radio station WMBD, which was broadcasting all of Bradley's tournament games back to Peoria from New York.

"By the end of the 1949–1950 season," Patty Edwards-Lindstrom wrote in *Victory, Honor and Glory*, a history of Bradley basketball, "college basketball had become more than just a game in Peoria." Though Bradley had long been a basketball power, participating in four NIT tournaments in thirteen years, this was the first time the team had advanced to the finals, and interest had never been higher. "Peorians are talking, eating and sleeping basketball," the *Peoria Star* noted during the tournament. "All Peoria, young and old, are taking their basketball medicine in terrific doses morning, noon and night." On the day of the championship game, workmen wheeled electric scoreboards onto the stages of Peoria's movie houses; during the late shows the scoreboards would flash up-to-the-moment scores as the screens played *Dear Wife* and *The Outlaw*. A squad of messenger boys was hired to circulate among the night-shift assembly lines of the Caterpillar plant, shouting out reports of the game above the din of the machinery. By game time, an audience survey conducted by a local advertising agency reported that 69 percent of all the homes in the Peoria area were tuned to the radio broadcast—twenty-one points higher than the peak audience for the Truman-Dewey election returns.

It was a classic matchup, thus described in *Victory, Honor and Glory*: "Bradley, representing the small-town provincialism of middle America, versus CCNY, representing the diversity and sophistication of big-city life." Like the Kentucky Wildcats, the Bradley Braves had never had a black player. The team's greatest star, Paul Unruh, was the son of a Baptist minister (he had come to Bradley on a half-athletic, half-clerical scholarship) who wore his hair in a crew cut; in the *Collier's* All-America issue the description of him read, in part, "Paul works in a Peoria haberdashery after school to buy gas for his 1937 jalopy"—a sentence that may be the purest possible distillation of small-town teen sensibility. Bradley University hosted a welter of fraternities and sororities, and the school year was a whirl of Valentine's Dances and Garden Balls and Spring Frolics. Bradley had a Christian Fellowship but, unlike City College, no Frederick Douglass Society nor Marxist Cultural Society; it had a BREW (Bradley Religious Emphasis Week) but not, as at City, a schoolwide Conference on Discrimination. The fans of the Bradley Braves and the City College Beavers looked at each other from across a vast cultural divide: from two territories of America for which, in the public imagination, the respective capitals were Peoria and New York City.

Inside Madison Square Garden, the basketball court shone with the glow from twenty-nine spotlights. In the mezzanine the Garden's official timekeeper, Caspar Lane, checked and double-checked the row of switches that controlled the working of the mammoth minute and second clocks. At the broadcasting tables nearby sat Marty Glickman, who would be covering the game for radio station WMGM, and Jack Quinn, the veteran radio announcer for WMBD of Peoria. The American Broadcasting Company would be televising the game across a twenty-six-city network, the play-by-play announcer an up-and-coming young sportscaster named Curt Gowdy. Scattered around the arena, newsreel cameramen stood behind cameras set up on tripods, their twin black film reels sticking up like Mickey Mouse ears. Reporters from newspapers around the country and all the wire services sat at the press table, while photographers sat on folding chairs, their heavy Speed Graphic flash cameras resting at their feet. Across the court, by the team benches, the two starting fives huddled with their coaches; for the City College Beavers, that coach was Nat Holman.

Holman had arrived in the Madison Square Garden locker room not long before, accompanied by his physician—who, Nat explained, would sit beside him on the bench during the game. He did not look like someone who had just risen from a sickbed: His salt-and-pepper hair was as perfectly coiffed as ever, and he wore a brown three-piece suit set off by a white pocket handkerchief, everything just so, all the way down to his pearl cufflinks. Holman was resolute in his determination not to miss this game, and he would never show up without looking his very best, even in the midst of a flu, even through gale-force winds; it was a testament to the powerful personal drive that had once made him basketball's most celebrated player. "I joined the team in the locker room," Holman later recalled, "[and] reviewed the pregame strategy and assignments." ("I made all the assignments," Bobby Sand would tell an interviewer years later; describing that meeting in the locker room,

Sand said of Holman: "He doesn't know anything—what we've done, what we've assigned.")

The two starting fives took the court, City College in their black uniforms, Bradley in white trimmed with red. The teams positioned themselves around the center circle and Eddie Roman and Elmer Behnke stepped inside it. Referee John Nucatola tossed up the basketball; Caspar Lane started the clocks.

Controlling the opening jump, Behnke tapped the ball to his teammate Bill Mann, who passed it ahead to Gene Melchiorre in the right corner; Melchiorre dribbled back across the lane, then stopped, feinted right, and turned left to bank in a hook shot for the first points of the game. On the next possession Irwin Dambrot took the inbounds pass and drove the length of the court for a layup. Behnke dropped in a jump shot; on the other end, Roman let fly a high-arcing hook shot that seemed to take forever to descend, then bounced gently off the backboard and into the net. In the early going City College took a 12–11 lead, but as the minutes passed the greater experience of the Bradley Braves began to assert itself. Every time a City player drove to the hoop he was immediately surrounded by Bradley players, an aggressive team defense that Dambrot later compared to a snake pit. The City fast break was sputtering, passes flying just out of reach, layups bouncing off the rim; eight times in the first half the Beavers sped downcourt on a fast break only to come up empty and have to retreat on defense, shaking their heads in frustration.

The Beavers also seemed to have lost their composure at the foul line, missing eleven out of twelve free throws, while Bradley—whose players, in the older style, shot free throws underhand—made eight of their first nine. After fourteen minutes the Bradley lead had grown to eleven points, 29 to 18, and a nervous rumble was coursing through the Garden crowd; for the first time during the tournament, City College would have to mount a comeback. Nat Holman sent in Norm Mager, and almost immediately Mager's tough, confident presence on the court seemed to calm his teammates. On his first time down the court Mager fought for an offensive rebound and coolly laid the ball back in amid a crowd of Bradley defenders. Then Dambrot intercepted a pass and tossed the ball ahead to Ed Warner streaking to the basket for an uncontested layup; the score now stood at 29 to 22 and the Beavers were finding their rhythm. In one stunning sequence Dambrot grabbed a rebound and fired a pass along the left sideline up to Mager, who immediately hit Warner flashing across the top of the keyhole; Warner drove to the left baseline, drawing the defenders toward him, and then, leaping, dropped the ball down to Eddie Roman under the basket, who laid the shot up backward, off the backboard and in. Mager had checked in to the game with six minutes remaining in the first half; Bradley did not score another basket during that time, and when the halftime buzzer sounded, the Beavers had pulled to within three, 30 to 27.

In the second half the game seemed to have become, as much as anything, a battle of nerves; it was, wrote Irving Marsh in the *Herald Tribune*, "a tight, tense battle of speed and strategy." Six times the game was tied, and seven times the lead changed hands. Midway through the half, Gene Melchiorre made contact with Floyd Layne as he drove to the basket and was called for his fifth personal foul, which fouled him out; as Melchiorre walked dejectedly toward the bench, Eddie Roman took a moment to come over and shake his hand, bending his head to speak quietly to the much shorter man. With Melchiorre out of the game the Braves increasingly turned to their All-American, Paul Unruh, and he sank a jump shot from the left corner to pull them ahead 56 to 55; on the next possession Roman hit a one-hander from well beyond the top of the keyhole, the ball bouncing on the front rim before going in, to regain the lead for City. After a Bradley miss, Dambrot followed with a gorgeous twisting jump shot and was fouled; he converted the penalty shot to make it a three-point play. The teams were maintaining a furious pace and on both benches the reserve players leaned forward, hands knotted into fists, cheering on their teammates.

With one minute and fifty seconds remaining and City up by four, Eddie Roman fouled Elmer Behnke as he drove to the hoop. Behnke sank the free throw to make the score 64 to 61; but rather than City taking the ball out under its own basket, both teams headed to the nearby foul circle for a jump ball. During the 1949–50 season, games at Madison Square Garden were played under a short-lived format known as "thirty-eight plus two": In the last two minutes of the forty-minute game, every foul shot was followed by a jump ball at the shooting team's foul line, with each coach choosing one of his players then on the floor to jump. Not surprisingly, Bradley head coach Forddy Anderson sent

out the team's tallest player, six-foot-seven Elmer Behnke; stepping into
the circle for the Beavers, though, was Ed Warner—the shortest man
on the floor for City College. Warner would generously have been described as standing six foot three, and indeed the Madison Square Garden program for the game listed him as six two and a half. It seemed
foolhardy to send out a player at least four inches shorter than his opponent for a jump ball, but everyone around the Beavers knew that
Warner could jump higher than anyone else on the team (the players
still spoke with awe of that palm print he had left on the ceiling outside
German class), and with the game balanced on a knife's edge, Holman
would rely on him.

The referee made the toss; the two players leaped, straining for the
ball, but Warner rose higher and with his outstretched left hand he
tapped the ball to Floyd Layne, who passed upcourt to Al Roth. Trailing
by three points and needing to regain possession, Bradley looked to foul,
but the Beavers were passing quickly, keeping the ball moving as in a
childhood game of keep-away; finally Bradley guard Fred Schlictman
grabbed Roth before he could get rid of the ball and the referee blew his
whistle at the 1:35 mark. Roth stepped to the foul line; the crowd seemed
to gather its breath for a moment, then exhaled in disappointment as
the shot sailed wide to the right. With the score still 64 to 61, Behnke
and Warner returned to the CCNY foul circle for another jump ball. The
two players leaped, and for the next several seconds time seemed to be
repeating itself: Again Warner tapped the ball to Layne, again the Beavers went into a weave, and again Schlictman fouled Roth. Again Roth
stepped to the line and again he missed the free throw, the ball bouncing this time off the back rim. Once more the players gathered around
the foul circle, and once more Warner won the jump ball; fifteen seconds later Roth was fouled, and he missed the free throw for a third
time, after which Holman replaced him with Norm Mager. Sixty-five
seconds now remained in the game. By this time Forddy Anderson had
seen enough of Elmer Behnke and he sent in his star player, Paul Unruh,
to jump against Warner. Though Unruh was renowned for his leaping
ability he fared no better; this time Warner tapped the ball straight
ahead to Eddie Roman standing in the foul lane, who hit a quick turnaround jump shot that brought the score to 66–61. In the final minute Anderson sent out the six-foot-six Jim Kelly to jump against Warner,

then Kelly again, and once more Paul Unruh, and each time Warner retained possession for City College. With each successive jump the crowd grew louder, eighteen thousand uproarious at the spectacle unfolding before them: Ed Warner, like the hero of a war movie, single-handedly holding off the enemy platoon.

In the last two minutes of the game Warner won seven consecutive jump balls, and during that time City's lead grew from three points to eight. It was, Holman would say later, "the finest exhibition of held-ball leaping I have ever seen."

In the closing seconds the Bradley Braves gave up the strategy of intentionally fouling, and as the Beavers passed the ball around, the crowd began a sustained cheer, realizing that the City College of New York—the team the Associated Press had dubbed "the darkest of dark horses"—was going to win the National Invitation Tournament. City's bench players were now standing, some of them jumping up and down like kids, waiting for the final buzzer, and then at last it came: Marty Glickman shouted, "And there's the buzzer! City College wins!" and the fans roared and City's reserve players rushed onto the court as the Bradley squad walked forlornly to the bench.

Announcer Jack Quinn, broadcasting back to Peoria on radio station WMBD, gave his listeners the final score—City College 69, Bradley 61; then, overcome by the moment, Quinn broke down and cried into his microphone.

As fans swarmed the Garden court the players laughed and hugged, some of them just walking around with dazed smiles on their faces. "The Garden went berserk when the buzzer sounded," reported a correspondent for the *Observation Post*. "Dambrot will be wiping lipstick off for days yet." Eventually authorities managed to clear the floor for the postgame ceremonies. The members of both teams received watches for their participation, followed by the awarding of the Kelleher Memorial Trophy for the winner of the National Invitation Tournament, accepted by Nat Holman on behalf of City College. Then there was one final award to present, and the arena hushed as the president of the Metropolitan Intercollegiate Basketball Association stepped to the microphone to announce, "And now the winner of the Most Valuable Player award is . . . Edward Warner of City College," and the crowd roared its approval as Warner walked smiling onto the court to be handed the silver loving cup, his name now included among those of some of the sport's greatest players. Ed Warner was the first sophomore ever to receive the tournament's Most Valuable Player award, and the first African American. Among those sitting in the balcony that night was a fifteen-year-old Harlem resident named Howie Evans, who would go on to become a sportswriter for the *New York Amsterdam News*, the city's leading African American newspaper. Recalling the game sixteen years later, Evans would write, "My heart thumped with every play. It thumped even louder as the Harlem boy walked to mid-court to receive the outstanding player award. It was a moment I'll remember for a long time."

By the time the players finished taking photos and signing autographs and had made it back to the locker room, Nat Holman had left, driven home by his doctor. As it turned out, no celebration had been planned for after the game, and Sam Winograd circulated through the locker room distributing the postgame stipend money just as he always did. Seeing the disappointment in the players' faces, Bobby Sand pulled Winograd into a corner, and after a bit of discussion they announced that they would take everyone out that night to Leone's restaurant. Leone's was a big, festive Italian place near the Garden, where patrons were welcomed at the tables with huge wedges of cheese and overflowing baskets of bread; the sportswriters and rival coaches always met there after games, often staying until the early hours of the morning, drinking and talking and eating the sliced steak sandwich known to all as "the basketball special." None of the players ever went to Leone's because they couldn't afford it, but tonight was different: Tonight was a celebration, and someone else was paying.

The next day, Sunday, they could rest up. On Monday a lunchtime rally for the team was scheduled for the college quadrangle, after which they would be driven to City Hall for an official reception with Mayor William O'Dwyer.

CHAPTER 15

In 1948, William O'Dwyer's portrait had appeared on the cover of *Time* magazine, smiling over a cartoon New York City landscape with swaying skyscrapers and undulating subway trains crawling like earthworms out of their tunnels, above the caption A HELL OF A TOWN. New York "is the biggest, richest city the world has ever seen," the magazine informed its readers, adding wondrously, "It is the world's greatest port, the world's greatest tourist attraction, the world's greatest manufacturing city and the world's greatest marketplace." All of that, O'Dwyer firmly believed, was true, but only a mayor could really comprehend what was required to keep it so. Within a month of his taking office, in February 1946, a strike of tugboat workers had shut down the harbor, keeping out the fuel the city needed to keep warm; after nine days he closed the city's schools, dimmed streetlights, ordered homes to be heated to no warmer than sixty degrees. "An air of unreality hung over the city," reported the *World-Telegram*. "Incidents took on a staccato, dream quality; sharply etched, touched with hysteria, cockeyed." The mayor had shown his mettle, though, and New Yorkers rallied around him, and the very next day the tugboat workers agreed to negotiate.

This city had nineteen thousand policemen, eleven thousand firemen, more than a hundred thousand other municipal employees, and all of them, he felt, depended on him. Sometimes at night he would walk up and down the long back porch of Gracie Mansion and gaze across the river at the lights of Astoria shimmering in the distance, and he would think, "Good Lord, I'm the mayor of this town." It was a marvel to which he had never quite reconciled himself. He felt much the same in the back seat of his Cadillac as they crossed over the Brooklyn Bridge, seeing Lower Manhattan's wall of stone towers loom above him like a cliff. In those vertiginous moments he had to admit to himself that he was frightened; in those moments he felt the job was too much for him—too much for any man, really. "You know, the city's too big," he confided once to a reporter. "It's too big for one government. . . . You can take that Andrew Green—the fellow who was responsible for unifying the five boroughs back in 1898—and you can build him a statue, and then, as far as I'm concerned, you can cut off his head and you can cut off his tail and blow the rest of him up."

In his autobiography William O'Dwyer would allude to the "personal problems and the pressures of office" that had beset him in 1950. The city's crises continued to mount: budget deficits, traffic tie-ups, a housing shortage, labor unrest. In his first term, facing an intractable budget deficit, he had raised the subway fare from a nickel to a dime, a decision that no previous mayor had dared contemplate; now he faced the unhappy prospect of having to raise it again. The job was the last thing he thought about when he went to bed at night, and his sleep was often broken up by dreams of work so real they left him exhausted. He was "a victim of one of the world's hardest jobs," *The New York Times* observed of Mayor O'Dwyer in December 1949, noting, "His most active political opponents would never deny that he works at that job with a soldierly devotion to duty and gives it the last ounce of his strength."

By himself at night in Gracie Mansion (his new bride, Sloan Simpson, was spending the winter in Florida), he felt increasingly restless and disturbed. Sometimes he sat up late in the mansion's library with a glass of Scotch, but the books he had always loved, of Irish poetry and American history, were less of a comfort than they once had been. Blunt-spoken and occasionally profane but always controlled, more and more now he heard himself shouting at underlings; he paced in the office, often refused phone calls, fumed at his treatment in the press. Questions were being raised in the newspapers about the dealings of his top aide, James Moran, and others in his administration with bookmakers and gangsters, suggestions being made of widespread bribery. He could still remember how proud he'd felt when he first put on a police uniform in 1917; an idealistic rookie, he had told a friend on the force, "Look, I'll never put my hand out. You don't have to. And I despise guys who do."

He felt weighed down by his own history, the partnerships and compromises he'd made to get to where he was. Two days after taking office as mayor, for instance, O'Dwyer had appointed a retired police captain named Frank Bals to a post as deputy police commissioner. The two men had maintained a productive friendship since the 1930s, when O'Dwyer was still in private practice as a defense attorney; at the time, Bals was the police captain in charge of the Bath Beach section of Brooklyn, a waterfront area that was a favorite spot for mobsters looking to dispose of their victims' bodies, and in that capacity he could send potential clients O'Dwyer's way before anyone else even knew that a crime had been committed. As a deputy police commissioner, Bals was assigned to oversee a special fifteen-man plainclothes squad that was supposed to investigate organized gambling in New York City. In fact the job the members of the squad undertook most energetically was to conduct shakedowns, and before long the city's bookmakers had begun to complain to their political friends that Bals's men were charging exorbitant rates for protection. After just two months O'Dwyer shut the squad down ("It's a manpower shortage problem and other things I can't tell you about," he explained to reporters), and ordered the city's chief investigations commissioner, John M. Murtagh, to conduct a report on the squad's activities.

Murtagh was young and zealous, and it wasn't long before he had uncovered the locations of numerous bookmaking operations, as well as the names of policemen said to be protecting them. He had plenty of information with which to proceed, but in addition to being young and zealous he was loyal and ambitious, and word around City Hall was that Mayor O'Dwyer, who had known Murtagh since he was a boy, was grooming him to be his successor. Murtagh believed that the investigations commissioner should make the mayor's job easier, not harder (he once referred to himself as "the Bromo-Seltzer for the mayor"); not wanting to put O'Dwyer in the awkward position of having to respond to his findings, he never filed a report. In public, he proclaimed himself unconvinced that there was even a problem to be investigated. "It would be silly to deny that a person can place a bet," he admitted to reporters. "But that is far from organized gambling. I know exactly where organized gambling is located. It is not located in New York City."

During the years of the O'Dwyer administration an estimated four thousand bookmakers were operating in New York; so open was bookmaking in the city that a 1948 guidebook advised tourists looking to place a bet, "All forms, except on-track pari-mutuel, are illegal, but you will have little trouble finding bookmakers and policy-slip sellers." In Champ Segal's restaurant just down the street from Madison Square Garden, bookmakers took bets on phones brought tableside by waiters, the enterprise protected by off-duty detectives wearing $200 suits and eating complimentary steak dinners. At the end of 1949 many high-ranking City Hall officials could be seen sporting monogrammed gold tie clasps; it was no secret that the clasps were Christmas gifts from the powerful bookmaker Frank Erickson, who, it was reported, had paid Tiffany $29,000 to have them made.

By this time James Moran was busily running a private business within the municipal government. Bookies paid for police protection each month as a matter of course, and 1949 had proven especially lucrative because it was an election year—one single Brooklyn bookmaking operation had contributed more than $300,000 to the O'Dwyer reelection campaign, the money collected by high-ranking police officers who made sure the bookies understood that if they didn't kick in with their share they would be shut down. Still, his steadiest income derived from the bribes extracted for oil burner inspections: He was making half a million dollars a year from that scheme alone.

He might have been coarse-spoken and prone to rages, and little trusted even by his friends, but Moran instinctively grasped the system of favors and tributes and emoluments that kept the city running, that got statutes passed and buildings built and candidates elected and, for some, fortunes made. For generations, bribery had been if not a pervasive, then at least a routine aspect of the New York economy, especially on those borderlines where private enterprise came into contact with government: A manufacturer seeking a city contract puts a politician's unemployed relative on the payroll; a bookmaker, needing to keep his business open, gives a policeman an envelope stuffed with cash; an attorney funnels money from a defendant to a judge while keeping a piece of it for himself. (Once, walking through a law library, New York governor Al Smith pointed to a student poring over a textbook and observed, "That boy is learning to take a bribe and call it a fee.") Bribery was the force that could overcome institutional inertia, set into motion wheels that might otherwise be intractable—a function acknowledged in the expression commonly used for the practice: *grease*.

Moran's schooling had never gone past the high school diploma the Franciscan brothers handed him at St. Francis Prep in Brooklyn, and though he was often heard to bemoan his lack of formal education he inevitably shrugged it off as incidental: "Oh, well, no matter," he would say. "I have a certain amount of gutter wisdom."

In January 1950, at the end of an otherwise routine press conference, Mayor O'Dwyer had surprised everyone by suggesting that the state of New York should legalize betting on public sporting events. "After forty years in this city," he said, "I am satisfied that the public generally is interested in sports not only from the standpoint of the sports themselves but also from the pleasure they get from betting on sports." The problem, he pointed out, was that "millions of decent citizens want to bet"—the newspapers themselves understood that, with their daily listings of point spreads and results from racetracks all around the country. To criminalize gambling, as drinking once had been criminalized, was simply a vestige of an outmoded Puritanism; in legalizing it the state could be unburdened from the corruption that came from unwise prohibition while opening a lucrative new source of government revenue. He announced that he would ask the leaders of the state senate and assembly to take immediate action to end the constitutional prohibition against gambling. *The New York Times*, though, reported that "the Mayor's proposal was met with amazement and disbelief, and few legislators of either party gave it any chance of passing." Governor Thomas Dewey called the notion "shocking and immoral."

Two days after making his ill-fated proposal, Mayor O'Dwyer left for a month in Florida, still recuperating, City Hall aides said, from the "thyroid ailment and virus infection" that had led to his earlier hospitalization. When the mayor returned on Valentine's Day, a host of pressing matters awaited him: a bus fare increase, contract demands by transit workers, plans for slum clearance projects. On March 17 he watched the St. Patrick's Day parade from the official reviewing stand, glowing with pride as marchers who passed by waved at him and called out "Up for Mayo!" in tribute to his own roots in Ireland. Three days later he was asked to preside over the reception celebrating the City College Beavers' victory in the National Invitation Tournament.

The ceremony was to take place outside City Hall, on the broad flight of steps that swept up to the columned marble portico at the front of the building. The steps were a frequent gathering spot for press conferences and political speeches, as well as public receptions for distinguished visitors; this was the first time a college basketball team would ever be received there.

The team had been driven by chartered bus from the uptown campus, following a noontime rally before twenty-five hundred wildly cheering students. Now they stood grinning as they awaited the mayor's arrival, awkwardly on display in front of a large welcoming crowd at the foot of the steps. Noted one newspaper account, "It was such an important occasion that City Hall employees, who generally cold-shoulder these things, unanimously invoked a work stoppage to take it in."

A cheer went up as Mayor O'Dwyer appeared at the front door of City Hall. Wearing a dark double-breasted pinstripe suit with a checked tie, he strode briskly across the portico, jaunty as ever, flashing his trademark grin. One by one he shook the hand of each City College player and pronounced: "I congratulate you for making the city of New York so proud."

Then it was the photographers' turn, and for a while there was some confusion about how the guests of honor should arrange themselves for the photos, but eventually it was decided that Irwin Dambrot and Joe Galiber, the team cocaptains, should stand on one side of the mayor, with Ed Warner, the tournament's Most Valuable Player, on the other. Nat Holman was still at home recuperating, and it was assistant coach Bobby Sand who handed the Kelleher Memorial Trophy to Mayor O'Dwyer, who in turn passed it off to Dambrot and Galiber beside him; then Sand gave him the MVP trophy, and O'Dwyer—now playing a bit to the crowd—pivoted to his right, handing the silver cup to Warner. ("It was a nice bit of teamwork," noted Leonard Lewin in the *Daily Mirror*. "The mayor handled his assignment so smoothly that there's no doubt Holman would use him as a floor man—if he has the marks to get into CCNY, that is.") Then the team was arranged into two rows and commemorative basketballs were handed out to four of the players in the front row, each ball inscribed with the score of one of the tournament victories; the mayor grasped the bottom of the NIT trophy as Dambrot and Galiber each held one of the handles, and once that positioning was in place they could all smile for the photographers and the newsreel cameramen.

After winning the 1950 National Invitation Tournament championship, members of the City College basketball team pose with New York Mayor William O'Dwyer on the steps of City Hall. From left to right: Eddie Roman, Norm Mager, Ed Warner (holding the tournament's Most Valuable Player trophy), Mayor O'Dwyer, Floyd Layne (over O'Dwyer's left shoulder), Irwin Dambrot, Joe Galiber. Assistant coach Bobby Sand can be partially seen at the top right, over Galiber's left shoulder. Archives, The City College of New York, CUNY

Though it was the first day of spring the temperature had been hovering around the freezing mark, the sky a low gray slate, and the wind, though far less furious than on Saturday, swept unbroken across the broad expanse of steps. Unlike the players, the mayor was not wearing an overcoat, and it was to be expected, given his recent ailments, that some City Hall aides would express concern about his standing too long in the cold. So after a couple of minutes for the photographers, Mayor O'Dwyer thanked the players again and wished them luck in the upcoming NCAA tournament, and with that he took his leave and marched back into City Hall.

CHAPTER 16

After the NIT championship game, some of the sportswriters, dazzled by Ed Warner's play under the basket, had asked him about the possibility of one day joining the Harlem Globetrotters. At the time the Globetrotters were the nation's best-known basketball team, a powerhouse touring club that in 1948 had beaten the champion Minneapolis Lakers, but Warner dismissed the idea. "Only two men on that outfit make any money," he said, adding, "If we want to turn pro, this City College team might stick together and do it after graduation two years from now." Along with Bobby Sand's notion of winning the 1952 Olympic gold medal in Helsinki, that was a dream the sophomores had occasionally allowed themselves—if the Kentucky starters had been able to move as a team straight into the NBA after graduation, they figured, they were good enough to do so as well. Of course, there was a major difference: The Beavers had two black players among their starting five, and the National Basketball Association had not yet allowed in any black players.

For Floyd Layne, to play in the NBA was his deepest desire: to receive that recognition as one at the top of his profession, to test himself against the greatest players in the game. And, of course, to play in the NBA meant putting an end once and for all to the kind of stories that he had grown up hearing, told by the older black men who hung around watching the games at the Harlem YMCA: stories of the barnstorming life, driving all night on rough back roads in a broken-down, rattling bus and then tumbling out tired and sore to play against the local team in front of a hostile, jeering crowd in a school gym or Masonic lodge, when they knew they weren't going to get any calls from the referees; driving through vast swaths of the country where service station owners, some carrying rifles, wouldn't let them have any gas even though the driver had cash in his pocket, and the players had to pick up their meals in bags around the back of diners like hobos, if they could get any food at all, and sometimes slept in jails because no hotel would take them in. The stories had the quality of tall tales, but they were for the most part true, and the amusement with which they were often related served to mask the deep pain and anger of the men who told them, at the close of careers marked by deprivation and exclusion, with great talents never fully recognized.

For Floyd, entrance to the NBA meant validation of the hard work he had put in to get there, and it especially meant making his mother proud, and paving the way for all the kids coming up after him. All he needed, he felt, was to be treated fairly and he could prove himself indisputably good enough. Bobby Sand had friends in the front office of the NBA, and he felt confident that the league would soon integrate, and Floyd did too. He believed that by the time he graduated from City College the NBA would be open to him—because he was an optimist by nature, but also because he had seen it happen before, had been given the example of Jackie Robinson.

Floyd loved baseball as much as he did basketball; he had grown up playing stickball in the street, dodging cars between plays, teaching himself how to impart wicked bounces and spins by subtly adjusting the pressure of his fingers on the pink rubber Spaldeen. Now he played first base on the City College baseball team and pitched as well, a tall, lean southpaw with a nasty curveball. It was not always easy to be a Dodgers fan living in Yankee territory in the Bronx, but when the weather turned warm he liked nothing better than to take the subway down to Brooklyn and spend an afternoon in the bleachers at Ebbets Field, cheering especially the nifty double-play combination of the white Kentuckian Pee Wee Reese and Jackie Robinson. "Jackie Robinson was everything to me," he would say later.

Though he was too modest to speak this aloud, Floyd felt that he possessed some of the qualities that had enabled Robinson to survive his

ordeal as Major League Baseball's first African American player—and
not just survive but excel, winning the very first Rookie of the Year
award in 1947. Floyd was not a naturally excitable person; he prided
himself on going about his business, taking one day at a time. On the
court he worked to keep his emotions in check, directing whatever ani-
mosity he might have felt into energy and focus, using it to build his
game. Bobby Sand had a long list of "morale builders" that he would
sometimes impart to the players, lessons about everything from court
tactics to winning attitudes, one of which was "Control your temper.
Basketball games can get rough." Floyd took Bobby's lessons to heart,
but there was one in particular that he tried to follow: "Live the part—
think of the game on and off the court." Arriving home after a practice,
when the subway doors opened high above the street at the elevated
station at Prospect Avenue, chances were good that he was thinking
about the previous game or planning for the next one. Floyd was the
kind of guy that no one could dislike, always smiling and ready with a
kind word; inside, though, he was also a fierce competitor, seeking out
the detail that someone else might overlook or discount but that might
provide him with an edge.

Later, a young man who had grown up watching Floyd play basketball was to say of him: "This guy was the ultimate gentleman and a
quiet assassin on the court."

Floyd was sure that both of the Eds, Warner and Roman, were good
enough to play in the NBA, and he believed he was too, though his particular skills were less immediately apparent. He made contributions to
a team that a casual observer would not notice, like the way he moved
so intelligently without the ball, or how accurate his passes were, or
how he never overguarded on defense so that he wasn't faked out of position. A younger player at City, Harold Bauman, would recall: "I was in
awe of how well Floyd Layne played the game. Just by watching him, he
made me a better player. My first instinct had always been to look for the
shot; now my instinct was to look for the open man." In the St. John's
game earlier that season, Eddie Roman had led the scoring with twenty-
three points and Ed Warner had added seventeen; although Floyd had
scored only two points, Stan Isaacs of *The Daily Compass*, watching from
the press table, decided he was the best player on the court. That month
the *Compass* ran a photo of him on the front page of the sports section,

with the caption "Most underrated player in city, according to many hoop fans, is CCNY's Floyd Layne, 6 foot 3 soph."

Asked about the sense that he was underrated, Layne replied with a laugh: "Hell, that's a compliment. When they start calling you 'underrated,' they've already started overrating you."

The City College Beavers were now, in the words of the *New York Journal-American*, "New York's darling." The question that occupied everyone's minds, as the *Journal-American*'s basketball writer David Eisenberg asked succinctly, was "Will they go stale?" Eisenberg pointed out that it was rare for a college basketball team to be able to play at its highest level for more than five or six consecutive games, and to pull off the double championship, City College would have to win seven in a row—the four they'd won in the NIT plus three more in the NCAA—and do so against the very best teams in the country. The team it would face in the opening round of the NCAA tournament, Ohio State, had finished the season with a record of 21 and 3 and was ranked number two in the Associated Press poll, behind only Bradley. The Buckeyes were led by an All-American forward named Dick Schnittker, six foot five and so fast and powerful that he also starred in football as a wide receiver. While the Beavers were playing Bradley for the NIT championship, team manager Al Ragusa had flown out to Columbus to watch the Buckeyes play their final game of the season. He returned with an extensive scouting report, but as for advice to Irwin Dambrot about how to guard Schnittker, Ragusa said later that he offered only a single word: "Pray."

That game would prove to be as physical and hard fought as any City College had played all year. In his scouting report, Ragusa had correctly anticipated that Ohio State would adopt a 2–3 zone, seeking to crowd the middle and prevent inside drives from City's two best scorers, Eddie Roman and Ed Warner; instead City would have to shoot over the zone, and to do so the Beavers turned to Norm Mager and Floyd Layne, the best long shooters on the team. The two sank shot after shot—Layne shooting two-handed from an almost vertical posture, Mager winding up before each shot, snapping his right knee forward like a prancing horse. Schnittker led the Buckeyes with fifteen points, and at halftime the score was deadlocked, 40 to 40.

In the second half the pace slowed considerably—at one point the Beavers passed the ball for four straight minutes without attempting a shot—the lead never more than four points either way. With two minutes remaining and City College up 55 to 53, Schnittker stole the ball from Irwin Dambrot and was fouled by Al Roth before he could drive in for a layup. Shooting underhand, he converted the first free throw but missed the second shot that would have tied the score; shortly afterward Schnittker fouled Dambrot and was forced to leave the game with his fifth personal foul. Dambrot sank the free throw to bring the lead back to two points, and under the NCAA's two-minute rule (during the last two minutes of a game, the fouled team retained possession of the ball after the foul shot), City passed the ball in from midcourt. Swiftly the Beavers moved the ball up and back and around, faking this way and that, as Buckeye defenders raced from man to man, doing everything they could to intercept a pass or knock away a dribble; the frenetic movement opened a brief gap in the Buckeye defense, and Dambrot noticed it and rifled a pass into Ed Warner standing alone near the basket. All Warner had to do was turn and sink the layup to give City a four-point lead, but he seemed startled about finding himself so open and was momentarily unsure whether he should shoot or continue taking time off the clock; the slight hesitation was enough that by the time he passed the ball back out to Floyd Layne the referee had whistled him for a three-second violation, returning possession to Ohio State. Warner's gaffe, wrote Stan Isaacs in *The Daily Compass*, "seemed like a fatal gesture," but on the Buckeyes' next trip down the court Eddie Roman was fouled while going for a rebound and he was awarded a free throw. Over the course of the season Roman had made 64 percent of his free throws; this time, though, the ball hit the back rim, then the front rim, and, to the crowd's groans, caromed out. The score remained 56 to 54.

Clinging to its narrow lead, City went back into its rapid weave, but with eighteen seconds to go and the game seeming to hang in the balance, Roman lunged awkwardly for an errant pass. Unable to stop his motion, he collided with Buckeye guard Bob Burkholder and the referee's hand shot up to indicate a foul. Burkholder sank the free throw to bring Ohio State within one point. The Buckeyes took the ball out again from midcourt, and with the clock winding down and the Garden crowd on its feet, forward Jim Remington's short jumper from the right side, which would have won the game for Ohio State, bounced off the front rim. Dambrot leaped high to grab the rebound and then dropped the ball off to Warner, who passed to Roth along the right sideline; Roth clutched the ball in his arms until the final buzzer sounded and then ran off the court still holding the ball, followed by his teammates, as though they wanted to get into the locker room before the referees could change their mind.

The North Carolina State Wolfpack were extremely confident heading into their Eastern Regional semifinal game against City College. NC State was a team on the rise, a prime example of the new power and popularity of college basketball in the South. As Kentucky was putting the finishing touches on its new basketball arena, Memorial Coliseum, North Carolina State had just opened an arena of its own, named after the late tobacco magnate William Neal Reynolds; the Reynolds Coliseum seated 12,400 fans, making it the largest on-campus facility anywhere in the nation. With its new arena NC State began to host a college tournament of its own, the Dixie Classic, featuring four North Carolina teams and four teams from around the country. "All visiting teams were smothered with Southern hospitality," notes a history of NC State basketball, "from the time they arrived at the airport until they lost their last game in the tournament." The hospitality, however, extended only so far: Before participating in the tournament, each of the teams had to agree to comply with the policy of racial segregation maintained inside Reynolds Coliseum. At the inaugural Dixie Classic, for instance, held the previous December, the head coach of Penn State had left the team's sole black player, Hardy Williams, at home while the rest of the players came to Raleigh. (The following year, the University of Oregon athletic director would not consent to the same request, and Oregon's invitation was withdrawn.)

Ranked fifth in the nation, NC State was coming off an 87–74 demolition of fourth-ranked Holy Cross in the opening round, the eighty-seven points an NCAA single-game scoring record. Led by their standout guards Sam Ranzino and Dick Dickey, the Wolfpack played a wide-open style of basketball, and most other teams simply couldn't keep up with them—that season they had beaten both the University of North Carolina and Louisville University by twenty-six points, and Wake Forest University by thirty-eight. City College, though, was another story; the Beavers had always believed that they could run with any team in the country, and to the great pleasure of a noisy capacity crowd in Madison Square Garden, they matched NC State break for break, shot for shot, all the way down to the wire.

It was a fast-paced, hard-fought game, with lots of personal fouls called. At one point Norm Mager tied up Dick Dickey for a jump ball, and as the two struggled for possession they almost came to blows and had to be separated by the referees. Another time Floyd Layne was fouled while shooting and went to the line for two free throws; as he later related to his friend Dick Kaplan, a sportswriter for the *Observation Post*, some of the NC State players began heckling him as he stood at the foul line—just loud enough for him to hear, doing what they could to rattle him and upset his concentration. Layne assessed them for a moment and then said with a smile, "You boys better shut up and start playing ball, or you'll be back picking cotton tomorrow."

"From then on," Kaplan wrote, "the Carolina hecklers were remarkably quiet."

Much like the opening round game against Ohio State, the North Carolina State game was almost impossibly close; the score was tied fourteen times, and with twenty seconds remaining NC State was down by only two points, 75 to 73, and had possession of the ball. But guard Vic Bubas fouled Layne while trying to rebound his own missed shot; Layne stepped to the line and sank the free throw, the ball rattling heart-stoppingly around the rim before going in. Again, under the two-minute rule, City retained possession, and with the arena in an uproar Layne received the ball from the referee under the basket for the inbounds pass; he tossed up a soft pass, just beyond the reach of the Wolfpack defender, to Ed Warner standing at the top of the keyhole, who drove down the left side of the line and put up a two-handed scoop shot that started somewhere around his knees and floated above two leaping defenders, then somehow spun off the backboard and into the net. The score was now City College 78, North Carolina State 73, and that was how the game would end.

Madison Square Garden was filled to the rafters that night, and though there had not been a hand-shaking incident, as with the Kentucky Wildcats, many of the local fans were disturbed by the sight of hundreds of North Carolina State supporters cheering on their team while waving Confederate battle flags. "We confess that we found deepest social significance in City's triumph over North Carolina State," observed the *New York Post* in an editorial.

> Nothing personal in this; State has a hard-fighting team and several magnificent players. But we were slightly sickened by the array of Confederate flags which belligerently waved (and finally drooped) among the Carolina rooters who followed their team to Madison Square Garden. It may be an old Southern custom to pretend that the Civil War never happened or that Grant never took Richmond; we have no desire to alter the quaint habits of Southern cheering sections in their own backyards. But outside of Dixie (as any college student should know) the Confederate banner remains the symbol of slavery and oppression. It is a peculiarly pointed affront to Negroes who play side by side with white students on every team in this city, demolishing master-race doctrines with each lay-up.

Meanwhile the Bradley Braves had been working their way through the Western half of the NCAA tournament draw, easily dispatching the UCLA Bruins and then surviving a two-point scare against the Bears of Baylor University. As almost seemed inevitable, the NCAA championship game would be a rematch of the NIT championship game. City College was now a single win away from a double championship, the Grand Slam, a feat never before accomplished; for its part, wrote one sportswriter, Bradley had been given "the opportunity for revenge the Braves prayed for."

CHAPTER 17

For weeks, interest in the team had been steadily growing, moving outward from City College students to basketball fans and, with the prospect of the double championship on the horizon, to New Yorkers generally. The night after the semifinal victory against North Carolina State, Ed Sullivan was hosting his weekly television show, *Toast of the Town*, from the Maxine Elliott Theater on West Thirty-Ninth Street. After Eileen Barton sang her hit song "If I Knew You Were Coming, I'd Have Baked a Cake" and a trick golfer performed a variety of shots using a professional jockey as a "human tee," Sullivan came onstage for a special introduction. "When City College of New York won the basketball championship," he said in his distinctive piping voice, arms folded, body slightly swaying, "there was just an outpouring of affection—for the team, of course, and for its very brilliant coach, Nat Holman. So let's hear it, New York, here is Nat Holman." Holman was supposed to simply stand at his seat and acknowledge the applause of the crowd, but the ovation was so loud and sustained that Sullivan called him up on stage—"Nat Holman, here he is"—to congratulate him and shake his hand.

A phrase was now being used to describe the team: "Cinderella kids." Comparing the Beavers to filmdom's tough but lovable gang of street urchins, the *Daily Mirror* observed: "Those riotous Dead End Kids from St. Nicholas Heights have become the darlings of New York." The newspapers ran photos of the players doing perfectly ordinary things, as they would with movie stars on holiday—on the day of the final game, Eddie Roman and Herb Cohen even made it onto the front page of the *Daily News,* looking studious with their textbooks, while inside the paper another photograph showed a smiling Ed Warner getting a haircut.

The afternoon of the championship game—March 28, 1950—the team held a brief practice before returning for an early dinner at the Paramount Hotel. After that the players retired to their rooms to rest before the game; a short nap would have been ideal, but everyone was too keyed up to sleep now. They knew that they were entering unmarked territory, a place no other college team had ever gone. All of them had grown up playing pickup ball; sometimes the games were five-on-five but more often they were three-on-three, and a game was to eleven or thirteen or sixteen points depending on how many teams were waiting, and it might be winners or losers out after making a basket, and other variations applied by neighborhood, but one rule remained constant: A team could hold the court for as long as it continued to win, and that was what the Beavers had done. They had beaten teams ranked twelve, six, five, three, two, and one, and now, standing at the edge of history, they would have to beat the top-ranked team once again.

The game, the second of the evening's doubleheader, would begin at ten o'clock; Bobby Sand's knock on the door came just before eight. Downstairs the players gathered in the lobby before leaving the hotel. For the final time they turned right on Eighth Avenue and as a group began walking uptown to the Garden. The streets were lined with saloons, delicatessens, all-night drugstores, the wind whirling newspapers in the gutter like tumbleweeds. At Forty-Ninth Street they turned left into the Garden players' entrance.

Handing their keys and watches and wallets to team manager Al Ragusa, they changed into their uniforms and one by one went to get their ankles taped. A few minutes still remained for them to stretch and use the bathroom, and maybe toss a medicine ball back and forth to warm up, and then Nat Holman called the team together for a last word. Holman was not usually one for pregame pep talks; though he was much in demand as an after-dinner speaker, and prided himself on his ability to impart advice and inspiration to his listeners, he did not feel comfortable giving his players aphorisms or anecdotes and generally confined his remarks to game strategy. This night, however, was different, and after a review of the Bradley lineup he stood silently for a few moments, regarding them with that distinctive expression seen in countless advertisements, one eyebrow raised and the jaw set somewhere between a smile and a scowl.

"You're one win from immortality," he said quietly, his tone all the more striking because it was one they had not heard from him before. "You're going out there tonight to play one game of basketball—just one game. But what you do over the next hour will be something you'll remember for the rest of your lives." He paused to let the import of his words sink in. "Now," he told them, "I have someone I want you to meet."

The players turned as one toward the door, and into the room walked Jackie Robinson.

He wasn't especially tall, just shy of six feet, but he was solidly built and handsome, with a strong jaw and a penetrating gaze, and he carried with him an irreducible aura of glamour, as though surrounded by the popping of flashbulbs. "Our mouths dropped open," Floyd Layne was to say later. "We were in awe."

Robinson knew all about City College; he had visited the campus just the year before to speak to the school's Sociology Society about his off-season work with kids at the Harlem YMCA—the very same Y where Floyd Layne and Ed Warner first played basketball together. And back in 1946, after Robinson's first year in the minor leagues, it was City College's Social Research Laboratory that had conducted a six-month survey of his case and four others, concluding that white Southern ballplayers would be hostile to the idea of a black teammate but would not actively oppose one, and that integration of Major League Baseball was "feasible and imminent" and "would be significant for better race relations in general."

Now Robinson sat down on one of the benches, pulling up his trouser legs as he did so; it was incongruous to see him in a suit and tie, out of the royal-blue Dodger cap and baggy flannel uniform in which he was instantly recognizable. At the age of thirty-one he was a man at the apex of his profession, the reigning Most Valuable Player in the National League—and at one time, as they well knew, he had also been a college basketball star. "Fellas," he said, "this is a great moment for you." His voice was higher-pitched than might have been expected, with a nasal twang that hinted at his Southern origins. "You've worked hard to get here, and I'm proud of you. You're exactly the sort of group I like best— the group that works together."

It was teamwork that had gotten them there, he reminded them, the ability to trust each other and play as one, and he urged them to keep playing that way, cooperatively and unselfishly and intelligently, and if they did he was sure it would pay off for them, because that was the kind of approach that won ballgames. They were, he said, a special group of players. He spoke for only a couple of minutes and in that time he never mentioned race, yet the idea of racial integration seemed somehow to underlie everything he said, and those listening intently in the room could not help but recall that in their seven postseason games they had faced only a single black opponent, Chuck Cooper of Duquesne; and some of them surely knew as well that in all the years of the NCAA tournament there had never been a black player on a championship team, and so they were standing at the edge of history in more ways than one.

Before long the locker room attendant came in and told them it was time to go. Robinson shook their hands and wished them the best of luck and departed, carrying that glow of celebrity with him. There was just time now to gather for one last team handshake, and after that they trotted through the concrete tunnel and out into the arena, the darkness so thick and vast that it was like plunging into the ocean at night.

A lone spotlight searched out each starter as Barclay Cooke announced his name, the crowd applauding in response as he dribbled to center court and then rolled the ball back to the bench. After the introductions the house lights came back up, 325 of them, the effect so dazzling that on the court the players had to blink for a moment to adjust their sight.

It was ten o'clock. Across the city bartenders reached up to change the channel from professional wrestling or *The Life of Riley* to WJZ, channel 7, where the NCAA championship would be shown. In kitchens families switched on little tabletop radios made of plastic and Bakelite; in living rooms they gathered around wooden consoles large and sturdy enough to be another piece of furniture, Zeniths and Philcos and Motorolas, the knobs and glowing dials tuned to 1050 WMGM. With his familiar rat-a-tat newsreel voice Marty Glickman set the scene for his listeners, describing the two squads as they huddled on the court to receive final instructions from their coaches. As the cheerleaders leaped and shouted on the sideline, the two referees stood conferring at midcourt. One of them hailed from the West and one from the East, selected by the NCAA to help ensure impartiality. Lou Eisenstein had worked numerous City College games in Madison Square Garden; Ronald Gibbs was a referee in the Missouri Valley Conference, Bradley's conference, and was himself an Illinois resident. That day the *Peoria Star* had called Gibbs's work "most satisfactory" and assured its readers, "Those who were dissatisfied with the officiating in the NIT tournament can rest assured that the officiating tonight will be fair and square with no prejudice being shown towards either team."

At eight minutes after ten the players took their positions around the center circle; Ed Warner would be jumping against Bradley center Elmer Behnke. All at once the crowd stilled, everyone wondering what the coming minutes would bring. Eisenstein tossed up the ball and the players leaped, Warner tapping the ball to Irwin Dambrot, who immediately took charge, dribbling fast down the center of the court and dishing the ball off to Al Roth in the left corner, who was fouled as he made a pass. Roth missed the free throw, and the Braves brought the ball back downcourt, where Bill Mann hit a turnaround jump shot for the first points of the game.

It had been an even more tumultuous week for the Braves than for the Beavers. After their defeat in the NIT championship game they had flown back to Peoria, where they were met at the airport by a throng estimated at upward of seven thousand fans. (Some on hand explained to reporters that the team needed a welcoming crowd more after a loss than a win.) A motorcade drove the players through downtown Peoria back to the college, and that night they were honored at a sold-out banquet at the local Shriners mosque. The next day the team flew to Kansas City for another game, defeating Kansas University to qualify for the District 5 slot. After winning two more Western Regional games, the Braves had arrived in New York only the day before, their TWA Constellation circling the city for two hours due to a persistent blanket of fog; the team hadn't arrived at the Paramount Hotel until close to eight o'clock at night. To start the game, Bradley head coach Forddy Anderson had decided to use a zone defense—in part because he hoped that guarding a section of court rather than having to chase around after an opponent would take less of a toll on his already exhausted players.

The best way to counteract a zone was with the fast break, attacking the defense before it had a chance to set up. But the Beavers were tired too, so City looked instead to go over the zone, bombarding the basket from long range. Holman sent in Norm Mager to replace Al Roth, and Mager responded with a couple of set shots. Eddie Roman, too, was stretching the Bradley zone, hitting jump shots from all parts of the court; he scored twelve points in the first twelve minutes of the game, his form as unconventional as ever, the shot beginning from somewhere around his right ear, legs splayed out wildly beneath him. On Bradley's end, Aaron Preece knocked down several shots around the basket, and Gene Melchiorre, not even five foot nine, drove in time and again for baskets against much taller men.

It was a rough game, played throughout with the sort of intense, desperate energy seen in most games only in the closing minutes, players contending for every rebound and fighting for every loose ball. With fifty-seven seconds remaining in the half, Mager grabbed a rebound and then turned quickly upcourt just as Preece reached in for a steal, and in a flash their two heads slammed together like bat against ball, the thud resounding sickeningly through the arena—the two players knocked sprawling, Preece motionless on his back, Mager holding his head and writhing in pain. They lay flat on the court for several long minutes,

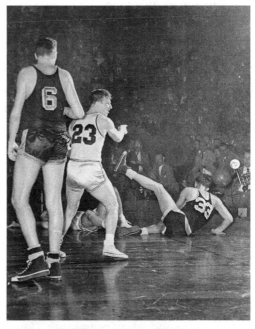

Bradley player Aaron Preece lies flat on the court after colliding with City College player Norm Mager (33) as the ball bounces away (to the right, just past Mager's head). Bradley's Gene Melchiorre (23) and City College's Eddie Roman (6) stand nearby.
Bettmann / Getty Images

hidden from view by a concerned crowd of teammates and Garden medical staff. Eventually Preece managed to get up and walk away, gingerly working his jaw, but Mager had to be helped woozily into the locker room, blood trickling down the side of his face, to be tended to by the Madison Square Garden house physician, Dr. Vincent Nardiello.

Nardiello had the countenance of an old-time bank teller, with round steel-rimmed eyeglasses, a small mustache, and hair parted in the middle. He had often seen the sort of injury suffered by Norm Mager, though it was far more common among hockey than basketball players. The collision had opened a deep gash two inches long on Mager's forehead that would require five stitches to close; Nardiello bent over Mager to do his work, giving him a piece of balsa wood to bite down on for the pain. In the meantime, team manager Al Ragusa had to shoo away half a dozen physicians, all of them CCNY alumni, who had shown up in the locker room offering their services. The only visitor admitted was Norm's mother, Regina Mager, who had been a horrified witness to the collision and immediately rushed downstairs to be with her son. Ragusa hastened to tell her that Normie was all right, and from the trainer's table Norm himself, though still groggy, also reassured her that it wasn't so bad, he looked worse than he felt, but Mrs. Mager was adamant in her insistence that Norman should not be permitted to go back into the game—not "after losing all that blood."

Mager, though, would come out for the second half, looking especially swashbuckling with a bloodstained strip of bandage on his forehead. As the second half got under way, City College was ahead 39 to 32. Eddie Roman had been playing one of the best games of his life, but with nine minutes remaining he was called for his fifth personal foul and, in anger and frustration, had to leave the court to watch the remainder of the game from the bench. By that point the lead had grown to ten and Bradley moved to a full-court press, hounding City's ball handlers from one end of the court to the other, and the crowd lapsed into a tense silence as Bradley patiently chipped away at the lead. With a minute and a half remaining, Gene Melchiorre deflected a pass out of Al Roth's hands and sped off for an uncontested layup that brought the score to 66–63. The Beavers went into a freeze, trying to take as much time as they could off the clock, and dribbling along the sideline, Mager was fouled by Preece. Under the NCAA's two-minute rule, there was no possibility of a rebound, so Mager stood alone at the foul line, the two squads watching from opposite sides of the court; coolly he sank a two-handed free throw to bring the lead back up to four. Floyd Layne, City's most reliable passer, stepped to the sideline to make the inbounds pass.

On the bench, Nat Holman had been gripping a rolled-up program tightly in his hand; he watched the action with his face set in a fighter's sneer, eyes darting over the court. Now, in this critical moment, Holman called in one of City College's few designed plays. It had been drawn up the year before by Bobby Sand, who dubbed it the Four Horsemen play because it began with four players lined up in a row at the midcourt line with their backs to the basket. Al Roth stood at the farthest end of the line, with Ed Warner next to him, then Ron Nadell, and Irwin Dambrot in the position closest to the passer. The Bradley defenders clustered tight around them, poised to intercept the pass as it came in. The referee handed the ball to Layne and blew his whistle to start play. Instantly Roth broke straight ahead toward the City side of the court, bringing two defenders with him as Layne faked him the pass; Warner turned left and headed upcourt, trailed by Nadell. At the other end of the row, Dambrot feinted to the left, as though to follow Nadell, and then abruptly curled back around to the right, breaking toward the basket and causing one Bradley defender momentarily to screen another; Layne threaded a perfect overhead pass to him, just out of the reach of the pursuing defender, which Dambrot caught two-handed like a wide receiver racing downfield. Stopping short under the basket to let the defender go flying by, Dambrot then calmly banked in the shot to make the score 69 to 63, a seemingly insurmountable lead with only fifty-seven seconds remaining—but as Louis Effrat was to note in *The New York Times*, "what happened in the last minute almost defies description."

The steady rumble in the arena had built to a crescendo with Dambrot's basket, the noise turning the action on the court into a kind of pantomime as the Braves passed the ball around, looking desperately for an opening in the City defense; as Joe Stowell dribbled across the lane, Warner made contact with him and was called for a one-shot foul—a critical mistake, because it allowed the Braves an opportunity to score without taking additional time off the clock while still retaining possession. Stowell sank the free throw; the lead was now five, and the crowd had quieted as Bradley brought the ball in again from the sideline. Melchiorre took a pass and skittered to the hoop, moving left while spinning a right-handed layup off the backboard and in: 69 to 66.

Receiving the ball from Roth near the basket, Dambrot turned and made a long pass upcourt that was intercepted by Fred Schlictman; two Bradley passes brought the ball back to Melchiorre above the keyhole, who again went straight for the hoop, lifting a scoop shot that floated gently down into the net. Melchiorre had made three baskets in less than a minute and the lead was down to a single point.

Thirty seconds remained in the game—remained in the season. Nat Holman sent Norm Mager back in; Mager received the inbounds pass and then sent the ball over to Floyd Layne. Layne began moving upcourt, searching for an open path, dribbling this way and that, hounded all the while by guard Charlie Grover, but he was surprised by another defender coming over to trap him and he stopped his dribble. Not yet across midcourt and fearing that he was about to receive a ten-second violation, he rushed a pass toward the sideline, which sailed high over the leaping Mager and out of bounds. Astonishingly, the Braves had the ball again, and the Garden crowd sat in grim, watchful silence as the Beavers set up their defense, trying to protect the slimmest of leads.

Bradley had time left for only one possession. Everyone in the arena knew that the ball would be coming in to Melchiorre, who needed just one more basket to complete the improbable comeback and cement his legend in Peoria, and with seven seconds remaining he took a pass on the left side near midcourt and without hesitation lowered his shoulder and dribbled across the keyhole and down the right side of the lane; but this time the path to the basket was blocked by Dambrot, and a trio of City defenders closed around Melchiorre in a moment that would be endlessly dissected and debated, the game film studied as though it were evidence from a crime scene. Melchiorre drove toward the basket, and as the ball went by him Roth's hand flashed out, as fast and precise as a pickpocket's, and going up for the shot, Melchiorre lost control of the ball. Sure that he had been fouled, Melchiorre immediately looked around for a call from the referees, but the call never came, and meanwhile Dambrot had grabbed the basketball out of the air and in a single motion tossed a long left-handed pass to Mager, who had broken downcourt as soon as Melchiorre passed him and was now streaking fast toward the other basket with Bradley's Fred Schlictman hard on his heels. Just past midcourt Mager caught Dambrot's pass in full stride; with two dribbles he drove to the left side of the hoop and leaped, twisting his body to shield the ball from the defender, and with a flick of his right hand laid the ball off the backboard and into the net, just before Schlictman crashed into him and sent him once again careening to the hardwood. It was Dambrot to Mager—the final play of both of their college careers.

The score now stood at 71 to 68 and the arena was in a frenzy, eighteen thousand people on their feet and roaring, and Schlictman took the inbounds pass and began dribbling upcourt, but he rushed his dribble and knocked the ball off his knee and could do nothing but watch helplessly as it rolled untouched out of bounds under the City basket. Layne passed the ball safely to Warner, the final buzzer sounded, and the Beavers stepped into history. On the other end of the court Mager clenched his fists and raised both arms in triumph, though only for a moment, as if he were suddenly too exhausted to keep them in the air, and his teammates came rushing off the bench to surround him and fans began pouring onto the court as though a floodgate had been opened, and Mager disappeared inside a swarm of well-wishers only to emerge again, grinning in disbelief, as he was lifted atop his teammates' shoulders and carried off the court at the end of the second half, as he had been helped off at the end of the first.

Madison Square Garden was bedlam, Marty Glickman having to shout into his microphone to be heard over the din. In the upper balcony the uproarious City College students chanted endless rounds of Allagaroo, the nonsense syllables merging into a deep locomotive roar. They whooped and cheered, pounded one another on the back, or just gazed dumbfounded at the spectacle going on below them; some, overcome by emotion, broke into tears. On the court Bobby Sand wandered around beaming madly, hugging everyone in sight, not quite sure what to do with himself. Many of those in the arena stood calling Nat Holman's name, and Floyd Layne and Leroy Watkins, who were standing beside him, laughed and hoisted him onto their shoulders—an awkward, tilting seat, as Watkins was so much

The City College Beavers celebrate after defeating Bradley University to win the 1950 National Collegiate Athletic Association title. Players Leroy Watkins (at left) and Floyd Layne hoist head coach Nat Holman onto their shoulders. Eddie Roman's younger brother, Richie, who had served as a ball boy for the game, stands to Watkins's right. Bettmann / Getty Images

taller—and a jubilant Holman raised his open hand high as though reaching for a brass ring.

Irwin Dambrot was voted the outstanding player of the tournament; he had led the Beavers with fifteen points while holding Bradley's All-American, Paul Unruh, to only eight. Sitting at the press table, Leonard Koppett composed a lead for the next morning's edition of the *New York Herald Tribune:* "Irwin Dambrot is a tall, handsome, agile young man of many talents, but he has never considered himself an author. Yet in front of 18,000 delirious people at Madison Square Garden last night, he wrote the textbook on how to finish one's college basketball playing career."

The International News Service informed newspaper readers around the country that City College was "a sophomoric team that looked like fate's fall guys when the season started but proved a team of destiny"; the Beavers now "belonged to the basketball ages." The other wire services were scarcely less exuberant. The United Press said that City had "carved a chunk of history through Bradley's zone defense." Norm Mager's final basket, reported the Associated Press, "gave a story book finish to one of the most amazing sagas of college basketball."

It had been a consummate team effort. To Dambrot's fifteen points Norm Mager had added fourteen, most of them in the second half after his injury. Ed Warner had fourteen points as well, while Eddie Roman had twelve, Floyd Layne eleven, and Al Roth five. In the crowded locker room the players, exhilarated but weary, sat in their uniforms smiling and quietly accepting congratulations; some stood to pose for photographs or spoke a few words to reporters who moved from one to another looking for quotes.

Among those in the City College locker room that night was a young reporter for *The Daily Compass* named Stan Isaacs. Isaacs had grown up in Brooklyn; when he was six years old his father had taken him to Ebbets Field to see the great Dizzy Dean pitch. Since that time he had devoted himself to sports of every kind, had witnessed all manner of victory and defeat, but watching the City College players receive the congratulations of their family and friends he realized that he had never been as thrilled as he was at that moment. "This was more than a basketball victory," he would write. "It was a triumph for a school, for a city. A bunch of kids from the alleys and gutters of New York, Jewish and Negro kids mostly, had licked the best the rest of the country had to offer. City College, a school so long mocked for no other reason than that a kid could get a free college education there, had achieved something no other school ever had."

Looking back twenty-one months later, Isaacs would decide that nothing could take away that triumph: that it would stand forever as a fine and wonderful thing.

CHAPTER 18

I t was 'Allagaroo' through the canyons, the side streets, on Times Square, Fifth Avenue, and all over the borough of Manhattan through the night and late into the afternoon," reported *The New York Times*. "Nearly all of New York seemed yesterday to be discussing City's dramatic triumph," the *Herald Tribune* noted. "There was," said the *Daily Mirror*, "a distinct lavender tint to the city."

That afternoon, for the first time in its history, the City College of New York suspended classes, and by noon waves of students were pouring onto the sun-filled quadrangle for a victory celebration, forming impromptu conga lines, waving banners that proclaimed the Beavers the greatest basketball team in history. In the upper floors of the Gothic buildings that bordered the quad, students tore up newspapers, phone books, notepads, and tossed the scraps of paper from the windows, the homemade confetti wafting down on the spring breeze. Arrayed in their crisp white-and-lavender uniforms, the forty-piece City College band started up the merry polka melody of the "Beaver Fight Song," the air filling with the rumble of drums and flourish of brass; snake dances wound through classrooms, growing ever longer as they picked up students along the way. On Convent Avenue, which cut through the center of campus, young men climbed onto the roofs of parked cars and began making speeches, about nothing really, seemingly just for the joy of declaiming amid such good cheer.

Atop the Main Building, the tower bell slowly tolled seven times, once for each tournament victory. That bell had not been rung for as long as anyone could remember, and indeed that morning a member of the custodial department had informed the dean of student activities, James Pearce, that the bell *couldn't* be rung, as it no longer had a clapper. Dr. Pearce insisted that the department should do whatever was necessary to ring that bell, even if they had to send a man up there with a sledgehammer. "That's just what they did," he was to say later, adding, "Pleasantest tolling you ever heard."

On the steps a makeshift platform had been set up, with a standing microphone wired to a pair of loudspeakers attached to the top of a lamppost. Before long the quadrangle had filled with several thousand students, some climbing into the trees and onto the tall base of the flagpole, hoping to get a better view. One by one the members of the basketball team in their jackets and ties were paraded up to the platform; each was introduced to roars of approval from the crowd, then shyly leaned

Nat Holman addresses students and faculty at a campus victory rally after the double championship. Associated Press/John Rooney

into the microphone to murmur a slight variation on a single theme: "Thank you for coming here. I'm glad I go to City College."

Nat Holman had been reluctant to address the crowd that afternoon, preferring to let the team's play speak for itself, but finally he was persuaded to do so, and he made a short speech with Churchillian echoes. "Never was so much owed to so few," he said. "The victory was not due to luck, but to cooperation and that wonderful CCNY spirit."

Somebody handed Eddie Roman a basketball, and, grinning, he held it up as though to shoot, a moment captured in the next day's *Daily News*, a wide-angle photograph that showed him towering over a crowd that stretched nearly as far as the eye could see. ROMAN HOLIDAY ON THE CAMPUS, the *News* captioned the photo, with the text below: "Hero-worshipping CCNY students lionize Ed Roman, brilliant 6 ft. 6 center, one of the players who helped make basketball history in the Beavers' unprecedented sweep to two titles."

Norm Mager had barely slept from excitement and a throbbing head, but he rose early that morning to take the subway in from Brooklyn for a midterm exam on the downtown campus; he rushed uptown when it was over, arriving as the rally was already well under way, his appearance on the platform sparking an uproarious ovation. He was, he admitted to a reporter, "a little rocky" but otherwise in good spirits.

One professor was watching the proceedings as he puffed furiously on a pipe; after a while he turned to a reporter and said: "Greatest thing that ever happened in the hundred-and-two-year-old history of this venerable institution."

At City College, basketball had always seemed the sole activity capable of unifying a busy and fractious student body. "We were all basketball fans," says Selma Wassermann, who in 1950 was a senior in the School of Education. "The team gave us a kind of status that we didn't have as students. We were the kids who didn't have enough money to go to NYU or Columbia. We were all very smart, we all had to pass a tough entrance exam that gave us the opportunity to move up the rungs of social status—but we always knew that we would never be in the same league as Columbia, and Harvard was not even speakable. So we trudged along every day with our lunches in brown paper bags. The basketball players were our heroes; they were the only heroes we had. They were formidable, and they made us formidable." Those who had managed to get into the City College of New York might envy classmates who had entered the Ivy League; might wonder about their prospects in the job market; might worry about political blacklists or an Army call-up; but they could be confident, at least, about two things: They were well educated, and they had an outstanding basketball team—or, as one of their cheers had it: "City College! Basketball with knowledge!"

That sense of distinction reached its pinnacle with the double championship. "There was elation on campus," says Mort Sheinman, who had entered City College that January as a freshman. "You know, in the bookstore you could buy these textbook covers that had the City College logo on it in lavender. And I remember riding the subway to school holding that thing up like a badge: Yes, I was a City College student."

For all the pride they took in their college, and in themselves for having merited admission to it, CCNY students also understood that they were attending a tuition-free commuter school on an overcrowded, increasingly dilapidated campus offering little of the undergraduate merriment that had come to define American college life in the public imagination, that cheerful Andy Hardyish world of mixers and send-off rallies and homecoming bonfires—theirs was, in *The Saturday Evening Post*'s description, a "college without frills or fun." Now, almost overnight, City College seemed to represent something entirely different. "From one end of the country to the other, City College was now recognized as the college of national champions," journalist Marvin Kalb, a CCNY student of the time, was to write. "Even kids in San Francisco were chanting 'allagaroo.' "

The City College Beavers had defeated all comers, from every part of the country, in much of which the idea of a home team comprising only blacks and Jews would have been met with amusement or derision or contempt. "We were the immigrants and the ghetto kids, the socioeconomic underdogs," says Jerry Jacobson, the cofounder of the student booster group the Allagarooters. "The real America, we had always felt, was out there in Peoria. We were just a bunch of ghetto snipes."

Though the basketball players could not help but stand out, if by sheer height alone, they were still a regular part of City College campus life, and except for their distinguishing talent, much like everyone else—they sat through lectures for the same required courses, had a table in the cafeteria just as the art students and the Trotskyites did, rode to school jammed tight with the other morning commuters on the subway—so it was not hard for their fellow students, even those with no interest otherwise in athletics, to root for them and even to feel, like the most devoted of sports fans, that their own fortunes were somehow tied to the success of their team.

"Everybody shared in the victory," team member Ron Nadell was to say later. "It wasn't just a victory for the ten or twelve guys that played it. It was for everybody."

There was another champion in the city, of course. The New York Yankees had won the World Series three times in the previous four years. But that was different. The Yankee players, like the players on every major league team, came from all over the country, from distant places, and had been brought to the city by business arrangement. Players spent the season living in hotels and furnished apartments, and much of the time they returned home after the last game had been played. To root for a professional team was, in a sense, to root for one's own collection of hired guns against the hired guns of a rival enterprise. But those who played for CCNY were all, by definition, hometown kids. The *Herald Tribune* referred to them affectionately as "our boys," the *Daily Mirror* as "our champs." They were children of the city (every single member of the varsity team was a public school graduate), had learned the game in parks and schoolyards paid for out of city taxes— and indeed, the day after winning the NIT championship Eddie Roman could be seen in Claremont Park, playing a Sunday pickup game just as always.

Like so many of their fans, the players had grown up, in the words of the old song, on the sidewalks of New York. They felt entirely at home in the melting pot of the city; they knew the immigrant neighborhoods, where the side streets reverberated with the cries of the cash-clothes men and the knife sharpeners, the itinerant vendors pushing little tin stoves from which they would pull, as in a magic act, jellied apples or salted chickpeas in a burst of smoke. They remembered scrap paper drives and air raid blackouts, had passed summer nights sleeping on rooftops, the tar beach that stretched overhead across the city. They shared those memories, were part of that common experience: bundled afternoon papers tossed against newsstands, and the chiaroscuro of sunlight peeking through elevated tracks, and old men pushing lemon ice carts, and the dazzle of the movie palaces along Broadway.

Says Hannan Wexler, then a sportswriter for the *Observation Post:* "It's not that they did it for us. It's that they *were* us, and they did it."

Almost every night, it seemed, the players were feted at another celebratory event. "We were invited to a lot of dinners," Herb Cohen recalls. "We ate a lot of chicken." On Monday, April 3, Floyd Layne, Ed Warner, and Joe Galiber were among the featured guests at a pro wrestling show held at Harlem's Renaissance Ballroom, three of the "glittering array of celebrities" that also included Congressman Adam Clayton Powell, Jr., and boxing champions Sugar Ray Robinson and Ezzard Charles. On Friday morning Irwin Dambrot and Eddie Roman appeared on the popular *Tex and Jinx* radio show, beginning their segment with a lively Allagaroo.

That week's issue of *Life* magazine included a full-page photograph of the team gathered around a bronze bust of Abraham Lincoln in front of the Main Building. The bust was a beloved feature of the City College campus (it was student tradition to rub Abe's nose for luck before an exam, and though the rest of his head had darkened with age, his nose shone brightly); for *Life*, though, the clear implication was that the basketball team seemed to embody Lincoln's dream of a freer, more welcoming nation, one less consumed by racial hatreds.

The photograph showed the team's starting five as well as super-sub Norm Mager (still sporting his bandage), flanked by Nat Holman and Bobby Sand. Originally Holman had objected to Sand's being included— "Nobody allows the assistant coach to be part of the setup," he said— but the players insisted that they wouldn't take the picture unless Bobby was part of it.

"He says, 'Why should he be in it?'" Sand would recall bitterly in an interview thirty-seven years later. "It didn't mean anything to him. He was the key guy, the world revolved around him."

By this time the Sands had finally moved out of Sylvia's parents' apartment on Rockaway Parkway to one of their own a few blocks away. After the Grand Slam victories Bobby wanted to host a party for the players, but their new place was too small, and so they held it at her family's apartment. "My father got us up and dressed and we went over there," recalls Bobby's daughter Wendie, who was seven years old at the time. "The players came in, they were hugging each other, talking, going over moves they had done in the tournaments. Everything was being said all at once. Practically the entire team was there, laughing and talking, and my grandmother was in the kitchen cooking like crazy."

There was brisket and roast chicken, and potato latkes, and stuffed cabbage and kugel, washed down with glasses of seltzer and cherry soda. Norm Mager was cracking up the guys with tournament war stories, like how in the Kentucky game he had taken a hard foul and turned around and told the guy to "kiss my white Jewish ass." Some of the players were sporting their newly acquired jewelry: They had each received a pair of commemorative Bulova watches from Madison Square Garden, and City College also gave each of them a ten-karat gold ring, inscribed on the front with the letters *NIT* and *NCAA* and an image of the Garden. Bobby had received a tournament watch as well, and the players had gotten together a collection among themselves and that afternoon they gave Sylvia a watch, and they had also bought Wendie a doll carriage, a modern-looking one in pink-and-gray plaid.

Bobby served as genial host, refilling glasses, moving in and out of the general jubilation, the bursts of laughter that erupted around the room; he watched in delight as some of the guys took turns giving Wendie rides on their shoulders. At times he found himself almost overcome with emotion, on the verge of tears. Above all he was happiest that the guys had proven how good they could be, proven it not just to the world but to themselves; that was a knowledge they would carry with them always.

Back in Peoria, the Bradley Braves had been welcomed by an even larger and more enthusiastic crowd than had greeted them after the defeat in the NIT final game. "It looked," said Bradley's student newspaper, *The Scout*, "as if the whole town had come to meet them at the airport." A hundred-car motorcade drove the team downtown, past thousands more cheering in the streets, past the Palace Theater where the marquee read WELCOME HOME BRADLEY'S GREATEST TEAM OF ALL.

The marquee of the Madison theater carried a different message: WAS SQUEAKY FOULED? YOU BE THE JUDGE! (Among Bradley fans, Melchiorre was affectionately known as Squeaky, a reference to his high-pitched voice.) For weeks, four of the local movie houses played newsreel film of the controversial final play; according to the *Peoria Star*, "the movies show 'Squeaky' driving in, as usual, and also show three of the eastern boys giving him the business under the basket." There was no one in town who doubted that Melchiorre had been fouled as he drove in for the potential game-winning layup, despite the fact that the referee representing the West, Ron Gibbs, maintained that there had been "definitely" no foul on the play. Years later, Paul Unruh was to recall that Gibbs was "one of our home-state boys. We wondered how a local boy could let that happen." Unruh's teammate Aaron Preece said bitterly, "We didn't lose. They took it away from us."

Bradley's head coach, Forddy Anderson, had insisted to reporters after the game, "I still think we have the number one team in the country." Responding to Anderson's observation, the *New York Post* asked facetiously, "This is a fascinating remark. Did he mean that New York is out of the country?"

Norm Mager was taken in the National Basketball Association draft that spring, selected by the Baltimore Bullets in the fifth round, the forty-ninth overall pick. Irwin Dambrot was the first-round selection of the hometown New York Knicks, the seventh overall pick; though it was initially suggested that he would be willing to join the Knicks, at least for a while—the *Observation Post* noted that "the offer was just too good"—ultimately Dambrot decided to refuse the selection and attend Columbia Dental School instead.

On the evening of June 15, 1950, the 104th commencement of the City College of New York was held in Lewisohn Stadium. The graduates filled the playing field, their families and friends watching proudly from the concentric tiers of stone benches above them. College president Dr. Harry N. Wright awarded the degrees. Sixty special awards were con-

ferred, including the Nat Fleischer '08 Award, for Outstanding Academic and Athletic Achievement; it went to Irwin Dambrot, the most
celebrated among a graduating class of 3,710.

After the degrees were conferred, Chief City Magistrate John M.
Murtagh stepped to the podium. Murtagh was the official who had been
assigned by Mayor William O'Dwyer to ascertain whether the Police
Department's plainclothes squads were accepting bribes from gamblers
and bookmakers. The investigation had determined that they were—
indeed, that in at least one case "members of the plainclothes squad
eventually and actually became part and parcel of the bookmaker's
operation"—but Murtagh had never submitted a written report to the
mayor.

Raising his right hand, Murtagh administered the Ephebic Oath of
Loyalty to the City of New York, an oath patterned on one from ancient
Athens, which for decades had been sworn by every City College gradu-
ate:

> We will never bring disgrace to our city by any act of dishon-
> esty or cowardice, nor ever desert our suffering comrades in the
> ranks;
>
> we will fight for the ideals and sacred things of the city, both
> alone and with many;
>
> we will revere and obey the city's laws, and do our best to incite
> a like respect and reverence in those about us who are prone to
> annul them and set them at naught;
>
> we will strive unceasingly to quicken the public's sense of civic
> duty;
>
> and thus, in all these ways, we will strive to transmit this city not
> only not less, but greater, better, and more beautiful than it was
> transmitted to us.

The voices of the thousands gathered together; the sound echoed
through the arena, then rose into the night and disappeared.

PART TWO

The Bridge of Sighs

The "Bridge of Sighs" in downtown Manhattan, which linked the Criminal Courts Building to the city prison. Peter Keegan / Getty Images

CHAPTER 19

The Borscht Belt, it was called, a stretch of hotels that ran through the southwestern part of New York's Catskill Mountains, a couple of hours up Route 17 from the city by ramshackle bus or overflowing family sedan. The Catskills had been discovered as a vacation spot around the turn of the century, when in the summertime Jewish immigrants fled the heat and noise of the city to experience the simple pleasures of country food and an after-dinner walk under the stars; as time went on, a steady stream of Jews from the Lower East Side began making the trek upstate, word having gotten around about the wonders of the mountains—the beautiful scenery, the healthful air, the deliciousness of butter and eggs from cows and chickens you could actually see. Soon farmhouses were converted into boardinghouses, and boardinghouses multiplied into bungalow colonies, and then came the hotels, sprouting like toadstools around the lakes and under the pines.

By the 1940s a Catskills vacationer had hundreds of places from which to choose, hotels for every budget and sensibility, from rustic homesteads to the most opulent modern palaces with tennis courts and golf courses; there were vegetarian health resorts and dude ranches and leftist retreats where the evening's entertainment might be a Pete Seeger or Woody Guthrie concert, or the restaging of a Clifford Odets play, or a musical pageant with a title like *Peace in a World of Equality*. Some hotels catered to families, while others were understood to be destinations for single people, or married people who arrived without their spouses, and there the evening dances took on a different quality, and couples made abundant use of parked cars and distant linen rooms, and the rules about employees fraternizing with guests were less strictly enforced. One of the hotels, the Sha-Wan-Ga Lodge, was widely known as "Schwenga Lodge," from the Yiddish word for pregnant. The comedian Joey Adams had a joke: "Every year thousands of girls come up to the Catskills looking for husbands—and thousands of husbands come up looking for girls."

The life of the hotel was carried on to the soundtrack of the public address loudspeaker, summoning bellhops for new arrivals, reporting lost children and phone calls waiting in the lobby, announcing upcoming activities: volleyball games, art classes, riding lessons, cha-cha lessons by the pool. (The Hotel Brickman offered lessons in so many activities that the owner, Murray Posner, once quipped, "You should get a diploma, not a receipt, when you leave my hotel.") Almost all of the hotels provided three gargantuan meals a day, which in the larger hotels became four meals, including a self-service "midnight supper." Nightly there was dancing—many hotels had two house orchestras, one that played American big band standards and the other specializing in the latest crazes of mambo and rumba—and on the weekends the fancier hotels also offered nightclub routines by stars like Martin and Lewis and Sophie Tucker and Danny Kaye and comedians like Milton Berle and Myron Cohen and Henny Youngman. ("A drunk was brought into court. The judge says, 'My good man, you've been brought here for drinking.' He says, 'All right, judge, let's get started.'") In some of the hotels it was common practice for the comedian to tell the joke in English but reserve the punch line for Yiddish, for that extra ethnic zing, that *zetz*: "Mr. Goldman," the policeman asks the old man lying in the street who's just been run over by a truck, "are you comfortable?" The old man raises his head and replies, *"Nu, me makht a lebn."**

Like the jokes, the members of the audience seemed to exist in two cultures at once: They weren't immigrants anymore but they weren't precisely American either, though some of the older ones had in their youth changed their names to more American versions, lopping off extra syllables like sidelocks, with one swift stroke converting Old World

---

* "Well, I make a living."

to New. Many of them still spoke with accents and belonged to mutual aid societies that derived from towns in the ancestral homeland, and even their children, making their way into the wider society, understood the reality of educational quotas and professional restrictions, recognized that while the most talented among them might someday become a Supreme Court justice like Louis Brandeis, none could hope to be president, or even gain admission to many of New York's elite private clubs. For a few weeks out of the summer, though, they could forget about their cares and do morning calisthenics and games of Simon Says, or just sit in the sun and do nothing at all, and three times a day, or four, they could eat to their heart's content, and order more than they needed, and send back plates with scraps of food still on them, and in so doing thumb their noses, at last, at generations of scarcity.

Of late there had been a new and exceedingly popular attraction in many of the hotels. In the postwar years some of the hotel managers realized that basketball games featuring college stars would be a low-cost form of entertainment for their guests, and almost overnight the region became, in the phrase of *Scholastic Coach* magazine, "hoop-crazy." By the late 1940s dozens of the Catskills hotels had their own basketball teams, with hundreds of college players recruited each summer. They weren't officially paid to play basketball, because that would have nullified their amateur status—they generally worked as waiters or busboys, or, if the hotel had a lake, on the waterfront—but it was basketball that had gotten them the jobs in the first place; at Young's Gap Hotel, the first question asked of a prospective waiter or busboy was this: "Where did you play your ball?"

In the summer of 1950, Eddie Roman worked at the Hotel Brickman. Every morning he rose at 7:30 and sleepily put on the black pants and the white shirt, tied the narrow bow tie, wrestled himself into the crisp white waiter's jacket, and made his way to the main dining room for a quick breakfast before work. There was never enough time to eat as much as he wanted—nor was the food served to the help anywhere near as good as that provided to the guests—and so, like most of the waiters, over the course of the day he supplemented the staff meals with bites of the guests' leftovers, an uneaten slice of steak or the end of a chocolate éclair popped into the mouth on the way back to the kitchen, a practice known as "scarfing" and which the management tolerated as long as it was done discreetly and in moderation. By 8:30 Eddie had already set out the silverware on his tables, laid out the platters of Danish and rolls to greet the guests, arranged the grapefruit halves and slices of honeydew on the sideboard, and beside them little glasses of juice: orange and grapefruit and tomato and prune. As the guests began filing in he could imagine the murmurings among them: *That big guy's Ed Roman, he plays for City.* Many of them had paid to watch him play, had cheered for him and followed his exploits in the papers, and now here he was wearing a different uniform, responsible for four tables, forty guests in all, times three meals a day. Even breakfast had six courses, and for two hours he schlepped herring and lox and cereals hot and cold, eggs fried and shirred and poached and scrambled, pancakes and French toast and whatever else the guests desired on the menu or off, shuttling between dining room and kitchen, carrying trays loaded with plates until he could barely raise his arms, and after everyone had left he set the tables for lunch and if he was lucky he had an hour to himself before he had to return to the dining room at noon for staff lunch.

Lunch was from one until three, and then Eddie had three off hours in which he might take a dip in the pool or scrimmage a bit on the basketball court, but a good deal of work still lay ahead of him, and much of the time he was so exhausted that he returned to his bungalow and took a nap. Then he changed back into his waiter's uniform for an early dinner and then dinner service until 9:30, when on most nights the guests repaired to the casino for dancing. Many of the husbands worked in the city and did not arrive until Friday night; this meant that during the week more women than men were staying at the hotel, and the management en-

The Hotel Brickman in South Fallsburg, New York, in the Catskill Mountains, where Eddie Roman and Al Roth waited tables and played basketball in the summer of 1950. Patricia Posner

couraged the waitstaff to change out of their serving uniforms into suits
and ties and dance with the female guests. Eddie did that as well, though
his workday had begun thirteen hours earlier and the prospect filled
him with apprehension.

Eddie had never had a problem talking to reporters, who liked to
go to him for quotes because he was articulate and winningly self-
deprecating, but outside his immediate social circle he was constitutionally shy; he found it hard to shake his idea of himself as the
enormous kid with bad skin and a runny nose, and the unkind laughter
and nicknames like Goose still rang in his ears, and sometimes, in his
lower moments, he even despaired of himself as the product of his
mother's anxiety and his father's silence. He was physically awkward,
too, not a skillful dancer like his pal Bob Zawoluk of St. John's, who was
working in the Grossinger's boathouse that summer, nor smooth with
women like Al Roth and Herb Cohen, who were both with Eddie at
Brickman's. At the evening dances he was a wallflower, though it was
hard to recede into the background when you stood a head taller than
everyone else in the crowd, which only intensified his feelings of self-
consciousness, and much of the time as the couples waltzed and jitter-
bugged around the room he stood by the stage with a cup of punch in
his hand and pretended to concentrate on the music of Ned Harvey's
Orchestra.

Still, there was no denying the lift that had come with the Grand
Slam, all that acclaim, the sense of personal accomplishment that remained with him like the commemorative gold ring he never took off;
he had just turned twenty, and little by little, to his surprise and relief,
he could feel himself opening up. In May, after the tournaments were
over, the Beavers had played an exhibition game against the City College women's varsity basketball team in the Main Gym. The game was
played for laughs, and in front of the packed crowd Eddie unexpectedly
found himself flirting with the opposing center, whose name was Clara;
she stood only four foot ten, and once when he was holding the ball he
allowed her to push him off his feet—the referee, a professor from the
economics department, of course called him for a traveling violation, to
the delight of the crowd—and another time Eddie pulled a Globetrotter-
ish gag by replacing the basketball behind his back with a red balloon,
which with a flourish he handed her like a bouquet. He hadn't asked her

out, though; he couldn't imagine dating a girl nearly two feet shorter than he was, but in truth he had never asked a girl out. So nights at the Hotel Brickman he'd watch Fats and Herbie circulate around the casino, so self-assured, and then return to his bungalow, maybe with some cupcakes and a glass of milk scarfed from the kitchen, and a discarded copy of the day's *Times* to read before bed.

Except on Fridays—in the Catskills, Friday was basketball night. It seemed that nearly all of the star players from the postseason tournaments were up in the mountains that summer. Irwin Dambrot and Norm Mager were ineligible to participate because they had been drafted by the NBA and were thus considered professionals, and Floyd Layne preferred to stay in the city to play baseball, but Ed Warner was a busboy nearby at Klein's Hillside Hotel. Sam Ranzino of North Carolina State was at the Tamarack Lodge, and his backcourt mate Dick Dickey was at the Harmony Country Club. Grossinger's Hotel and Country Club had a virtual All-Star team, including Bob Zawoluk of St. John's and Sherman White of LIU. For its part, the Ambassador Hotel had dispensed with individual recruiting and just imported the entire Bradley starting five from Peoria. Some of the most prominent head coaches in the sport had also been hired to run the hotel teams, among them Ed Diddle, Jr., of Western Kentucky University, of whom it was reported that on his first day at Kutsher's Country Club he saw sour cream listed on the menu and, turning to owner Milt Kutsher, asked in astonishment, "You serve spoiled food to your guests?"

It was hard to imagine a more idyllic setting for basketball than outdoors in the mountains on a summer night, amid the pines with a bright moon overhead and, at many of the hotels, a lake sparkling in the distance. Moths swarmed around the floodlights high above the court, tall poles surrounded by nimbuses of light like puffy white dandelions; the games went on in a strange half-light between darkness and glare, the players casting long shadows on the court as they ran up and back. The hoops, with white-painted backboards, were attached to the top of elaborate wooden structures like lifeguards' watchtowers. Spectators crammed together on bleachers pressed tight along the sidelines, older guests watching the game from rocking chairs; on the cooler evenings some of them sat wrapped in lap robes, passing thermoses of coffee back and forth. In one game that summer, the ball was passed wildly off the court and play was delayed for ten minutes as the referees, armed with flashlights, went hunting for it in the deep grass.

The games were played on Friday nights and often on Sundays as well, and beforehand it was common practice for a member of the staff to circulate among the hotel's guests with a hat containing numbered slips of paper. A guest would pay a dollar and select one of the numbers in the hat, which corresponded to the combined number of points that might be scored in the game—if the final score was, say, 50 to 47, the winning number would be 97. After the game, the collected money went to the patron who had picked the correct final score.

Though gambling was by no means the prime attraction in the Catskills, criminal rackets had established casinos throughout the area and had installed their own bookmakers in some of the hotels; many of the larger hotels operated gambling concessions, hosting big-money poker games in which players gave the hotel a percentage of the bets in exchange for refreshments and waiter service. Scattered among their regular clientele—dentists and secretaries and garment workers and the like—the Catskills resorts had their share of itinerant gamblers, professionals who went from hotel to hotel, winning the confidence of fellow poker players over a period of nights before making the kill on the final night, and then, billfold heavier, moving on to another hotel in a nearby town. Along with the other guests the gamblers liked to attend basketball games in the mountains, and some among them perceived an opportunity to turn a wager into a sure thing. The proposition was simple enough. Before the game the gambler would contribute his dollar and pick his number out of the hat, and then he would pull aside a few key players from each team and make them an offer: If the players could produce the number that he wanted, they would receive a cut of the winnings, which could often run to several hundred dollars.

It was in those Borscht Belt exhibition games—where lots of money was bet and the outcomes didn't matter—that many college basketball players first made the acquaintance of professional gamblers and became comfortable with the notion of shaving points, that they first learned how to control a game by allowing a flurry of baskets or freezing the ball in the last few minutes, fine-tuning the score like a radio set. Said Lou Goldstein, the famed social director of Grossinger's: "Teams didn't throw games—they threw scores."

• • •

Among the guests at Grossinger's that summer was a jewelry manufacturer from New York named Salvatore Sollazzo. At the age of forty-five, Sollazzo was stout—a once muscular body having begun to run to fat—with thinning hair and a tight, crooked smile. To outward indications he was just another high-living man-about-town. His suits were custom-made, his shirts monogrammed; he owned season tickets for the Polo Grounds and Yankee Stadium, and he was a habitué of the Belmont and Aqueduct racetracks and the midtown nightclub the Latin Quarter, where he was known among the hat check girls as a lavish tipper. Sollazzo's personal history, though, was far spottier than his appearance might indicate. It included a youthful marriage and divorce, the bankruptcy of his family's Lower East Side jewelry store after he took it over, and a five-year term in Sing Sing for acting as a lookout in the armed robbery of a midtown jewelry store.

After his release from prison, Sollazzo had gone to work as a jewelry salesman in his brother's business; eventually he saved enough to start a company of his own, and here, at last, one of his gambles came through. Always looking for a big score, Sollazzo had been taking out loans to speculate in platinum. For a while it looked to be a bad bet, but during the war years the United States government declared platinum a scarce war material and the value of Sollazzo's stockpile skyrocketed. New customers flocked to him, having heard of his vast supply, and his company grew into one of the country's leading makers of wedding and birthstone rings. He opened a second company, and between the two firms he had annual sales of between one and two million dollars, supporting a workforce of some eighty employees. Yet even this newfound success was not sufficient for him, and he arranged a scheme to have out-of-state customers order products through a pair of shell companies and then deposited their payments into phony bank accounts, thus reducing by more than half a million dollars the income taxes he would otherwise have owed.

In his forties Salvatore Sollazzo could finally begin to live the life he had always imagined for himself, with exciting, sun-filled days at the track and nights in dark, glamorous places, surrounded by showgirls and mobsters. He married again, this time a woman half his age, a chorus girl and model named Jeanne Wright, who was taller than he was and had dark, sultry looks—the newspapers would often describe her as "raven-haired." In the summer of 1950 she was often seen lounging around the Grossinger's pool; Sollazzo was not averse to using his wife's striking beauty to attract the attention of the members of the basketball team, and among the most attentive was a Long Island University player named Eddie Gard.

Gard had been fixing basketball games since his sophomore year at LIU, when an older player had introduced him to the practice; by his senior year, the 1949–50 season, he was in charge of the team's point-shaving activities, negotiating payments from gamblers for several games. Though he was not academically inclined he had a dexterous mind, able to instantly calculate all the angles—"He could have been a bookie," says Herb Cohen in some admiration—and even in casual conversations he seemed always to be sizing up the situation, evaluating what might be gotten from it, like the kid who, entering a candy store for the first time, immediately assesses the distance between the candy counter and the front door. Recalls Sid Trubowitz, a star CCNY player of a few years earlier, Gard was "a wheeler-dealer. . . . There was something with him that always seemed not quite on the level." He was dapper and charming, with a round, open face, and he brought to all his activities an infectious enthusiasm, a delight in what the world was starting to provide him; he would sometimes bring friends into his bedroom and open a dresser drawer to reveal that it was filled with cash, marveling along with them at his unexpected good fortune. As one of the local sportswriters would later say, "Eddie was lovable, but he was larcenous."

Like many of the top college players, Gard spent the summers in the Catskills, working first at the Pines Hotel and then at Grossinger's. He was an invaluable find for Salvatore Sollazzo, for by 1950, despite his apparent wealth, Sollazzo was in deep financial trouble. By his own characterization he was "a diseased gambler, just like a diseased narcotics user." He bet on baseball, bet on basketball, bet on the horses and the fights; said one acquaintance, "Sollazzo was the kind of a guy who would bet on two cockroaches running across the floor." As a gambler he was especially inept; the hunches he was so sure about seemed never to work out, and yet he couldn't give up the pursuit, that irreplaceable thrill of hope and danger when the clock wound down or the finish line grew near and money was on the line. Nor could he ever shake the feeling that his luck was sure to change, and so he chased each bad bet with two more, and as time went on he fell further and further behind, losing much more than he could afford. While his four-bedroom apartment cost him $450 a month in rent, in three years of gambling he lost a quarter of a million dollars.

After the war Sollazzo had devised a scheme to sell gold for a steep profit on the black market, and for a while that gambit forestalled the threat of bankruptcy; in 1950, though, he learned that the Internal Revenue Service wanted to examine his books, and suddenly he faced the prospect of losing it all, the life of opulence on which he and his wife had come to depend: the plush apartment, the cars, the mink coats, the obedience classes for Jeanne's French poodle. He needed to find a way to bring in large sums of money, quickly and reliably. Sports betting had been his downfall, but now he thought it might also be his salvation.

That summer Sollazzo entertained Eddie Gard lavishly, taking him to nightclubs and buying him drinks and dangling the prospect of easy money if he would agree to fix some games. He found in him an enthusiastic partner, for though Gard still had a semester left on his scholarship he was not planning to return to school. He had bigger, more audacious dreams—he no longer wanted to organize point-shaving for just a single college, as he had for LIU. He imagined instead running a whole city full of crooked teams, grew dizzy calculating how much he could make by offering gamblers a lock on both the NIT and NCAA tournaments. Gard was twenty-three years old and felt he was already knowledgeable and experienced enough to handle the day-to-day activities that would be involved. All he needed was someone willing to finance that operation, and Salvatore Sollazzo, he believed, could be that man.

CHAPTER 20

Day after day District Attorney Miles McDonald's rookies continued to raid bookmaking joints across Brooklyn; many of those arrested in the raids then received subpoenas to testify behind the twin smoked-glass doors of Room 405 of the Brooklyn County Courts Building. In that room twenty-two grand jurors—among them a former suffragist who had once campaigned for the right of women to serve on grand juries—sat for hours on end as a parade of witnesses took the stand. The grand jury heard testimony from policemen and bookmakers alike; bankers testified about the accounts of police officers suspected of receiving bribes, while representatives of brokerage houses detailed the officers' stock trades. McDonald's investigators, reported *The Brooklyn Daily Eagle,* were edging ever closer to a "bookmaking ring whose ramifications are reported to extend high into the borough's social and political levels"; they were "hot on the trail" of "a top borough racketeer with choice political connections."

Miles McDonald had not yet found the elusive Mr. G.

In April, rookies from McDonald's squad had raided a restaurant in the Bay Ridge section of Brooklyn and arrested the owners, Salvatore and Thomas Starace, for bookmaking. The Staraces indignantly protested that they "had paid the cops regularly"; the brothers refused to say whom exactly they had been paying off, but several policemen from the local precinct were subsequently called to testify before the grand jury. One of them was Captain John Flynn, who explained under questioning that he had heard of bookmaking going on in the Staraces' restaurant and sent a uniformed officer to investigate, but the officer found no evidence. After his testimony, Flynn was excused, and he was not required to return.

Three weeks later Captain Flynn checked in for work at the precinct house; in the captain's room he lay down on the daybed, pulled out his service revolver, and shot himself in the right temple.

Flynn left a note denying that his suicide was related to his testimony, but in police circles he was widely believed to be a casualty of the McDonald investigation. On the day of his funeral some six thousand police officers gathered at the funeral home in Queens where Captain Flynn, in a flag-draped coffin, received a Solemn Requiem Mass. At the end of the service a group of reporters clustered around the mayor to ask for his reaction. For days O'Dwyer had been saying privately that Flynn had been "hounded to death"; now he could not resist the impulse to use the occasion to inveigh against McDonald's investigation. "Nobody had the guts to say that Johnny Flynn was a clean man," answered the mayor, "but six thousand policemen walked by his children to tell them so. I'm not opposed to the gambling investigation in Brooklyn. I have aided it when asked. But I am opposed to witch hunts and the war of nerves made popular by Hitler."

O'Dwyer believed that linking McDonald with Flynn's death would, as he assured aides, "finish that knucklehead who used to work for me," but he had miscalculated the impact of his words. Raising the dark specter of Hitler only five years after the end of the Second World War, in a city still deeply traumatized by the Holocaust, seemed shockingly inappropriate and only intensified the widely held suspicion that Bill-O was losing his political touch, losing the ability, finely honed over two decades in public life, to understand and express the problems and desires of everyday New Yorkers—for while the people of the city were not especially concerned about the activities of bookmakers, they *were* concerned about the idea of police officers accepting bribes to protect those bookmakers. In his autobiography O'Dwyer acknowledged the error: "It may have been a justifiable label," he wrote, "but it was not good politics to say so, and I paid the price for the rash statement."

• • •

He was doing what he could in those months to maintain his rapport with the people of New York, the easy give-and-take that cheered him and gave him hope for the future. Often on sunny Sundays he would wander onto the lawn of Gracie Mansion and chat with neighbors through the bars of the fence; sometimes he and Sloan Simpson would stroll hand in hand through nearby Carl Schurz Park, the mayor tipping his homburg to those who passed by. O'Dwyer had also begun appearing on a new television show called *At the Mayor's Desk,* broadcast every other Thursday night. For half an hour he and various government officials would sit in his City Hall office and informally discuss the problems of New York, but as the *New Yorker* correspondent Philip Hamburger noted, "the Mayor himself is unquestionably the star of the show. Not only is he a fine figure of a man but he could give many television actors a lesson or two in how to behave in front of the cameras."

All of the great deeds he planned for his second term and that he so loved to talk about on his show—the juvenile aid initiatives, the water pollution control programs, the new highways and public housing complexes—were being overtaken by the bookmaking scandal in Brooklyn, a vast and splendid landscape dimmed by a single dark cloud. The mayor had always maintained amicable relations with the press; now he complained incessantly about the treatment he was receiving in the papers, refusing to speak to reporters for days at a time. He himself seemed unable to let go of thoughts of the burgeoning scandal, even on the most unexpected occasions. During a ceremony welcoming Australian prime minister Robert Menzies to City Hall, he praised the prime minister's "ready wit and sense of humor," then could not refrain from adding, "I am sure, sir, that you will agree that a sense of humor saves a man in public life from worrying over the machinations of his political enemies." For New Yorkers it was discomfiting to see their mayor, long known for his charm and geniality, appearing to brood in public about his "enemies."

At the end of July, Samuel Leibowitz, the judge overseeing the Brooklyn grand jury, summoned the mayor to what the newspapers termed a "peace parley." Accompanied by Police Commissioner O'Brien and several top aides, Mayor O'Dwyer drove to Brooklyn to meet Judge Leibowitz and the foreman and assistant foreman of the grand jury. Sitting down with the visitors in his chambers, the judge reminded them that his job was to ensure that the grand jury's work continued free from interference. "It seems to me," he told the mayor, "that you and other officials in this city ought to work together" rather than "engage in acrimonious newspaper debate." He had just released forty-one pages of grand jury testimony, he said, which demonstrated conclusively that Captain Flynn had been treated with the utmost respect and consideration and that his honesty had not been impugned in any way.

For his part, Mayor O'Dwyer affirmed that he had always tried to aid the inquiry—had even offered his top investigator to lead it—but that all his efforts to bring a sense of objectivity and professionalism had been thwarted by the district attorney. After half an hour the police officials departed; Samuel Leibowitz had always been known for the directness of his speech, and now, with the policemen gone, he loosened his tongue, telling the mayor that he had been acting in a partisan and intemperate manner, and then he went even further, suggesting to O'Dwyer that his usefulness as a mayor had ended and that it was in his interest and the interest of the city for him to leave office as quickly and as gracefully as possible.

Afterward, reporters were waiting for the mayor back at City Hall. "I went to Brooklyn," O'Dwyer told them, "to give Judge Leibowitz and the grand jury assurance that there would be complete cooperation from the mayor and the Police Department."

"Was there any criticism of the district attorney?" asked one of the reporters.

O'Dwyer hesitated for a moment, then said only: "No comment."

"Do you still think that Mr. McDonald is conducting a witch hunt?"

"No comment."

"Do you still think the grand jury is pursuing Hitler tactics?"

"I never said that, and I told the grand jury that today."

Despite Judge Leibowitz's sterling reputation in the city, O'Dwyer deeply distrusted him, considering him a headline chaser and a political climber. Still, he considered it a remarkable day when a County Court judge felt free to tell the mayor of the City of New York that he should resign. Rumors were flying about what the Brooklyn grand jury was learning. They were zeroing in on the big man, it was said, the bookmaking kingpin with the political ties; there was talk that wiretaps conducted by McDonald's squad had captured conversations between bookmakers and cops that included the names of New York City political officials—even that of the mayor. Years later he would write of that period, "I somehow felt things getting away from me."

Late nights he often rambled around Gracie Mansion, worrying and brooding, the only one awake in the house other than the security detail, who dared not intrude on his privacy. Sloan was always urging him to attend the social functions for which he had less and less patience; she preferred to go out at night, escaping the tension that had begun to pervade the house. After returning from their Florida honeymoon she had set out to redecorate the mansion, hanging Irish paintings on loan from the Metropolitan Museum of Art, rearranging the living room so that more people could sit in one area for after-dinner conversation. Of late, friends had begun to remark on the wistfulness that had crept into his talk, the stories of his boyhood in Bohola. It was a little world of bogs and stone huts and star-filled nights, where he had no dreams greater than to become a village schoolteacher like his parents; his father, though, had wanted him to test his mettle in America. "In the USA," he said, "you'll either be a bum or a man." Now he lived in a colonial house overlooking the river, with pictures of Irish scenes on the wall; it was a beautiful home, far better than any other he would ever know, and he would be sorry when he had to leave it.

One night in August, reading by lamplight in his study, he received a most unwelcome visitor.

Edward J. Flynn had run the Bronx Democratic machine for the previous twenty-eight years. During that time the Bronx had not elected a single Republican official; a political candidate nominated by the local machine was such a shoo-in to be elected that he was said to be "in like Flynn."*

Ed Flynn confounded every stereotype of the urban party boss: He was patrician in manner, tall and silver haired, an avid horticulturalist with a taste for literature and fine art, likely the only political boss ever to have his memoir excerpted in the pages of *The Atlantic Monthly*. Intro-

---

* Though the phrase is widely associated with the actor Errol Flynn, etymologist Eric Partridge indicates that it originated with Ed Flynn, whose "Democratic Party machine exercised absolute political control over the Bronx. . . . The candidates he backed were almost automatically 'in'—and he himself permanently so."

spective and aloof by nature, prone to bouts of melancholia, Flynn was uncomfortable in crowds, which for a big-city politician of the time was akin to a physician who recoils at the sight of blood. He abhorred back-slapping and glad-handing and rarely appeared at the benevolent association dinners and police smokers on which William O'Dwyer had built a career. He much preferred to spend time at his upstate farmhouse or the ranch where he bred racehorses, or pass the evening playing gin rummy or Russian bank at home with his wife. Flynn maintained his control of the party machinery in large part through the adroit dispensation of patronage—including jobs for leaders of the local Republican Party, as he understood that this would reduce the incentive for genuine opposition. Though he was a strong supporter of Franklin Roosevelt, he was continually frustrated by New Dealers ("amateur politicians," in his disdainful phrase) who were willing to provide patronage even to those not connected to party organizations; Flynn firmly believed that politics was important enough that, like medicine or engineering or the law, it should be left to the professionals.

Under Flynn's command the Bronx was, by percentage, the most heavily Democratic territory anywhere north of the Mason-Dixon Line, reliably providing huge numbers of votes to elect Democratic officials statewide and deliver the state in national elections. In 1940 he had been named chairman of the Democratic National Committee, and he had served as the campaign manager for Roosevelt's 1940 and 1944 presidential campaigns. Along with the Manhattan Tammany Hall chieftain he was also responsible for putting together the Democratic ticket in New York City elections, negotiating various constituencies to create an optimally balanced ballot line, with candidates representing the Democratic strongholds of Manhattan, Brooklyn, and the Bronx, and ideally including at least one Irishman, one Italian, and one Jew. He was the consummate political professional, able to read even the gentlest of political winds, and it was not hard for him to see how damaged William O'Dwyer had become; Flynn recognized that the McDonald investigation was going to expose serious public graft and police corruption, and he believed it would be prudent for the Democratic Party to remove those tainted by the bookmaking scandal before the voters next went to the polls.

Furthermore, a New York gubernatorial election was scheduled for that coming November. The Republican incumbent, Thomas E. Dewey, was a popular governor, and the only way he might be defeated was to dramatically increase Democratic turnout, especially in New York City—and the most effective way to increase the city's turnout was to hold a mayoral election on the same day. O'Dwyer, however, had only just been reelected, and the seat would not open up again until 1953. And so, Flynn reasoned, it would be necessary to hold a special mayoral election that coming November, with a new field of candidates, and that would mean persuading O'Dwyer to resign.

So Ed Flynn traveled to the White House, where he met with President Harry S. Truman in the Oval Office. In 1944, when Franklin Roosevelt wanted Truman to be nominated as vice president, it was Flynn to whom he entrusted the important and delicate task of convincing party leaders around the country to support the choice; Truman had not forgotten the service, and after he succeeded Roosevelt he retained Flynn in the informal position of the president's man in New York. Now Flynn explained to President Truman that for the good of the party, Bill-O had to be gotten rid of.

Flynn's proposition to Truman had an almost fiendish cleverness: In 1948 O'Dwyer had publicly suggested that Truman should be replaced at the top of the Democratic ticket, because, he argued, Truman could not beat the Republican presidential nominee, Thomas Dewey. The notion of increasing Democratic turnout in the gubernatorial election by means of a special New York City mayoral election thus presented Truman with the gratifying prospect of dispensing with both O'Dwyer and Dewey in a single blow.

As it happened, the president had recently received the resignation of the career diplomat Walter C. Thurston, who had been serving as U.S. ambassador to Mexico. He would send O'Dwyer to Mexico, Truman told Flynn. There was just one problem: The ambassadorial position paid only $25,000 a year—would O'Dwyer be willing to take a $15,000-a-year pay cut?

"Don't worry," said Flynn. "He'll take it."

It was nearly midnight when Ed Flynn arrived at Gracie Mansion. O'Dwyer himself answered the door; together he and Flynn walked through the grand foyer and into the living room. Earlier in the evening the mayor had attended a political dinner, and he was still wearing his black dinner jacket, with a starched white shirt beneath. Flynn was dressed, as he always was, in an expensive, finely cut suit with a boutonniere in the lapel and a flowered Charvet tie. He settled into an easy chair as O'Dwyer poured them a pair of whiskeys.

The two men sat contemplatively with their drinks; from beyond the darkened window they could hear the mournful call of the foghorns on the river. After a while Flynn said, "I guess you know why I'm here, Bill."

"Yeah," O'Dwyer replied in a quiet voice. The lamp above his head had whitened his graying hair, so that he appeared unexpectedly old.

"Well, how do you feel about it?"

"How can I feel?" The indignation of his tone seemed briefly to energize him, and for a moment it was as though he were back on the campaign stump reciting his own accomplishments, as he reminded Flynn of the years of service he had given New York, the countless favors he had provided for their friends in the party.

"It's pretty late, Bill," Flynn interrupted. "Now, look—we want you out just as soon as possible. Maybe within two weeks."

With that O'Dwyer seemed to crumple a bit, and for a long while he just sat silently, staring at the carpet. Then he raised his head and said, "What have they got for me?"

"You're lucky," Flynn replied. "I've been to see the president. He says, if nothing goes wrong before then, you can be ambassador to Mexico."

O'Dwyer sighed. He had spent so many nights strolling the long porch outside, even snowy nights, stormy nights, just marveling at the lights of the city shimmering in the distance. He would, he knew, never get New York out of his head. At last he said faintly, "All right."

"Very good," said Flynn. "You'll be hearing from me." He rose and left the room, leaving the mayor sitting alone in the lamplight.

At six o'clock on the evening of August 14, Mayor William O'Dwyer boarded a Pennsylvania Railroad express train bound for Washington, D.C. No explanation was given for the sudden trip, though it was generally understood that he would be meeting the next day with President Truman at the White House. As it turned out, they met for no more than twenty minutes; afterward came an announcement from the president's secretary that Mayor O'Dwyer would resign his office at the end of the month and would then be appointed United States ambassador to Mexico. "I had a conversation with the president that made up my mind," O'Dwyer explained to reporters in the drawing room of the train returning home. "What that conversation was I am not going to disclose."

The next day O'Dwyer attended a meeting of the city's Board of Estimate at City Hall, the final such meeting he would oversee as presiding officer. In a voice choked with emotion he told those gathered in the chamber, "I am saying this morning my official goodbye to the city. I want you to remember that a city that took in an immigrant forty years ago, gave him every opportunity, and step by step honored him over and above his just deserts. . . ." There the mayor's voice broke, and he paused to wipe his eyes with a handkerchief. "We pray," he continued after a moment, "that when we leave we will leave a city, state, and nation better for those who follow us. I haven't words to say any more. I have tears, but you don't want them."

With that he resumed his seat, putting on his tortoiseshell reading glasses and lighting his curved-stem pipe. For the next hour, the Board of Estimate proceeded to hand out $116,000 worth of raises to various officials on the city's payroll. The mayor's two police chauffeurs were promoted to deputy police commissioner; his bodyguard, Detective Joseph Boyle—the man who had claimed that he'd accidentally started the fire in the mayor's hospital suite—was likewise made a deputy police commissioner. Not surprisingly, the most prized appointment of all went to Bill-O's closest aide, James Moran: He was named a commissioner of the city's Board of Water Supply, a well-paying lifetime appointment and not subject to the discretion of future mayors. Moran's only apparent qualification for the job was his career of service to William O'Dwyer. It was, reporters Norton Mockridge and Robert Prall noted in their book *The Big Fix*, "one of the most shocking appointments ever made by any mayor in the history of New York."

• • •

On September 2, 1950, the city clerk received a letter bearing the official seal of the city. It read simply: "Dear Sir: I hereby resign as Mayor of the City of New York. Very truly yours, William O'Dwyer."

Thirteen days later, Chief Investigator William Dahut and another detective burst into Room 1116 of the Towers Hotel in Brooklyn Heights. The room was furnished with richly upholstered chairs, thick carpeting, and gold brocade draperies, and it opened onto a terrace that commanded a magnificent view of New York Harbor. Though it was almost eleven o'clock in the morning, the room's occupant, a paunchy young man with slicked-back black hair and manicured nails, was unshaven and wore only pajama bottoms.

"We're from the district attorney's office," said Dahut, flashing his badge.

Harry Gross nodded. "I've been expecting you fellows for some time," he said.

CHAPTER 21

Months earlier, a tip from an irate gambler with the Dickensian name of Danny Fagin had led Miles McDonald's investigative squad to a different Brooklyn hotel, the Hotel St. George. A search of the register found that room 724 had been signed for by Harry Gross, and after discussions with hotel officials, a detective named Theresa Scagnelli began work as a chambermaid assigned exclusively to the seventh floor.

Each morning she and one of the hotel's maids worked together making beds, emptying wastepaper baskets, vacuuming carpets. She never entered room 724 until Gross had left; then, as she cleaned, Detective Scagnelli conducted a surreptitious search while the other chambermaid—who knew nothing of her partner's true occupation—was busy in another room in the suite. On the third day, rummaging around in a dresser drawer, she found an unexpected treasure: a small black address book, which she glanced through and then quickly replaced. The following day she slid the book into an apron pocket as she called out to her partner that she was going to use the bathroom; with the door closed, she hurriedly copied a few names and phone numbers onto a slip of paper that she hid in her brassiere before returning the book to the drawer. Each day Scagnelli would take the address book into the bathroom and copy out as much as she could without drawing suspicion, and each evening, back at headquarters, she would relay the information she had obtained to Miles McDonald and William Dahut.*

To simply take the address book would have alarmed Harry Gross, of course; the plan, instead, was to keep watch on him while he unknowingly led the investigative squad to all of those with whom he did business. Dahut assigned rookie cops to tail those in Gross's book, and before long the squad had discovered dozens of betting parlors throughout the city, hidden like secret compartments in the back rooms of taverns and candy stores and auto repair shops. One day, however, Gross abruptly checked out of the Hotel St. George, leaving no forwarding address. Questioning of employees revealed that he had been paying some of the hotel's phone operators twenty-five dollars a week to let him know if they ever heard his name mentioned on a call; an operator had reported that one of the maids assigned to his floor was actually a police detective, and without delay Harry packed up his things and left.

The trail had once again grown cold, and it would be some time before Harry Gross was sighted again and followed to his new place of residence, the Towers Hotel in Brooklyn Heights. By that point McDonald and Dahut had also learned the telephone number of Gross's "wire room," the clearinghouse into which all of his bookmakers called in the bets they had received. The number was listed to a business address in the town of Inwood, just beyond the city line on Long Island. Judge Samuel Leibowitz signed a warrant for a wiretap to be placed on the phone lines leading into the Inwood office; a patrolman who had formerly worked for the phone company ran an underground line that stretched across three counties back to the investigation headquarters in Brooklyn, where all of the calls coming into or out of the wire room were listened to and recorded. The phones there rang all day long, transferred by the switchboard operator to one of the four clerks on duty. It was all in a day's work for Gross's clerks, but for the investigators wearing the headphones, bent over their desks penciling long columns of digits into their notebooks, the numbers were truly staggering. The amount of money that passed through Gross's gambling ring was far greater than

* In later years, under her married name, Theresa Scagnelli Melchionne, she would become the first female deputy commissioner in the history of the New York Police Department.

anyone on the squad had ever contemplated—his bookmakers turned out to be handling at least $75,000 a day in bets, or more than $20 million a year.*

Investigators also listened in as the manager of the wire room placed a call to Gross to tell him that he had heard talk that the room was "hot"—under surveillance—and that they should probably clear out before it was raided. When this conversation was relayed back to investigation headquarters, McDonald called together his top aides; they had to strike quickly, he decided, before Gross moved and they once again lost the trail. The squad of rookie cops was broken up into teams assigned to locate Gross's bookmakers throughout the city in preparation for arrest. A special team led by an assistant district attorney and accompanied by several Nassau County policemen would raid the Inwood wire room. The time was set for the next day at 12:30.

Just before eleven o'clock that morning, September 15, 1950, Chief Investigator William Dahut knocked on the door of room 1116 of the Towers Hotel.

Even as a boy Harry Gross had been known around his Brooklyn neighborhood as fast-talking and quick-witted, always looking for a scheme that might bring him some money. As someone who knew him then would recall, "He had a sharp mind and a baby face and he could take you for your last dime." After school, when other kids gathered for a game of stickball, he'd rush off to a local newspaper vendor to pick up a stack of papers to sell. Harry never sold them himself, though; he passed off the papers to a gang of younger boys to hawk on street corners, then took half of their profits as the "distributor." Around this time, in sixth grade, Harry fell down the stairs in his apartment building, breaking his leg. When his friends came by to visit he would casually suggest that they play casino or blackjack to pass the time, just for small stakes; he always ended up winning, and it was a couple of weeks before one of the kids noticed that Harry was switching cards under the table with others that he had hidden in his plaster cast.

Though he was bright, Harry had no interest in school, and at the

---

* $20 million in 1950 is equivalent to about $213,000,000 in today's currency.

age of fourteen he announced to his parents that he was through with his education and persuaded them to sign his working papers. Before long he had gotten a job in a drugstore; in his spare time he also ran errands for a local bookie, and when the bookie asked if he wanted to go to work for him, taking bets over the counter of the drugstore, Harry immediately agreed. When the other bookies who did business in the drugstore discovered what he was doing, though, they complained to the owner that the kid was trying to chisel in on their territory, and Harry was fired. He found work at a different drugstore, but soon he was dismissed from there too, and when the same thing happened at a luncheonette, Harry decided that it was time to begin working for himself.

On a winter's day in 1941—he was now twenty-four years old—Harry was standing on a Flatbush street corner taking a bet from a customer when he was approached by a patrolman. He was operating like a small-timer, the cop told him, making book without police protection; he should smarten up and work out an arrangement with the plainclothes squad, who could give him the okay so that he never risked arrest. For fifty dollars the cop agreed to set up a meeting at a nearby restaurant, where Harry and some of the plainclothesmen of the local division worked out a system of regular payments. One night later that year Harry won a luncheonette from a restaurateur in a big craps game in the Edison Hotel. He renamed it the H and G Luncheonette and instructed the countermen to let it be known that from now on, customers who wanted to could lay a bet on a horse there, or buy a shot of liquor under the table at a lower price than the local bars were charging. With the profits from the luncheonette he opened a couple of horse rooms in other neighborhoods, and before long, payments only to the local plainclothes squads did not suffice; he needed protection on a larger scale, and he began paying squads that had jurisdiction across Brooklyn.

Harry was short and thick-set, with wavy dark hair and heavy brows and a jowly face with a permanent five-o'clock shadow; he was a meticulous dresser, his wardrobe running to monogrammed shirts, hand-painted ties, and linen handkerchiefs with hand-rolled edges. Though he wasn't conventionally good-looking, women often found him attractive, for he was animated and talkative and had an apparently unshakable self-confidence. In 1942 he married a secretary named Lila Oransky; before long they had a son and a daughter, and Harry bought the family a house by the ocean on Long Island, which is where he lived when he wasn't staying in the city on business, overseeing his betting parlors and the handouts to local cops.

Among the policemen Harry was then paying off was a young plainclothes officer named Jimmy Reardon. Reardon was said to be very well connected within the Police Department—so much so that he had never even worn a uniform, having moved straight from the Police Academy to a plum position in the squad assigned to the police inspector. Reardon was a heavy drinker with a loud laugh and a volcanic temper who was known to be good with his fists; handsome and debonair and carrying a persistent whiff of violence, he was a commanding physical presence in the Sinatra mold, and Harry Gross immediately sensed that the two of them could establish a formidable partnership. Reardon, too, had dreams of a bigger life for himself, one that included an uptown pied-à-terre away from his wife and kids during the week and, for the weekends, a family house in Connecticut and membership in a private golf club: the sort of country-squire life he could never hope for on a policeman's salary. After only a brief career in plainclothes he quit the force and threw in with Gross full time.

Reardon set to work winning the backing of his many friends in the department, paying for drinks and dinners in expensive restaurants and getting them tickets to Broadway shows and the fights at Madison Square Garden, and over time it became known that most of the plainclothesmen in the city were on his side. With the weight of the Police Department behind him he was able to put the squeeze on rival bookies, demanding that they join the Harry Gross syndicate or close up shop. Gross and Reardon established betting rooms throughout the city, all operating with the consent of the local precinct houses; often, when trying to decide where to open a new place, they consulted with the cops walking the beat.

The protection money (the "ice," as Harry liked to call it) was doled out according to payment plans that had been negotiated in meetings conducted inside precinct houses, an intricate and carefully scaled taxonomy of graft. A police lieutenant, for instance, would receive fifty dollars per month for each of the bookmaking locations in his district, as would the captain; the sergeants also got their assigned share, as did the detectives, and the plainclothesmen, and the foot patrolmen, and the men in the squad cars. At Christmas everyone got an extra payment as a holiday gift: "double ice."

Gross made his main headquarters in the Dugout Cafe, an otherwise nondescript bar and grill not far from Ebbets Field in the Flatbush section of Brooklyn. Despite the neon sign out front that promised DINING & ENTERTAINMENT, the Dugout was mostly a dark, quiet place, except on afternoons after Dodger games, when throngs of fans would raise glasses of Rheingold or Schaefer to toast a victory or drown a defeat—and on the first and fifteenth of every month, payoff days. On those days a steady stream of police officers, in and out of uniform, would slip into the restroom only to emerge a few minutes later holding a thick envelope or, if they were collecting for an entire precinct house, a package. The pickup man for Captain Frank Bals's "super squad"— the special squad that Mayor O'Dwyer had set up ostensibly to investigate police corruption—would arrive at the Dugout with an empty bushel basket, and Gross's cashiers would fill it with money.

In April 1948, having received a complaint of bookmaking being conducted at the Dugout Cafe, a justice of the New York State Supreme Court directed the Police Department to install a wiretap on the restaurant's phones. Incredibly, the plainclothes officer charged with setting up the wiretap informed the Dugout's owner ahead of time that he would be doing so. At the back of the restaurant was a vacant lot, and the policemen who conducted the wiretaps would station themselves in the lot from noon to two o'clock, clearly visible not only to the patrons of the restaurant but to anyone passing on the street. "The basic objective of tapping the wire of the Dugout was obviously frustrated by the physical manner in which the said police officer tapped these wires," noted the Brooklyn grand jury in its final report. "It is scarcely necessary to add that no evidence of bookmaking was obtained as a result of said wire-tapping." In fact, the police were using the wiretap for an entirely different purpose: The officers on duty would listen to the conversations and mark down the names of the bookies who got mentioned—and then check out each one to make sure he was paying his protection money as required and therefore not subject to arrest.

At the end of each day the officers conducting the wiretaps destroyed the tapes on which the conversations had been recorded; the police lieutenant charged with supervising the wiretap never ordered his men to make written reports to him, nor did he ever instruct them to retain their notes of the conversations. "There should have been a written record at Police Headquarters," District Attorney Miles McDonald would later complain, "a summary of the conversation overheard if not a fully detailed record."

That records of wiretaps were not being properly maintained at police headquarters—and that tapes of potentially incriminating conversations had not been preserved—would later prove to be a crucial element in the city's other notorious bookmaking scandal.

By the close of the 1940s, Harry Gross had become Mr. G, a bookmaking kingpin with thirty-five betting parlors operating throughout New York City and its suburbs. He was laying out more than a million dollars a year in ice, not to mention the hundreds of gifts that he lavished on his friends in the Police Department, the cars and watches and cases of top-shelf liquor, the custom suits from Manhattan's finest clothiers. For the Graziano-Zale middleweight championship fight in 1947, Gross invited five policemen to join him and Jimmy Reardon on an all-expenses-paid trip to Chicago, complete with nightclub passes and a day at the Arlington Park racetrack. That was the same year that a veteran police lieutenant asked him for a favor: He had $135,000 in five-hundred-dollar and thousand-dollar bills that he needed to exchange for smaller denominations, and Harry was happy to convert the money into tens and twenties, no questions asked. There seemed almost no favor that Harry Gross could not provide, no wish he was unable or unwilling to grant— like the time he used his influence to gain admission for a policeman's daughter to her chosen college, Sweet Briar in Virginia.

It was more than just business: Harry loved socializing with cops, relished the sense of invulnerability that their companionship imparted, and they loved socializing with him, too, hobnobbing in a private box at the racetrack or corner table in one of the clubs where all the maître d's knew him by name, reveling in how easy everything seemed to be with Harry around, easy laughter and easy money and easy women. Twice a week Harry would rent a suite in an expensive hotel and invite eight or ten members of the police force to join him for a small party. He always chose his guests according to their rank; one night only deputy police inspectors would be invited, while on another night it might be only lieutenants and captains. Arriving at the suite, the guests would be greeted by Gross and Reardon and four or five beautiful young women wearing evening gowns; they would sit on couches and in easy chairs for cocktails and conversation, until there was a knock on the door and a team of bellhops would roll in a multicourse dinner under silver domes for everyone to enjoy, and after a couple of hours the men would relax with brandy and cigars and someone would begin playing a piano, and in the dim smoky light the women would stand and remove their dresses; and more liquor would flow, and as the hour grew later the music became louder and the laughter more uninhibited, and the guests were invited, if they liked, to escort one of the women (each of whom Gross was paying fifty dollars for the evening) into one of the adjoining bedrooms.

It wasn't long before Harry Gross's self-confidence had bloomed into arrogance, the conviction that he had the system beat, that he could outsmart anyone who came after him, and that, with the Police Department in his pocket, he was untouchable. Harry did have one problem, though, which was that he was a gambler himself—and while he was an exceptional bookmaker, he was a very poor gambler, in large part because he always believed he could find an angle on a bet even when there was none to be found. Nor was he satisfied with a small wager when he might win so much more with a big one, and once he had ready cash at his disposal he began to bet very big indeed, sometimes as much as $5,000 on a single ball game, and while he won often enough to keep himself interested, most of the time he lost. "You fat jerk," said Jimmy Reardon when he found out about the gambling, "from now on you leave the betting to the suckers."

But Gross couldn't stop, not when he was losing and was sure that he could figure out a way to get even. He was placing his bets with Frank Erickson, the powerful Manhattan bookie who was also known to be the bookmaker for other bookmakers; all through the summer of 1949, Gross bet on baseball, and then in the fall he switched to football, and with each week his losses mounted. Hoping to change his luck, he switched to the horses, and despite a long losing streak he still kept betting, and eventually something snapped inside him and that weekend he went on a horse-playing binge; he became, in the bookie's term of art, a plunger, desperately chasing the next winner, calling in bet after bet for more and more money, but if anything his luck grew even worse, the hole he was in ever deeper, and after three days, when he was finally too drained to bet any more, he had lost nearly $170,000.*

He was now virtually broke, no longer able to pay the money he owed the winning bettors in his own bookmaking syndicate. Exhausted and terrified and not knowing what else to do, he threw some suits in a bag and, after stopping by a couple of his own betting parlors to pick up several thousand dollars in cash, raced to Newark Airport, where he boarded the first flight to California.

Harry took a room at the Hollywood Plaza Hotel; it was several days before he could bring himself to call Jimmy Reardon and tell him where he was. Reardon cursed him out, just as Harry had expected he would, even threatening to fly to California and beat him up personally, but after a while he calmed down a bit and told Harry to sit tight while he figured out what to do.

A shock wave ran through many of the city's police precincts when word got around that Harry Gross had been forced to close up shop. Hundreds of cops had come to rely on the ice that arrived every other week, as steady and dependable as a government paycheck; they counted on it when planning for family vacations or enrolling their children in parochial school, when buying a new car or a more expensive home. Now that extra income had suddenly dried up.

After several weeks, in November 1949, Reardon sent word to Gross that it was safe for him to return to Brooklyn. Harry rented a suite in the Hotel St. George, where he was visited by a delegation of New York City detectives. One hundred thousand dollars had been put together for him by three high-ranking members of the Police Department; it was not a gift but a loan, meant for Harry to recapitalize his bookmaking operation and start the protection money flowing again.

By this point the police were no longer merely Harry Gross's beneficiaries; now they were his business partners.

· · ·

---

* $170,000 in 1949 is equivalent to about $1,770,000 in today's currency.

"Make yourself comfortable," Harry Gross said to Inspector William Dahut. "Mind if I get dressed?"

Dahut indicated that he should feel free, and Harry stepped into the bathroom, where he washed and shaved; then he returned to the bedroom, still wearing only his pajama bottoms, and after some consideration picked out a pearl-gray flannel suit. As he dressed, Harry kept up a constant conversation, bragging about the quality of the twenty-two pairs of shoes that lined the floor of the closet, noting how when he found a shirt he liked he always bought a dozen or so. When he finished he gave himself a last look in the mirror. He turned to Dahut. "What are we waiting for?" he said. "I'm ready. Let's go."

Dahut checked his watch: it was only just noon. "No, not yet," he said. "We've got half an hour to wait."

"You got something else going this morning?"

"Yeah. Matter of fact, we have. A little job out at Inwood."

For just an instant Dahut saw a nervous tic flicker across Harry Gross's right eye, an involuntary suggestion of weakness that over time the detective would come to know well. Harry slumped down on the bed. "Christ," he murmured under his breath. Then he turned to Dahut and said, "Well, I guess it figures. But it's the damnedest thing—I was gonna move the joint next week."

At precisely 12:30 Dahut told him to get his things, it was time to go. "That's yours. Take it," Dahut said, gesturing to the bureau, where a thick wad of bills lay in a gold money clip. Gross looked at him for a moment, as if considering the angle, then just nodded and slipped the clip into his pants pocket. It was the first time, he would later say, that a cop had ever let him pick up his own money.

Miles McDonald's rookie squad made thirty-five arrests that day. Inside the Municipal Building in Brooklyn, the normally sedate district attorney's office had erupted into chaos, with loudly protesting bookies being hauled in and out, shepherded into any available room to be interrogated by detectives and assistant district attorneys as stenographers took down the conversations and handed off their notes to secretaries who typed the reports onto thick sheaves of white paper and purple carbons.

Rather than being brought to the district attorney's office, Harry Gross was taken to the investigation headquarters at 184 Joralemon Street. He sat by himself for an hour until finally Assistant District Attorney Julius Helfand entered and took a seat across the table. "It's nice to have you with us, Mr. Gross," he said.

"Well, enjoy me while you can," Gross said. "I won't be here long."

Helfand smiled mildly. "No?"

"No. How long can you hold me? Only twenty-four hours at the most. Then I've got to get out on bail. And I don't care how high you make the bail, I'll get it up. Even if you make it fifty thousand, I'll have it in ten minutes."

Gross, though, was unaware that he would not be held on a bookmaking charge. Instead, District Attorney McDonald planned to hold him as a material witness in a case against corrupt police officers, and as a material witness he could be held at astronomical levels of bail; in this case, a quarter of a million dollars—more money than even Harry Gross could produce.

Gross was driven to the Raymond Street jail, a grim, turreted stone fortress known as Brooklyn's Bastille. His expensive gray suit was exchanged for a set of prison grays and he was placed in a tiny, dimly lit cell. He had been in jail before, as a young bookmaker without police protection, but never for more than a couple of hours; now he sat for days on end, in deeper trouble than he had ever contemplated, a place even his friends in the Police Department seemed unable to reach. He had been a part of so many crimes over the years, the bookmaking of course but also bribery and money laundering and prostitution, plus misuse of police property and likely dozens of other charges he didn't even have names for but was certain that McDonald did, and sitting in jail he felt a rising panic: he had seen what happened to guys who turned state's evidence. Look at Kid Twist, the star witness against Murder, Inc. when O'Dwyer was Brooklyn DA—he had been placed in the tightest possible police custody, provided with his own special detail to watch him around the clock, and yet he had still ended up dead five floors beneath his hotel room window in Coney Island.* And Harry

* Kid Twist (whose real name was Abe Reles) would enter New York City lore as "the canary who could sing but couldn't fly."

knew all too well which police officer had been in charge of Kid Twist's protective detail—it was Captain Frank Bals, who would later be appointed head of Mayor O'Dwyer's anticorruption squad, the one whose payoff man used to show up at the Dugout with the empty bushel basket.

Now Lila was threatening to divorce him; he knew that his unannounced flight to California had not helped the situation, nor the fact that he spent most nights in the city. She certainly wasn't going to wait for him to finish a long prison sentence, but on the other hand he wouldn't be any good to her dead, either. No matter how hard Harry looked he couldn't figure out a play; for four nights he tossed and turned on his prison cot, increasingly distraught, unable to decide whether to testify. Finally, on September 19, 1950, he requested an interview with Samuel Leibowitz, the county judge overseeing the work of the special grand jury.

The two men met in the judge's chambers in the Criminal Courts Building. Dark crescent moons of sleeplessness waxed under Harry Gross's eyes; his cheeks were the gray of a newspaper photograph. He had a difficult decision to make, he told the judge. If he wanted to, he could tell a story of vast corruption in the Police Department, spill it all, provide whatever information the grand jury needed: names, dates, amounts paid. Still, he had a conscience and he couldn't help but worry about the policemen who would be implicated by his testimony; he considered these men to be not just business associates but friends—he had been in their homes, had attended the graduations of their children. He wondered how he could ever face them again if he testified. The words poured out in a torrent. He had come that day, he said, because he felt he could sit down and talk with the judge at least—could hear from him if he was doing right or wrong. Harry turned to face the judge directly, his eyes filled with tears. "Your Honor," he said, "what should I do?"

Samuel Leibowitz had close-cropped white hair and bushy dark eyebrows, and his expression as he listened to Harry Gross was stern but kindly. It had been his experience, he said, that the only honorable path lay in the truth. "Tell the truth without fear or favor—that is my advice. If there is any fear that you have of anybody doing you any harm, you can rest assured that the arm of the court will stretch out to protect you. These are things that are not new in the world. A man makes a decision about whether he is going to stand on the side of truth and on the side of law and order, or on the other side of the line. That decision he must make himself. Now, my advice to you is to go ahead and tell the truth."

The two men talked for a while longer, and when the meeting was over Miles McDonald and Julius Helfand led Harry Gross back down the corridor to the elevator.

Harry turned to McDonald. "You know," he said, "I have a hunch there are going to be a lot of worried people in the city soon."

CHAPTER 22

Before the 1950–51 college basketball season began, a United Press poll of thirty-five leading basketball coaches ranked City College the number one team in the nation—a finding that in any other year a newspaper reader would surely have goggled at and concluded was a misprint, but now was only to be expected.

City College head coach Nat Holman, though, could not help but wonder: Would the Beavers be able to repeat? It was a question asked of him everywhere he went—by an usher during intermission at the theater, by a waiter at Leone's, even by a reporter who tracked him down while he was on vacation with his wife in the Berkshires. He gave the same response each time: "I wish I knew." Faculty manager of athletics Sam Winograd had put together a grueling schedule for the Beavers that season. It included trips to Detroit, Chicago, Cleveland, Boston, and Philadelphia, with only a single game out of twenty-one in the college's Main Gym. Every one of their opponents, Holman understood, would treat the game against City College like a tournament game, seeking the prestige that would be conferred on the squad that finally dethroned the reigning champs. He was confident about this year's team, though by no means overly so. Irwin Dambrot was irreplaceable, of course, but fortunately he still had the two Eds, Warner and Roman. Together they had the potential to be the most devastating one-two scoring punch on any college squad in the country, and before the preseason workouts began, he named them team cocaptains.

While in earlier years the preseason workouts had been relatively secluded affairs, now the City College gym regularly hosted a throng of reporters. The practices began promptly at four o'clock each afternoon, at which time, one reporter observed, "a strange electrical charge seems to pervade the atmosphere of the College's main gym." It was not only that the gym had been fitted with new fluorescent lighting, nor that the court had been varnished to such a high sheen that the players could see themselves in it. The players themselves looked spruced up: Though only half a year had passed since the tournaments, they seemed more mature, sleeker somehow, not quite so much the scruffy kids from the streets of New York. Floyd Layne, for one, now sported a mustache. Eddie Roman wore his championship ring (he never took it off, not even during practices), but a handkerchief no longer dangled from a belt loop on his shorts, as though that holdover from his high school playing days, that banner of sinus problems, was not suitable for a team cocaptain and the college's all-time leading scorer.

For the most part the practices were conducted with little conversation, in a deliberate, businesslike manner. None of those inside the gym, either as participant or observer, could ignore the question that swirled outside it: *Can they repeat?* An especially acute pressure was felt by the juniors who would make up that year's starting five, the players who, having won the Grand Slam as sophomores, now faced two seasons of the highest possible expectations; Leonard Ansell of the *New York World-Telegram and Sun* wrote of a general perception that the "club must repeat as titleholders or look bad." Another reporter in attendance during the first week noted that an unusual tension seemed to pervade the practice, with the players moving "quietly and cautiously on the yellow floor of the Main Gym . . . silent as they displayed their skills." During one break in the action, Al Roth and Floyd Layne took a moment to get a drink of water. At the water fountain Roth turned to Floyd and said, "You know, this is the quietest team I ever saw."

Al Roth had been talking to Eddie Gard since the previous summer about the possibility of shaving points. At the time, Gard was serving as Salvatore Sollazzo's go-between: introducing him to the basketball players with whom Gard worked at Grossinger's, driving together through the Catskills in Sollazzo's black Cadillac to visit the hotels where Gard knew some of the players. Among them was his fellow Brooklynite Roth, who was working at the Hotel Brickman. There was something about Sollazzo that Roth found unnerving, his sharp eyes and thin lizard smile, a sense of threat and desperation that seemed to lurk beneath the air of bonhomie. "The first time I met Sollazzo," he was to say later, "just looking at him scared the shit out of me." Gard, though, gave his eager spiel about how he had big plans for his operation, how he was reaching out to all the top college teams in the city, how City wouldn't want to be left out in the cold—and Fats, in truth, did not require much convincing. He said that he would talk to Eddie Roman.

Eddie had shaved points during the previous season, of course, in games against Southern Methodist and UCLA (the second one a makeup for the previous blown attempt), but he hadn't liked doing it and had dropped out of the deal as soon as he could. Even so, he had to admit in retrospect that everything had worked out okay, just as Norm Mager had promised: The points had been shaved and the money delivered and even though they lost a few games they should have won, the Beavers had still gone further than anyone could have dreamed.

That year had been without question the most eventful of Eddie's life, and in returning to City for his junior year he found that he was oddly discontented. "I'm back in school now, and things are just as normal as they ever were," he told Leonard Ansell that fall, adding enigmatically, "Somehow when you're young everything seems so much more important than it actually is. I mean winning the championships and everything. It was wonderful, but somehow it didn't turn out exactly the way I thought it would be." Ansell noted that Eddie had developed a broader outlook than was typical in the college players he interviewed, that he seemed somehow "liberated from the boundaries of the Bronx"; at the age of twenty he spoke with a gravity and sense of purpose that the sportswriter described as "the wisdom of a much older person."

Eddie wasn't sure about doing business with Gard, he told Fats, but in any case he knew he didn't want to come in unless Ed Warner did too. Roth agreed, and he conveyed this provision to Eddie Gard, explaining that Warner was City's best player, and they worried that over time he might begin to wonder why he wasn't getting the ball in key scoring opportunities and might bring his concerns to Nat Holman—and if Nat got even a whisper, Roth said, that would be the end of them.

That rationale was improbable, to say the least, as they had shaved points several times the year before without Warner's expressing any suspicions; moreover, Warner had virtually no relationship with Holman, and given Warner's friendliness with professional gamblers in Harlem and his background as a numbers runner, there seemed no chance that he of all people would report them to the authorities. It seems far more likely that Roman did not want to get involved without the participation of his cocaptain, unwilling to re-create on the team the implicit racial division that Eli Kaye had earlier established in his fixing, in which only white players were trusted to shave points. Roman could be confident that Warner would want in on the scheme, just as Floyd Layne, who was the straightest arrow he knew—an actual Boy Scout—likely never would; he felt uncomfortable even bringing the subject up with Floyd.

Eddie Gard assured Roth that he would get Warner. He had begun talking to him over the summer as well, in the Catskills, where Warner was working as a busboy at Klein's Hillside Hotel. Initially Warner had not seemed interested, but Gard persisted in his recruitment efforts all through the fall, telling him that he could make as much as $15,000 a year, reminding him how much money the colleges were making off them while the players weren't getting a dime, exploiting every means at his disposal, including an appeal to racial antagonism. "When Eddie Gard recruited me, he sold hard," Warner would say later. "And what he sold was that my teammates were doing it the year before and why should they make money and cut me and Floyd out? In a way, he made it sound like black versus white. He turned me against them for a while. He knew how to do that. And at the time I thought Roman wasn't in it either, because we were close. But I was wrong about that, too. I was poor and I wanted my piece of the action."

By November, Warner had told Gard that he was in, and he would see what he could do to get his pal Floyd Layne in too. In early December, Roth reported to Gard that he still didn't know about Roman. By that time City College had won its first two games of the year, against St. Francis College on November 25 and a week later against Queens College. The third game was the following Tuesday against Brigham Young

University, and Gard suggested that after the game he take Roth and Roman to see Salvatore Sollazzo, that he was sure they could all come to an arrangement.

Brigham Young was one of the toughest opponents on City College's schedule, and on December 5 the two teams played a close, hard-fought contest that the Beavers finally held on to win, 71 to 69. Gard met Roth and Roman outside the Garden, and together they drove uptown.

Salvatore Sollazzo lived on Central Park West, one of New York's most desirable residential avenues, on the eighteenth floor of a high-rise building called the Majestic—an unabashedly boastful title, so unlike those of the squat apartment houses Roman knew from the Bronx, most often with names like the Lillian or the Rhoda, in honor of the owner's wife or mother.

The Majestic was made of orange brick that glowed warmly in the streetlights, with a ziggurat of terraces and large wraparound corner windows that provided a clear view of the park; it rose to a pair of stately towers, in which one of the penthouses belonged to Frank Costello, New York's most powerful underworld boss. At the front of the building the three were greeted by a uniformed doorman who saluted Eddie Gard and said "Good evening, Mr. Logan" as he called up to the apartment to announce the visitors. (It was an alias, Gard would explain to his bewildered companions; you had to have an alias in matters such as this.) The lobby had polished terrazzo floors and walls of marble and zinc, and the elevator was manned by an operator who closed the door behind them and pulled a large lever like one on an amusement park ride that delivered them smoothly to the eighteenth floor. There they were met by a man with thinning hair and narrow eyes and a hawklike nose, and a leering smile that seemed to communicate less friendliness than complicity. He extended his hand to Roman; on it, a star sapphire pinky ring gleamed in the light.

They stepped into the apartment; it was like that dazzling, unexpected moment in *The Wizard of Oz* when the world suddenly transforms from black-and-white to glorious color. Eddie Roman had lived in one place for his entire life, that two-family home on Teller Avenue with its unrelieved palette of whites and grays, five rooms crowded with lumpy couches and chairs that were too small for him, plus an extra unheated room above the front porch that his older brother, Mel, slept in because there was not enough space for all three of the children downstairs. The foyer of Salvatore Sollazzo's apartment opened onto a sunken living room with green chairs and lustrous gold drapes and curvaceous porcelain lamps with fringed shades that looked antique and not simply old; there was also a love seat upholstered in red velvet, a piece of furniture unlike anything Roman had ever seen. The room was large and high-ceilinged, and, as in a stage set, the light seemed to emanate from everywhere and nowhere in particular. From somewhere deep in the apartment came the trill of an unseen canary.

The four of them settled into chairs. He wanted to make it clear from the very beginning, Sollazzo said, that he would not be unreasonable—no one would ever ask them to lose a ball game. They could go as far as their talents would take them, just as long as the victories in the games in which they worked together were by margins narrower than those specified in the point spread. He assured them that they would earn "a considerable sum of money" with him as their partner; they would receive a flat fee, with the payment to be made in cash after each game in which the score was successfully controlled, and it hardly needed stating that they were not to tell anyone about what they were doing.

Sollazzo's voice bore traces of his childhood in Sicily, and as he talked he kept giving them that vulpine smile, one that seemed to appear and disappear at random moments unconnected to the conversation. Still, he had a likable directness about him, an inclination to dispense with unnecessary pleasantries and get down to business. (*Tukhes afn tish*, Roman's older relatives would say admiringly: a man who puts his "backside on the table.") He spoke like a factory owner, someone who expected others to pay heed to his words, and though he was the shortest man in the room, his body possessed a bulk that conveyed authority rather than, as in Roman's own case, awkwardness. Roman couldn't help but marvel that he was listening to someone who each night walked home across the same marbled lobby as Frank Costello; the notion was both thrilling and unnerving, and though no explicit reference had been made to any underworld ties that Sollazzo might have, the coincidence seemed too obvious to ignore. Unlike his parents' crowd of house painters and schoolteachers and luncheonette proprietors, this was a guy who had cornered the market in platinum, like Lamont ("the Shadow") Cranston or one of the other dashing millionaire heroes from the radio dramas of Roman's youth, and as a result of his boldness he now lived in the kind of Manhattan apartment sung about in Cole Porter songs. He also had a young, gorgeous wife who (Eddie Gard had let it be known) liked to host lavish parties for basketball players, sometimes cocktail parties there in the apartment, she and her friends slinking around in evening gowns, and other times more intimate affairs in hotel suites that Sollazzo rented for the evening.

Sollazzo told them that he was anxious to get moving—the upcoming game against Missouri would provide a comfortably large point spread. The players would each receive $1,500 if City came in under the points. Fifteen hundred dollars: It was an amount to make Roman's head spin, nearly one-quarter of the mortgage his parents and his aunt and uncle had remaining on the house. And all the while Gard and Roth—confident, stylish guys with their Ivy League clothing and teen-idol pompadours—kept smiling and nodding at everything that Sollazzo said. He reminded them that he was planning to bankroll several of the local teams, and of course their teammate Ed Warner would be included as well. He talked as if this were already a settled matter, as if Gard had not communicated to him any hesitation that he, Eddie Roman, might have had about participating, and in any case by this time Roman had ceased thinking about the doubts and anxieties of the year before, when he had quit shaving points as quickly as he could and resisted all solicitations to get back in; if he had been at all reluctant when he entered that apartment, he no longer was upon leaving it.

The first time Ed Warner had approached Floyd Layne about shaving points was in October, in the City College locker room after a practice. "Forget it," Floyd said right away. "I'm not interested."

Floyd wasn't especially surprised to hear that point-shaving was being discussed; he had read about the Brooklyn College scandal in the papers, and over the years he had heard lots of vague rumors about this or that school doing business. The gambling talk was like the low hum from a cheap radio: It was always there in the background, but you did what you could to ignore it and just focus on the music. As the conversation continued, though, Floyd was shocked to hear from Ed that point-shaving had been going on the year before, on his very own team. "That stopped me in my tracks," he was to recall. "That's what it did to me—it stopped me in my tracks."

He went home from practice in a kind of daze. Before long, that initial sense of shock gave way to confusion at the notion that Eddie Roman had never told him what he was doing, and anger at having been excluded, but in the end Floyd decided that he was thankful not to have known: He wouldn't have wanted to disappoint his teammates, nor to challenge, much less report them, and in retrospect he was glad simply to have a clean conscience about that season.

Over the next few weeks Floyd did what he could to put the conversation with Ed out of his mind and focus on his schoolwork. By this time he had declared his major to be physical education, with the idea that he might go into coaching when his career as a professional athlete was over, and nights that fall he often holed up in his bedroom with thick textbooks for classes that included Principles of Secondary Education, Human Anatomy, and Physiology of Exercise and Kinesiology. He sat home with his books, he once said, like they were his best friends.

In November, though, Ed Warner brought up the subject again, and again Floyd insisted that he would not get involved. He couldn't explain why the notion of point-shaving felt like a violation; he only knew that he would be ashamed to let his man score when he always took such pride in his defensive play. Everyone knew that he was a stickler for doing things the right way; indeed, some of the players used to laugh about how you couldn't walk anywhere with Floyd, because if he saw a couple of kids playing a pickup game he would stop and coach them on proper technique.

Floyd and Ed had themselves been kids when they first started playing together at the Harlem YMCA, where the athletic director, Clarence Small, seemed to spend half his time shooing away the gamblers who wanted to offer the better players bribes—"cakes," they used to call them. Later on it was Floyd who convinced Ed to apply to City College, and at City, Floyd had always looked out for him, encouraging him to attend his classes and to make use of the student tutors Bobby Sand offered them both; now Ed relished the opportunity to repay him. He looked at Floyd sorrowfully, and with what seemed real pity at his friend's misguided stubbornness, as though he were refusing a surefire stock tip or denying himself necessary medicine on religious grounds. Then he just shrugged and said, "Well, I'm going to make sure you get something anyhow."

At the end of November, Floyd and Ed attended a Knicks game together at Madison Square Garden. Leaving the Garden, the two of them ran into Eddie Gard standing on the corner of Forty-Ninth Street; the seemingly chance encounter struck Floyd as suspicious but he said nothing about it, and his suspicions grew as Warner and Gard climbed into Gard's car that was parked nearby and gestured to Floyd to get in as well. By now it had been six weeks since Warner had first approached him. Gard launched right into the hard sell; he talked for what seemed like a long time, promising them that they could each make a thousand dollars a game, maybe even fifteen hundred, and he assured Floyd that he wouldn't have to deal with anyone but him. "I'm the payoff man," he said. "You'll get the money directly from me."

Floyd said that he needed time to think it over. An uncomfortable silence filled the car until finally Warner told Gard that they would let him know.

"You might as well get in on it," Warner advised him as they headed home. "You know others will make the money if we don't."

Don't be a sucker, Gard had kept admonishing him; lots of other schools would be doing it. So would all the other sophomores from the championship team's starting five, including both of the Eds, the guys his mother referred to so delightedly as "my other sons." There was no way, Floyd understood, that he could ever tell her about any of this. She never tolerated anything that smacked even slightly of dishonesty. Every night she wanted to know where he had been that day and with whom—she needed him, she said, to account for his whereabouts. Lina had done everything in her power to make sure he stayed safe. One day, he recalled, she was watching him play youth football in Crotona Park and he took a hard tackle and was bent over gasping for breath, and after the game she had said "You better put a stop to that" and demanded that he turn in the uniform and pads even though she had already paid for them, with what was surely many hours of work.

She rose early in the morning, in the dark on the coldest winter days, bundled up in a heavy coat with her work clothes folded in a paper bag, and waited for the bus that would take her to a nicer neighborhood to the west or south, where she would spend endless hours beating mattresses, changing dirty sheets, scrubbing floors, washing and ironing the clothes of other women's children, for which she hoped to earn as much as a dollar an hour after the employment agency took its cut. What little money was left over from the household expenses went to pay for Floyd's uniforms—Scout and athletic—and his music lessons. Now here was the prospect of fifteen hundred dollars, half a year's work for her, just to miss the occasional basket (when in truth he missed most of the time anyway), to alter a final score that no one would remember even a week later; fifteen hundred dollars, when you could get a washing machine for just one hundred, or a refrigerator for a little more than that.

He began to get excited thinking of all he might buy, and he discovered that once he truly contemplated having that money, it was hard to give it back, even in his imagination. Others would make the money if he didn't. Maybe he *was* a sucker for not getting in; like Ed had said, they were going to do it one way or the other, with or without him. One of Bobby Sand's morale builders was "Don't be a prima donna or a lone wolf. Five men make a team." Roman, Roth, Cohen, Warner, Layne: the five sophomores, and he the only one not accepting any outside money. It didn't make sense, none of it did; but this was the way things were now.

On the morning of the game against the University of Missouri, a City College student named Ira Citron ran into Al Roth on the subway in Brooklyn. Citron knew Roth from Erasmus Hall High School, where they had played together on the team that won the city championship. He was a devoted basketball fan, and as the two of them chatted, he asked—in a jesting way, because the answer seemed self-evident—who was going to win the game that night.

Roth smiled and replied, "Bet on Missouri." He said it in that half-kidding, half-sneering way he had, but still, something in his tone caused the remark to lodge in Citron's memory. "It was a joke," he recalls, "but it wasn't a joke."

That afternoon another City College student, Larry Gralla, was sitting in the sports department of *The New York Times* building on West Forty-Third Street. Gralla covered sports for *The Campus* but worked on the side as a stringer for several local newspapers, including the *Times*, and at one point the veteran reporter Michael Strauss turned to him. "Hey, kid," he said, "don't put any money on your guys tonight—they're going under the points."

Though Gralla was not personally a gambler, he paid close attention to the remark, because Strauss had been covering basketball in New York for many years and because it seemed to confirm some of what he himself had been hearing. "I understood very quickly what he meant," says Gralla. "There were a lot of rumors going around at the time."

In a matter of days the point spread for the City College–Missouri game had dropped sharply; initially City had been favored to win by twelve and a half points, but by game time the margin was down to six. It was an indication that a lot of bets had come in on Missouri to cover the points—that is, to win the game or at least lose by less than the point spread—and the bookmakers were narrowing the spread in an effort to encourage betting on City College and equalize the money wagered on each side. There was no obvious reason for the late surge in betting on the Tigers; as the *New York Journal-American* basketball writer David Eisenberg put it bluntly, "Missouri did not rate highly at all."

In the previous season Missouri had compiled a pedestrian 14 and 10 record, and this season it had lost the only game it played. For two straight weeks, however, the Tigers had been preparing to play the defending champions, and they adopted a disciplined ball control strategy, patiently moving the ball around while setting screens designed to free up their best player, Bud Heineman, for open shots. Just that afternoon a dentist had pulled two of Heineman's teeth in an emergency procedure, but as one sportswriter noted, "He played as though he had had a blood transfusion instead." He smoothly dropped in jumpers from all over the court, scoring fifteen points in the first half alone. Meanwhile none of City's players could find a consistent shooting rhythm; over the course of the game the Beavers connected on only twelve out of sixty shots, a lackluster .200 percentage. "There is little question that City did much to damage its own cause," observed Michael Strauss in the *Times*, perhaps inviting the paper's readers to read between the lines.

In one eight-minute span in the first half, the Tigers scored seventeen consecutive points, and after that they never relinquished the lead. For their part, City's players strained to change the momentum and get back in the game, too often forcing a pass or taking a premature shot or committing an overly aggressive foul, the errors cascading, each miscue seeming to bring on another. When the game came mercifully to an end, Missouri had won by a score of 54 to 37. Warner led the team with eleven points on three-for-ten shooting; Layne was two for twelve, Roth one for nine, and Roman three for seventeen. The only Beaver to make even half his shots was the sophomore reserve Harold Hill, who sank the single shot he attempted.

It was the worst game that anyone could remember, and when it was over the City players walked off the court shaking their heads in confusion and dismay and the fans filed out of Madison Square Garden trying to find answers for what they had just witnessed. Some of the more sanguine among them reasoned that no team went undefeated for an entire season, that the Beavers had won twelve games in a row, had not lost since February—and even the best teams were entitled to a bad game every now and again. "The team should become better," David Eisenberg predicted confidently in the next day's *Journal-American*, "now that it has learned that you can't win this year's games on last year's clippings."

One evening a few days after the Missouri game Eddie Gard picked up Floyd Layne and Ed Warner on Fifth Avenue near midtown; when they got in the car he said that he had arranged for them to meet his friend at ten o'clock and then they would get their money. He also mentioned, almost in passing, that Al Roth and Eddie Roman had worked the Missouri game for someone else and so they weren't going to get paid. This was a startling piece of news, and Floyd felt a pang of dread in imagining the reaction of his teammates. He wondered, too, almost despite himself, if what Gard had said might possibly be true.

They drove around the city for a long time. Outside the temperature was dropping and a damp, biting wind had picked up; a crescent moon cast a silver glow on a sheet of clouds. Finally Gard made a turn and began heading west. He stopped the car on West Street, on a lonely, deserted stretch of warehouses and parking lots. They got out of the car. Standing there was a heavyset man in his forties wearing a bulky overcoat and a light-colored fedora, whom Eddie Gard introduced as Sol. Sol greeted them pleasantly, but when he spoke of their two teammates the warmth drained from his voice. He explained that some of the bookmakers had taken the Missouri game off the boards—had refused to accept bets on it—and as a consequence he had not been able to lay all of his bets; he was convinced that their friends, Roman and Roth, had been working the game for someone else and that news of the fix had gotten out and spooked the bookies. That had not been part of the deal, so their friends would not get paid.

When the conversation was over the three of them got back in Gard's car; still no money had changed hands. Gard started the car and began driving uptown along the river. The black water shimmered with what seemed a thousand crescent moons; narrow piers jutted out from the shoreline like the teeth of a great saw. After several minutes Gard turned right onto 158th Street, and at Broadway he pulled the car over and shut off the engine. He lowered one of the sun visors and took out a wad of cash that was clipped there: The money had been in the car all along. He counted out fifteen hundred-dollar bills for Ed and another fifteen for Floyd.

Gard got out of the car and walked with them to the corner. "You see," he said, "my friend is okay." He told them he would be in touch again soon, and then he got back in his car and drove off.

Floyd and Ed walked to the IRT station a block away; it would be a long trip home for each of them. Floyd rode downtown to Ninety-Sixth Street, where he transferred to the Dyre Avenue train to the Bronx. At 149th Street the train emerged from the tunnel and began running aboveground; Floyd could see himself reflected in the window, seeming to hang in the air like a ghost looking mournfully back into the lighted car. It was very late when he arrived at the Prospect Avenue station. He hurried along the darkened street, the storefronts barred like prison cells, unlocking the front door of his building and bounding up the stairs to the second floor. In his bedroom he could finally pull the money out of his pocket; he wrapped the bills in a handkerchief and buried the bundle in a flowerpot, making sure to smooth out the dirt on top so that no one could tell.

CHAPTER 23

Watching from the bench during the Missouri game, assistant coach Bobby Sand had become increasingly frustrated with the team's poor play, and several times he turned to the freshman coach, Mike Wittlin, to say, "What the hell's happening out there?" These were smart, experienced players, and it wasn't like them to take those low-percentage shots or commit that sort of clumsy foul. Finally in exasperation he said, "Nat, get them out of there. Put in the second team." Holman, though, waved off the suggestion: These were his best players, he said, and if he lost with them there was nothing else he could do.

On the way home, Sand ran into some friends on the subway, who told him they had heard rumors that the game was fixed and that some bookmakers, alarmed by the unusual betting patterns, had taken it off the boards. Sand was troubled by the information, and the next day he brought his concerns to Frank Thornton, a fellow economics professor and a member of the Faculty Athletic Committee, the group that oversaw the college's athletic programs. "Frank," Sand said, "you've got to do something about it—you've got to have an investigation to clear up this situation now. Otherwise we're in trouble."

Thornton had heard similar talk from one of his students, and that day he called faculty manager of athletics Sam Winograd and suggested that the committee look into the matter. Winograd sounded skeptical about the claim, but he agreed to bring the story to the attention of Frank Lloyd, chairman of the hygiene department, and to Nat Holman.

Lloyd told Winograd that he didn't think an investigation was warranted "unless you have hard evidence." Holman asked whether Thornton had provided any specifics, beyond what appeared simply to be rumors; speaking of Holman, Winograd would later say, "He wanted something on which he could hang his hat, and I couldn't give an answer to him." No investigation was ever pursued.

As Floyd Layne had anticipated, Eddie Roman and Al Roth stoutly denied working with anyone else on the Missouri game, and they were irate about being stiffed on the payment they were owed. Floyd said that he understood and would do what he could to get the money for them. A meeting was arranged a few nights later for the corner of Central Park West and Seventieth Street, a block from the Majestic.

Eddie showed up at the appointed time and was shortly joined by Fats; they were two unusually tall young men standing by themselves on a street corner, and under the circumstances they could not help but hope that nobody would recognize them and stop to talk about the previous game or the next one. It was mostly quiet here, where the park met the city; streetlamps cast pools of light on the sidewalk, hexagonal paving blocks meticulously fitted together by long-gone workmen. Eventually Salvatore Sollazzo appeared, strolling down Central Park West. He was wearing horn-rimmed glasses, which with his wide-brimmed fedora and camel's-hair overcoat gave him the mien of a prosperous businessman, and he didn't seem quite as intimidating in the open air as inside his golden apartment. Eddie gathered himself for a moment and demanded their money; they were entitled to it, he said indignantly, just as much as Floyd and Ed were. Sollazzo pointed out that he had not been able to make all of his bets, that word had somehow gotten out before the game and he suspected that they—who, unlike their two teammates, had worked with other gamblers in the past—were doing business with someone else. In a rush of words Eddie and Fats insisted that they had not told anyone, that they were not double-crossers, they had a deal only with him and if he just paid them what they were owed for the Missouri game they would continue to work with him in the future. Sollazzo seemed satisfied with their assurances and, given the prospect of additional fixed games, agreed to pay them what they were owed; he said he didn't have the money with him but would get it to them soon.

Meanwhile Sollazzo wondered what they thought about their upcoming game against Washington State University—that is, what they thought the outcome might be. The Cougars had won their four games that season, but they were not regarded especially highly by basketball aficionados, and Eddie and Fats both expressed confidence that City would win by a large margin. Sollazzo said that he appreciated the information, and he promised to pay the four players $250 each if the Beavers exceeded the point spread that night. If they wanted him to, he told Fats and Eddie almost as an afterthought, he would lay that money on the game for them—if they did beat the spread, two hundred fifty could turn into five hundred.

Fats and Eddie looked at each other; they had never contemplated betting on themselves before. Unlike most instances of point-shaving, in this case they were being asked simply to perform as well as they were able, which is exactly what they would be doing anyway, what any athlete did as a matter of course. The two players told Sollazzo to go ahead and place their money on City College. Sollazzo said that he would arrange with Eddie Gard to get them their money, and they said goodbye and the players turned and walked to the subway. Only later did it occur to them that Sollazzo did not seem to have included Floyd and Ed in the betting on the Washington State game, and that it would probably be best if they kept that information to themselves.

Only 10,473 fans were in attendance for the Washington State game, slightly more than half of capacity; many rows of the arena were empty, and Madison Square Garden, which had on so many occasions shaken with excitement from floor to rafters, on this night often fell into the weary, slightly embarrassed silence of a Broadway audience sitting through a flop. The small crowd, Irving T. Marsh observed in the *Herald Tribune,* "yawned, although politely" during the opening game of the doubleheader, as City College "toyed with Washington State and won as it pleased." The Beavers had a ten-point lead at halftime and eventually built it to twenty-two, at which point Nat Holman rested his first team and began sending in substitutes. The final score was 59 to 43, a solid victory for City College and comfortably above the bookmakers' ten-point spread.

The Beavers had played with confidence, and the outcome of the game had never been in doubt; still, there were some distressing indications for the team, particularly regarding absences in the lineup. Herb Cohen, whom Holman had originally projected to be the fifth sophomore on the starting five, had been out the entire season with a case of jaundice. More troubling, Ed Warner had sprained an ankle at the end of the game against Missouri, and although the injury was not considered serious, he may have been still unsteady on that leg, because in the Washington State game he took a bad fall and staggered painfully off the court. In the locker room he was examined by the Garden physician, Dr. Vincent Nardiello, who determined that he had pulled lateral ligaments in his right knee. He missed the second half of the game and for the next week he showed up to practice on crutches.

A few days after the Washington State game Al Roth met Salvatore Sollazzo just north of Rockefeller Center; Sollazzo hailed them a cab, and in the back seat he handed Roth an envelope containing $4,000 in cash—the three thousand he owed Fats and Eddie for the Missouri game plus another $500 each, as promised, for the Washington State game. Floyd and Ed would receive only $250 apiece. Ed Warner picked up the money from Sollazzo in a bar near Rockefeller Center. Sollazzo, he recalled years later, "was covered in gold jewelry. He gave me a ring and I threw it away. There were always good-looking women around him. I was kinda crazy but I wasn't stupid. I would get my money and get as far away from him as quickly as possible."

Not long after the double championship, the Crown publishing company had gotten in touch with Nat Holman, wanting him to write a book about basketball strategy. Holman asked Bobby Sand to ghostwrite the book for him for a flat fee of $800, and he had agreed to do it. Bobby had been writing furiously all through the fall, turning out page after page on his lined yellow notepaper, and in December, Crown released *Holman on Basketball*. More than three hundred pages long, the book discussed every aspect of the game, from passing, dribbling, and shooting to team offense and defense, and provided advice to young coaches as well as "scouting points" that Sand had compiled over his years of researching opponents and potential recruits; it also included dozens of play diagrams and sequences of photographs from game films that illustrated various maneuvers step by step. (Sand had set up a film-strip projector in his living room so that he could select frames while he was writing.) *Holman on Basketball* opened with a foreword by Ned Irish that lauded Nat Holman as one of basketball's "greatest personalities and technicians" and assured the reader that "Nat Holman the author is as skilled and thorough as Nat Holman the coach." Sand's name appeared nowhere other than in the introduction, in which Holman wrote, "In the preparation of this book I have had the invaluable assistance of Bobby Sand, Assistant Coach of C.C.N.Y., whose services and contributions I desire to acknowledge with deep gratitude."

The reviews were glowing. *Scholastic Coach* began its review of the book this way: "The greatest basketball technician of all time, a man equally at ease with the spoken and written word, Nat Holman is ideally qualified to write on the game. And if you want any proof, just grab hold of his latest book. You won't have to get much past the opening tap to realize you are reading the greatest technical text on basketball ever written."

Concluded *Scholastic Coach* (one of the magazines for which Holman had forbidden Sand to write): "The book is a four-star beauty. Chalk up another remarkable achievement for 'Mr. Basketball.' "

One day in December, Floyd Layne dug through the flowerpot to retrieve the bundle he had hidden there; he pulled a couple of bills from the handkerchief and then replaced it, carefully smoothing the dirt again. Stuffing the money into his pocket, he headed out to Fordham Road, a few blocks from his apartment, where the appliance chain Davega had one of its stores. The store was large and well lighted, its many aisles lined with the dazzling goods of postwar American abundance: refrigerator-freezers, electric ovens, television sets, pop-up toasters. All were displayed to advantage: The porcelain gleamed, the chrome sparkled, the wood veneer was lustrous. These were items that Floyd had never even considered purchasing; now, if he wanted to, he could buy anything in the store.

The washing machines looked like robots from a science fiction movie, with cylindrical white bodies and head-like automatic wringers on top, and a long black hose in the back that attached to the kitchen faucet. The model he selected cost $110. Floyd paid in full—no need for any layaway plan for him—and arranged to have it delivered before Christmas.

Until then, he worried about how he was going to explain the purchase to his mother. When Christmas came and she looked in amazement at the huge box, he told her that he had been saving up for a long time, that he had used the money he earned after his high school graduation, when he'd spent part of the summer working in a brush factory on 169th Street. Lina knew Floyd was like that—he was careful with his money—and she believed him, which imparted a certain sadness to the gift but was still far better than the alternative.

He was indeed careful with his money; when he came home that day from Davega he returned to the handkerchief the money left over from his purchase, and he never again removed any of the bills buried in the flowerpot.

Salvatore Sollazzo had wanted the players to shave points on the Christmas Day game against Brooklyn College, but they refused—it was asking too much to do business on Christmas, and there was no way they were going to try to come in under the points and risk losing against Brooklyn, a team that City had beaten fifteen straight times. Ed Warner was still sidelined with an injured knee, and in his absence Eddie Roman dominated the game. He finished with thirty points, three times as many as anyone else and the most ever scored by a City College player at Madison Square Garden. The final score was 64 to 40.

Sollazzo and Eddie Gard persisted in their solicitations, and the four players agreed to shave points in their next game, three days later, against the University of Arizona, in which City College was favored by nine points. Warner was included in the deal, although he wasn't sure he would be ready to play, and now, surprisingly, Roman was questionable as well. At some point during the past week he had gotten a cut on one of his toes; he didn't think much of it at first, but after the Brooklyn game the cut seemed to have become infected, because by the next practice the toe was an angry red, tender and throbbing, making every step a misery. Gamely he hobbled through practice until finally he asked the team's trainer to cut a hole in his sneaker, to allow more room for the swollen toe, and that seemed to help a bit. For the rest of the week Eddie did what he could to tend to the problem, keeping the toe clean and bandaged, and he saw a doctor to have the affected area lanced and drained, but by Thursday night the toe was still no better, and in the Madison Square Garden locker room before the Arizona game he sat down with Nat Holman, trainer Al Maxtutis, and Garden physician Vincent Nardiello to decide how to proceed.

Holman suggested that the bad toe might be injected with novocaine to dull the pain and allow him to play, and neither member of the medical staff objected to the idea. After Eddie consented to the procedure, Dr. Nardiello removed a hypodermic syringe from his bag and filled it from a small glass vial; he inserted the tip of the needle into the toe, injecting first one side and then the other, and each time Eddie felt a moment of excruciating pain, followed by a slight tingling and ultimately—it was the strangest sensation—a total absence of feeling, as if his toe had been replaced by a length of wooden dowel. The trainer then taped up the toe and his ankles; Eddie put on two pairs of socks (cotton socks next to his feet and woolen ones over those), and the pair of sneakers with the hole cut in one of them, and he was ready to play.

Ed Warner's game status was similarly hazy. Talking to Holman before the game, Al Maxtutis said that Ed's knee was bad, that he had been complaining about it all week, and in his opinion he shouldn't be allowed to play; Bobby Sand was also there, and he agreed with Maxtutis. Holman, though, said that he had discussed the matter with Warner at practice that afternoon; he had asked, "How's the knee? Will you get off your feet?" and Warner had assured him that everything was all right and that he wanted to play.

Ed Warner did start the game, but he was visibly limping, listing like a smashed ship, and after only two minutes, shaking his head in pain and frustration, he returned to the City College bench, where he would remain for the rest of the game.

Although Eddie Roman's toe didn't hurt at first, he still felt an unusual pressure inside his shoe; as the game went along, he found that the novocaine was wearing off, that he was increasingly aware of the pain in his foot like a police siren growing ever louder, and even before the first half had ended he understood with a kind of desperate feeling that he was not able to adequately plant himself to take a hook shot or lift for a jump shot or make a sharp move on defense. He did what he could to keep his team in the game, blocking out for rebounds and shooting whenever he was open, and City managed to overcome an early twelve-point deficit and midway through the second half took the lead. In the *Journal-American* David Eisenberg wrote that Eddie played "nobly" despite his injury, scoring nineteen points, twelve more than anyone else on the team.

In the end the Beavers fell 41 to 38; it was the team's third loss of the season against five victories.* After the game an angry Holman told reporters that he didn't know what to do with his starters, that he couldn't go in there and play for them himself, that Roth and Layne especially seemed lethargic, and finally he said in exasperation, "Right now they look like a one-man ball club—Ed Roman."

Eddie Roman, the *Post*'s Sid Friedlander pointed out after the Arizona game, "has been playing great ball, better than last year both offensively and defensively." In eight games he had scored 153 points for a 21.8 average—more than four points per game better than the previous season, when he broke City College's single-season scoring mark. Meanwhile, all around New York basketball fans were wondering about the outlook for Tuesday, January 2. The annual City College–St. John's game was always the high point of the regular season, and the previous year's game (won by City when Ronnie MacGilvray's last-second shot rolled out) was already considered one of the more memorable entries in the colleges' thirty-year basketball rivalry. The prospects for another classic, however, were doubtful at best. Ed Warner was still nursing his injured knee; for his part, Eddie Roman skipped the team's workout entirely on Saturday, and on Sunday he glumly watched the practice in street clothes. By Monday—New Year's Day—the infection in his toe

---

* On December 21, City College had lost to the University of Oklahoma, 48 to 43, in a game in which no one was taking money; the Beavers were simply outplayed by a deep and capable team at a time when Ed Warner was sidelined with a knee injury.

seemed to have spread, for Eddie was now laid up with a 101-degree fever and had to have the toe lanced and drained once more. It was a perfectly miserable beginning to 1951.

Complaining about his team's poor play after the Arizona game, Nat Holman had predicted, "St. John's will beat us by fifteen points." In fact, with Warner's and Roman's participation undetermined, bookmakers were a little kinder, installing St. John's as a nine-point favorite. St. John's coach, Frank McGuire, believed the game would be close and hard fought, and on New Year's Day he made a confident prediction, telling a reporter: "You can take five stars on one side and five pigs on the other. If one group is City and the other St. John's, the coaches might as well sit in the balcony. The game is going to be a rat race and I don't care which side it is that's got the pigs."

McGuire could make another prediction with a fair degree of certainty: that the team's number one fan, William P. O'Brien, would as usual sit directly behind the St. John's bench, as he had been doing for years. The main difference now was that O'Brien was no longer police commissioner of the city of New York.

Harry Gross had started to talk.

CHAPTER 24

William Patrick O'Brien was, in the phrase everyone used, "a cop's cop." A burly man with a prominent nose and icy blue eyes in a perpetually florid face, he had a gruff voice and spoke out of the side of his mouth, which gave even his weightiest pronouncements a slightly comical effect. (His was an especially pure example of the Brooklyn accent of an earlier period, in which the word *first* is pronounced "foist," while *foist*, in turn, becomes "first.") For thirty-three years O'Brien had moved slowly but steadily up through the Police Department; he had long been one of William O'Dwyer's close friends, and in 1949 the mayor appointed him police commissioner of the City of New York.

The commissioner's private office, in police headquarters downtown on Centre Street, was a darkly paneled sanctuary that would not have seemed out of place in an English manor house, everything burnished and finely crafted and larger than would be expected, including iron chandeliers, a massive wood-burning fireplace, and a desk that one observer suggested was about the size of a double bed. This was the office in which Commissioner O'Brien held his meetings, and in the grim days of September 1950, those meetings were most often with Chief of Detectives William Whalen and Chief Inspector August Flath. They were the highest-ranking members of a force of nineteen thousand, and together they seemed to embody the palace guard that had so concerned Brooklyn district attorney Miles McDonald, a faction that would do everything in its power to thwart his investigation. When they got together that month, the three men always locked the door behind them and did not invite a secretary to take notes, as would ordinarily have been the case, and, according to those who worked in the commissioner's outer office, upon emerging from those meetings they appeared nervous and agitated. They had good reason to be, for they were privy to information that was not yet widely known: that all three, earlier in their careers, had received "ice" from Harry Gross.

On September 15, the day of Gross's arrest, Judge Samuel Leibowitz called O'Brien and Flath to his courtroom for an extraordinary night session. The two men arrived at 9:30; the chief inspector was described by a reporter as "visibly nervous," the commissioner as "pale and grim." The two officials sat at one of the counsel tables, with District Attorney Miles McDonald and Assistant District Attorney Julius Helfand at the other. Judge Leibowitz gazed down at them from his bench; he had personally signed the order for a wiretap to be placed on the phone lines leading into Harry Gross's Inwood wire room, he said, and he wanted the commissioner and the chief inspector to listen to one of the recordings that had been made, as an example of what the investigators were finding. At an instruction from the judge, the "play-back machine" was turned on.

Within seconds, the voices of a pair of bookmakers, "Artie" and "Mickey," filled the room. Artie, who handled bets in Brooklyn, was heard to complain that the cops in his neighborhood had said that because of the investigation, things were hotter now, and they would need $350 a week instead of the $300 they had gotten before. Not only were the cops demanding more money, Artie complained, but they also said they "had to make a pinch quick." Mickey, who worked in the Inwood wire room, told Artie that he should stand for the arrest himself; Artie complained that he had "stood for seven already." Mickey told him to pay somebody to be a stand-in; Artie said that he did not know anyone willing to be arrested. Mickey said he should ask "the Weeper"—the Weeper was always up for a pinch.*

Back and forth the conversation went; it was like the syncopated

---

* Irving Goldstein, a garment cutter known in gambling circles as "the Weeper" for his tearful excitability, would later testify that he had accepted an offer of a hundred dollars from Arthur Karp to take an "accommodation arrest" from a plainclothes policeman.

patter of an old vaudeville routine, but no one here was laughing, and when the recording came to an end the two police officials sat wordlessly in the silent courtroom.

"Commissioner," Judge Leibowitz said after some time, "I thought it important that you get this information right from the record, and it may be that you have some real, constructive, forthright suggestions on how to clean house."

O'Brien stood to address the judge, the action unavoidably reminiscent of a defendant preparing to receive his sentence. He said, "This is a rather unusual proceeding. I was glad to come, and glad to listen. The police commissioner of the City of New York does not take his hat off to anybody in this city in his desire to have a clean Police Department, and to have each and every member worthy of the badge he wears."* He congratulated Mr. McDonald and Mr. Helfand for the great service they were doing for the Police Department and for the people of New York. "We have given them every assistance possible," he insisted. "We intend to give them every assistance possible. We are as much interested in this as anybody in the city."

The next day Commissioner O'Brien announced that he was ordering a special departmental investigation of "possible police involvement with graft." The man assigned to lead the investigation was none other than Chief Inspector August Flath.

On September 24 the lead story in *The Brooklyn Daily Eagle*, citing "unimpeachable sources close to Manhattan police headquarters," reported that Acting Mayor Vincent Impellitteri had decided to fire Police Commissioner William O'Brien.

The very next evening, Monday, September 25, 1950, police graduation exercises were held in the 71st Regiment Armory on Park Avenue. At 9:30 a row of dignitaries stood on the stage with their hands over

---

* Commissioner O'Brien's reference to taking off his hat might well have struck some as ironic. On a different occasion O'Brien had given his policemen these remarkable instructions: "Nobody takes a bribe. Of course, at Christmas if you happen to hold out your hat and somebody happens to put something in it, well, that's different." In the New York Police Department a twenty-dollar bribe would, in tribute, come to be known as a "hat."

their hearts as a police band played the National Anthem; then they sat down and the commissioner stepped to the podium. William O'Brien wore a dark double-breasted suit and a tie with wide diagonal stripes. He congratulated the 496 members of that year's graduating class, reminding them of the noble history of the department and the special honor and great responsibility that came with the privilege of being a police officer. His gruff voice, so evocative of an earlier time, resounded through the vaulted hall. He paused for a moment and then said, "After thirty-five years as a policeman, I find it my regretful duty to turn in my shield. It is a hard thing for a policeman to do." Six months earlier he had been offered an "attractive position" in private industry and had considered retiring then, but District Attorney McDonald's investigation "of a small segment of my department was in progress, and under the circumstances I deferred my resignation." He was retiring now because his position had become "untenable" and he believed that to remain in office "might prove harmful to one of the finest citizens of our town, Acting Mayor Impellitteri."

With that the outgoing police commissioner returned to his seat. The acting mayor spoke next. Vincent Impellitteri—Impy, as he was known to all—was small and slight of frame and spoke with none of the rhetorical flourishes and broad gestures that New Yorkers had come to associate with their mayor, after seventeen years of La Guardia and O'Dwyer. "Since certain disclosures last week," he said, "I have had several conversations with Police Commissioner O'Brien. I have known the commissioner for a long time. I honestly believe that his personal integrity is not involved in the present situation. I also feel that his position has become untenable. During our conversation it was mutually agreed that his resignation at this time would go far toward restoring the public confidence and strengthening any morale of the police force that has been weakened." Impellitteri announced that the next morning he would nominate Thomas F. Murphy, assistant U.S. attorney for the Southern District of New York, as the new police commissioner.

In El Centro, California, where he was vacationing while awaiting Senate confirmation of his ambassadorship, William O'Dwyer received a call from Ed Reid of *The Brooklyn Daily Eagle*; it was Reid's exposé of gambling in Brooklyn that had sparked the McDonald investigation in the first place. "I believe Bill O'Brien is as honest a man as I have ever

known," O'Dwyer told Reid. "I don't know the facts, but if there is corruption in the Police Department it is the result of disloyalty by members of the department to Bill O'Brien."

The widening bookmaking scandal, which had already forced the
resignation of Mayor O'Dwyer, had now claimed Police Commissioner
O'Brien as well.

So O'Brien was out as police commissioner, to be replaced by Murphy,
who in turn would be replaced by Monaghan, and subsequently by
Adams, Kennedy, and another Murphy; the previous commissioners
had been, in order, McLaughlin, Warren, Whalen, Mulrooney, Bolan,
O'Ryan, Valentine, and Wallander. For several decades the New York
Police Department, like the Fire Department, had been overwhelmingly
Irish Catholic in its membership and leadership alike—so much so that
it was not until 1952 that Irish members of the force set up their own
fraternal organization, the Emerald Society, as had earlier been done by
Italian, Jewish, African American, Puerto Rican, and Polish police officers; before that time, noted one observer, "an organization of Irish policemen in New York might have resembled a committee of the whole."

Though many of the Catholic colleges in the New York area, such as
Manhattan College and Fordham University, maintained basketball
programs, the strongest one unquestionably belonged to St. John's University of Brooklyn, and the Redmen were the team of choice for many
of the city's Catholic college basketball fans, even those who had not
attended the school—much as many New York Jews instinctively rooted
for City College, and as African Americans throughout the United States
became Brooklyn Dodgers fans in 1947 with the signing of Jackie Robinson. A strong Redmen rooting section had long existed among the
members of the police force; still, in all of the New York Police Department there had been no more fervent or more visible St. John's fan than
William P. O'Brien.

O'Brien had himself been a talented basketball player in his Brooklyn youth, and through his years as assistant chief inspector and then
as police commissioner he attended all of the St. John's home games,
sitting in the front row directly behind the bench. O'Brien, said *The
Brooklyn Daily Eagle*, was "the number one St. John's rooter." In a testi-

monial to him shortly after he was appointed police commissioner, Manhattan district attorney Frank Hogan amusedly remarked that O'Brien was "kidded a great deal about being called assistant coach to Frank McGuire of St. John's."

Frank McGuire was himself the son of a New York cop, and until he discovered basketball in his youth he had thought that he would grow up to be a policeman. In 1950 the best player on St. John's was center Bob Zawoluk, whose own father had been a New York City policeman until he suffered an unfathomable tragedy: One day while he was directing traffic at a busy intersection in Brooklyn, a Department of Sanitation truck swung too fast around the corner, and a broom hanging off the back of the truck knocked him down and his head hit the street; he died the next day. Since that time the two Zawoluk children had been supported by a widow's pension and looked after by members of the department including their uncle John, who was a policeman as well. As it happened, McGuire's father had also died on the job in the most unlikely of circumstances—of jaundice that he had contracted from an infected hypodermic needle after being bitten by a rabid dog—and Frank, too, had been looked after as a boy by his late father's colleagues on the force. It was an unhappy connection, but one that proved instrumental in bringing Bob Zawoluk to St. John's. "When McGuire showed up at Zawoluk's home one evening and began to discuss St. John's," noted sportswriter Milton Gross, "interspersing his comments with Police Department stories, Zawoluk's mother virtually measured him for a red and white uniform."

McGuire was tall and lean, with devilishly arched eyebrows and a dimpled chin; like Nat Holman he was immaculate in his personal appearance, but while Holman seemed as substantial and prosperous as a bank president or the head of a movie studio, McGuire was younger and flashier, more like a sports car salesman or a cardsharp, from the high crown of his wavy red hair and his immaculately manicured fingernails down to his polished alligator shoes. He had many friends who were cops but he also had friends who were criminals, and from his early days at St. John's there were whispers about how he afforded his expensive wardrobe, his fancy car, and his lakeside vacation home on a coach's salary. "He may not have conspired with gamblers or the Mafia members who often underwrote their activities," wrote Bethany Bradsher, a historian of college basketball, "but no one who knew him disputes that McGuire probably associated with some of the characters who engineered those deals. The son of a city cop, he always kept close association with both the law and the Mob." (On one occasion, after he had left St. John's to coach at the University of North Carolina, McGuire asked the UNC team manager, Joel Fleishman, to request additional tickets for an NCAA tournament game at Madison Square Garden. Fleishman asked for two groups of tickets on opposite sides of the arena; the Garden official handling the request suggested that it would be more convenient to obtain a single large block of tickets to accommodate McGuire's family and friends. "No, no, you don't get it," Fleishman told him. "We have the cops and the priests on one side and the Mob and the convicts on the other side.")

While he was coaching at St. John's, McGuire had what Milton Gross called a "personal rooting section"—two men on opposite sides of the law. One was a childhood companion who in later years had gone wrong and served time in prison for armed robbery; the other was New York Police Commissioner William P. O'Brien. "Both are McGuire's friends," wrote Gross. "They're for him and he's for them, no matter what."

"Frank McGuire and the commissioner were very close," recalls Frank Mulzoff, a St. John's player of the time. "I remember the commissioner would often visit the locker room before and after the games."

In 1950, the New York police commissioner was one of the head coach's closest friends (said to be for him "no matter what"). The coach maintained friendships with many members of the police force, and himself came from a police family; so, too, did the team's star player, who was described in an admiring profile in *Sport* magazine as "something of a ward of the police department."

The New York City Police Department, *Sport* noted, "has more than a rooting interest in St. John's."

CHAPTER 25

For New York's college basketball fans, the St. John's–City College rivalry was special in large part because the two teams were usually the strongest in New York; for the players themselves, the games had an added edge because many of them had been competing with one another for almost as long as they could remember: They had grown up playing on the same courts around the city, had worked together in the summers in the same Catskills hotels. "We were great friends with the guys from City," says Frank Mulzoff, the St. John's cocaptain.

The Brooklynites on the City squad, like Al Roth and Herb Cohen, often participated in the pickup games at the 108th Street playground in Far Rockaway, where the McGuire brothers (Al was a St. John's cocaptain, and Dick, a former St. John's star, now played for the New York Knicks) could be found almost every Sunday morning after early mass at St. Camillus. Eddie Roman, for his part, was a close friend of St. John's center Bob Zawoluk. Eddie and Zeke—as Zawoluk was known among his friends—had been roommates at the Waldemere Hotel in the Catskills; they had waited tables and played basketball, and on amateur talent nights they donned wigs and ill-fitting skirts and put water balloons under their shirts and lip-synced to Andrews Sisters songs, an act that never failed to bring down the house.

Zeke was the same height as Eddie, six foot six, but he was lean, with a rawboned Gary Cooper quality; the famed entertainment columnist Leonard Lyons had met him in the Catskills and was so impressed by his looks that he urged him to get a Hollywood agent and take a screen test. Zawoluk was well aware that he was handsome, and he cultivated this asset much as he did his basketball ability; he preferred suits to the more casual sport jackets or cardigans most of the players wore, and in the St. John's locker room he was notorious for the extreme care he took with his hair—his teammate Ronnie MacGilvray had timed one of his hair-combing sessions and found that it lasted a full twelve minutes. Tall and well dressed, a smooth ballroom dancer as well as a basketball star, and burdened by a tragic family history, Zawoluk was devastatingly attractive to women in a way that Eddie Roman could only dream about. As a basketball player, though, Zeke's game was much like Eddie's, and in the days leading up to the City College–St. John's game, the press was full of stories comparing the two centers. The players themselves didn't take the individual competition very seriously and often practiced together, offering each other shooting tips as they played, prompting Bobby Sand to suggest gently to Eddie that he hold off on coaching Zawoluk—at least until after the St. John's game was over.

Once again Roman received a novocaine shot before the game, and in the first half he matched Zawoluk with twelve points apiece; in the second half, though, the pain in his toe came back full force. He hobbled around the court, couldn't get open for a shot, and was able to manage only two points. Despite that, noted David Eisenberg of the *Journal-American*, Roman was "at his best in the second half," guarding his man so tightly that for fourteen straight minutes Zawoluk was not able even to touch the ball. "Apparently there are times when the hero does not win the gal, the gold, or the gonfalon," lamented the *Post*'s Sid Friedlander. "Big Ed was quite a ball player last night at the Garden, but when it was all over the best he could get was the short end of St. John's 47–44 decision over City College."

"To the victors it did not matter that they failed to live up to their six-point favorite's line," observed Louis Effrat in the *Times* about the St. John's Redmen. "Their aim was victory at any score and let the points fall where they may." Indeed, the game had turned out to be a spirited and hard-fought affair, and closer than most people had anticipated, and those who had bet on City College to cover the points went home that night especially pleased.

• • •

Sports editor Max Kase of the *New York Journal-American* was fifty-three years old and had been working in the newspaper business since the age of fourteen. Heavyset, with an open, jowly face, Kase was a consummate New York newspaperman, renowned for hounding his reporters to give him information about teams or players that he could include in his daily column, "Brief Kase." As a respite from his writing and editing duties, Kase also ran a regular nighttime pinochle game in his office in the sports department; this was by no means the only gambling to be found inside the *Journal-American* building. "Every third guy in the joint is a bookie," the city editor, Paul Schoenstein, liked to tell his son Ralph. "They put out the paper on the side." In fact, sports betting was so commonplace there, and conducted so openly, that a young assistant district attorney once ordered the police to raid the newspaper office on South Street. The longtime Manhattan district attorney, Frank Hogan, canceled the operation as soon as he found out about it, and then telephoned his friend Paul Schoenstein to share a laugh about the newcomer's overzealousness. "I'm sorry you called off the raid, Frank," said Schoenstein. "I had thirty reporters on the scene."

Kase had long heard rumors that certain college basketball games played at Madison Square Garden were being fixed by gamblers; as the 1950–51 season began, the rumors seemed to be growing louder, and that fall, Kase began spending time in establishments where he knew gambling went on, discreetly asking questions, seeing what he could learn. One night a source finally gave him a name, and Kase passed it along to two young basketball writers on the *Journal-American* staff to see if they could track down any supporting material. By the beginning of 1951 the reporters were confident about the name provided by their source, but they worried that publishing the information might disrupt an ongoing law enforcement investigation. Kase decided to hold off on publication, at least temporarily, other than to insert a suggestive blind item in his "Brief Kase" column of January 9, 1951: "Those reports of basketball fixes and dumps are much too persistent for the health of the game."

Instead, Kase contacted the Manhattan district attorney, and the following day he and a veteran *Journal-American* sportswriter named

Lewis Burton were ushered into the private office of District Attorney Frank Hogan on the eighth floor of the Criminal Courts Building.

Like all visitors, Kase and Burton understood that the Manhattan district attorney was to be addressed always as Mr. Hogan, never as Frank. He was a polite, formal man of forty-eight, square-jawed, with a dignified, almost clerical manner—so much so that the prostitutes who passed in and out of the nearby House of Detention would sometimes refer to him, not unkindly, as Father Hogan.

Kase explained to the district attorney his newspaper's investigation of rumors of game fixing in college basketball. His staff had received a tip about a fixer that subsequent inquiries seemed to confirm; he suggested that the DA's office would do well to watch the activities of a former Long Island University basketball player by the name of Eddie Gard.

Frank Hogan had long been interested in fixed sporting events at Madison Square Garden; almost exactly two years earlier, his detectives had arrested four gamblers for attempting to bribe the captain of the George Washington University basketball team to shave points in a game against Manhattan College. Hogan's investigators had been looking into recent rumors of fixed basketball games but had not made any substantial progress, and he was grateful for the tip from the *Journal-American* that he subsequently described as "very, very helpful."

He would pursue the matter vigorously, Hogan told them, but in the meantime he hoped that the *Journal-American* would not print any stories about it. In return, he promised that he would give the paper inside information, including exclusive interviews with him, once the case finally broke; Kase agreed to the deal.

When Kase and Burton left, Hogan immediately ordered that a wiretap be placed on Eddie Gard's telephone, and that detectives watch him around the clock.

The following day brought another unaccountable loss for City College at Madison Square Garden, this one to the Eagles of Boston College. City had started out as an eleven-point favorite, but by game time the spread was down to seven points—a narrowing caused, perhaps, by the news that Ed Warner's injured knee would once again prevent him from playing. Eddie Roman led the team with sixteen points but fouled out midway through the second half. Without Roman and Warner the Beavers were badly out-rebounded; Boston College scored nine of the last ten points and won the game 63 to 59.

Salvatore Sollazzo had promised Roman, Roth, and Layne $1,500 apiece for the Boston College game, and $500 for Warner even though he wasn't going to play. When Roth met Eddie Gard afterward, though, Gard handed him an envelope containing only $1,400—thousands less than what the City players had been promised. Gard explained that bookmakers were getting nervous about handling action on games in the Garden, and some had pulled the Boston College game off the boards; Sollazzo had been able to bet only $2,500. He was giving this money to Fats as a down payment, Gard explained; Sol needed the rest of it to bet on the upcoming LIU game against Duquesne, and when he got his winnings from that game he would give them what they were owed.

Roth brought the money back to Brooklyn and put it in a safe deposit box.

During the 1950–51 season, City College lost every one of the games (against Missouri, Arizona, and Boston College) in which members of the team had intended simply to shave points. Something about point fixing apparently prevented them from playing well enough to win. Perhaps it was that unnatural sense of watching oneself at all times, having constantly to decide if this was a moment to compete wholly or instead ease up just a bit, inescapably aware of the game inside the game, all the while wondering how one's performance looked to the coaches and the crowd and to teammates both on the take and not. Or perhaps it was simply a lingering consciousness of guilt that proved debilitating. In contrast, Eddie Gard's former team, the LIU Blackbirds, seemed oblivious to these concerns; they possessed a remarkable ability, in the gamblers' term of art, to "control the points": that is, to win the game while still remaining under the point spread. Favored by seven against Kansas State, the Blackbirds had won by a single point; favored by four against Denver, they won by two; favored by eleven against Idaho, they won by two; favored by seven against Bowling Green, they won by six.

The LIU players taking money from Salvatore Sollazzo that season were the three stars of the team—guard Leroy Smith, forward Adolph Bigos, and center Sherman White. On January 6 the three had managed to bring the team in under the points against Bowling Green, as they had promised, but Bowling Green had offered very little opposition, and in order to keep the game sufficiently close they had needed to play far more poorly than normal, missing one foul shot after another and tossing passes out of bounds, the blunders so glaring that the *World-Telegram and Sun* reported that fans "howled in indignation."

Afterward the three were unnerved by how transparent their artifice had been, especially when two days later head coach Clair Bee showed them an anonymous letter he had received accusing the players of shaving points. Though Bee accepted their emphatic denials, they could feel the heat beginning to rise, and before LIU's next game against Duquesne, the three decided that they were not going to shave points any longer. When the players walked onto the court, White waved his hands at Eddie Gard to indicate that the deal was off. Gard pointed at Sollazzo, who was staring stonily at White (later White would say, "I thought it was over. I thought he was going to kill me"), but the players were resolute that they would play the game on the level. The result was a pure demolition, with Long Island University winning 84 to 52. In the stands Sollazzo watched with a growing sense of alarm: He had bet $30,000 on Duquesne to cover the points.

By now Sollazzo was into his bookies for $75,000 and was scrambling desperately to find a way to pay off the debt. Since 1934 the federal government had tightly controlled gold sales to the general public, but as a jewelry manufacturer Sollazzo was legally entitled to purchase 160 ounces of gold a day; he had concocted a scheme to sell the gold on the international black market and now he was laying off gold as fast as he could, selling his allotment each day to jobbers in the jewelry trade who were willing to handle it, while also cooking his own companies' books, sending his young accountant out each morning to the Railway Express office to convert the jobbers' cash into American Express money orders purportedly made out to him by out-of-state jewelry dealers whom in fact he had invented. Much of Sollazzo's life was increasingly a fiction, including the veneer of wealth he maintained to keep his young wife happy (intent on climbing New York's social ladder, she had recently joined the fundraising committee for the ASPCA ball at the Waldorf-Astoria, other members of which included a Rockefeller and a Vanderbilt), as well as the fantastic notion he had sold to the players: that he was flush with cash, and as long as they kept their part of the bargain his payoffs were as dependable as dividends from General Motors or IBM.

The City College players, though, had been hounding Eddie Gard for the money they were owed, and he kept putting them off with one explanation or another. While he had always been excitable, Gard now seemed simply jumpy, his entrepreneurial optimism and relentless bravado having begun to drain away, and after that catastrophic doubleheader he finally admitted to Floyd Layne: "The big boss took an awful loss and now he hasn't got the money."

The LIU and Manhattan doubleheader had taken place on January 16; the following day the Bronx district attorney's office announced the arrests of two former Manhattan College players,* Jack Byrnes and Hank Poppe, along with three professional gamblers, on charges of having attempted to bribe the current Manhattan star, six-foot-eight-inch center Junius Kellogg. Byrnes and Poppe had been the cocaptains of the 1949–50 Manhattan Jaspers, but as it turned out the two had been receiving a forty-dollar-a-week retainer from a gambling syndicate during that entire season, and in addition had been paid $5,000 apiece to fix five games. Now, in his postcollege life, Poppe was awaiting a job with the New York Fire Department. In the meantime he was working for his old gambling syndicate, and he showed up at Kellogg's dorm room one night to offer him a proposition: one thousand dollars to fix the upcoming game against DePaul.

Twenty-three years old, Junius Kellogg was an Army veteran and the first African American ever to play basketball for Manhattan College. He was there on a basketball scholarship, and he feared that he would lose his scholarship if word of the bribery offer ever got out. He told Poppe that he would consider the proposal, but instead he went to his coach, Ken Norton, who took the information to the president of

---

* Despite its name, Manhattan College is located in the Bronx.

Manhattan College, who in turn notified the police. Later that week Kellogg and Coach Norton met with a group of detectives at the Bronx district attorney's office; they fitted Kellogg with a hidden wire for a subsequent meeting with Hank Poppe, in which Kellogg pretended to accept the offer. "It's easy, Junie," Poppe assured him. "Everybody's doing it all over the country."

DePaul had been favored to win, and the syndicate wanted Manhattan to lose by at least ten points. Though Kellogg was not taking any money for the game, he found (much as Eddie Roman had in the previous year's game against Niagara) that the mere awareness of the scheme rattled him so profoundly that he could hardly play. He scored only four points while committing several fouls, and eventually Ken Norton had to pull him out; his replacement, though, shot eight for eight for seventeen points and Manhattan ended up winning 63 to 59. After the game, Poppe did not appear at the arranged-upon meeting place, Gilhooley's bar near Madison Square Garden, to deliver the money, but he and Byrnes and three associates were arrested in their homes later that night.

The news was splashed across the front pages of all the city's tabloids, the articles running alongside photos of the athletes and gamblers, eyes averted in shame, being hauled in to the local precinct house for booking. Prominent figures from all branches of sport vied to outdo one another in the extravagance of their denunciations: NBA president Maurice Podoloff referred to the attempted bribe as a "cancer"; Coach Ken Norton called the gamblers "termites"; in the *Journal-American* Max Kase condemned the players' "calloused greed for their Judas pieces of silver."

Sid Friedlander of the *New York Post* telephoned Nat Holman in Hollywood Beach, Florida, where he was vacationing during the midwinter break. Holman expressed shock at the news and said, "I don't like to see anything happen to a great game. I don't want to see the fans lose confidence. But I don't believe we coaches can do any more than we are doing. We alert our kids to the dangers at the beginning of each season and we urge them to do their best at all times. I tell my boys to report to me at once anything that might not be strictly on the level."

"It seems unbelievable," commented Clair Bee, head coach of Long Island University, who nine days earlier had shown his star players an anonymous letter accusing them of fixing games. "I can't even imagine such a thing."

Only a week before the Manhattan College arrests, Stan Isaacs of *The Daily Compass* had written a column entitled "Oh, It's Dumping Time Again Among the Court Hotshots," which he began by asking a single blunt question: "Is basketball honest?"

> No one can say for sure yes, and those who would know otherwise aren't going around telling the world—at least they shouldn't be.
>
> Each year with the start of the mad carrying-ons in the Garden, there are rumors on top of whispers about shady developments. On the street corners, in the poolrooms, in the school yards and in the hotel lobbies—wherever basketball fans move—there's whispering about dumps.

Like most of New York's sportswriters, Isaacs knew many gamblers; in the wake of the Manhattan revelations he wrote a column in which he asked one of them the best way to clean up the game. The gambler replied, "They want to stop this stuff, those phony cops, I'll tell them how. Instead of making these big raids on the bookies and talking about busting another gambling ring, why don't they put a tail on some of these highfalutin' college boys for a few days. They'll find out things."

"That may sound harsh," Isaacs advised his readers, "but it's a solution." He was not yet aware that this measure—police following college basketball players suspected of taking bribes—was already well under way.

The anonymous gambler quoted in Stan Isaacs's column was implicitly referring to District Attorney Miles McDonald's ongoing bookmaking investigation in Brooklyn, and just six days after the Manhattan College arrests, the central figure of that investigation—Harry Gross—pleaded guilty to sixty-six counts of bookmaking and conspiracy to violate state gambling laws. His plea came shortly after Assistant District Attorney Julius Helfand revealed in court that Gross possessed the official police records for certain members of his syndicate; the records had been removed from Police Department files—presumably by cops on the pay-roll of Harry Gross. The revelation, noted the reporter for the *Journal-American,* was "startling."

Several months earlier, McDonald's grand jury had discovered that the taped and written records of wiretaps conducted at Gross's head-quarters, the Dugout Cafe, had routinely been destroyed. Now New Yorkers learned that police records, which might have been presumed sacrosanct, were in fact not safe: like, it seemed, so much else in the city, they could be had for the right price.

CHAPTER 26

Eddie Roman and Al Roth were in the Catskills on vacation over the midwinter break when they heard about the arrests of Hank Poppe and Jack Byrnes. The news was unexpected and frightening, for although there was no obvious connection between them and Manhattan College—they didn't know any of the gamblers who had gotten pinched—it was still unsettling to see guys they had played against standing at the desk of the precinct house waiting to be booked like ordinary criminals, and the natural tendency was to imagine yourself facing the very same fate, even if you didn't actually believe it would happen to you. Besides, once the police investigation got going, no one could predict where it would end up. Poppe himself had lamented to reporters at the station house, "Why pick on us when others are doing the same thing?" and amid its extensive coverage of the arrests the *Post* had run an article with a headline guaranteed to send a chill across campuses around the city: OTHER COLLEGE FIVES FACE FIX PROBE. In their darker moments Eddie and Fats even considered turning themselves in to the cops, just admitting everything in hopes of obtaining leniency, but ultimately decided against the idea, in large part because they couldn't bear the thought of having to face their families afterward.

Fats brooded constantly about Eddie Gard's big mouth; Gard seemed constitutionally unable to resist dropping suggestive hints about the big point-shaving scheme he had put together. A few weeks earlier Eddie and Fats had attended a Christmas party that Salvatore Sollazzo threw at his apartment on Central Park West, when for the first time they had the run of the place and could gape at the swanky master bedroom with the gold velvet bedcover and ruffled green drapes, the recreation room with a pool table, the television room with a twenty-inch TV set. Sollazzo himself wandered here and there, slapping players on the back and filling their glasses, the atmosphere as festive and inviting as could be. About a dozen players attended the party, and of course Eddie Gard had been invited too, but there were other, older guys they didn't know, not to mention lots of Jeanne's good-looking girlfriends. Now, looking back, Fats wondered who they all were, began to suspect informers everywhere. Sometimes, he said, when he went out at night he had the feeling that he was being followed; he could swear, too, that he heard clicking noises when he talked on the phone at home, as though the line was being tapped. Eddie worried that Fats was growing paranoid; Fats had even started to consider the possibility that Ed Warner was working his own side deal with other gamblers—surely there were guys up in Harlem that the rest of them had no idea about. By the time they returned home from the Catskills, Eddie and Fats knew they were done with point-shaving. They would collect the money they were still owed for the Boston College game and that would be it.

Floyd Layne and Ed Warner agreed with the decision not to work any more games, and the four players were glad to focus once again solely on basketball. On January 30 the City College Beavers set off on an eleven-day road trip that would take them through Cleveland, Detroit, Boston, and Chicago. The midwinter break had come at just the right time—Ed Warner's strained knee had finally healed, and the infection in Eddie Roman's toe had cleared up—and the Beavers won all four of their games; they returned to New York on February 11 with a record of ten wins and five losses and a realistic prospect of being invited to the postseason tournaments to defend their twin championships.

By that time, detectives had been watching Eddie Gard for a month, tailing him around the clock and listening in on his phone calls. As it turned out, Gard loved to talk in code on the phone, employing a set of aliases that were almost comically easy to decipher. When talking to Roth or Roman, he called Salvatore Sollazzo "Sally"; when talking to Sollazzo he referred to the CCNY players as "the uptown girls." Roman was "the girl with the big nose" or "the big-nose sweetheart," while Roth was "Nosey's friend."

Before long, detectives had identified several college basketball players they suspected of doing business with Gard and Sollazzo, and the investigation quickly expanded. Handwritten detectives' notes reveal that at the end of January, court orders were issued for wiretaps to be installed on additional phone lines, among them TAylor 7-8353, belonging to Augusta Zawoluk of 217 Hendrix Street in Brooklyn, mother of Bob Zawoluk of St. John's University, and JErome 8-1686, belonging to Julius Roman of 1372 Teller Avenue in the Bronx, father of Ed Roman of City College.

On Saturday, February 17, the City College Beavers traveled to Philadelphia to play their final road game of the year, against the Owls of Temple University.

Temple came into the game led by the nation's top scorer, Bill Mlkvy ("the Owl without a vowel"), and the team played with skill and sharpness, but the Beavers set a furious pace right from the opening tap, scoring basket after basket, and as the minutes passed the Temple players became increasingly discouraged, their shoulders starting to slump, as the realization set in that, on this evening at least, their best would not be good enough.

Eddie Roman hadn't felt this free on a basketball court for a long time. That night in Philadelphia the hoop seemed as wide as a circus ring, and when he shot he released the ball unhesitatingly and with full confidence that it would go in. By the end of the first half he had twenty-one points; midway through the second half he had twenty-five, having missed only four shots all night, and at that point the victory was assured and Nat Holman felt confident enough to sit him down with the rest of the starting five.

The final score was 95 to 71; Temple, the Associated Press reported, had been "trounced." Noted the *Observation Post*, "The Lavender five was as good or better than the Grand Slam champs of 1950. Everything they did was with the finesse of champions." The Beavers' ninety-five points were more than any team had ever scored in the history of Convention Hall; it was unquestionably their best game of the year, boding well for a strong finish to the season.

After everyone had showered and dressed, the team walked together to the nearby railroad station, where they would catch the 11:26 train, the *Potomac*, bound for Pennsylvania Station in New York. A light rain had begun to fall, and on the train platform the players shivered a bit in their winter overcoats. City College did not enforce a strict dress code on road trips, but the players were all dressed neatly, in varying degrees of formality. Eddie Roman was outfitted like a junior executive, in a gray topcoat over a dark suit and striped tie; instead of a jacket and tie Ed Warner wore a knit two-color sports shirt and slacks beneath a double-breasted overcoat. Tossing their coats and hats and gym bags on the overhead luggage racks, the players settled into the upholstered seats of the Pullman car, arranging their long legs as comfortably as they could. Bobby Sand sat at the front of the car with the student managers; Nat Holman, as was customary, had taken a private roomette. Some of the players closed their eyes and tried to catch a bit of sleep, while others played cards or perused the sports sections of the evening papers. The car was filled with cheerful voices and the easy laughter of a ballclub at long last in full command of its powers.

Two passengers had come aboard with the team in Philadelphia; they were middle-aged white men, one short and one tall, dressed for the weather in belted trench coats and fedoras. One of the train's other passengers was a City College student named Ina Segal, who worked as a typist for Nat Holman and Sam Winograd in the athletic office. Ina noticed the two men in trench coats, she would say later, because unlike the other passengers they did not take seats but instead stood wordlessly between cars. After the train passed New Brunswick, New Jersey, the shorter of the men stepped inside Nat Holman's roomette, closing the door behind him.

Holman was alone in the car. The man identified himself as Abraham Belsky, a detective with the office of Manhattan district attorney Frank Hogan. He sat down beside Holman, explaining that another detective was waiting outside, and that they had arrest warrants for four of his players and they hoped the arrests could be conducted quietly and with a minimum of disruption. "I think you ought to do it this way," he said. "We don't want a scene. Maybe when the train gets into Penn Station you ought to take the players aside and talk to them."

Holman agreed to do so. He asked whether he might accompany the players to the police station.

Belsky said that the district attorney would prefer it if he didn't, and Holman did not pursue the matter any further.

Forever after, Nat Holman would insist that he had been thoroughly shocked by the detective's notification, but it seems likely that the revelation only confirmed a suspicion that he had been nursing for some time. Holman had often asserted that it was inconceivable to him that, as he put it, "a City College man" would ever be guilty of underhanded practices. However, he knew of a bribe offer that one City College player had made to another as early as 1945; in 1948 he had been notified ahead of time about the possibility of a fix in a game against Syracuse University (this was the game in which Norm Mager claimed to have stumbled upon a City College point-shaving scheme); and earlier that season, after the game against the University of Missouri, Sam Winograd had alerted him to rumors that the game had been fixed. There was also something else: Years later, the son of Honey Russell, head coach of the Seton Hall basketball team, would reveal that on one occasion during the 1950–51 season, the two coaches, longtime friends, sat together in an empty Madison Square Garden and Holman "told my father of his fears about his City College team—some weeks before the news broke of the 1951 point-shaving scandal."

When the train entered the tunnel leading into Penn Station, Nat Holman emerged from his roomette and made his way down the center aisle; in the players' car he stopped and murmured brief instructions to four members of the team, telling them simply to wait outside the train when they arrived, that he wanted to have a talk with them.

With a squeal of brakes the train pulled in to the station, slowly coming to a stop alongside the dimly lit platform. Inside the enormous train shed the world seemed to have resolved itself into tones of black and gray and white; a complicated pattern of steel girders rose like tree trunks into branches that arched high overhead to support a canopy of glass. Clouds of steam billowed around the idling trains, then rose like breath in the air and disappeared. Even at this hour the air was filled with the shrill of whistles and the shouts of conductors and the polite calls of white-jacketed porters hurrying up to the street with suitcases in their hands and under their arms. Max Kase, the sports editor of the *New York Journal-American*, was already waiting on the platform; he was the only newsman to have been notified by District Attorney Frank Hogan about what was to take place there.

The black iron hands of the clocks hanging overhead now read 1:30. The four players—Eddie Roman, Al Roth, Ed Warner, and Ron Nadell, a little-used reserve—stood silently on the platform holding their gym bags, waiting for Holman to speak to them. The two detectives from the train stood just to one side; they had now been joined by two other men, similarly dressed in trench coats and fedoras.

Holman approached the group; his face was drawn, and when he spoke his voice had none of its usual vigor. "These men are detectives," he said to his players. "Go with them. Go without fears. Tell them everything they want to know. If your consciences are clear, you are all right and cannot get into trouble.

"If not," he said sadly, "I'm very sorry for you."

Holman then instructed Roman to call him when he got back home. With that he turned and walked off down the platform, coat collar up, hands thrust deep into his pockets, and before long he had disappeared into the darkness.

It occurred later to Eddie Roman that those were the last words Nat Holman ever spoke to him.

Nat Holman did not insist on accompanying his players as they were taken in for questioning, accepting without argument the detective's explanation that the district attorney would "prefer" that he not. In his brief talk to the players on the train platform Holman did not inform them that the college would arrange for legal representation, nor did he advise them not to speak to investigators until attorneys had arrived. He seems to have made no provision to safeguard the rights of his players as they were taken away to be interrogated on serious criminal charges; he did not contact any attorneys that night, nor did he call the president of City College. Instead, by his own account, he simply returned home and stayed up until dawn awaiting a call from Eddie Roman—but, as he lamented to a reporter from the *Post* the next day, "Roman never called."

Nor did Holman assure the players that as their coach, he would take it upon himself to phone their parents and tell them what had happened. That task he had already assigned on the train to his assistant Bobby Sand, who would make the four calls when he arrived back home in Brooklyn.

Eddie Roman's parents, Julius and Sarah, had been attending a cousin's wedding that night, and they returned home late and were surprised to see that Eddie was not yet there. Their disquiet grew stronger as the minutes passed without word from him. The time moved slowly past two o'clock, then two thirty. Eddie's mother feared that his train had crashed; only two weeks earlier a Pennsylvania Railroad commuter train had derailed on a bridge in New Jersey, killing eighty-two people, and the grisly photos had been splashed across the pages of the city's tabloids. Sarah's older sister and her husband, who lived upstairs and had also attended the wedding, sat up with them to await Eddie's arrival; there was both relief and terror when the phone suddenly rang, the sound of the bell echoing like a gunshot through the silent house.

On the train platform, the four detectives led the players to the exit doors and up to the street for the ride downtown.

Floyd Layne watched in amazement as his teammates were taken into police custody; he turned and headed safely home, feeling himself in the presence of a miracle.

The unmarked police cars drove without sirens through the quiet streets, the tires humming on the wet pavement, wipers beating a steady rhythm on the windshield. Rain beaded and streaked the windows; outside, the city looked smudged, distorted, the bright letters of the neon signs dissolving into indistinct oranges and blues. In the back seat the players responded to the detectives' polite inquiries in hoarse whispers, their voices crumbling in their throats; each was lost in his own thoughts, wondering what the next few hours held. Al Roth, for one, took some comfort in the fact that Ron Nadell—who he knew was innocent—had been picked up along with the rest of them. He would say later, "I saw them grab Ronny and I figured they don't know nothing. They're just fishing, because Ronny was playing, what, maybe two minutes a game? Who was gonna try to fix him?"

After only a few minutes the cars pulled up alongside the huge and imposing Criminal Courts Building on Centre Street. High above the street, a windowed walkway connected the courts building to the city prison next door; the walkway was known as the Bridge of Sighs, because it offered a prisoner a final, sorrowing glimpse of the world outside before he had to begin his sentence.* The detectives led the players past the revolving doors of the main entrance to a doorway around the corner, the district attorney's private entrance. They walked by the policeman who sat at the reception desk in the lobby and crowded into the elevator.

The seventh floor, home to the Rackets Bureau, was normally a noisy, agitated hive, occupied by dozens of lawyers, investigators, accountants, secretaries, stenographers, and process servers; now it held twenty detectives and a scattering of attorneys, grim-faced men in white shirts and dark ties obviously awaiting their arrival. The district attorney himself, Frank Hogan, was in his suite of offices on the floor above; he had arrived at ten o'clock that evening, in anticipation of the arrests, and in the meantime was occupying himself with various ongoing cases. The four City College players were led to separate interrogation rooms at the back of the office.

Inside one of them, Eddie Roman was invited to take a seat. The room was already crowded with men. One of the investigators, tall and slender with light wavy hair and a cleft chin, introduced himself to Eddie; his name was Harold Danforth, but everyone called him Dan. Danforth talked for a while about why they were there that night. He spoke in a confidential, sympathetic tone, referring obliquely to "the basketball situation at the City College of New York." He said that he understood Eddie wasn't a criminal; they had done some checking and

---

* The nickname "Bridge of Sighs" originates from a poem by Lord Byron in which he imagines the misery of prisoners as they walk across a bridge from the Doge's interrogation rooms into the prison in Venice. The earlier incarnation of New York's city prison had an elaborately decorated bridge, four stories above the street, that connected it to the Criminal Courts Building of the time; the newly constructed version of the bridge was shorter, higher, and more utilitarian in style, but the nickname remained.

he knew that Eddie was an A student, a good kid, and not a rich kid either, and he could understand why a player like that might avail himself of an opportunity to "make some change." He wondered whether Eddie had ever discussed with anybody the possibility of making money on a basketball game. One of the detectives sat with an open notepad in front of him, prepared to take down everything Eddie said, like a ghastly parody of a sportswriter after a game. Eddie could not help but wonder how many of them had watched him play in Madison Square Garden, cheered for him during the tournaments. It was hard to concentrate with everyone staring at him like that; he could not think of how to craft a confession that did not also implicate his teammates, which he couldn't bring himself to do, and so he maintained a demeanor of polite bewilderment.

He was asked about the people he knew, the deals he had made. The men around the table seemed disappointed with the quality of his responses. They crossed their arms, stood up and sat down again, exchanged whispers outside the door. They brought one another paper cups filled with coffee, took long drags on their cigarettes and then stubbed them out angrily in the ashtray. Some of them, it became apparent, had not slept in a long while. Over time their tone became sharper, less patient. They informed him that his teammates had already confessed, had given him up to save themselves. If he didn't confess as well, they would be forced to make the charges based solely on what his friends had to say. It wouldn't do for him to be the only holdout, not when it came time for his sentencing. The word lingered pungently in the air like smoke. They needed him to understand that he was part of a criminal conspiracy and faced the real possibility of many years in jail. Again and again they cajoled him: "Tell us what we already know." In fact they seemed not to know very much. Eddie could not help noticing that they never mentioned anything about point-shaving during the previous season; apparently he was the only one in the room who knew about the dealings with Eli Kaye. He shifted his bulk uncomfortably on the chair; he tried not to think about his parents, how frantic with worry they must be. If he just admitted what he had done, the men promised, they would release him and he could go home. At some point, when they seemed unable to come up with any new variations on their questions, Harold Danforth asked for the recording device.

A technician wheeled in a large hinged box that opened up to reveal a complicated-looking mechanism of wires and dials. The technician threw a switch and suddenly the room was filled with voices; it took Eddie a few seconds to realize, with a start, that one of them was his own, and that the other belonged to Eddie Gard. The detectives around the table gazed meaningfully at him as he listened. The implication was clear: They already had all the evidence they needed for conviction.

At a nod from Harold Danforth the technician turned off the sound. Now Danforth said there was someone they wanted him to see—it was like a bizarre version of *This Is Your Life*—and in a few moments one of the detectives returned to the room with Eddie Gard himself. Gard was wearing a rumpled white shirt without a tie, and he had dark shadows under his eyes and his face looked to be stained with tears: He seemed at once much older and much younger.

Gesturing across the table, Danforth asked Gard, "Did you give this boy money, Eddie?" His tone was reminiscent of a schoolteacher making an example of a wayward pupil.

"Yes, I did," Gard mumbled.

"How much, Eddie?"

"Fifteen hundred."

Eddie was shocked to see Gard like this, utterly abject, trying to gain favor with the police by going room to room to accuse his accomplices. Gard was older than they were, had served in the Merchant Marine; if he had broken, then surely Eddie's teammates had too, just like the detectives had said. There seemed no point in remaining silent, taking the fall for guys who were not willing to do the same for him. Maybe he didn't have to name names; maybe he could just apologize and give the money back. He hadn't touched it, after all, not a single cent. If he confessed, he could at least get out of that room and go home to his family, try to recover the life he had before, when on a Sunday morning like this one he and his little brother Richie would walk to 170th Street to buy fresh rolls and rye bread at the bakery. It seemed outlandish that the cops were so interested in him that one had climbed a telephone pole in front of his house and planted a bug on it so they could eavesdrop on his private conversations. Thinking of it he felt exposed, as if a stranger had been peeping into his bedroom window, but even more than that he felt ashamed because the investigators must have listened to his parents and brothers as well, whose only offense was to have him as a family member. This was what he had done to his family: betrayed the hopes they had invested in him, exposed them to public ridicule and disgrace. The odor of corruption would forever after attach to them because of what he had done; in trying to bring them security he had brought them only shame, and in contemplating that, Eddie understood that in fact nothing would ever be the way it was before, that he was indelibly marked now, and so were the people he loved, and there was nothing he could do about it; and a wave of misery swept over him and he began to cry, his large body shuddering with sobs. Later that day Frank Hogan would note in his diary that Eddie Gard had been the first to break, followed by Al Roth, and that "Roman was next—pitiful—a brilliant student."

It was close to five o'clock in the morning when Eddie Roman began to talk; Ed Warner confessed shortly afterward. By then the players were exhausted, hungry, disoriented. They had not been permitted to call their parents, and so their own feelings of fear and humiliation and self-reproof were compounded by guilt and worry about their families.* More critically, the players had not been granted the opportunity to speak with attorneys, and as a result they did not understand that the evidence presented by the investigators as the most damning imaginable—the wiretap recordings—could never be used against them in a court of law.

The legality of wiretapping had been a deeply contested issue from the very start, and not just because there seemed something tyrannical, not to mention morally shameful, in the notion of the government secretly listening in on the private conversations of its citizens—which often involved those not suspected of any wrongdoing. Intercepting personal communications in order to obtain incriminating testimony was also widely seen as an infringement of Fourth Amendment protections

---

* Al Roth finished his confession in tearful despair over the shame he believed he had brought upon his mother and father. At that point he rushed blindly to the window and pulled it up, as if to throw himself to the sidewalk seven floors below; however, the windows of the interrogation rooms had been designed to open no more than three inches, in anticipation of circumstances exactly like that one.

against unreasonable searches and Fifth Amendment protections against self-incrimination.

In 1934 the United States Congress passed the Federal Communications Act; section 605 of the act stated: "No person not being authorized by the sender shall intercept any communication and divulge or publish the existence, contents, substance, purport, effect, or meaning of such intercepted communication to any person." However, the phrase "intercept . . . and divulge" seemed to create a loophole in which the government was permitted to intercept private communications as long as they were not also "divulged"—that is to say, presented in court—and for years attorneys general permitted federal officers to tap phones solely as a means of gathering evidence. This practice was likewise followed in the ten states that permitted police wiretapping, New York among them, and indeed in New York City wiretapping became an especially widespread investigative technique. In 1949 *The New York Times* reported that wiretaps were used in about 350 police cases in the city every year, and in 1951, the year of the basketball investigation, the Manhattan district attorney's office alone received court authorization for eighty-one wiretaps in twenty separate cases. For more than two decades New York's law enforcement officials maintained a careful balancing act: Investigators were allowed to conduct wiretaps to lead them to evidence that could be confirmed by independent sources, but the wiretap recordings themselves were not to be used in court.

The City College players, of course, had no way of knowing this. Instead, the wiretap recordings were presented to them as prima facie evidence of their guilt, used as a lever to pry out their confessions—the actual evidence prosecutors could use to charge the players and obtain convictions.

Like his fellow City College players, Ron Nadell had been taken to a separate room for questioning. The detectives, however, seemed less interested in him than in the other three, and after a brief interrogation he was excused but not released from police custody.

As he waited through the night Nadell saw another college basketball player, St. John's star Bob Zawoluk, enter the office. Zawoluk was the seventh player to be brought in (Connie Schaff of New York University had been arrested with Eddie Gard that afternoon, and another NYU player, James Brasco, had also been questioned), but in his case there was one substantial difference: Unlike the others, Zawoluk was accompanied by an attorney.

In fact, Henry L. Ughetta was more than merely an attorney; he was a justice of the New York State supreme court. He was, as well, a prominent figure in New York Democratic circles, and in 1941 he had served as the treasurer for William O'Dwyer's first unsuccessful campaign for mayor. In addition to his many legal and political connections, Ughetta was well known inside the city's sports establishment through his close friendship with Brooklyn Dodgers owner Walter O'Malley, who had appointed him to the team's board of directors. He also served on the boards of numerous charities and religious organizations; he was described by one biographer as "a high-ranking Catholic layman," regularly appearing at events on behalf of the Brooklyn diocese. In 1949, for instance, Ughetta was one of six members of the laity selected to preside at a ceremony for a local Catholic retreat house; among the other five dignitaries was Police Commissioner William P. O'Brien.

In the district attorney's office Justice Ughetta refused to allow Bob Zawoluk to be questioned outside his presence, and the examination that followed seems to have been more perfunctory than might have been expected. Zawoluk, after all, was one of the handful of basketball players who had attended Salvatore Sollazzo's New Year's Eve party at the Latin Quarter nightclub; Zawoluk had also worked at Grossinger's Hotel in the Catskills with Gard and Connie Schaff the previous summer, when Gard first began planning his point-shaving operation. Detectives considered Zawoluk's potential involvement in the case to be significant enough that he was one of the few players for whom a home wiretap was requested, authorized by a judge, and installed. Still, despite all of this, Zawoluk was subjected to only a brief interview in the district attorney's office and was subsequently released.

"I am convinced this boy is absolutely innocent of any wrongdoing," District Attorney Frank Hogan told reporters the next day.

By that afternoon—Sunday, February 18—seven persons connected to the basketball investigation had been placed under arrest: Salvatore

Sollazzo, Eddie Gard, the three CCNY players, Connie Schaff of NYU, and a gambler named Robert Sabbatini, who was said to have made bets on Sollazzo's behalf. Frank Hogan would later write out four pages of notes in which he summarized the basics of the case, including the names of the defendants, how they had each come to work with the others, the charges on which they were being held, the three games in which point-shaving was alleged to have occurred (the University of Missouri, the University of Arizona, and Boston College), and the amounts paid for each game. On the final page Hogan also included a section with the heading "Payments made variously by Sollazzo and Garde [sic]." There he cited two additional games:

> *Dec 14, 1950 Wash State*
> *Jan 2, 1951 St. John's*

Hogan indicated that "R & R" (Roth and Roman) had received $500 each for the Washington State game and $250 each for the St. John's game as "good will bonuses." The payment for the Washington State game would eventually be cited in the *Outline of Proof as to Various Counts of the Indictment* prepared by the district attorney's office in preparation for trial; the payment for the St. John's game, however, was never mentioned.

Ron Nadell sat in the district attorney's office for thirteen hours, until at last he was informed that he was in the clear and could go home. On his way out of the office that Sunday afternoon he ran into Eddie Roman, who had just finished several hours of interrogation by Assistant District Attorney Vincent O'Connor and was now waiting to be booked. Eddie had not slept all night and still had a very difficult day in front of him, surely the worst of his life; he looked terrible, drained, barely able to string a sentence together. "He was glad to see someone he knew," Nadell was to recall. "He couldn't talk much. He kind of stumbled and stammered."

Eddie spoke briefly with his teammate; as they talked, the sense of regret seemed to build up inside him, until in a burst of emotion he yanked off his gold championship ring and blindly tossed it away. Said Nadell, "It was hard to watch."

• • •

That afternoon detectives from the district attorney's office brought the accused downstairs to be booked at the Elizabeth Street precinct house. The police station was four blocks away, and the players walked dazedly through the narrow streets followed by a scrum of reporters and photographers and curious passersby, a crowd of more than one hundred in all. The detectives pulled open the double doors and led the defendants to the long oak counter inside. Detectives and other observers crowded in several deep behind them, taking up every square inch of space; the hum of conversation resounded off the pressed tin ceiling and the marble staircases that wound upstairs to a dozen prison cells, punctuated every few seconds by the muffled explosion of a camera bulb. The scene was a tableau of white men in fedoras; Ed Warner was the only African American in the crowd, and Eddie Roman, hatless, towered over them all. He stood beside Eddie Gard, who some thirteen hours earlier had confronted him with his guilt.

After a long night of interrogation, college basketball players and gamblers await booking at the Elizabeth Street police station. From left to right: Ed Warner, Al Roth, Connie Schaff, Detective James Cashman, Salvatore Sollazzo (in lighter-colored fedora, hiding his face), Robert Sabbatini, Eddie Roman. Eddie Gard is hidden behind Roman. New York Daily News / Getty Images

Later that evening, having subsequently been brought to police headquarters to be photographed and fingerprinted, the accused were taken back to the Criminal Courts Building for a special night session of felony court. There they stood before Chief Magistrate John M. Murtagh. Eddie Roman was still in his dark suit and striped tie, his overcoat folded neatly over his left arm like a commuter waiting for a train; he stared stoically straight ahead, his unshaven jaw clenching and unclenching as he listened to the judge read out the charges of having violated Section 382 of the New York State Penal Code, which prohibited bribes to lose a sporting contest or to limit the margin of victory. With that, the magistrate declared, he would determine bail, based on the charges and the criminal history of the accused.

Salvatore Sollazzo excused himself to interrupt, wanting to explain the circumstances behind his earlier convictions for grand larceny, armed robbery, and jewelry theft, for which he had served two prison sentences.

John Murtagh had auburn hair and deep-blue eyes that flashed now in anger. "You will get no sympathy in this court," he responded sharply. "You appear to have corrupted these young men and brought disgrace on a great institution. I happen to be an alumnus of that school."

Murtagh was a City College graduate, class of 1931; at the 1950 graduation in Lewisohn Stadium he was the public official chosen to administer the Ephebic Oath, the one that began *We will never bring disgrace to our city by any act of dishonesty or cowardice.* His successful career he owed in large part to the patronage of William O'Dwyer, who had been a close friend of Murtagh's father, Thomas, since their boyhood together in County Mayo, Ireland. During his first mayoral administration, O'Dwyer appointed Murtagh investigations commissioner, assigning him to lead an inquiry into police involvement with gamblers. One month after this night session, Murtagh himself would be called to testify before District Attorney Miles McDonald's grand jury in Brooklyn, where he declared that as investigations commissioner "no one did more to fight organized gambling than I did." Judge Samuel Leibowitz seemed skeptical, asking him, "Did you finally come to the conclusion that some cops were involved with bookies?"

"No, sir."

"Never?"

"Never." Murtagh claimed that despite an "exhaustive" investigation—

which discovered that some policemen assigned to gambling squads had accumulated assets of $30,000 or more—he had never found any evidence of corruption and as a result he had not felt a need to report his findings to the mayor. He explained to Judge Leibowitz, "I would rather be humane than a dogged, unfair persecutor."

Now Murtagh set bail for each of the three City College players at $15,000*; Connie Schaff's was set at $10,000. They would each remain in custody until bail was posted. Salvatore Sollazzo would be held without opportunity of bail, and Eddie Gard, who had indicated his willingness to cooperate with the district attorney's office in every possible way, would be held in protective police custody at an undisclosed location.

The four players were taken from the Criminal Courts Building to the city prison, across the Bridge of Sighs.

Jeanne Sollazzo and her brother-in-law arrive at Manhattan's Supreme Court in an unsuccessful attempt to have fixer Salvatore Sollazzo released on bail. Author's collection

* $15,000 in 1951 is equivalent to about $151,000 in today's currency.

CHAPTER 27

Eddie was all right, Bobby Sand had told them; he was safe, but he had been taken to the district attorney's office in Manhattan on charges of conspiring with gamblers. "The sword has fallen," he said, his voice breaking. Hearing the news, Eddie's parents burst at once into tears, and Bobby wept along with them.

All the next day Julius and Sarah remained by themselves in their bedroom, Julius emerging only occasionally to greet family members who arrived bearing baked goods and platters of cold cuts, as in a kind of shiva. The line of guests extended from the kitchen through the dining room and into the living room, which had always been reserved for special occasions, the conversations carried on in hushed tones in English and Yiddish. Many of those in the house that day referred to what had happened simply as "the trouble," an all-embracing phrase redolent of Eastern European sorrow. Sarah's older sister Bashke and her husband, Hymie, lived just upstairs and they had come down as soon as they heard, and later they were joined by their son Charlie and their daughter Rae and her husband, George. George worked downtown at the Ted Brooks clothing store; he was the only one in the family who had any money, and therefore his opinion was accorded special weight. Before long he had put together a plan to raise the $15,000 in bail money by putting up several thousand dollars of his own savings and using the Romans' house as additional collateral. Much of the discussion centered on finding an attorney. It was generally understood that they had to find one with "connections"—that was, everyone agreed, Eddie's only chance. Someone remembered a girl from Taft High School who had been friends with a number of the players on the basketball team; her father was a lawyer who was thought to be politically well connected. Phone calls were made, and by the end of the day he had been hired.

Every so often the doorbell would ring and instead of a friend or family member it was a reporter looking for the family's response to the news; they were now, unexpectedly and through no intention of their own, the focus of the city's most fevered attention. "He's a good boy," the relatives insisted again and again—a sweet boy, an honor student, not at all the sort of person who would get involved in this sordid business. "It's a terrible shock, just terrible," Eddie's older brother, Mel, told the reporter from the *Post*, Alvin Davis. "There may be a more sorrow-struck family somewhere in this city of eight million," Davis wrote, "but it would be hard to find."

Julius and Sarah refused to come out of the bedroom to talk to the press. Mel's wife, Harriet, described their condition to a reporter as "near hysteria." Sarah in particular was inconsolable, and she spent the day in bed sobbing, refusing all offers of food or other forms of comfort.

The tragedy she had long awaited, the one that would ruin the life of her family, had finally arrived.

At his Sunday press conference announcing the arrests, District Attorney Frank Hogan told reporters, "This entire business is loathsome, and at the same time pathetic. I cannot feel the joy of accomplishment in this sickening business. These stupid and dishonest men broke down when they admitted their guilt. Their tears of remorse and self-reproach should be an object lesson to others who would toss away their honor for tainted money."

In his diary, Hogan would note that the press conference had received "nation-wide coverage," that he had gotten "calls from newspapers all over the United States." Stories about the City College arrests appeared on the front page of all of New York's daily papers; even *The New York Times* ran the article on page one, with an accompanying photograph just below the masthead—the only photo on the page. Four columns wide, the photograph shows the accused players and gamblers, surrounded by plainclothes detectives, standing at the front desk of the Elizabeth Street precinct house. None of the men is looking at any of the others, each seemingly trapped in his own private anguish, which gives the image the feel of a Renaissance painting of guilt and sorrow. In the foreground at the left edge of the frame Ed Warner is unexpectedly smiling, as though the desk sergeant has just told him a joke, but the smile belies the look of hurt and confusion in his eyes; directly to his left Al Roth stares grimly ahead; at the center of the image Connie Schaff holds his hands crossed in front of him in what appears a gesture of supplication, one wrist above the other, as though he were already wearing handcuffs; at the other edge Eddie Roman looks sheepish, his eyes downcast, wearing a half-smile to disguise his pain and embarrassment.

In the *Times*, the City College basketball story ran directly alongside an article about a proposal to set up special "watchdog" grand juries across New York City "for the express purpose of investigating political or government misconduct," a proposal inspired by the revelations emerging from Miles McDonald's Brooklyn grand jury investigation. Throughout the coming months, stories of the two scandals, the basketball scandal and the Harry Gross scandal—each one connected to sports gambling, each one shocking in its revelation of previously unfathomed corruption—would often run side by side on the front pages of the city's newspapers.

On Monday morning the office of Dr. Harry N. Wright, president of City College, issued a statement on behalf of the school. "The news of the latest basketball scandal comes as a deep and terrible to shock to us," it began.

> We are heartsick at the recent revelations. In particular we extend our sympathies to the families of the boys.
>
> At present we expect to fulfill our contractual obligations and complete the remainder of the schedule. As far as the future is concerned, the college authorities are making a thorough examination to determine where we will play our games next season and beyond that.

City College has a long and honorable tradition of service to the community and the nation, and athletics have always played an important part of the educational program. The leadership in basketball as provided by Professor Holman is of the highest caliber. We have constantly been on our guard to prevent what has taken place. This year, as in the past, the members of the team were continually instructed as to the possible dangers of this kind.

The statement concluded with a sentence that was sure to send shock waves reverberating across the campus: "This morning, the three boys involved, Ed Roman, Al Roth, and Ed Warner, were suspended from the college until further notice."

That Monday was unusually warm for February in New York, the temperatures climbing into the mid-60s, the clouds low overhead and the air damp and heavy. On St. Nicholas Heights in upper Manhattan the weather seemed entirely in keeping with the general mood: "The college with the concrete campus was in mourning today," noted the *World-Telegram and Sun.* Says Mort Sheinman, a CCNY sophomore of the time, "It was as if this gray cloud of gloom had settled over the campus. People didn't know what to say." The feeling was one of collective grief, of a sort that Sheinman says he would not experience again until the assassination of President Kennedy, and even decades later the City College students of the time consistently describe the revelation of the arrests using analogies of sudden, shocking, even violent loss. "Everybody was so disheartened," says Myron Neugeboren, a student at the downtown campus. "It was like they had lost their best friend."

"It was like somebody died in the house," says Gloria Schulman, who had just graduated. "We were all in mourning—my parents, my family. It was like we had lost a member of our family."

"It was," says Leonard Dauer, a senior that year, "like putting a knife through our hearts."

Walking to their Monday morning classes, the students found that they had been joined on campus by reporters from radio, television, newspapers, and newsreels; inevitably the media interest called up memories of the morning after the second tournament championship, but now instead of easy exhilaration many of them found that they didn't know how to respond to the questions, what exactly to say or even to think. It was still too new, too strange, too upsetting. Oscar Zeichner, a professor of American history, walked into his classroom and saw all of his students with their heads lowered, as though already taking an examination: They were deeply engrossed in newspapers on the desks in front of them. When the bell rang to start class he said, "This is a class in history, and I think we would do well to spend the first five minutes reading the newspapers."

For the next several minutes there was not a sound in the classroom other than the rustle of pages being turned. "Now," Zeichner finally said, breaking the silence, "do you want to get anything off your chests?"

Someone muttered something about how they used to call Ed Roman "the noblest Roman of them all"; the nickname, he seemed to be saying, was no longer appropriate.

Another student spoke up. "I've read all the stories," he said. "I just can't believe it. It must be a hoax. Those guys just couldn't do this to us."

One of the women in the class said that she thought they should take the basketball team out of Madison Square Garden—the atmosphere there was too commercial for college games—but a young man in the seat beside her said that he didn't think it would make any difference, that gamblers could find the players in small gyms as well as big ones.

All that gray morning, students huddled talking in clusters around the campus; as with the student in Oscar Zeichner's class, the sense of betrayal seemed most often to be directed at Eddie Roman. "He never got a big head, even after last year's Grand Slam basketball championships," one student said, his tone pitched somewhere between wonderment and bitterness. "He was always writing letters to fans. He never refused to sign a kid's autograph book. How could he do something like this?"

How could he do something like this? He was the team's cocaptain and leading scorer, a second-year honors recipient, a candidate for Phi Beta Kappa, by every account thoughtful and hardworking and modest, seemingly the player least likely to succumb to corruption. The notion of Eddie Roman taking bribes from gamblers simply didn't comport with what they thought they knew about him; and yet apparently he *had* done it, had been photographed in the papers standing side by side with criminals, and the very incongruity of that picture seemed to call much else into question: All at once the sturdy bedrock of City College seemed to be shifting beneath their feet. "Something that I had thought was so beautiful and so clean," says Dorothy Steinmetz, a sophomore that year, "was just shattered."

By noon, word had gotten around that a rally had been called for two o'clock in the Great Hall, to publicly demonstrate support for the school and the remaining members of the team. Long before two, the hall was filled to overflowing, every one of the twenty-four hundred seats on the main floor and in the balcony already taken. Beginning the proceedings, the president of the student council, Jerome Levinrad, stepped to the podium to read aloud President Wright's written statement. Many of the students had not yet heard it, and they cheered the news that the team would play out the remainder of its schedule, and gave a warm round of applause to the words of praise for Coach Nat Holman.

Holman himself was not present at the rally; he was downtown at Leone's restaurant with Sam Winograd, attending the weekly luncheon of the Metropolitan Basketball Writers Association alongside the coaches from New York's other basketball powers: Long Island University, New York University, and St. John's University. When he stood to speak he expressed his shock and dismay at what had happened and vowed to fight as hard as possible in the three games left in the season. "Who knows," he said, a touch of wistfulness in his voice, "the team may be better than ever—they say a repaired garment can sometimes be stronger than the original." Winograd as well emphasized the great distress he felt over the situation, but he took care to note that he did not believe that playing in Madison Square Garden exerted any sort of corrupting influence on college basketball, and he expressed confidence that the public wouldn't turn against the City College team due, as he put it, to the "moral deterioration" of three of its players.

The chairman of the college's athletic department, Dr. Frank Lloyd, attended the Great Hall rally in Holman and Winograd's stead, receiving a burst of cheers when he declared: "Eight months ago [*sic*], the city, the country, and the world honored a group of men representing City

College: a group that carried CCNY to an unprecedented honor. We all basked in the glory of the team's victory and now we must not let our support dwindle. Let's show the world that we are behind the team."

Before long what might have been a kind of memorial service had turned into a pep rally, the crowd hailing the speeches given by representatives of the faculty and administration and roaring for Edward Cohen, president of the Student Athletic Association, who exclaimed, "I want every student to come to next Thursday's game against Lafayette and support these other players! I don't think we students are guilty of anything and only guilty people are afraid to stand up!" At that the crowd leaped to its feet, the noise rising to a crescendo when Cohen called to the stage six members of the basketball team who had been sitting anonymously among their fellow students. Most of them were sophomore reserves who had never received the cheers of the crowd, but overnight they had turned into stars, and as the tall young men walked shyly up to the platform, the audience gave them a sustained standing ovation, the whoops and whistles and cheers echoing through the vast room and ending only when a member of the athletic booster group jumped onto the stage to lead the crowd in what one *Campus* reporter described as "the most rousing Allagaroo ever heard at the college."

Floyd Layne was in a chemistry lab on Monday afternoon and so could not attend the Great Hall rally. A reporter for *The Campus* caught up with him that day to ask for his response to the arrests, but Layne had little to say. He had not noticed poor play by any particular individual that season, he said—"the whole team didn't function well." To the *Observation Post* Layne said only that he was "shocked" to hear about the conspiracy among Roman, Roth, and Warner, and that he felt "as badly as the three of them. What else can I say?"

Another student rally was scheduled for the next morning, though, and Layne did attend that one with the rest of his teammates. More than two thousand students jammed into the auditorium of the downtown business school while the members of the team sat in a long row on the stage. Though other members of the college community briefly

addressed the audience, Coach Nat Holman was the most highly anticipated speaker. He began his remarks by expressing how surprised and
disappointed he was that City College students had been implicated in
the basketball scandal; still, he explained, "Ideals and good citizenship
don't mean much sometimes when a dollar bill is flashed in front of the
eyes." Every week for years Holman had listened to the debates from
Town Hall on the radio, learning how to turn a phrase or hold an audience's attention; now his cultured voice rang strong and clear through
the auditorium. "Some of our boys made a mistake," he said, "a terrible
mistake. I know they're sorry, but I was close to those boys and I repeatedly told them that if they wanted to dance they would have to pay the
piper."

Holman urged the students to turn out for the next game, against
Lafayette College. With a flourish he pointed to the reconstituted team
and declared emphatically, "Now is the time to come to the support of
these kids—they haven't got a price!"

With that, Holman announced that the new cocaptains would be
Ron Nadell and Floyd Layne, and the two players smiled modestly and
waved in turn as the cheers of the crowd washed over them. The response was affectionate for Ronny, as the other students called him, for
he was the only senior on the team and was known to them especially
well as a fellow student on the downtown campus; by far the stronger
outpouring, though, was reserved for Floyd Layne. Floyd, after all, was
now the sole remaining member of the previous year's double-
championship starting five, the last link to that more glorious time,
which was only eleven months in the past but already seemed preserved
in amber; more important, he was the only one of the current stars who
had resisted temptation—who, in Nat Holman's formulation, didn't
have a price—and while he had always been among the most popular
members of the team, he had now grown into something more, not just
a basketball player but a genuine hero, who would compete on behalf of
the school with dignity and honor. He seemed the exemplar of who they
themselves wanted to be as City College students, and the ovation they
gave him was thunderous, and from all around the auditorium students
called for him to *speak, speak, speak,* the pleas so loud and insistent, the
desire to hear him so strong, that decades later many who had been

there would remember him as actually having made a speech when in fact he simply rose from his chair and awkwardly acknowledged the cheers of the crowd before sitting down again. "I could never get myself to do a thing like that," Layne would later write. "I never said a word."

The two rallies seemed to have provided a kind of catharsis, and over the next few days the feelings of hurt and disappointment and anger that had initially prevailed among the students, while never disappearing entirely, began to evolve into something larger and more inclusive. "We, as a group, are closer than any other to these athletes," the editors of *The Campus* reminded their fellow students. They had sat beside the players in class; had eaten with them in the cafeteria; had cheered them on, again and again, as they brought the college undreamed-of glory. Though it was taken as a given that the players bore primary responsibility for their own disgrace, some students began to ask whether the college, too, was in some measure accountable, for having placed the players in the big-time atmosphere of Madison Square Garden, exposing them to easy money and bad influences. "We throw a handful of youths into a snake pit," the *Observation Post* noted acerbically, "and solely blame the boys for being bitten." The players, it was often pointed out, had not entered the college already corrupted; something had happened in the intervening years that caused them to fall. Was it simply that these young men had an especially slack morality, or might there be deeper temptations at work to which even a good person might over time succumb? The members of the team, after all, came from the same neighborhoods they did, from families much like their own. From this acknowledgment it was but a small step to wonder: Faced with that situation, might I not have done the same thing?

In classic City College fashion, the debates went on all over campus, students and professors alike asking themselves to what, and to whom, they should be loyal.* Amid the crisis, many tried to resist the moral

* *Loyal* was an especially loaded word at City College, at the very moment when CCNY graduate Julius Rosenberg was about to go on trial with his wife, Ethel, for atomic espionage; one of their codefendants, Morton Sobell, was a City College classmate of Julius's. There was something deeply discomfiting about the notion of City students engaged in conspiracies; it seemed to reinforce the perception of City College

superiority that allows pain to be converted into vengeance; such a response seemed inimical to long-standing and deeply held City College values such as justice, rationality, and mercy. As a senior named Ted Zimmerman would write in a letter to *The Campus,* City College "is not simply a series of Gothic buildings stuck together by some wet Allagaroos. It's a community for social and intellectual interaction, a dynamic and vital community. We don't resolve our crises by getting hysterical nor by accumulating tar and feathers." While acknowledging that the three players should not return to the basketball team—their transgression was too serious for that—many students began to suggest that they should be allowed to reenter the college to complete their education: to rehabilitate themselves as students so that they might someday redeem themselves as citizens. "What if we don't permit them to return?" a student named Phyllis Schwab asked in a letter to the *Observation Post.* "If we, the ones they betrayed, cannot or will not forgive them, who will? Who will give them the chance to transcend their disgrace? Who will let them prove their integrity the stronger for being through the Hell of remorse? Nobody for many years—perhaps for the rest of their lives. A school can conquer its disgrace in time; a man cannot without help."

Though some disagreed, little by little a kind of consensus began to emerge on campus. Before the week was out the Student Council had passed a resolution calling for the three suspended players to be reinstated; the vote was twenty-five to one. The chairman of the college's Sociology Department, Burt W. Aginsky, told the *New York Post,* "I've canvassed a number of the members of my department and the feeling seems to be, the guilt lies in the total situation. We feel we have a responsibility to these youngsters. We feel this shouldn't be the end of their usefulness and opportunity. We hope an application for reinstatement next semester will be favorably considered." A spokesman for the school's alumni association said that "the general alumni sentiment is that we should help these boys in every way without condoning what they did."

---

as an untrustworthy institution, outside the American mainstream. The writer Avery Corman recalled a City student in his Bronx neighborhood receiving the news of the basketball arrests: " 'For years they've been saying everyone at City is a Communist,' she said, despondent, 'and now this.' "

Editorials in all of the college's student newspapers likewise advocated reinstatement. "They are not incorrigible," insisted *The Campus*. "The justice that we know is deeply rooted in the tradition of City College beckons to them: come back to school as students; you have little else!"

The newspaper of the business campus, *The Ticker*, adopted a larger perspective in an editorial entitled "For Reinstatement": "Even though we might not like to hear it, we, *all of us*, share the blame that has been thrust upon the involved players. Being component segments of a society which idolizes the money god, we share the guilt which must fall on that society."

Not everyone who accepts bribes goes to prison, the *Ticker* editors pointed out—indeed some, like Congressman James A. Garfield, had been elected president. Nor had banks and large corporations been free of corruption and the other base practices "which have all-too frequently associated themselves with our money-mania. . . . In deciding the penalty, if any, which may be meted out to the players, we should appreciate the fact that our entire social structure is off-balance when money becomes an end rather than a means. And that's what it has become for most of us.

"It is said that the action of the 'fixers' was immoral. That we concede. But it is immorality based on, and caused by, an already corroded code of ethics."

CHAPTER 28

Nat Holman stood before the City College Beavers in his office on the second floor of Lewisohn Stadium. A single window overlooked the playing field; in warmer weather, and happier times, Holman had often enjoyed listening to the "Stadium Symphony Orchestra" rehearse outside while he worked. The office now had the uncomfortable, apprehensive air of a physician's waiting room. "Boys," he began, "I wanted to talk to you about this unfortunate thing that has happened to you fellows, to myself, and to the college. I know how you all feel—how shocking it was to me and to you. We have three more games. How do you feel about them? Shall we play them or call the season finished now?"

It was a line of questioning that seemed to allow only one response—especially as Holman himself had already publicly announced that he intended to play out the remainder of the schedule, and a schoolwide rally had been convened to help boost student ticket sales for the upcoming game. "Play them," a voice responded after a moment. Said another, "Sure—play," and that sentiment was echoed by several in the room.

"I'm glad you agree," Holman said. "I feel nothing should interrupt our program, which means so much to the college. I'm so glad you agree. It makes it easier for me to say what I want to say."

He began to pace in front of them. "It started so far back. The Missouri game, and those three showing straight faces when we talked and were together. It's a terrible thing. There's a lesson to be learned from this, boys, but it's a terrible price to pay for it. Believe me, boys, I have no sympathy for them if they are guilty, because they did as fine a double-crossing job on me and on you as has ever been done." Holman repeated for the players what he had told the basketball writers earlier that day, about how a patched garment could be stronger than the original. He said, "When you go out on the floor now, all eyes will be on you. You've never had so many behind you as you will have now. You didn't have a price. The others did. The money was fabulous . . . a guy like Fats . . . a nice guy . . ." Holman's voice began to trail off. After a moment he asked, "Is there anything else you want to say?" No one spoke. "That's all, then," he told them. "Go down to the gym. I'll be right down."

The players, as it turned out, were not the only ones sitting in Nat Holman's office that afternoon. The door to his private bathroom had been cracked open an inch while the meeting was going on; inside, the *New York Post* sportswriter Milton Gross was busily taking notes for his column the next day. In the column Gross would write that Holman had chosen to hold the team meeting in his office rather than the City College gym because he wanted "privacy"; if privacy was the goal, however, it was only reasonable for the players to wonder why Holman had encouraged them to speak freely while a newspaper reporter hid in the bathroom recording everything that was said.

Gross's column would relate Holman's talk to the players virtually word for word; it began to seem that the true audience was not the players but the public, that Holman had staged his talk to reinforce the idea that he had been blindsided by the point-shaving revelations. "We were used as a foil for him," Herb Cohen would later say about that meeting. That was why they had been invited up there, many of the players came to believe; that was why they were seeing the inside of his office for the very first time.

As the week went on, the scandal only intensified. Along with Nat Holman, Long Island University coach Clair Bee had given a speech at the basketball writers' luncheon after the arrests were announced. "I'm very disappointed in Eddie Gard," said Bee. "But the rest of my boys are innocent. I swear it on the heads of my children." Before the day was out, three members of his team had been arrested by Frank Hogan's detectives and confessed to accepting money to shave points in seven games over two seasons.

By the end of the week, Manhattan district attorney Frank Hogan announced that $20,540 in bribe money had been recovered from the arrested players. Ed Warner had folded up the money and stuffed it in a shoe inside a shoebox he kept in the basement; he had been saving up to move out of his aunts' apartment and someday get a place of his own. Eddie Roman had put the money in an envelope and asked his cousin Charlie to hold it for safekeeping. He was planning to give the money to his mother, who fretted constantly about the family's expenses. Al Roth, who placed the money in a safe-deposit box, had intended to use it to set himself up in business once he got out of school.

To get an apartment, to run a household, to start a business: These were decidedly middle-class aspirations. The bribe money had not been spent on expensive cars or swanky clothing or any other of the trappings of the underworld life as represented by, say, Harry Gross with his Cadillac and closetful of suits; instead it had been set aside, largely untouched, in hopes of providing a more secure future. "This was not to be spending money," op-ed columnist Max Lerner observed in the *New York Post*, "but rainy day money, business-starting money, career-insuring money." Lerner had entitled his column "Why Did They Do It?" It was a question that for a while preoccupied much of New York; yet the motivations of the players were perhaps not as puzzling, their desires not as far-flung, their corruption not as essential—nor as isolated—as observers might have liked to believe.

"Basketball is the slot machine of sports," the veteran sportswriter Jimmy Cannon observed in 1951. "The teams have the appeal of the black and red of the roulette tables." One year earlier Milton Gross had written, "Gambling and her odorous sister, bribery, still hover like obscene buzzards over the grand old winter sport of basketball. Nobody knows just when they will circle down again and befoul the scene. But they will. That's better than an even money bet—and no point spread." Gross's own newspaper, the *Post*, like nearly all of the city's papers, published point spreads for both the professional and college games. Privately most of the editors in town would admit that there was something at least slightly disreputable about a newspaper regularly devoting space to an illegal activity—not to do so, though, was to risk losing customers to one's competitors. (Indeed, the press's complicity with the gambling industry was so open that at the beginning of the 1950–51 college basketball season the *Post* "gave" an imaginary hundred dollars to each of its three basketball writers—one of them was Milton Gross— with which to place bets against the listed point spreads, and tracked their cumulative total each week.)

Though no one, least of all Madison Square Garden promoter Ned Irish, liked to talk about it, a large share of the Garden's hefty gate receipts for college basketball games likewise derived from gambling. While the arena's balconies were dominated by students who paid little for their tickets and exuded raucous school spirit, downstairs many of the more expensive seats were occupied by fans who cared less about who won or lost than about which team covered the points. Noted Jimmy Cannon: "Many a guy, I suppose, attends basketball for reasons of sentimental attachment to a university. Some are interested only in the action of the contaminated game. But more than any sport I cover, except horse racing, basketball attracts those who gamble." Though Irish made a big show of policing gambling inside the arena, little meaningful action was ever taken to actually prevent it. The week after the CCNY point-shaving scandal broke, a group of New York University students attending an NYU–Notre Dame game made a series of simulated bets, using stage money, in full view of the Garden's special police. "A student would leave his seat," reported the *World-Telegram and Sun,* "walk to another pretending to be a bookmaker, whisper to him and accompany him to a spot near an usher or patrolman. There the stage money was passed and the bookmaker jotted down a memorandum." No effort was made to halt the apparent betting.

For Ned Irish, noted Dan Parker of the *Daily Mirror,* college basketball was nothing less than "a gold mine." It was college basketball, after all, that had paid for Irish's Park Avenue apartment and his New Jersey lake house, out of the percentage of the gate receipts that he retained after expenses. Contractually, a popular local team such as City College received 12.5 percent of that night's gate, which worked out to approximately $3,000 per game, or more than $50,000 over the course of a season—enough to subsidize the other twelve sports in City's athletic program. Each season, the City College Beavers played only one or two out of perhaps two dozen games in their own school gymnasium; the rest were played in Madison Square Garden or one of the arenas in the other nine cities around the country for which Ned Irish also promoted college basketball games. Like almost all of New York's significant college basketball programs (Columbia University alone refused to play in the Garden), City College had ceded control of its schedule to an outsider who was motivated primarily by profit—but this was a deal the school was more than willing to make, for City now collected as much money from a single Garden appearance as it had once earned, before Ned Irish, from an entire season of basketball.

A kind of financial triangle had thus been created that connected gamblers, the colleges, and Madison Square Garden, each one needing the others in order to thrive. For a school to keep its status as a premier attraction, however, it was imperative to maintain a winning program; this meant recruiting the most prized local basketball prospects, having to compete for them with state universities that routinely offered full scholarships, free use of cars and apartments, and monthly living expenses. At Long Island University, head coach Clair Bee (who in addition to his coaching duties was vice president of the university) rewarded his players with tuition waivers, easy student jobs, and private rooms in a house near the college, and also enrolled them in courses that in the 1950–51 academic year included Oil Painting, Camp Administration, and Lifesaving: Diving and Small Craft. City College, of course, charged no tuition, and thus scholarships were unnecessary; for housing, the college offered only the occasional use of one of the bunk beds in Army Hall, and for spending money the possibility of part-time student employment. That, at least, was what the college admitted to providing. Behind the scenes, as Eddie Roman well knew, other promises were sometimes made (if not always fulfilled), such as a seat in a graduate program for an older brother, or even, for a father, a new job. And while City had long heralded its special status as a college that maintained rigorous academic standards for admission, in the case of certain desirable basketball recruits, such as Al Roth, even this worthy principle was not immune to violation.

Like Floyd Layne and Ed Warner, Al Roth had graduated from high school with a grade point average too low to gain admittance to City College. Unlike Layne and Warner, though—whom Bobby Sand had enrolled in evening session courses designed to bring up their averages—Roth was allowed to proceed directly into the college's general program. As it turned out, there was a reason for that. In the wake of the point-shaving scandal, the city's Board of Higher Education hired a private investigator named Andrew O'Neil to examine CCNY official transcripts, and in the course of his examination O'Neil discovered that while Roth's high school average was only 70.4, someone had entered it onto the entrance transcript as 75.5. Even that doctored number was still too low for admission, but candidates for City College also had to take an entrance examination, the results of which were combined with the high school average to produce a final score. Apparently Roth had done extraordinarily well on this exam, receiving a final score of 89.40; when O'Neil rechecked the exam, however, he determined that the score should actually have been 70.63.

Roth's Erasmus Hall teammate Herb Cohen was likewise undistinguished academically, having completed high school with a 74.5 average, but O'Neil discovered that on his college transcript the 7 had been turned into an 8—in so doing raising the average ten points and, with a single stroke of the pen, turning an ineligible candidate into an eligible one.

Nor were the cases of Roth and Cohen isolated examples. Andrew O'Neil ultimately uncovered no fewer than fourteen cases, dating back to 1945, in which academic records of athletes had been "fraudently changed in such a way as to raise the high school average sufficiently to establish eligibility for admission to the college."

The altered transcripts, the relaxed academic standards, the arena where a blind eye was turned to illegal gambling: Through it all the talented young basketball player came to understand that the rules governing the lives of others could, in his case, be adjusted as necessary. Perhaps, then, he too might seek to adjust the rules just a bit—might alter the score of a basketball game without actually having to lose it.

The college players caught up in the burgeoning scandal were white and black, Jewish and Christian, good students and poor. Most came from families that could loosely be described as working class, though some were slightly better off than that, and some a good deal worse. They were much like their classmates in all ways but one, which was that they had a surpassing talent for basketball, and as a result they found themselves in a circumstance almost singular in American society: They could generate enormous profits for others, but they were not permitted to keep any of those profits for themselves.

It was an especially fertile field in which a culture of bribery could take root. Of course, bribery was already rife in New York's political and business circles, but these college basketball players were unusual in that they were working class and yet consequential enough to be offered bribes. In this regard they were something like police officers—and it is not hyperbolic to suggest that the basketball player who turned down a bribe to shave points was about as uncommon as the policeman who turned down a payoff to protect the activities of the local bookmaking syndicate.

Cops were on the take everywhere in the neighborhoods in which the players had grown up, the crooked cop as much of a local fixture as the bookie taking bets in the pool hall or the numbers runner going door to door like a meter reader or Bible salesman. It was a world of hidden money: of transactions, accommodations, payoffs, pulling of strings. The painters' union to which Eddie Roman's father had belonged, once a proud Socialist redoubt, had been seized by mobsters who took a piece of all the contracts they negotiated; the family's political representatives in the Bronx had been chosen by a party boss who dispensed jobs and favors to all, even those from the opposition party, who agreed not to challenge his authority. When the players got into trouble with the law, everyone understood that their strongest hopes lay not in an attorney who was legally astute but one who was politically well connected. And when the players sought bail, they stood before a judge who was a lifelong friend of Mayor O'Dwyer and who had advanced his own career by protecting the mayor from charges of conspiring with bookmakers. The corruption was not abstract; it was both intimate and pervasive, a rotten smell that seemed to hang in the air, seeping into all aspects of their lives, reminding them always that this was the way things were done in the city, this was the real game.

Every night at home Floyd Layne waited anxiously for the step in the hall, the knock on the door. His three former teammates had been released on bail; before long they would be called before Frank Hogan's grand jury and surely they would name him—they would not dare risk adding a charge of perjury to ones of bribery and conspiracy. Of course he had considered going to the cops and turning himself in; often he felt that arrest would be preferable to this relentless anxiety, the leaden dread that he could never shake. He lived with a kind of sword of Damocles hanging above his head, threatening at every moment to fall. Yet still there was that single thread of hope that somehow he might escape detection, that eventually the investigation would end and he could walk away untouched.

As the days passed and still he said nothing, the notion of confessing became ever more implausible; meanwhile he was being lionized at school, hailed by his classmates as a paragon of honesty and integrity, the only one of the four sophomore starters on the double-championship team who had resisted temptation, who had not sold the school out to the gamblers. Each accolade Floyd experienced as a blow, because it seemed only to emphasize his own duplicity, his cowardice in not having held to his convictions when he had the opportunity. At one time he had thrilled to his conspicuousness, how he could scarcely walk a block down Convent Avenue without someone waving or calling hello; now he could hardly bear the hopeful eyes turned his way. That rally of support for the team had been for him an hour of agony. He could not bring himself to confess, but at the same time he didn't want to lie—or anyway, lie by commission rather than omission. So what could he say when the reporters asked him for comments about his crooked teammates? All he could think to do was mumble a few platitudes and plead ignorance, hoping to allay suspicion while deflecting whatever attention he could from himself. This evasion was in turn misinterpreted as admirable modesty.

The next game was Thursday night against Lafayette College. Not since the tournaments had the campus experienced this level of excitement; the upcoming game was an opportunity to demonstrate that City College still believed in honest basketball, that the school as a whole refused to be defined by the misdeeds of a few. By game time, 3,291 students had purchased tickets—a college record.

Inside the Garden that night the balconies were filled to bursting, which made for a striking contrast with the quiet, sparsely populated sections downstairs. Total attendance that night was listed as only

7,493, less than half of capacity. (In the wake of the point-shaving scandal, noted City student Mort Sheinman, the arena was now "empty of the bookmakers and the gamblers and the hustlers.") Under normal circumstances City College would have been a heavy favorite against Lafayette, but with the Beavers missing three-fifths of their starting lineup the game was regarded as a toss-up. A great roar erupted from the balconies as the teams took the court, the students whooping and cheering and shaking cowbells, and cutting through the din a bugle brought the call to charge. "It was sentimental and wonderful and joyous as youth should be," the *Post*'s Jimmy Cannon noted of that moment, "and managed to defeat the cold climate of the public building where college athletes are alien amateurs."

Nat Holman had decided that Floyd Layne would start that night at center; Floyd had not played center since his days at Benjamin Franklin High School, but he understood that with the two Eddies gone, Nat had no one else on whom he could depend. Now he stepped to the center circle; the referee tossed up the ball and the game was on.

In the early minutes Floyd appeared a bit tentative, like a musician picking up an instrument that he has not played in years, but little by little the memory seemed to return to him, and by the middle of the first half he was dominating the game. To the spectators he looked to be operating at a different tempo from the other nine players, darting this way and that, taking the full length of the court in just a few graceful strides. Always in the past he had deferred to the greater scoring power of his teammates, preferring to focus on passing and a suffocating defense that shut down the other team's best shooter; now, though, he seemed to grant himself permission to shine, and he grabbed rebounds and blocked shots and on offense he slid smoothly into the pivot position, swooping one way for a left-handed hook shot or reversing back toward the hoop for a twisting, off-balance layup. "He played the position as though he invented it," marveled the reporter for the student newspaper *Main Events*.

In the closing seconds of the first half, Floyd took a pass at the midcourt line and, as the clock wound down, tossed up a shot from nearly fifty feet out; the ball soared high and fast above the players' heads and then descended, like a circus aerialist fired from a cannon, right through the hoop. Like the best circus tricks, the shot was met in the arena first with a moment of stunned disbelief and then, as the players jogged off the court, a roar of delight. On this night, it seemed, anything was possible. The Beavers led 37 to 25, and Floyd Layne, who had never scored more than seventeen points in a game, had scored fifteen in the first half.

In the second half, with City maintaining a large lead, Floyd began feeding his teammates for baskets, everyone on the squad moving fluidly and fast, as if they had been playing together for a long time; when the final buzzer sounded the score was 67 to 48, a far larger margin than anyone could have predicted or even imagined, and though the team as a whole had shown admirable resilience and unexpected skill, everyone in the arena understood that the victory really belonged to a single player. The City College players and their fans swarmed onto the court, where they mobbed Floyd, wringing his hand and pounding his back, and then a few of them lifted him up and carried him off triumphantly on their shoulders. Under the most adverse of circumstances he had played the best game of his life.

"I played against Lafayette and scored nineteen points," Floyd would later write. "I didn't feel anything. I was numb from what was happening."

For the City College fans in the crowd, though, their joy was not yet exhausted, and after the game some two thousand students swarmed out of the Garden and began an exuberant march down Eighth Avenue to Times Square, where they sang and danced in the streets as if it was New Year's Eve, resplendent in the brilliance of the Great White Way; then they marched twice around the Times Building, demanding to see the game score displayed on the rotating news ticker just as the reports of the arrests had been, until finally a contingent of mounted policemen dispersed the crowd and everyone descended into the subway.

"They were deliriously happy," recalled an article in the college yearbook, the *Microcosm*, "for hadn't City College shown them all?"

The game against Lafayette took place on Thursday, February 22. At three o'clock the following Tuesday afternoon Floyd Layne was leaving class when the instructor called him aside and quietly informed him that a couple of men were waiting for him in the hall.

They were detectives from the district attorney's office, James Petro-sino and James Cashman.

"Well, I was expecting it," Floyd said as he surrendered himself to their custody. The detectives would later tell reporters that he "appeared relieved and evidently hadn't been sleeping well." He put on a tan top-coat over the red-and-black lumber jacket he was wearing, and together the three men walked downstairs to the detectives' car.

In the district attorney's office Floyd readily admitted that he had accepted $3,000 in bribes—$1,500 for the Missouri game, $1,000 for the Arizona game, and $250 each for the games against Washington State and St. John's; he had been promised another $1,500 for the Bos-ton College game but had never received it. Subsequently he would write, "The sickly feeling and deadly self-reproach were lifted from my mind as I told of my part in the mess."

After the interrogation, Floyd and the detectives got back in the car for the long drive to the Bronx. This was the moment he had most been dreading. He had not confessed at first because he was confused, and then because he was scared, but most of all because he could not bear the thought of having to explain himself to his mother, admitting what he had done, how he had lied to her; every time she saw that washing machine she would be reminded of it.

Lina was home when they arrived. Though her eyes widened in alarm when she saw them, her initial concern was for his safety. As the three walked into the apartment she momentarily tried to block the way, asking, "What are you doing with my son?"

The detectives looked to Floyd to respond. By way of explanation he could bring himself to say only, "These gentlemen wanted to see me."

Floyd led the two detectives into his bedroom, where a single plant sat on the windowsill. He dug his hand into the flowerpot and brought out a rolled-up white handkerchief that he handed to Detective Cash-man. Turning on the desk lamp, Cashman examined the contents. Carefully he counted out twenty-three $100 bills, one $50 bill, fourteen $20 bills, twenty-five $10 bills, and two $5 bills—$2,890 in all. It was the full amount that Floyd had received for the point-shaving, except for the $110 he had spent on the washing machine.

Now, with the money recovered, there was nothing left but to re-turn downtown for booking.

Lina was still standing by the front door. When they emerged from the bedroom she took in the grim expressions on the detectives' faces and the shame in Bunty's downcast eyes and understood at once what had happened. "He's a good boy," she told them helplessly. "My son is a good person."

Floyd Layne stands between detectives James Petrosino and James Cashman while being booked at the Elizabeth Street police station. He had been arrested at City College earlier that afternoon. Associated Press/John Lent

CHAPTER 29

At 9:30 P.M. on February 22, as Floyd Layne was thrilling City College basketball fans in Madison Square Garden, New York's new police commissioner, Thomas F. Murphy, was being interviewed on the radio about the point-shaving scandal. "I share the resentments of all New Yorkers who have been revolted by this outrage," Murphy said, adding for good measure, "New York City, despite its physical size and teeming population, is one of the cleanest cities in the country, has the best Police Department, and its vigilance is never relaxed, even for an instant."

Earlier that day a story had broken in *The Brooklyn Daily Eagle* that called those confident assertions into question. The *Eagle*, of course, had prompted District Attorney Miles McDonald's bookmaking investigation with Ed Reid's eight-part exposé that linked police officers to organized crime. In recent months, a young basketball writer named Ben Gould had been breaking stories about point-shaving in college basketball on what seemed an almost daily basis; later that year Gould would receive the George Polk Memorial Award for distinguished achievements in metropolitan journalism. Time and again the *Eagle* had demonstrated that its reporters had cultivated invaluable contacts inside the worlds of sports, gambling, and law enforcement—and on February 22, bringing those three elements together, the paper published what might have been its most spectacular exposé of all.

For more than a year, the *Eagle* charged, the New York Police Department had possessed "detailed evidence of a gigantic college basket-ball 'fix,' involving every metropolitan team that played in Madison Square Garden." The evidence came in the form of forty wiretap record-ings that the department—then under the leadership of Police Commis-sioner William P. O'Brien—had made before and during the 1949–50 college basketball season; the recordings "were said to involve players from every big-time team in and around New York," the corruption ap-parently so widespread that "publication of this data . . . would result in driving every college team in the city out of the Garden."

The information, however, had been suppressed by the police—Commissioner O'Brien had the recordings, but he had not acted on them on the order of a "higher authority." The allegation was nothing short of stunning, and it provoked an immediate denial from O'Brien, who stated, "To my knowledge no recordings were ever made. Positively none were ever called to my attention."

In the wake of the *Eagle*'s article, Commissioner Murphy announced that he was launching an internal search of the Police Department's files. Murphy, a civilian, had been hired by Mayor Vincent Impellitteri for the express purpose of cleaning up the Police Department amid the Harry Gross scandal. And yet the police official he assigned to search the police files was none other than Chief Inspector August Flath: the very same man whom Mayor O'Dwyer had sent to Miles McDonald's of-fice with a request that the Police Department oversee his rookie squad; the very same man whom Commissioner O'Brien had placed in charge of an official investigation—never actually undertaken—to probe "pos-sible police involvement with graft."

Though Commissioner Murphy assured the public that the search for the alleged wiretap recordings should require no more than two days, the week passed without word of the results. Not until March 9, more than two weeks later, did Murphy announce that Inspector Flath's search had failed to locate any records of telephone conversations re-garding basketball fixes. There the matter ended—though by this point confidence in the results could not be assured. After all, the city's paral-lel gambling scandal, featuring Harry Gross, had shown that evidence involving bookmakers was not necessarily safe inside the New York Po-lice Department.

Eight months later, Chief Inspector August Flath would submit his resignation from the police force. In his statement the fifty-three-year-old Flath explained, "There is a limit to human endurance—for me to remain longer would seriously impair my health." Not long afterward, Harry Gross revealed that for a period of about two years he had been giving Flath $200 a month in payoffs. Among the various other gratuities Flath received was a seat at a hundred-dollar-a-plate benefit dinner for the Brownsville Boys Club in Brooklyn. Nine more police officials sat at the table that night alongside Harry Gross and his friends; one of them was William P. O'Brien, shortly to be named police commissioner of the City of New York.

Floyd Layne was the thirteenth player to be arrested, including six from Long Island University, four from City College, two from Manhattan College, and one from New York University. The scale of the point-shaving scandal was growing ever larger, and around the city, rumors were rampant that another college would soon become involved. The *New York World-Telegram and Sun* advised: "A university thus far not mentioned may be included in the ever-broadening inquiry." *The Brooklyn Daily Eagle* likewise reported that the district attorney's investigators were closing in on three players from "a college not yet implicated in the bribe scandal."

The DA's investigators were said to be especially interested in the New Year's Eve party that Salvatore Sollazzo had thrown at the Latin Quarter nightclub in Manhattan. According to the *Eagle*, Sollazzo and his wife, Jeanne, had been joined by five "guests of honor," four of them former or current basketball players: Eddie Gard, Connie Schaff of New York University, an unnamed player from a college in Manhattan, and a player "of All-America standing at a school not previously named in the fix investigation." The identity of the fifth person was not revealed.

His name, as it turned out, was Meyer Alexander, known to all as Mendy. Though Mendy Alexander had been sought by Hogan's investigators, it was *Eagle* reporter Ben Gould who managed to track him down in Miami, where he had fled after the arrests of the Manhattan College players. Alexander was a close friend of Eddie Gard's who was said to have served as a liaison between gamblers and the LIU players; as such, the *Eagle* dubbed him "Mr. Go-Between." In the course of a long-distance telephone conversation, Gould persuaded Alexander to return to New York to speak to Frank Hogan; his testimony, Gould reported, in accordance with the recent conjecture in the press, "would involve at least one player from a school that has not yet figured in the investigation."

On March 6, Mendy Alexander arrived back in Brooklyn after a frenzied all-night drive from Miami. The next morning, accompanied by an attorney, he appeared at the district attorney's office in Manhattan, prepared to tell all he knew. Frank Hogan, however, ended up speaking to Alexander only briefly before dismissing him. "He is," Hogan declared, "of no aid in the investigation."

Two days later, *The Brooklyn Daily Eagle* published on its front page a photograph that had been taken by the Latin Quarter's house photographer on New Year's Eve. Captioned "'Fixer' Throws Party for the Boys," the photo shows four figures engaged in holiday revelry. In the forefront, grinning as he holds up a woman's hat, is Mendy Alexander. Behind him is Alexander's pal Eddie Gard; standing beside Gard, a bejeweled Jeanne Sollazzo beams as she waves at someone in the distance, looking like a movie star at a premiere; smiling beside her, tall and handsome in a dark suit, is Bob Zawoluk of St. John's (the player the *Eagle* had earlier identified as being "of All-America standing at a school not previously named in the fix investigation").

Perhaps hoping to counter the public association of Bob Zawoluk with the fixer Salvatore Sollazzo, the Reverend Dr. John A. Flynn, president of St. John's University, invited several newspaper reporters to interview Zawoluk that afternoon in his office. Earlier that same day, Manhattan district attorney Frank Hogan issued a statement clearing Zawoluk and his friend Jim Brasco of New York University of any involvement in the scandal. "We questioned Zawoluk the night of February 17," Hogan affirmed. "He denied any implication whatsoever and we have every reason to believe he is telling the truth."

To meet the reporters, Zawoluk was accompanied—as he had been for his questioning by the police—by New York Supreme Court justice Henry Ughetta, identified as "a legal advisor of the university and a personal friend of Dr. Flynn." The interview lasted about twenty minutes, and several times, as Zawoluk was about to respond to a reporter's question, Ughetta interrupted to caution him, in the manner of an attorney advising a client at a deposition, "Wait a minute, Bob—and think."

The story Zawoluk recounted for the reporters was an anodyne one: the story of a shy, sheltered young man apparently too naïve to comprehend what was going on all around him. He had known Eddie Gard for a long time and liked him, Zawoluk said; he had never heard any game fixing stories about Gard, though, and he insisted, "I never suspected him." The two, of course, had spent the previous summer working together at Grossinger's Hotel and Country Club, at the very moment when Eddie Gard met Salvatore Sollazzo and began developing his point-shaving scheme. Gard's primary role in the operation was to entice top-rank local players; eventually he would draw in Connie Schaff of NYU and Sherman White, Adolph Bigos, and Leroy Smith of LIU—all of whom also played basketball at Grossinger's that summer—and it is unclear why he would not likewise solicit the leading scorer for one of the most important college teams in the city. All the rest of the hotel's starting squad ended up involved in the scheme, and Gard, who was renowned for his inability to keep his thoughts to himself, even introduced him to his coconspirator Salvatore Sollazzo during the summer; yet apparently Zawoluk alone was unaware of Gard's activities.

Zawoluk said that he met Sollazzo again not long afterward, in September, when he and Gard were walking together on Broadway and the two of them, seemingly by coincidence, ran into him. (The chance encounter seems to have been something of a modus operandi for Gard, as on the night he happened to meet Ed Warner and Floyd Layne after a Knicks game at Madison Square Garden—an encounter that quickly turned into a joint effort to persuade Layne to join their game fixing scheme.) It was especially fortuitous that the St. John's center would cross paths with Gard and Sollazzo at the very time they were putting their point-shaving plans into place; even so, the two fixers chose not to avail themselves of the opportunity that fate had provided them. Zawoluk recalled of the meeting, "He was introduced to me as just plain Tarto and nothing else"—Tarto was the nickname used by Sollazzo's friends—and after a few minutes of casual conversation "we went on our way."

About a month later, Gard was with Zawoluk and NYU star Jim Brasco when Gard suggested that they all go up to Sollazzo's apartment on Central Park West because he wanted them "to meet some friends of mine." It was, to be sure, an unusual suggestion, as this would now be the third occasion on which Zawoluk had "met" Sollazzo, after the previous encounters in the Catskills and on Broadway. The two players agreed, and Gard took them to the Majestic Apartments (where presumably the doorman announced him not as Eddie Gard but as Mr. Logan, an oddity that seems not to have registered on Zawoluk).* Salvatore Sollazzo turned out not to be at home; Jeanne, however, was there, and according to Zawoluk they all "spent about forty-five minutes watching a television program," at which point the players decided to leave.

Zawoluk told the reporters that this was the only time he ever visited the Sollazzos' apartment. Yet only a year later, in an adulatory profile in *Sport* magazine that was clearly informed by extensive conversations with his subject, Milton Gross wrote: "On several occasions, Zawoluk visited Sollazzo's luxurious Central Park West apartment."

The next acknowledged encounter with Sollazzo came on New Year's Eve. Once again Gard was with Zawoluk and Brasco, in the gym of the Williamsburg YMHA, and at the end of the workout he asked them, "What are your plans for tonight?" Remarkably, neither of the two college basketball stars yet had New Year's plans, and Gard invited them to a party that Sollazzo was throwing at the Latin Quarter nightclub near Times Square. When the two players arrived that night they found Gard sitting at a table with Mendy Alexander, Salvatore and Jeanne Sollazzo, and two other couples whose names Zawoluk never learned. Everyone had a good time drinking and eating and watching the floor show; Salvatore was sitting next to Zawoluk at the table, and as the evening went along they talked about a number of light, inconsequential matters, not basketball related, until at some point Sollazzo grew more serious and made his pitch. St. John's, he noted, would be playing City College two days later. "I've got a good-sized bet on the St. John's–City College game," he said, and he was interested in having City

---

* Eddie Gard apparently used the alias Logan every time he arrived at the apartment. When he brought Sherman White of LIU to the apartment for dinner one night, the doorman saluted and said, "Good evening, Mr. Logan." The Sollazzos' housekeeper, Julia Davis, also told investigators that "both Mr. and Mrs. Sollazzo referred to him as Eddie Logan."

College lose "by a large score." If Bob could help make that happen, Sollazzo told him, "I might give you a present."

Zawoluk did not specifically state what his response to this was, other than to indicate that he didn't ask what the present would be and Sollazzo never volunteered the information. When a reporter asked him what he had thought about Sollazzo's offer, Zawoluk replied simply, "He had a few drinks in him and I paid no attention to his remark." The conversation moved on to other subjects. Zawoluk listened to the music of the Art Laner Orchestra, danced with Jeanne Sollazzo, and left the club at about 2:30 in the morning. He had, he said, not seen Sollazzo since.

Unlike Junius Kellogg of Manhattan College, who would trigger the point-shaving scandal when he informed his coach about the bribe offer from his former teammate, Bob Zawoluk did not report the offer to his coach, Frank McGuire, or, for that matter, to the police—his uncle, after all, was a police officer and Zawoluk had grown up surrounded by cops. Not only had he not volunteered the information, he had publicly denied ever receiving an offer from Sollazzo, or even having met him. As was pointedly noted by one of the reporters in the university president's office that day, "Zawoluk apparently experienced a change of heart, because several weeks ago he repeatedly denied reports that he ever had been approached by Sollazzo. He told the *World-Telegram and Sun* flatly that he had never had any contact with him, even though reports persisted that he and Sollazzo had met at least once."

Thus: He had met Sollazzo in the mountains; he had been introduced to him on Broadway; he would be taken to "meet" him in his apartment; he had been to Sollazzo's apartment once; he had been there on several occasions; he had been approached by Sollazzo to fix a game; he had never been approached by Sollazzo. It was a constantly shifting story that Zawoluk told about his contacts with the Sollazzos—not just with Salvatore, but with Jeanne as well.

In the university president's office, Zawoluk indicated that he had first met Salvatore and Jeanne Sollazzo the previous summer while they were staying at Grossinger's, the introduction having been arranged by Eddie Gard. The reporter from the *Journal-American*—perhaps sensing that something was amiss—paid a visit to Zawoluk at home later that night, at which point he presented a rather different story, in which he and Eddie Gard had socialized with Jeanne Sollazzo outside Salvatore Sollazzo's presence; according to Zawoluk, the two players "had been out on dates in the Catskills with Mrs. Sollazzo before he even knew she was married."

Apparently the *Journal-American* reporter did not pursue that line of discussion; it isn't exactly clear what "dates" means in this context, nor what is implied in the notion that Zawoluk and Gard had gone out with Jeanne Sollazzo socially—apparently more than once—without ever learning that she was married. This seems unlikely (especially as her husband was the man with whom one of them concocted a large-scale scheme to fix college basketball games), but it may comport with the belief that was widely, if privately, held among many of the local players: that Bob Zawoluk was having an affair with Jeanne Sollazzo.*

When the reporter from the *Journal-American* asked about her, all Zawoluk would say of his time with Jeanne Sollazzo was this: "She had class, was a wonderful dresser and a nice girl, and she certainly knew how to entertain." To that the reporter simply noted, "Mrs. Sollazzo, in previous interviews, indignantly denied she had entertained the college basketball players who were on her husband's payroll."

The *Outline of Proof as to Various Counts of the Indictment,* compiled by the Manhattan district attorney's office in preparation for possible trial, contains a statement given to detectives by Bob Zawoluk's friend Jim Brasco of New York University. In the statement Brasco says that he had been to Sollazzo's apartment on two occasions—once with Eddie Gard, and once with Gard and his NYU teammate Connie Schaff. Neither incident, of course, includes any mention of Zawoluk, despite the fact that

---

* The story of Zawoluk, Brasco, and Gard watching television with Jeanne Sollazzo is reminiscent of a story that the LIU player Leroy Smith later told the veteran sportswriter Jerry Izenberg about how he first got involved in the point-shaving scheme. According to Izenberg, LIU star Sherman White brought Smith up to the Sollazzos' apartment one afternoon when only Jeanne was there. The three spent some time talking and watching television, and at some point, says Izenberg, "Mrs. Sollazzo took him [Smith] into the other room, and he screwed her. And he came out, and then Sherman said, 'This is what we're going to do,' and he laid out the details of the scheme. And Smith said, 'I'm not doing that.' But Sherman said, 'You're *in* it now. You screwed the man's wife. Do you know who he is? He'll kill you.' "

Zawoluk himself acknowledged having visited Sollazzo's apartment with Brasco and Gard. Brasco's statement mentions Zawoluk only once, in passing, when he attests that he had gone to the Latin Quarter on New Year's Eve with Zawoluk and Mendy Alexander; this itself is a small but telling deviation from Zawoluk's own account, in which he claimed to have gone to the Latin Quarter with Brasco alone, thus downplaying his involvement with "Mr. Go-Between," Mendy Alexander (whom Ben Gould of the *Eagle* had earlier reported would inform District Attorney Hogan about "at least one player from a school that has not yet figured in the investigation").

Like Jim Brasco, Bob Zawoluk was never charged with any illegal activity. He, too, was questioned and released by the district attorney's investigators the night of the original City College arrests; he, too, was said to have turned down a bribe offer from one of the defendants. No statement from Zawoluk, however, is contained in the *Outline of Proof*— nothing about the offer made by Sollazzo at the Latin Quarter, nothing about Eddie Gard's effort to introduce him and Brasco to Sollazzo. Yet the *Outline of Proof* contains statements from witnesses as tangential as a woman who worked briefly as a housekeeper for the Sollazzos, whose only contribution to the case was to attest that on one occasion she had seen Sherman White in the Sollazzos' apartment.

Even more striking, the *Outline of Proof as to Various Counts of the Indictment* discusses in some detail the money paid by Salvatore Sollazzo to the City College players after the Washington State game, including statements from both Al Roth and Ed Roman describing the conversation with Sollazzo that led to his offer; about the St. John's payment, however, there is nothing at all.

In his autobiography *The Fastest Kid on the Block*, radio announcer Marty Glickman recalled a conversation he had on the team bus with a member of the St. John's starting five at the height of the point-shaving scandal. Noted Glickman, "He looked awful."

> "What's wrong?" I asked.
> "Well, there's a detective waiting for me at the Garden."
> "Is there something for you to worry about?"

"Shit, I don't know."

That was it. A guy who was in the clear wouldn't have been that worried. He was white as a sheet. He was sick. Was St. John's involved? Nobody from St. John's was ever implicated, but there were stories about the district attorney's office being sympathetic to St. John's. I recall only the sick look on that young man's face. He was never charged.

The former police commissioner, William P. O'Brien (who had been commissioner when wiretap recordings implicating every major college in New York were allegedly made), was among St. John's coach Frank McGuire's closest friends. According to Frank Mulzoff, the St. John's cocaptain during the 1950–51 season, O'Brien and McGuire had ongoing contact as the point-shaving investigation proceeded, and the information received from O'Brien was in turn passed on to the players. "The contact was very important," says Mulzoff, "because we gained a lot of warning about what was going to happen. Frank McGuire warned the team ahead of time about what was coming down. We all just assumed that the coach's friendship with the commissioner did it. I'm sure there were a lot of times when Frank and the commissioner were sitting together having a beer and the commissioner said to him, 'Hey, Frank, there are serious things going on. Take care of your boys.' I remember going to school one day, and the athletic coordinator said to me, 'Listen, there's a big problem—something's about to break about gambling in college basketball.' We all knew about it beforehand."

When Bob Zawoluk was called for questioning at the DA's office he arrived accompanied by an attorney, a clear indication that the college had been notified ahead of time. Frank Mulzoff also remembers detectives questioning certain members of the team not in a police station or the district attorney's office but on the campus itself—a courtesy not accorded the players of any other school.

Eddie Roman was especially close with Zawoluk, his former roommate at the Waldemere Hotel in the Catskills; in the words of Leonard Ansell of the *Sun*, it was "one of Roman's most cherished friendships." Among his family, at least, Eddie spoke openly about Zawoluk's involvement; recalls his brother Richard, "Eddie said he knew that St. John's was doing business. He was glad that Zawoluk didn't get busted—he really liked him—but still, St. John's got buried."

"We knew about St. John's," Bobby Sand told an interviewer near the end of his life. "It was no secret. . . . Bob Zawoluk and Eddie Roman were playing together in the Borscht Circuit, and he was telling Eddie what he was getting paid."

Discussing the scandal decades later, City College player Herb Cohen—who shaved points during the 1949–50 season—referred to a pair of players on St. John's as "the two biggest ganefs," a Yiddish word meaning a thief or otherwise dishonest character. "St. John's," he insisted, "did the same thing we did."

The son of one of the arrested City College players tells a story of sitting with his father many years later as they watched a member of the St. John's team discussing the point-shaving scandal on television, when his father exclaimed: "I can't believe he's talking like this—he was in it up to his eyeballs."

In the coming months the point-shaving scandal would stretch beyond the city, involving some of the most prestigious college basketball programs in the nation. In New York the scandal touched City College, Long Island University, Manhattan College, and New York University. Among the city's major basketball programs of the time, only one emerged unscathed—St. John's. By way of explanation, many who were there at the time use a single sardonic phrase: "divine intervention."

In New York in the 1950s, no figure was accorded greater respect, awe, veneration, and—in more progressive circles—antipathy than Francis Cardinal Spellman, archbishop of New York. Short and bald and round-faced, with dark, narrow eyes behind wire-rimmed spectacles, he was routinely characterized as the second most powerful Catholic in the world, "the American pope." "Beneath his soft demeanor, he was tough, calculating, and iron-willed," wrote Spellman's biographer John Cooney. "Adept at flattery and developing personal relationships, Spellman traded in favors, which he actively solicited and usually repaid in full." Canny and charming, friendly with every important figure in town, he operated much like a Renaissance cardinal, publicly disdain-

ing the exercise of political power while thoroughly engaged in it behind the scenes. "As far as I was concerned, he controlled Tammany
Hall," observed the well-known Catholic writer Rev. Albert Nevins. "He
made judges and other appointments, but you could never prove it.
There was never anything on paper in New York politics. It was always
done through the back door."

Perhaps nowhere in the city, outside the Church itself, was Spellman's influence felt more deeply than in the ranks of law enforcement.
The police force was overwhelmingly Irish Catholic, and when church
workers and their friends ran into trouble with the law, the cases were
routinely handled without arrests, away from public view. As John
Cooney noted, "Cooperation between law enforcement officers and the
Church in New York was nothing new. New York City police had long
granted the Catholic Church a special status."

Frank Hogan himself was an observant Catholic, and although he
had long been known for his personal probity, in the case of the 1951
basketball scandal there seems little question that he was not especially
zealous in pursuing avenues that might have led in the direction of St.
John's University, and in particular to a star player whose father was a
policeman killed in the line of duty. Despite his contact with both of the
fixers, Bob Zawoluk was questioned for only a short time, always in the
presence of an attorney, before being released. Even as the City College
players were still awaiting bail, Hogan characterized them in a press
conference as "pathetic" and "dishonest"; though Zawoluk had by his
own admission not reported the bribe offer from Salvatore Sollazzo,
Hogan publicly attested that he was "a player with a very fine character."

Hogan would have had little incentive to delve too deeply into the
involvement of St. John's, especially if—in the story that immediately
emerged—a special request had come from the cardinal himself. Hogan
had political aspirations, his name often mentioned in discussion of upcoming elections; he had been considered as the Democratic candidate
for the 1950 New York gubernatorial race, and now there was talk that
he would run in 1954 to succeed his predecessor in the district attorney's office, Governor Thomas A. Dewey. As a Democrat and an Irish
Catholic he could not have contemplated the possibility of success without the support of Cardinal Spellman. Recalls the veteran sportswriter

Jerry Izenberg, "The story I got was that Hogan wanted to run for governor. Spellman called Hogan and said, 'You know, I can get you every big Catholic donor. Period. But that team is not to be touched.'" The account of basketball writer Charley Rosen, who spoke with numerous players and coaches of the time, differs slightly; according to Rosen, "Spellman sent a Catholic detective to Hogan to [pass] the word to lay off the Catholic schools. They couldn't risk a face-to-face meeting, or even a phone conversation."

Unlike City College and Long Island University, which never again regained their status as major basketball powers, St. John's continued to maintain a top-flight basketball program. In 1951 the Redmen finished the season ranked ninth in the nation and were invited to both postseason tournaments; the following year they again participated in both tournaments, losing to Kansas University in the NCAA finals. Bob Zawoluk graduated in 1952 and was drafted by the Indianapolis Olympians of the National Basketball Association; he finished his college career with 1,826 points, a three-year St. John's record that stands to this day.

CHAPTER 30

A mong City College students, the range of emotions provoked by
the first arrests—shock, bewilderment, anger—had after Floyd
Layne's arrest given way to sadness and resignation, feelings that were
less sharp but somehow darker. They could not help but feel foolish
as well, thinking of how fervently they had cheered for Floyd at the
team rally and at the Lafayette game, how they had carried him off the
court on their shoulders, the memories shot through now with bitterness and regret, like those from a relationship betrayed and brought to
an end, and the understanding that the joyful sounds of that game, the
shouts and the cowbells and most especially the deep-throated Allagaroo, would not be heard again anytime soon. So no objections were
raised when—only half an hour after Floyd was taken away by the
detectives—CCNY president Dr. Harry N. Wright issued a statement
saying that "in view of the more recent developments" City College was
canceling its final two games of the season and reevaluating its future
involvement with Madison Square Garden. The students would continue to press for the academic reinstatement of the suspended players,
but they would no longer flock to the Garden to watch their team play;
everyone understood that this portion of their lives, and of the life of
their school, had come to end. The final sentence of the *Observation Post*
editorial about Floyd Layne's arrest was simply: "As for now, the roof
has caved in."

• • •

Nat Holman's wife, Ruth, had recently been ill, and he was sitting at her bedside in Mount Sinai Hospital when Sam Winograd called to tell him the news of Floyd Layne's arrest. The *Post* basketball writer Sid Friedlander called shortly afterward, and it was all Holman could do to murmur, "It's a tragedy, a horrible tragedy." Listening to him, Friedlander was struck by how different he sounded—like a man saved from drowning, his voice low and choked, his thoughts muddled. "I can't make sense of it," he was saying. "I can't find words to tell just how I do feel."

Before long, however, Holman's sadness had evolved into anger, fueled by a sense of personal betrayal. "What the hell has a guy like Holman got to say, when a thing like this happens to a coach!" he exclaimed to David Eisenberg of the *Journal-American*, referring to himself, as he often did, in the third person. "Here are four fellows, and a coach is breaking his neck to put a team on the floor. It's a terrible thing."

Nat Holman had devoted himself to the City College basketball program for thirty-two years, and the scandal broke just as he reached the pinnacle of his profession. That very month *Sport* magazine had named him its Man of the Year in Sport, hailing him as the "master coach," the "basketball genius" who had brought unparalleled success to City College. "True, it was the players themselves who had scored the baskets," the article acknowledged, "but everybody knew that Nat Holman was behind every shot, every defensive move, every surge down the court." Wherever he went, people stopped him on the street, wanting to talk, to congratulate him, filling him with a glow that he thought of as "that God-bless-America feeling, the top of the heap." Day after day he received letters of praise, invitations to speak to civic and business groups, to conduct basketball clinics around the country and around the world. Now, he recognized, his reputation would be forever tarnished; people would believe what they wanted to believe, and some of them would always believe that he had known his players were on the take—that he *must* have known, that "Mr. Basketball" was too astute not to have noticed when a player wasn't giving his all. And of course he could tell when a player wasn't shooting well or was committing foolish fouls on defense. That was part of the game; even the best players had off nights every now and again. But these outsiders didn't understand that although a coach could observe performance, he could not discern motivation, could not tell what was in a boy's heart. It wasn't his job, in any case, to teach them right from wrong, and if a young man arrived at City College without a firm sense of personal morality, then there was really not much he could do about it. Besides, he had warned the players about consorting with gamblers. They knew where his office was. Why had they not come to him?

Scarcely a month after Layne's arrest, Nat Holman had taken action: He announced that in the future, members of the City College team would be banned from participating in Catskills summer basketball. In his announcement Holman referred to the hotel teams as "schools of crime," but City College, like the other big-time college programs, had encouraged its players to work in the hotels, because they provided the toughest basketball competition to be found anywhere; as Ben Gould of *The Brooklyn Daily Eagle* noted, "Coaches have favored their boys working in these spots because they improved tremendously after two months upstate."

By this time President Wright had recommended to the Board of Higher Education that City College should withdraw from Madison Square Garden and return its games to the campus gymnasium. Though Holman himself had long opposed this idea, he refused to comment on Wright's recommendation, other than to affirm that he would continue to coach the Beavers regardless of where the games were played. "I wouldn't leave at a time like this," he said. "I think the college needs me now more than ever."

Shortly after the arrests of the three City College players, the members of the Bradley University basketball team held a meeting at which they voted to reject any future invitations to play in Madison Square Garden; the decision was widely seen as an assertion of the solid Midwestern values of Peoria against the corrupting influence of New York City. On the day after Floyd Layne's arrest, the *Daily Compass* sportswriter Stan Isaacs included a blind item in his column, one that did not name names but was so patent in its implication of Bradley and its All-American guard Gene Melchiorre that it scarcely merited the term: "There's the Midwestern school which at this very moment is righteously casting aspersions at the Garden and the whole Eastern basketball set-up. Yet this school, which built its name on the strength of its basketball teams, has a star player (an All-American) who is as much involved as any of the local players."

A few days later, the *Eagle*'s Ben Gould added his own spin to the story: "Would you be surprised to know that a certain team doesn't want to return to New York for any post-season event because its stand-out cager is afraid some gentlemen will meet him at Penn Station?"

Not long after the first three City College players were arrested, a group of CCNY alumni raised the funds to hire them a new attorney. His name was Jacob Grumet, and he was the epitome of politically well connected. A Republican, he had served as an assistant district attorney under the Democrat Frank Hogan; now in private practice, he had recently finished a term in the Court of General Sessions, and though he was known to his friends as Jack he preferred his clients to address him as Judge. Grumet was tall and slim with dark hair and a large-featured face—he had a long, fleshy nose, protruding ears, and exceptionally arched eyebrows, set off by a pencil-thin mustache, which together gave him the intimidating, slightly dyspeptic look of a banker father-in-law in a Hollywood romantic comedy. He was himself a graduate of the College of the City of New York, and he felt deeply for the institution as well as for the players. "This is a particularly heartbreaking experience for me," he told reporters upon announcing his appointment. "It is one of the saddest cases I have ever undertaken."

Grumet explained to the players that in his opinion their most advantageous strategy was to cooperate fully with the district attorney. Frank Hogan had indicated that he intended to bring multiple counts against each defendant, including bribery and conspiracy. The bribery charges were especially serious (they each carried a maximum sentence of five years in prison), but Grumet knew Hogan well and did not believe that he was inclined to put college basketball players behind bars. If the players would agree to testify against Salvatore Sollazzo, he was sure the district attorney would drop the bribery charges and ask for suspended sentences on the conspiracy. He advised them, "Tell the authorities everything they want to know."

Ed Warner, though, seemed troubled by something, and finally he admitted to Grumet that he had a juvenile arrest record. It was only one incident, he explained, a gang scuffle in Harlem when he was fifteen years old. In Children's Court he had been found guilty of fighting and released on probation, but the judge had warned that the conviction would remain on his record and could be used against him if he were ever to be arrested again.

Jacob Grumet told Warner not to worry about it. "Trust me, young man," he said, "you'll never go to jail."

Eddie Roman, too, was troubled, and later he would ask for a private meeting, at which he told Grumet that he had been thinking about the need to tell the authorities everything. The thing was, he explained, the games with Sollazzo hadn't been the only ones in which they had shaved points—there had been three other games during the previous season, handled by a fixer named Eli Kaye. He hadn't wanted to say anything, Eddie admitted, because it involved other teammates of his, guys not yet implicated in the scandal. Grumet listened carefully, and when Eddie was done he pointed out that sixty-eight detectives were working on the basketball case full time; eventually they would discover what had happened the year before, and he was sure they wouldn't look kindly on him if they decided he had been holding out. He had already scheduled a session for Eddie later that month with the district attorney; that would be the perfect opportunity to unburden himself of all that he knew.

These days Eddie was back living at home, after getting away briefly to a friend's house to avoid the presence of newsmen. Reporters from the *Journal-American* and the *Daily Mirror* had shown up on the front porch of the house as soon as Eddie was released on bail. He had told them each the same thing, which was that he couldn't talk until he had spoken to his lawyer, although he did volunteer a single rueful sentence: "I've been a sucker."

One evening a week after the arrests, Sam Winograd and his wife unexpectedly came to the house. Eddie's parents showed the Winograds into the living room, where they were joined by his two brothers and his sister-in-law. Winograd explained that he was "very much troubled," as he put it, and that he had come to see Eddie that night because he wanted to ask him a question: "What did we do in City College that might have caused you to do what you did—to bring such grief upon you and your family, and everybody connected with the college and your fellow students?"

The question was unexpectedly hostile, and Eddie struggled with what he could say to make Winograd understand. In the end he simply replied that he could not think of anything specifically, other than that some promises had been made to him before he came to City College, but at the same time he didn't want to rationalize—that was the word he used—and say that that was what had caused him to do what he did.

Winograd persisted. Who, he wanted to know, had made the promises?

Eddie indicated that he didn't want to name any names, but he explained about the student job he had been given, how everyone had said it was just a make-work job they gave to the school's athletes, and though he worked more than the other students did, one day out of the blue they cut his pay and he had been angry about that. He did not mention the job that had been promised to his father—for Julius, after all, was sitting right there, and discussing it in front of the rest of the family would only be an additional and unnecessary humiliation for him. So Eddie just noted, as though serving as a character witness for himself, that he had always taken his academic work at the college very seriously, and that he thought he had done well. He did not point out that he had reluctantly agreed to give up his preferred major, chemistry, because it interfered with basketball practices. Nor did he mention that he knew that Winograd, who in the summertime ran the athletic program at the Young's Gap Hotel in the Catskills, personally paid the hotel's college players out of the money collected for the basketball gambling pools; or that he knew that Winograd had taken money to play semipro ball while he was a City College student in the 1930s, using an alias like a common criminal; or that he knew about the shady deals for the college's athletic equipment that Winograd made with a friend of his who ran a local sporting goods store.* As much as Eddie might have wanted to get some of this off his chest, he recognized that it could not possibly

---

* Dr. Samuel Winograd would resign from City College in 1954 in the wake of a *New York World-Telegram and Sun* exposé of a two-year Board of Higher Education investigation revealing "possible irregularities involving the purchase of thousands of dollars in athletic equipment by certain City College executives."

help the situation, that if anything it would only turn Winograd further against him at a time when he hoped to be granted reinstatement to City College, and so he simply shook his head and mumbled again uselessly that no, he could not explain why he had done it, and Sam Winograd and his wife left shortly afterward.

Those first days after the arrest were the ones when Eddie most desperately wished that he could somehow rewind his life, run it back to an earlier, better moment, as though it were one of those game films they used to watch over and over at the beginning of the practice season, trying to identify and learn from their mistakes. The lawyer he had met with briefly before Grumet had advised him to go about his "routine, normal life," but that was a preposterous notion—his normal life consisted of school followed by basketball practice, both of which were forbidden to him now. He lived those days in an agony of waiting, punctuated by occasional moments of acute humiliation and shame. The scandal was in the papers just about every day, in the news section, the sports section, the editorial cartoons, the op-eds, the letters to the editor; everybody, it seemed, had an opinion. One letter to the *New York Post* noted that Eddie was beloved among the students at Taft High School, that he had often taken the time to come back and visit, and that a recent issue of *The Taft Review* had even voted him number one on a list of Taft students who had made good; having said that, the writer went on to wonder how those high school students were supposed to feel now that "a friend has stabbed them in the back." In another letter, a pair of writers provided the pithy observation that while some of the local college basketball teams would be depleted for the coming season, "the Sing Sing team's chances are looking better than ever."

The *Post* was actually one of the more sympathetic of the daily papers. The dean of their sportswriters, Jimmy Cannon, wrote several impassioned columns about the players he termed "the tall children of basketball." "They are amateurs exploited by a commercial alliance of culture and commerce," he wrote. "As much as $1,500 apiece was given them to throw a game. It is an immense fortune to kids who check coats at the Garden to pick up two dollars. But it is a miser's sum when you compare it to the enormous profits made from television and ticket sales at the Garden." The most left-wing of the city's newspapers, *The Daily Compass*, ran a three-part editorial that went so far as to advocate that college athletes should be paid. The amateur rule, editor Ted O. Thackrey asserted, served mostly to allow arena owners to obtain skilled players at "bargain basement prices": "One fact we refuse to face is that there are no amateurs in big-time college sports: there are only underpaid professionals."

In March the Senate Crime Investigating Committee (popularly known as the Kefauver Committee after its chairman, Senator Estes Kefauver of Tennessee) decamped from Washington to New York to take testimony on the infiltration of the city's politics by organized crime. The featured witness was the crime boss Frank Costello. Costello's attorney had demanded that his client not be televised, arguing that the image of him conferring with his lawyer during questioning would prejudice popular opinion against him. The television networks interpreted this as a directive against showing Costello's face, so they trained their cameras instead on his hands; for hours on end a rapt audience watched those hands twitch and gesture, tapping on the witness table, twisting a handkerchief, reaching for a glass of water, as off-camera Costello described his longtime friendships with many of New York's most powerful politicians.

Within the week the city's former mayor, William O'Dwyer, was called back from his ambassador's post in Mexico City to testify before the committee. In response to questioning, O'Dwyer admitted to having met Frank Costello, and he further acknowledged that one of the most important fundraisers for his 1945 mayoral race, a shirt manufacturer named Irving Sherman, was a collector for Costello in the garment district. Senator Charles Tobey of New Hampshire noted how popular Costello seemed to be among the city's politicians, and then asked, "Mr. Ambassador, what do you consider the basis of Costello's appeal?"

Replied O'Dwyer with admirable candor, "It doesn't matter whether it is a banker, a businessman, or a gangster—his pocketbook is always attractive."

It was the age of investigation, of official efforts to root out corruption in social institutions, to expose intrigue and thwart conspiracies. All of these things were happening at the same time in New York: In the Federal Building on Foley Square the former mayor, William

O'Dwyer, testified to dealings with known gangsters (while nearby Julius and Ethel Rosenberg went on trial for passing atomic secrets); in the Municipal Building in Brooklyn the bookmaker Harry Gross was detailing his payoffs of policemen and politicians; and in the Manhattan Criminal Courts Building a parade of college basketball players began to appear before Frank Hogan's grand jury.

The ballplayers, of course, had their own story, their own motivations; yet for the general public the temptation was very strong simply to blend them in with the others, the gangsters and the machine politicians and the crooked cops, to remove any complicating issues of power or exploitation and view them as just another example of municipal corruption. The case of the City College players was an especially heartbreaking example, because they were young and had achieved such glory, and because they had seemed to represent so much of what was good about New York and attended a school that occupied a cherished place in the life of the city. Wrote Max Lerner in the *Post,* "The corruption in this case . . . touches the one team that last year brought basketball to a degree of frenzy it will probably never again achieve, and turned thousands of fans into whirling dervishes. It involves the very men who had become the core of a hero cult." The players had betrayed the public's trust, had sold out to criminals, dispensing favors for money. That might have been expected from a cop walking the beat or a political functionary on the city payroll; it was far worse when the guilty party was a star player on the hometown team, who had stood and received the cheers of the crowd.

Thus fame was transmuted into notoriety; thus sports heroes turned suddenly, shockingly, into fallen idols.

The Sporting News made the connection between organized crime and basketball fixing explicit in an editorial that declared, "Honesty must be restored as the first principle of living and its precepts so thoroughly planted in the minds of all that there can be no more 1919 World Series and basketball scandals, no more necessity for Kefauver Senate crime investigations, no violations of the public trust." The linkage was further emphasized by Estes Kefauver himself, who announced to reporters that his Crime Committee had been investigating the fixing of basketball games "for some time." District Attorney Hogan laughed when he heard about that. "It's a surprise to me," he said.

On March 24, however, the Kefauver Committee did expand its inquiries into basketball game fixing, calling a Milwaukee gambler named Sidney Brodson to testify. Brodson told the committee that he wagered about a million dollars a year on college basketball and football games. However, he had long sensed something "abnormal" about basketball in Madison Square Garden—the tip-off was the rapid fluctuation in point spreads just before a game, which led him to conclude that insiders were placing large sums of money on teams they regarded as a "sure thing"—and as a result he refused to bet on games played in the Garden.

Two days after Brodson's testimony, the presidents of St. John's University, Manhattan College, and New York University announced that they would continue to play basketball in Madison Square Garden; the deal had been negotiated with Garden promoter Ned Irish over dinner in department store magnate Bernard Gimbel's apartment.

The following night, March 27, Herb Cohen, Irwin Dambrot, and Norm Mager were picked up by detectives working for the Manhattan district attorney. They were interrogated for more than twelve hours, at which point they were charged with violating Section 382 of the Penal Code. Cohen was a junior at City College; Dambrot attended Columbia Dental School; Mager played with the Baltimore Bullets of the National Basketball Association, but the season had recently ended and he was back in Brooklyn. The three had not been together since the tournament celebrations of the previous year; the unwished-for reunion could be seen in the photographs that appeared in the papers the next day: exhausted players standing before the police desk, surrounded by detectives.

The entire starting five of the City College double-championship squad had now been arrested, along with the top two reserves. The shame of the team was complete.

CHAPTER 31

Brooklyn district attorney Miles McDonald had always been cautiously optimistic about his investigation, but of late he was feeling actually hopeful. For the first time he felt that he had allies in City Hall and police headquarters; Police Commissioner Thomas Murphy, for instance, had ordered twenty-one police officers to testify before the grand jury in Brooklyn, the names having come from a list provided to him by McDonald himself.* More than anything else, though, McDonald was hopeful because Harry Gross was finally talking to the grand jury—"singing," in the verb favored by all the papers.

Inside the jury room Gross was as slick as always, dressed to the nines and his hair just so, smirking at Judge Leibowitz and cracking jokes and smoking cigarettes whenever there was a break in the action; all the same, though, he testified in minute detail, without benefit of notes, identifying individual policemen by name and explaining how he had assigned specific payouts according to rank, from patrolmen all the way up to chief inspectors, in so doing demonstrating a remarkable familiarity with the internal structure of the New York Police Department and the geography of the city as expressed in its precincts and divisions. Over time the members of the grand jury became conversant with the

---

* Murphy himself had come to believe that corruption in the Police Department's plainclothes force was so widespread that he demoted every one of its 336 officers back to uniformed duty; their places would be filled by policemen who had never served as plainclothes officers.

bookmaker's terms of art: how "ice," for instance, meant protection money, and the "pad" was the list of policemen to be paid off, and a "stiff" was a guy who agreed to take an arrest for a bookie, and a "shoo-fly" was a cop who investigated other cops. Gross told of packages filled with fifty- and hundred-dollar bills, gifts of television sets and mink coats and hundred-dollar suits. "Once he opened up, the whole story was on the table," McDonald would recall. "The information flowed like water."

In May 1951 the grand jury brought indictments against twenty-one members of the New York Police Department for conspiracy to obstruct justice, with another fifty-six officers named as unindicted coconspirators. The trial

Bookmaker Harry Gross faces reporters after testifying before the Brooklyn grand jury investigating police corruption. Tony Linck / Getty Images

would begin in Brooklyn County Court in September,* and Miles McDonald was taking no chances with his star witness. Harry Gross had been released from the Raymond Street jail after he agreed to testify (his prison sentence for the sixty-six counts of bookmaking to which he had pleaded guilty would be determined by his cooperation), and ever since then he had been allowed to come and go as he wished, as long as he was accompanied by a policeman. For the duration of the trial, however, McDonald ordered Gross to be held in the Hotel St. George in Brooklyn—as it happened, the very same hotel in which high-ranking officers once lent him money to recapitalize his business—guarded around the clock by a contingent of his rookie cops.

---

* The trial ultimately involved eighteen policemen rather than twenty-one; by the time it began two of the defendants had been granted separate cases and one had committed suicide.

As the trial got under way, Gross asked McDonald if he might visit his wife and children at their home in Atlantic Beach, Long Island. "It'll be the last chance I get to see them, if I'm gonna be locked up in that hotel every night," he explained. "Besides, I gotta get some suits and stuff."

McDonald knew that he would not need Gross during jury selection and opening arguments; moreover, he was well aware that his case hinged on Gross's cooperation and he wanted to keep him contented. So he assigned a pair of his policemen to the job, and that afternoon the three set off in Gross's black Cadillac convertible.

The Gross family lived in a two-story house on a quiet street only a block from the Atlantic Beach boardwalk. His wife, Lila, was there to greet them when they arrived, and after a bit of conversation Gross announced that he was going upstairs to pack. One of the cops, Joseph Cunningham, remained downstairs in the living room, while the other, Rubin Rabinowitz, went out to get something to eat.

Gross packed a couple of bags and brought them downstairs to the dining room, where he sat talking with Lila. Cunningham was sitting in the next room and could hear every word they said, including Gross's comment that he wanted to go wash his hands; he glanced up and saw him heading into the kitchen.

Before long Rabinowitz had returned from the restaurant. "Where's Gross?" he asked.

"He's in the kitchen washing his hands."

Rabinowitz listened for a moment and then said, "I don't hear anything."

"Then he must be in the dining room again," said Cunningham, and he went in to check, only to find Lila Gross sitting there by herself. "Where's Harry?" he demanded.

Lila looked surprised. "I don't know," she said. "I thought he was with you."

Cunningham rushed into the kitchen, which was empty, and then the two cops ran through the house, up and down the stairs, calling his name; then with sinking hearts they dashed outside—the Cadillac was not in the driveway.

Harry Gross was gone.

• • •

Miles McDonald was also staying on Long Island that evening, at his family's summer home in Stony Brook. When the phone rang he answered it himself. "Miles, this is Julie," said Assistant District Attorney Julius Helfand, his normally booming voice now quiet and strained.

"What's the matter with you?" McDonald asked. "You sound like you're at the bottom of a well."

"Miles, Gross is gone."

"Gone? What are you talking about?"

"He's gone. Just disappeared. Escaped. I don't know where he is."

"But how—"

"I don't know. He just walked out on the two cops. But what do we do now? Do we call the police or work on it ourselves?"

McDonald thought it over for a moment. "Don't call the police," he told Helfand. "Not yet, anyway. Don't take them into your confidence. Wait till I get there."

McDonald drove back to the city, his mind racing. All along he had known it was a gamble to depend on someone like Harry Gross, a guy who had made his first dollar cheating at cards and had not earned an honest buck ever since. Still, a prosecutor had to take his witnesses from those available to him, most of them of shady character: Nuns and librarians rarely got involved in this sort of enterprise. McDonald didn't want to think what might happen if someone who wanted him to stay quiet got to him before they did. And Gross was the linchpin of the case; without his testimony they would not have enough evidence to convict. It hardly seemed possible that all the work of the past two years, that slow and patient accumulation of links on the chain, would come to nothing. In the beginning McDonald had feared the end of his own career as a result of this quixotic campaign against corruption; lately, though, politicians from both parties clamored to be photographed with him. Contemplating a successful outcome of the case, he had allowed himself to entertain the hope that one day he might be nominated as a justice of the state supreme court, the position his father had always dreamed for him; now that hope might be gone as well, vanished along with the star witness.

It was, he knew, a selfish thought, and he felt even worse for having had it. So he tried to put it out of his mind as he drove, and instead began planning the search.

Harry Gross was happy as he drove in his Cadillac, the tires humming on the asphalt, a warm breeze blowing in off the ocean. It was one of the last remaining days of summer, and he didn't know when he would next see summer again. He was facing maximum time if he refused to testify, but if he did turn state's evidence he was a marked man, even with a permanent police detail. While he had long considered trying to make his escape, he had arrived at his decision only the day before, when he was passed a message at the hotel that a meeting had been arranged for him. He knew that he needed to get back to his house, where he might find a moment to slip his guards. They were mainly concerned about protecting him from harm; given the danger he faced on the outside, they didn't figure he would try to flee, and he had given them no reason to think otherwise.

Harry crossed the Atlantic Beach Bridge onto the mainland and then headed north. He drove through the Queens Midtown Tunnel and into Manhattan, along the sedate streets of the East Side, where the nightclubs and steak houses and discreet hotels were tucked away amid the brownstones and stately brick apartment houses. Rather than stop at any of the old haunts, though—he could only imagine the amazement on the boys' faces when they saw Harry Gross coming through the door—he just kept going west, into the Lincoln Tunnel; on the other side was New Jersey, where his business was to be conducted. By the time he arrived in Newark it was past dark, but he had no trouble finding the address that had been given in the message, a private house that looked like any other on the street. He was met at the back door and led to a room at the front of the house. Four men were waiting for him there, but only two mattered.

One of them, small and dapper with an intelligent, discerning gaze, was Meyer Lansky. Lansky was one of the original Jewish gangsters, who had gone into bootlegging with his childhood pals Bugsy Siegel and Lucky Luciano; after Prohibition he had set up casinos with Frank Costello, and now he ran gambling operations from New York to Hollywood and Havana. At the age of forty-nine Lansky was a legend in his field, and in meeting him Harry Gross must have felt some of the awe and admiration of a midlevel executive meeting the company's founder. The other man, a few years older than Lansky and with an open, jowly face, was Willie Moretti. Another associate of Frank Costello's, Moretti oversaw gambling in New Jersey and upstate New York, and he possessed enough political influence that Mayor O'Dwyer had appointed his brother-in-law deputy hospitals commissioner.*

Lansky and Moretti did not waste any time in setting out their proposal. They explained to Harry Gross that they were prepared to pay him $120,000, and all he had to do to get it was refuse to talk when he took the stand. This was life-changing money, Harry well understood, a guarantee of financial security for his family while he was away, and in that regard Lansky and Moretti assured him that everything had been arranged for his sentencing. He would not receive more than four years in prison; with good behavior he would be out in three, and then he would be permitted to return to his bookmaking activities if he so chose—a path, they scarcely needed to mention, that would be forever closed to him if he decided to testify.

No more than thirty minutes later Gross was back in his car, on his way to the seaside resort of Atlantic City. It was nearly midnight by the time he pulled up in front of the luxurious Chalfonte–Haddon Hall Hotel, but despite the hour he wore a pair of sunglasses as he walked into the front lobby carrying the two suitcases he had packed at home. He wanted an oceanfront room, he told the desk clerk, and he wanted it for ten days. He signed the register *Harry Green*.

Miles McDonald and Julius Helfand spent the night trying to track down Harry Gross, calling everyone who might have an idea where he had gone, but to no avail. The next morning they had to call Judge Leibowitz and explain what had happened; Leibowitz was understandably shocked

---

* Moretti would be dead within the month, murdered by gunmen over lunch in an Italian restaurant in New Jersey. He was supposed to have been joined for lunch that day by two friends of his, the entertainers Dean Martin and Jerry Lewis, but Lewis found out that morning that he had contracted the mumps and the two men did not show up.

by the news, but he agreed to a temporary adjournment of the trial. Next, McDonald and Helfand contacted the U.S. attorney's office, asking for a warrant to be prepared for Gross under the federal Fugitive Felon Act; that allowed the FBI to assist in the search, and within hours a thirteen-state alert had been issued. His photograph was published in the afternoon papers, his description given on the radio. He was the most wanted man in America.

Meanwhile Harry Gross was relaxing in Atlantic City. On his first day in town he just strolled the boardwalk, enjoying the sun and salt air, but by the next morning he was bored and hungering for some action. He put on a gray suit with a blue tie and a monogrammed gold tie clasp, set off by a pair of blue suede shoes, and after breakfast he drove to the Atlantic City Race Track. He spent the afternoon betting on the horses; as he was walking to the hundred-dollar window he was approached by a policeman, Robert Ryder, who thought he looked familiar and had noticed the initials *HG* on his tie clasp.

"Pardon me," Captain Ryder said, "but are you Harry Gross?"

Harry Gross acknowledged that he was.

"You're wanted up in New York."

"Yeah, I know," Gross said.

"Well, look," Ryder said, taking his arm, "there's an alarm out for you."

Harry Gross offered no resistance as he was taken to the nearby state police barracks, where he bantered with the troopers while a phone call was made to the Brooklyn district attorney to inform him that his witness was in custody. "Do you blame me for taking off?" Gross asked. "Got two cops with me day and night. District attorneys, assistant district attorneys, judges, all kind of guys, all the time. Never any time to myself. You blame me? I just wanted to get away and walk in the sun and make a bet at the track. That's all. Anything the matter with that?"

Miles McDonald, Julius Helfand, and William Dahut drove down to New Jersey with several detectives to pick up Harry Gross personally. On the way back to Brooklyn, Gross explained that he was sorry for any inconvenience he might have caused, but they should understand that he wasn't going on the lam, he just needed a little vacation, and now that he was back they could count on him. "Don't worry," he said. "I'm going to do just what you want me to do. I'll finger those cops and I'll shoot the works."

The trial resumed on September 17, with Assistant District Attorney Helfand making his opening statement to the jury, explaining that evidence would be presented of a criminal gambling syndicate operating with the cooperation of members of the New York Police Department; it was, he said, "a conspiracy without equal in New York City."

Testimony began the following day. The state's first two witnesses, a police inspector and a city clerk, drily instructed the jury about the structure of the New York Police Department. Then Helfand rose to call Harry Gross to the stand.

For his appearance in court Gross was dressed more conservatively than usual, in a solid navy suit, his dark cheeks powdered, his black wavy hair glistening with oil. After the swearing-in, Helfand led him through a brief account of his early career as a bookmaker; Gross answered the questions but he was plainly uncomfortable, speaking in a low voice that was occasionally drowned out by the rumble of the subway beneath the street, and as the questioning moved to his dealings with the New York Police Department, he pursed his lips and wiped his palms with a handkerchief. There was a moment of levity when Helfand introduced into evidence a large chart illustrating Brooklyn's police divisions, and as the chart was moved into place it fell off its stand and whacked Judge Leibowitz on the back of the head. The spectators laughed, and Leibowitz grinned at the crowd and said wryly, "Whenever the umpire gets hit the bleachers cheer," and everyone laughed again, but the disruption seemed only to agitate Gross even more. He clenched his fists and banged them lightly on his thighs, and when Helfand resumed his questioning he abruptly exclaimed, "Mr. Helfand, I refuse to answer any more questions! I refuse to answer now or any more! That's all!" and with that he burst from the witness chair and dashed out the side door.

Instantly the courtroom dissolved into chaos as the guards set out after Gross and the spectators leaped to their feet as one, like the crowd at a football game watching a runner suddenly break free from the defense, and reporters scribbled notes frantically and the eighteen defendants laughed and patted one another on the back; finally a stunned and shaken Julius Helfand returned to ask for a brief adjournment— a request that was quickly granted by the judge—and then he and his assistants hurried out again. An hour later Harry Gross was led back into the courtroom and Helfand explained to Judge Leibowitz that Mr. Gross was suffering from a gall bladder condition and as a result he had been rather jumpy lately, and while he was still upset he had agreed to resume his testimony the following morning. The judge ordered Gross to be returned to his hotel and directed a physician to attend to him overnight.

The next morning Harry Gross once again took the stand. On this day he was dressed less conservatively, in a light-colored suit with wide lapels, and a transformation seemed to have come over him; his earlier anxiety had now been replaced by surliness, his pursed lips with a contemptuous sneer, and when Julius Helfand addressed him he declared, "I won't answer any questions." Gross announced that he was sick and tired of talking, that he had already said everything he was going to say, and once again without warning he walked off the witness stand, calling over his shoulder, "I ain't coming back!"

Judge Leibowitz directed the guards to seize him, and when they had done so he roared at Gross, "If you don't come back to this stand, I'll order the court officer to chain you to the stand with handcuffs! You can't affront the dignity of the court this way!"

Gross complained loudly that he had been in solitary confinement in the Raymond Street jail for six months and the experience had taken twenty years off his life. Leibowitz replied that it hadn't been solitary confinement, and in any case he had nothing to do with the imprisonment, but in his courtroom the witness would answer the questions put to him. "If I have to give you a thousand years," he said, "I will give you a thousand years, and you'll have plenty of time to think it over."

Gross stared down at the floor for a long while; finally he lifted his head and asked the judge if he had any children.

Seemingly taken aback by the question, Leibowitz replied that he did.

"Well," said Gross, "if they ever have the misfortune to get into trouble, I hope they're tried before a judge like you."

At that Judge Leibowitz cited Gross for contempt of court and ordered him to be returned to the witness stand. Julius Helfand was now desperately trying to salvage the case, to find a way to get Harry Gross to affirm in court the information he had previously given to prosecutors. For the next hour he dispensed with direct questioning and instead read aloud passages from Gross's testimony before the grand jury; at the end of each passage he simply asked the witness to acknowledge that what he had said was true. Each time Gross refused to answer, and each time the judge levied another citation for contempt of court. Finally Judge Leibowitz had no choice but to acknowledge that it was useless, that Gross was not going to testify under any circumstances, and he turned to address the jury directly. "This man," he said, his voice rising, "has put a dagger through the hearts of the people of New York. No man in my memory has done more harm to law and order than he has. He deserves every day in jail I can give him. For a wretch like this to sit on the witness stand and thumb his nose at justice is something I will not condone. It's a shame that the power of the underworld and the rats working with them is strong enough, powerful enough, to paralyze the hands of those who are trying to make this community a clean, decent place."

By this time Miles McDonald had been summoned and was sitting beside Julius Helfand at the counsel's table, and on seeing him, Leibowitz was reminded of the countless witnesses who had testified before the Brooklyn grand jury he still oversaw, and the judge declared that Harry Gross was trying to undermine the good work that District Attorney McDonald had undertaken, a heroic effort that would have crushed many other men. "He fought even with a mayor of the city of New York castigating him and trying to thwart the investigation," the judge said, his words having now begun to assume, perhaps inevitably, a valedictory tone.

Amid the judge's fulminations Gross's natural brashness seemed to have returned; at the insults he laughed out loud, and once he even turned to face the spectators in the courtroom, like a comedian mugging in a vaudeville skit, and shrugged and winked. Now Judge Leibowitz ordered the security guards to place Gross before the bench. The courtroom grew silent as the judge tallied up sixty contempt citations; after more tallying he announced that with a fine of $250 and a sentence of thirty days for each one, Gross faced a penalty of $15,000 and eighteen hundred days—nearly five years—in jail for contempt of court.

Harry Gross replied sneeringly, "Why don't you just give me the chair and get it over with?" Then he turned and glowered at Miles McDonald as he was escorted out of the courtroom.

It was, McDonald would say later, the worst day of his life. The case on which he and his men had worked for nearly two years was coming apart before his eyes. Under the law of double jeopardy the defendants could not be tried twice for the same crimes; it dawned on him that the events had been carefully engineered to take Gross up to the point in the trial at which double jeopardy would take effect. McDonald had heard rumors of meetings being held with the defendants in hotel rooms, and now he felt he understood what those meetings had been about. The fight against police corruption was by no means over; he would seek to bring the accused cops before a departmental hearing, would do whatever he could to have them removed from the police force. He and Julius Helfand, of course, already had a full docket of other cases on which to focus. It was the rookie cops for whom he felt most deeply, the ones who had been plucked straight from the academy, who had endured the taunts and slurs of their fellow officers, had risked threats against themselves and, worse, against their loved ones, and who now, marked, would return to the body of the force only more firmly convinced of the power of corruption; that was the most heartbreaking idea of all, and in contemplating it McDonald felt his throat tighten and he realized that he had begun to cry. After a few moments he rose and approached the bench.

"Without Gross's testimony," he said quietly, "we have no case. Therefore, I move for dismissal."

"Granted," said Judge Leibowitz, banging his gavel, and the courtroom erupted, the cops cheering and shaking their attorneys' hands and embracing family members who rushed shrieking from their seats, and amid the tumult Miles McDonald, his cheeks still wet with tears, turned and walked silently out.

CHAPTER 32

Floyd Layne was working those days as a shipping clerk for a dress manufacturer in the Garment District, a City College alumnus named Harry Spielberg. Each day, as he stood wrapping and sorting bundles, he tried to maintain his focus on the private vow he had made: that he would never do another dishonest thing.

Those five blocks home from the subway after being released on bail had seemed the longest walk he had ever taken; by then everyone had read about him in the papers and he imagined being looked at from every window. Worse still were the pain and humiliation he saw on his mother's face when he arrived back home. "Bunty," she said quietly, "did you do it?" and it just about killed him to admit that he had. He holed up in the apartment for two or three weeks, not wanting to talk to anyone, feeling sorry for himself full time; eventually, though, he began to recognize that feeling sorry was not enough—it certainly wasn't enough for others (he could sense a certain reticence even in some old friends, a doubt in their eyes), nor did it set his own mind at ease, and by the time Bobby Sand called with his friend Harry Spielberg's job offer, Floyd had resolved that he wasn't going to rest until everyone stopped thinking of him as the guy who had sold out his school and himself; he was going to prove them wrong, however long it might take.

Even months after the arrests Floyd could see that Eddie Roman was taking the scandal especially hard; he seemed sunk in a depression, the endearing goofy grin and braying laugh relics of a bygone time. As the weather got a little warmer the two of them often took long walks together, Eddie perpetually slump-shouldered, Floyd swinging his arms, bouncing a bit on his toes as he walked. They walked to the clack and rumble of the El train overhead, passing liquor stores and kosher butcher shops, drugstores with newly printed FARMACÍA signs to cater to the growing Puerto Rican population, Chinese restaurants and tuxedo shops and dry cleaners and dance studios, all of them tumbledown and disconnected, seeming to have been blown together randomly like scraps of paper against a wall. This was where they both felt most at ease, on these mottled and disorderly streets; they were more comfortable talking here than in their own homes (Floyd's apartment now seemed off-limits for Eddie, the pain of the arrest still too raw for Lina to welcome him), and as they walked they recalled better times, like those weekend pickup games when they and Ed Warner would hold the playground court for what seemed hours at a time, taking on all comers. Sometimes, bittersweetly, they remembered games they had played together at the Garden, hearing again the roar of the crowd, its hoarse rise and fall like the surf at Coney Island.

That spring a friend had invited Floyd to participate in a basketball tournament at the Immaculate Conception church in the Bronx, and Floyd in turn invited Eddie to join him on the team. It had been months since they played, and they were nervous as they suited up and walked onto the court, wondering how the crowd would react to them. Not long after the arrests, Eddie and Sherman White had signed up for a YMCA tournament in New Jersey, but during the warm-ups they were ordered off the court by the tournament director and had to watch the game from the stands. Soon after the Immaculate Conception game began, though, Floyd got open in the corner and lofted up his trademark set shot, the one that ended with his hands together above his head like a diver, and to his relief the shot dropped straight in—*swish*, as Marty Glickman might have said. Only about four hundred people were there, a far cry from the eighteen thousand who used to attend the Garden games, but the cheer they gave him after that shot seemed the loudest Floyd had ever received, and he would say later that it had meant the most.

Floyd had felt himself floating around the court that night; the crowd's reaction, so generous and accepting, gave him hope that one day the players would be readmitted to school and given the opportunity to prove themselves honorable. Eddie was far more pessimistic. "It's all over, Floyd," he would say as they walked. "We might as well go down to the docks and start working right now. We'll never get another chance."

On July 5, fourteen former college basketball players, including seven from City College, pleaded guilty to conspiracy before Judge Saul S. Streit in General Sessions Court in New York. It was a deal that had been negotiated by the players' attorneys with the Manhattan DA's office; by pleading guilty to conspiracy and agreeing to testify against the fixers, the players avoided prosecution on the more serious bribery charges. The players still faced sentences of up to three years, but as Jacob Grumet had anticipated, Assistant District Attorney Vincent O'Connor would not be asking for jail time. He told the court, "We do not believe that the public interest requires that these young men receive felony convictions." Judge Streit set October 2 as the date for sentencing.

On July 24, eight members of the Bradley Braves, including the All-American Gene Melchiorre, confessed in Peoria to having taken bribes to shave points in three games during the 1949–50 season and another game the following year. (Like the City College players, the Bradley players refused to shave points during the 1950 postseason tournaments.) Two weeks later another college sports scandal hit the front pages: Ninety cadets at the United States Military Academy at West Point, including nearly all of the varsity football team, were expelled for having violated the school's honor code by cheating on exams. Before long, though, this new scandal had received an unexpected intervention: A church representative issued a written statement from Cardinal Spellman announcing that he had asked the presidents of three Catholic colleges in his archdiocese to accept any of the expelled West Point cadets who applied for admission. The Cardinal's statement was just two paragraphs long and began with a brief quotation: "To err is human, to forgive divine."

The months dragged by, especially after the date for sentencing was delayed from October to November. Eddie and Floyd filed official requests for readmittance to City College, but President Wright had not changed his position and the fall semester got under way without them. Floyd left his job at the dress factory in July when George Gregory, the executive director of Forest Neighborhood House, where Floyd worked as a counselor in the summers, hired him as an assistant group leader in its athletic program. "As far as I'm concerned," Gregory had told a reporter after the arrest, "I'm going out of my way to help this boy in any way I can," and his opinion was echoed by another Forest House official, Herman Forster, who pointed out, "If the Police Department sent us a boy who had gotten into several scrapes with the law, we'd turn our settlement house upside down to help him. Can we do any less for a kid who has an exceptionally good past record?"

Floyd had grown up without a father at home, but he had spent years watching the men who worked at Forest House and the Harlem YMCA, brilliant basketball players who were also compassionate and community oriented, none more so than George Gregory himself, the first black All-American and captain of the Columbia University basketball team, who had earned a degree in sociology before going on to work at the Children's Aid Society. Floyd had long tried to model himself on these men, studying their demeanor, how they carried themselves—as he would say later, "standing up straight, talking straight, dealing with problems head on"—and now he tried as best he could to carry on their example in his own work.

The kids at Forest House ranged in age from twelve to twenty-one, and though Floyd himself was only twenty-two he found that he was able to exert a kind of quiet authority, that kids quickly began to cluster around him seeking his attention and approval. "I'm with those kids every chance I get," Floyd said at the time. "I show them how to play basketball, sure. But I also show them a lot of the things I've learned, things that are a whole lot more important than losing your man on a give-and-go play. I know that all those youngsters who have been around me realize that just being a good player isn't enough. I keep showing them things to better themselves." As time went on George Gregory assigned him to some of the more troubled kids, those dismissed offhandedly as "juvenile delinquents," and Floyd began to venture into the community, speaking with parents, teachers, parole officers, trying to get the kids enrolled in Forest House after-school programs, doing whatever he could to give them a second chance, as Mr. Gregory was giving him a second chance, tracking them down on playgrounds and street corners, in principals' offices and, occasionally, in a courtroom, which was especially painful to him, as it could not help but call to mind the courtroom that he would soon be entering under very different circumstances.

That day finally arrived on November 19, 1951, the Monday before Thanksgiving. On the eleventh floor of the Manhattan Criminal Courts building, the Court of General Sessions was a high-ceilinged room with tables and benches made of richly burnished blond oak and long draperies that imparted elegance while muffling sound. Every one of the more than two hundred seats was taken that morning, a sense of tension thick in the air; at the front, a congregation of tall young men in suits and ties gazed nervously around the room, doing their best to smile at relatives or leaning down to murmur with their attorneys. For the players, at least (as opposed to the fixers Sollazzo and Gard), the sentencing was expected to be routine—the district attorney had made clear that he did not believe that justice was served by putting these young men behind bars; moreover, he was concerned that future investigations would be inhibited if players were jailed even after having given evidence against the men who organized the schemes. The players could also take comfort in reminding themselves that history provided no instances of athletes having been imprisoned for gambling-related offenses. This was true even of the Chicago "Black Sox," participants in the most notorious gambling scandal in the history of American sports, who had taken money to lose the 1919 World Series; the eight implicated players had been barred from professional baseball for life, but even they had not spent any time in prison.

Still, there was no telling what could happen, and the room was filled with an ecclesiastical hush as the bailiff called for all to rise. At the age of fifty-three, Judge Saul S. Streit was an impressive-looking figure, six feet tall and trim, with liquid dark eyes and brushed-back hair graying at the temples. Streit had been a judge for fifteen years but he had never had a case like this one; he was well aware of the intense interest and strong emotions it had provoked, and before taking his seat he asked the court attendants to escort the female relatives of the defendants from the courtroom—"to prevent," he explained, "any possible hysterical outburst."

Almost imperceptible ripples of confusion and unease ran through the room, and in the first rows several women rose to their feet, Lina Griffith Layne among them. They were dressed in outfits that might otherwise have been worn to a wedding or graduation, their faces now etched with lines of exhaustion and sorrow, and they made their way silently and with great dignity up the aisles and out of the courtroom, having been removed for an illegitimate reason but unwilling to protest because at this moment, when everything seemed to hang in the balance, they would do nothing that might dispose the judge in any way against their loved ones. Salvatore Sollazzo's wife, Jeanne, was there as well, looking both mournful and glamorous in a trim black dress set off by a single strand of pearls, and reporters clustered around her in the hallway as she explained that she was now earning her living as a receptionist and photographer's model, and that her husband's financial difficulties and newfound notoriety had forced her to move from their Central Park West apartment to smaller quarters, the location of which she preferred to keep secret. "I just want to be left alone to pick up the pieces," she said.

With the female relatives removed, Judge Streit asked the guards to lock the courtroom doors, a dramatic and unexpected gesture that only added to the tension inside the room. As the proceedings got under way, the judge heard impassioned pleas from the defense attorneys, including Jacob Grumet, who spoke at length on behalf of the players, noting that he was also conveying a plea for mercy from City College president Harry N. Wright as well as faculty manager of athletics Sam Winograd and head coach Nat Holman. Prison was not needed for these young men, Grumet argued, as the stigma of their crimes would be punishment enough for the rest of their lives. He urged Judge Streit to recall the action of Cardinal Spellman with respect to the West Point cadets: "The Cardinal said to err is human, to forgive is divine. He gave them an opportunity to straighten out their lives. They can be useful to the community. You, your honor, can destroy them."

Jacob Grumet's former boss, District Attorney Frank Hogan, also rose to plead for leniency. The players, he acknowledged, "couldn't have been prosecuted if they hadn't cooperated with the police and confessed. These men's rehabilitation began with their confessions. They purged themselves of perverted thinking. They will come out of this bigger men. The interests of society will adequately be served by suspension of sentence, and I earnestly make that recommendation."

Frank Hogan had not tried a case in eight years, nor led a grand jury investigation in six, and he rarely appeared in court; the fact that he had come personally to speak on behalf of the players was an indication of the importance that he placed on this case. Judge Streit, too, had taken a special interest in it, spending months interviewing college presidents, coaches, registrars, and numerous others. This was the only ruling of his that would be excerpted in the newspapers, and now he began to read it aloud; the ruling turned out to be forty-one pages long and required nearly an hour to finish.

Streit charged that the commercialization of big-time college sports had fostered a culture of gambling, corrupting athletes, coaches, administrators, and alumni alike. He described how talented prospects were feverishly recruited by colleges all over the country, offered money and gifts and phony jobs, often in direct violation of amateur guidelines. "To put it plainly and bluntly," he declared, "[the player] is bribed in the first instance to choose one college over another." In pursuit of athletes, colleges routinely lowered academic standards or ignored them entirely. One of the defendants, Sherman White, had placed 230th in a high school graduating class of 263, and after admittance to Villanova College, had been withdrawn for academic cause after one semester; coach Clair Bee then offered him a scholarship to Long Island University, where, almost miraculously, he was said to show "remarkable scholastic improvement." Ed Warner had graduated from high school 827th in a class of 942 and had been assessed at 2.3 years behind grade level, yet he was allowed to enroll as a regular student at City College after only a single semester of evening session courses. Al Roth and Herb Cohen likewise had poor high school grades, but those grades had plainly been altered on their entrance transcripts. Many of the players had obtained summer jobs in the Catskills, ostensibly as waiters and busboys and lifeguards but actually to play basketball. The games themselves were played in Madison Square Garden, "an arena not under college control and permeated with the most deleterious influences," where "the point spread was shouted from one end of the arena to the other." In effect, Streit observed, the players were "professionals masquerading as amateurs."

Finally Judge Streit came to the task of sentencing; he began, as was to be expected, with the fixer Salvatore Sollazzo, who faced heavier charges than anyone else. Sollazzo, the judge pronounced, "has no scruples, no sense of morals, nor any respect for the law. He is a menace to society and deserves no consideration from this court whatsoever." With that Streit sentenced him to eight to sixteen years in state prison.

Next was Sollazzo's partner Eddie Gard. Assistant District Attorney Vincent O'Connor had earlier pleaded on Gard's behalf, pointing out that Gard had been immensely cooperative with the state's investigation, but Streit set aside this appeal for clemency; declaring that Gard had "adopted the behavior pattern of one whose aim in life is the fast buck," who had "helped wine and dine the players and supplied them with women to soften them up for the kill," he issued a sentence of up to three years.

Now the judge turned to the players; ashen-faced and trembling, they stepped into the well one by one to receive their sentences. The first was Adolph Bigos of Long Island University. Bigos was among the most enthusiastic of the point shavers, who had fixed games during two seasons and encouraged others to participate in the scheme. "In my opinion," Streit observed, "this defendant is guilty of a series of briberies without regard for his honor or the public interest." Before coming to LIU, however, Bigos had served in the South Pacific during World War II, for which he received eight combat medals; Judge Streit (who would later display an "Americanism" award from the Veterans of Foreign Wars on the wall of his office) was not inclined to put a combat veteran in prison, and he suspended sentence for Bigos. Dick Feurtado and Nate Miller of LIU had war records as well, and to them the judge also handed down suspended sentences. Their teammate Leroy Smith had not served in the armed forces, but Streit noted that Smith's high school record was "uniformly excellent" and that he was "the son of industrious, law-abiding, God-fearing parents"; his sentence too was suspended. Next the judge summoned Norm Mager of City College.

The choice of Mager to start seemed ominous; if any of the City College players were to receive jail time, it would likely be him—after all, he had been the contact man for the fixer Eli Kaye, procuring players and then arranging the deals and handing out the payoff money. Mager, however, had served in the Army during the war, and after reciting his offenses, Judge Streit said sternly, "Mager, I should send you to jail, but it is only because of your service to your country that I am extending to you extreme clemency. Sentence is suspended." Streit then summoned in quick succession Irwin Dambrot, Herb Cohen, Floyd Layne, and Ed Roman, each of whom also received suspended sentences. "And now," he declared, "I come to the most distasteful part of my duty in connection with this tragic scandal."

Neither Ed Warner nor Al Roth had yet been called to step forward; nor had Sherman White of LIU or Connie Schaff of New York University. The judge continued, "I have exercised judicial discretion so as to be merciful in meting out punishment, for, in the ordinary case, a college boy who winds up a criminal is amply punished by his disgrace, even if he does not go to jail. However, there are a few who stand in a special position of guilt, and by virtue of their evil conduct are different from those whose sentences I have just suspended."

Now the four remaining players were called to stand before the bench. At six foot eight, Sherman White was the tallest among them; he was generally regarded as the best college player in the country, and it was understood that the New York Knicks planned to select him in the NBA draft. When White was fourteen years old he had appeared in Juvenile Court for possessing a stolen pocketbook, and at sixteen he appeared again on a charge of petty larceny and was twice cited for disorderly conduct. This, however, was not exactly the record of a hardened criminal, and a gasp went up in the courtroom as Judge Streit sentenced him to a year in the state penitentiary.

Next was Connie Schaff; when he heard his sentence—six months—Schaff fainted dead away and had to be helped to his feet by a court attendant.

Just as Ed Warner had worried about to Jacob Grumet, that single appearance in Juvenile Court as a member of the Sabers youth gang was cited by Judge Streit in pronouncing a six-month prison sentence. Al Roth, too, was sentenced to six months. By this point in the proceedings his face had turned a sickly gray, and as Streit read the sentence he raised an arm, as though to interrupt, but his attorney admonished him to wait; one of the reporters in the room observed, "He dropped his half-raised arm to his side as if it were weighted with lead." Roth and the three others were then escorted from the courtroom to a detention pen just outside.

In determining the sentences, Judge Streit claimed to have weighed what he called "four fundamental factors": The defendants were not simply victims of temptation, but had sought to corrupt others; they were "mature young men," at least twenty-two years old; their criminal acts were "persistent, continuous, and many"; and they "profited largely" from their dishonesty. "It was not an unreasonable set of premises from which to proceed," acknowledged author Stanley Cohen, "but it was difficult to know just how Streit had applied them. For on the basis of his own criteria, it appeared that the wrong players had been sent to jail."

Ed Warner, for instance, had been charged with taking bribes in three games—fewer than five of his codefendants, and no more than three others. The criminal acts of several defendants were not just more numerous but also more "persistent" than his; they had engaged in game fixing over the span of two seasons, whereas Warner was involved during only one. Connie Schaff, for his part, had shaved points in but a single game; he had attempted to induce just one teammate, James Brasco, and had failed even in that. As for profiting "largely," Schaff had received less bribe money than eight of the other defendants.

Judge Streit noted that the four to be imprisoned were all over the age of twenty-two, but this was a distinction without a difference, for every one of the defendants other than Eddie Roman was at least twenty-two years old. In fact, Roth had just turned twenty-two, and Warner was twenty-three; Bigos, on the other hand, was twenty-six and Mager, Feurtado, and Miller were twenty-five. Moreover, Bigos had brought Sherman White into a point-shaving scheme that was already going on at LIU, and according to the judge, Mager "had induced the defendant, Roth, to participate. . . . Then he influenced his teammates, Roman and Dambrot." Bigos and Mager seemed just as much the corrupters of others, yet they had gone free while Warner and White had not.

If strictly applied, the "four fundamental factors" would have led to the imprisonment of a different combination of players; only other factors, ones less firmly rooted in legal principles, could have produced this particular outcome. In justifying the sentence for Sherman White, for instance, Streit observed, "He became greedy and glamour-struck and developed an insatiable lust for night clubs and the company of girls." "Insatiable lust" was a phrase more suited to a scandal magazine than a judicial ruling; and in any case, by the judge's own acknowledgment, White was a "mature" young man of legal drinking age, who was entitled to spend time in nightclubs if he so chose, in the company of girls or not. Regarding Ed Warner, Streit noted that "the Probation Department reports that he was arrogant and resistive to efforts to interview him— that he was untruthful and evasive." Like being "glamour-struck," arrogance was a personality trait rather than a misdeed; in 1951 it was also, surely, a trait more readily identified in athletically gifted young black men with lucrative basketball careers ahead of them. As for being evasive, Warner had spent a lifetime trying to evade the attentions of white authority figures, all those principals and policemen and probation officers so quick to pronounce him "slow" and "sullen," few of whom ever seemed to have his best interests at heart, who could scarcely have failed to notice his many educational difficulties but who kept moving him through the system, from one school to the next, in large part because of his singular talent for basketball.

Al Roth, for his part, had no criminal record, but he had other marks against him: According to Judge Streit, "His basketball success turned his head and he became vain, aggressive, and greedy. His moral scruples deteriorated if he ever had any, and as I have indicated, he had insufficient grades to be admitted to City College."

Indeed, it was this last factor—insufficient grades—that the four sentenced players most obviously had in common. "White, Warner, Roth, and Schaff were not college students in the true sense of the word," observed the judge. Streit had discussed at length how Roth's high school transcript was altered to allow him to attend City College, and elsewhere he noted that Schaff's "scholastic record was uniformly bad." In the cases of Warner and White, in addition to reporting their unimpressive grades, the judge went so far as to cite their low IQ scores. Poor scholarship, however, is not a legal offense, and the fact that they were wrongfully admitted to college was a failing not of the players but of the school administrators. Judge Streit had devoted nearly ten thousand words to a description of how the colleges, pursuing young athletes, routinely lowered academic standards and violated amateur guidelines, but it was the athletes themselves who would be punished for it.

In the end, these four players were not sentenced to prison because they were more deeply involved than the others in criminal activity— they were not—nor because they had profited most handsomely from it. Nor were they sentenced because they were more "mature"; on the contrary, they might well have escaped prison had they been old enough to serve in World War II. They received prison sentences, instead, because they were poor students and the judge disapproved of their conduct: It was less a judicial verdict than a moral one.

Al Roth's mother was then gravely ill, and before Judge Streit dismissed the court he ordered Roth to be brought back in, at which point the judge permitted him to return home to visit with his family, extending his bail until the following week. (Ultimately a deal would be arranged in which Roth avoided jail time in exchange for enlisting in the Army.) Connie Schaff, too, was allowed to return home to attend to certain unnamed personal matters. No such allowances, however, were made for Ed Warner and Sherman White; the two of them—two of only four African Americans among the sixteen defendants—were taken from the detention pen to the city prison.

Mothers and sisters and aunts milled around in the hallway as the freed players emerged from the courtroom, many of them beaming, others weeping with relief. Floyd Layne and Eddie Roman stood side by side, surrounded by friends and family, the scene unavoidably reminiscent of the ones in the locker room after the tournament victories. In the full-page photograph that ran the next morning in the *Daily Mirror,* Floyd appears less exultant than dazed, gazing off into the distance, and in talking to reporters he focused not on his own freedom but on the imprisonment of the others. He noted grimly that Al Roth's mother was dying of leukemia, and shaking his head in disbelief he added, "The shock might kill her. When I heard the sentence I was shocked. I guess we all expected suspended sentences, not prison terms for some."

Eddie Roman spoke briefly with Sam Winograd to express his gratitude for having added his name to Jacob Grumet's plea for leniency. The president of City College, Harry Wright, had also added his name, and later that afternoon Eddie would call Dr. Wright to thank him and discuss the possibility of reinstatement, but the president remained noncommittal.

In the hallway Ed Warner's aunt Elizabeth Duncan was sobbing. "Is that justice?" she asked anyone who would listen. "The one who contacted Eddie is free on a suspended sentence. His mother and father are dead. Who can I turn to? He's been made the goat. He's suffering the brunt of it for the school." She turned helplessly to Sam Winograd standing nearby. "Professor," she said, "I don't understand this. They were all as guilty as my nephew, but they go free and he goes to jail. I don't understand it. Explain it to me." But Winograd could not explain it, nor could anyone else, and when she finally left the courthouse to make the trip back to 138th Street she was pinning her hopes on the possibility of an appeal.

Later that night, though, Elizabeth Duncan received a phone call from Jacob Grumet (who had earlier assured her nephew that he would "never go to jail"). He was sorry, Grumet told her, but there was nothing to be done; the defendant had pleaded guilty and so an appeal could not be made.

The next morning Ed was removed to Rikers Island to begin serving his sentence.

CHAPTER 33

In 1952, Harry N. Wright retired and the City College of New York named a new president, Dr. Buell G. Gallagher. Gallagher was a youthful, vigorous forty-eight and was widely extolled as an idealist and a reformer, although culturally he made an odd fit with City College: The son of a Congregationalist minister, he had grown up in parsonages in Minnesota, Montana, and North Dakota, and in an interview with the *Observation Post* he mentioned that his favorite pastimes included "fly-fishing for trout, and some occasional deep-sea fishing." He moved swiftly to address the lingering basketball scandal, initiating a shake-up of the hygiene department, the academic home of the athletic program: Frank Lloyd was removed as department head and reassigned to a teaching position, as was faculty manager of athletics Sam Winograd. Head coach Nat Holman was granted sabbatical leave, and he and his wife departed for an extended vacation in Spain.

Bobby Sand, for his part, was fired as assistant basketball coach. He was also dismissed from the economics department, where he had taught for eleven years, while his status within the hygiene department—in which he had tenure—was changed to "unassigned."

Alone among the members of the hygiene department, Sand had long advocated decommercializing basketball at City College. He liked to say, "Big-time basketball breeds big-time betting; big-time betting breeds corruption." In 1948 he had worked with editors from *The Campus* on an article that proposed a major realignment of the athletic program, calling for basketball games to be played in the Main Gym rather than Madison Square Garden and for athletics to be funded by a student fee rather than the profits from basketball. In the months before the suspensions, Sand had been interviewed by Andrew O'Neil, the investigator hired by the Board of Higher Education; O'Neil reported that some of the testimony given by college officials contained "inconsistencies, contradictions, and lies. . . . No discrepancies, however, were found in any of the testimony given by Sand." He concluded: "Since 1945 Sand told his superiors that the basketball climate was no good. He did everything in his power, short of resigning from the staff, to bring about a healthy program."

After the shake-up in the hygiene department was announced, an editorial in the student newspaper the *Observation Post* echoed the view widely held on campus, that Sand was being unduly punished:

> Bobby Sand did nothing that did not have the approval of the men above him. . . . When the scandal broke he was the one person we knew or heard of who showed compassion for the boys involved. Everyone else scurried for the safety of cynicism or ignorance.
>
> We think, of all the people close to the scandal, Bobby should be the last to take the rap, and here he is the only one without a job.

For two months Sand lived in a kind of professional limbo; then in November 1952 a special committee empowered by the Board of Higher Education to investigate the basketball scandal filed a report charging "neglect of duty" and "conduct unbecoming a teacher" by Frank Lloyd, Nat Holman, and Bobby Sand. Lloyd and Holman faced a variety of charges: Lloyd, for instance, was charged with having approved payments to local high school coaches to steer recruits to City College; Holman was cited for not having reported numerous instances of suspicious activities, including a bribe offered by one City player to another in 1945. "Our Committee is convinced," the report concluded, "that either Prof. Holman knew very well many of the aspects of big-time basketball . . . or else was so naïve about matters involving his own job as to throw doubt on his fitness as a teacher."

The charges against Bobby Sand arose from a letter he had written to Ed Warner after the championships. A promoter in South America had invited the City College team on a summer barnstorming tour of Brazil, Argentina, and Uruguay; Sand was to serve as coach in place of Nat Holman, though he agreed to participate only on the condition that he could distribute his stipend of $2,250 among the players participating in the trip. Holman wanted to ensure a representative team, and before the tour could be confirmed he required that at least four members of the starting lineup sign affidavits stating that they would participate. Floyd Layne, however, had injured his hand playing baseball and did not think he would be in shape for the trip, and Ed Warner said that he preferred to work in the Catskills. With the trip hanging in the balance, several of the team's players, as well as administrators including Sam Winograd, began to pressure Sand to obtain the necessary affidavit.

So one day in the City College cafeteria Sand sat down and wrote a letter to Warner at Klein's Hillside Hotel suggesting that Warner sign the affidavit even if he did not currently intend to go. He might change his mind later, Sand pointed out, in which case he would be glad to have signed; if he ended up not going he could always claim an injury and a replacement for him would be found—but at least then the trip would still be on. Sand reminded Warner that the players would each receive a share of his coach's stipend; additionally, he mentioned that the college's director of public relations, Lester Nichols, who was organizing the tour, had indicated that he would try to schedule an extra game, "with the 'kicks' going to the boys."

This last point—that a CCNY official would schedule a game for the express purpose of compensating amateur players—was an especially sensitive one, and in closing Sand urged Warner to destroy the letter after reading it. However, Warner read only the first page and then put the letter in his suitcase, and eventually he handed it over to Sam Winograd when Winograd got wind of its existence and demanded it from him. Winograd, in turn, informed Nat Holman and Frank Lloyd, and in a meeting at the college the three men agreed not to tell anyone else about the letter, storing it in a safe-deposit box in a nearby bank. ("I want to hold on to it," Winograd said, "and if Bobby ever gets funny sometime in the future I'll have this to use against him.") Ultimately the proposed South America trip fell through; however, Sand was charged by the committee with having "violate[d] basic amateur standards" by offering to pay the players with his own stipend and for encouraging Ed Warner to lie regarding the affidavit.

A Board of Higher Education trial would hear the charges against Holman, Lloyd, and Sand and, in the event of guilty verdicts, determine appropriate punishments. The day after the release of the committee report, President Buell Gallagher suspended the three without pay.

"If I have to go, that's okay," Sand told a reporter. "I'll offer my defense when the time comes, but I have no quarrel with an action that will finally clear up the situation. I felt a long time ago that basketball was the tail that wagged the dog here at CCNY. I can't think otherwise now that I've been hurt." Two days later, though, as the reality sank in of his new life without a paycheck, he was less forgiving; in *The Campus* he called himself a "scapegoat" and described the decision not to bring charges against Sam Winograd as "an injustice which cannot be expressed in words."

In the past Bobby had received several college coaching offers, but those offers had come before the arrests and the atmosphere of suspicion that now enveloped City's athletic program, and there was no telling whether he could find another coaching job until he was able to clear himself in court. Finally he concluded that he would have to look elsewhere. Many CCNY graduates worked in the garment industry, and Bobby had used his connections there to land Floyd Layne a job at the Harry Spielberg dress factory; before that he had gotten Ed Warner a summer job with Henry Rosenfeld, another dress manufacturer. Now, with no other prospects, Sand himself found work as a Rosenfeld dress salesman, earning fifty dollars a week, less than half what he had made at City College.

Financially, it was a desperate period: Bobby's daughter Wendie recalls his trying to sell his gold tournament watch to bring in whatever extra money he could.

The Board of Higher Education trial commenced on May 28, 1953, in a courtroom on the sixth floor of the New York Bar Association offices on

West Forty-Fourth Street. For years the two defendants* had sat side by side on a bench at Madison Square Garden; now they sat at a counsel's table, separated by attorneys, gazing up at a three-man committee of the New York City Board of Higher Education. The trial would last until December, with dozens of witnesses called and more than three thousand pages of testimony taken. Nat Holman insisted that he had had no involvement in high school recruiting, having delegated it to his co-defendant Bobby Sand; that he paid attention only to the games on the court, not to point spreads or rumors of game fixing; and that he could not function as a coach if he allowed himself any suspicion of his own players. In retrospect, he said, he had come to believe that the scandal owed primarily to the players' own moral deficiency: "I have reviewed this thing in my mind for some time, and I honestly feel that the cause was brought about mainly because the youngsters lacked the moral fiber to make a decision when they were faced with temptation, when these unscrupulous gamblers approached them . . . they just didn't have it in them at the time to say no."

Bobby Sand admitted that he had made a mistake in writing the letter to Ed Warner but explained that he had done it because he thought the players deserved the South America trip and he didn't want them to lose it over a single missing affidavit. Nor did he feel right in taking a generous stipend when the players would receive only a dollar per day in expense money; distributing his pay among them worked out to about seven dollars per day per player, which didn't seem extravagant, especially as they would have to cut short their work season in the Catskills. The Warner letter, he insisted, was "the only blemish on my record in eighteen years of service to the college."

When the trial was over, the committee voted 2–1 to recommend the dismissal of all charges against Nat Holman and to reinstate him with back pay for the period of the suspension. The committee unanimously found Bobby Sand guilty, directing that his back pay be withheld and that he be reinstated at City College but not permitted to teach or coach. The trial committee's recommendations were then transmitted to the twenty-one-person Board of Higher Education for a final rul-

---

* At the beginning of the trial the third defendant, Frank Lloyd, agreed to resign from City College and as a result the charges against him were dropped.

ing. It was expected that the board would simply rubber-stamp the recommendations, but instead the BHE reversed the decision on Holman, finding him guilty of having concealed the Sand-Warner letter, having failed to report the 1945 bribe attempt, and having been uncooperative with the board's investigation. In a decision that sent shock waves through the basketball world, Nat Holman was ordered to be dismissed from City College.

Holman's attorney called the reversal an "outrage and injustice," vowing to appeal the decision to Lewis A. Wilson, the state commissioner of education. Meanwhile, the board reprimanded Bobby Sand and upheld his suspension without back pay; however, it also expressed appreciation for his "cooperation, his frank admission of guilt, and his expression of repentance" and ordered Sand restored to his former faculty status, to be "assigned to such duties as the President of City College may designate."

Just before the start of the fall 1954 semester, Commissioner Wilson himself reversed the decision of the Board of Higher Education, ordering Nat Holman to be reinstated with full back pay. "Thank God, there's justice in America," Holman exulted upon hearing the news. "I thought the biggest thrill of my life was winning the double championship in 1950, but it isn't anymore. Today's vindication is my greatest victory."

Speaking to reporters, President Buell Gallagher said, "We at City College will of course be glad to have Mr. Holman back again." Gallagher noted that he intended to restore Holman to his position as head coach of the basketball team, explaining that "his interests and greatest skills are in the coaching field and it was the normal, natural thing to do. We have gladly welcomed him back to the College and wish him well as coach."

The president was far less forgiving of Bobby Sand. After the BHE decision, Gallagher announced that Sand would be assigned to the records department, where his duties were "to sift through the accumulated back records of the College and carry out the classification of materials in old files as well as to establish the process by which materials are regularly deleted and destroyed as they become no longer useful." Sand was still a tenured member of the hygiene department, and while Gallagher acknowledged that it was "unusual" for the college to employ a faculty member outside the department in which he had tenure, he stated curtly, "Mr. Sand does not now qualify for any instructional job."

For Bobby Sand, then, there would be no position making use of "his interests and greatest skills," as had been granted to Nat Holman. Before long, Sand was reassigned to the Division of Planning and Design in Eisner Hall, a modern brick building at the northernmost edge of the campus. Holman continued to coach the City College Beavers while Sand was delegated a succession of dispiriting tasks. He was put in charge of a campaign to save paper; he served as a liaison between the college and the city's Board of Estimate; he was loaned out to two community colleges in Queens and the Bronx to help them map their facilities. Editorials in the school newspapers referred to him as "the Forgotten Man."

In 1956 an editor for *The Campus* named Sheldon Podolsky devoted his final column to Sand's plight. "I think of Bobby Sand sitting at his desk in Eisner Hall," Podolsky wrote, "a broken man after years of devotion to the College. He made one mistake and will never stop paying for it." By that point it was clear to Sand that Buell Gallagher wanted him to become so frustrated that he would simply quit, but he refused. Sylvia would not hear of leaving New York, where her family and doctors were near at hand, and besides, City College was his second home and he believed that one day he would clear his name and be allowed to return to teaching and coaching. All through the 1950s and into the 1960s Sand remained in a kind of exile on the farthest reaches of the campus. "Bobby worked in hidden offices, dusty attics, and damp basements," recalled a colleague from that period. "It was as though they didn't trust him around kids anymore. He used to be bright, warm, and loving, but they cut out his heart."

At the close of the 1952–53 college basketball season, Manhattan district attorney Frank Hogan announced that he was bringing his investigation to an end. In all, thirty-three players had been arrested from seven schools: Manhattan College, City College, Long Island University, New York University, Bradley University, Toledo University, and— perhaps most shocking—the University of Kentucky.

Back in August 1951, after the arrests of the Bradley and Toledo players, Kentucky head coach Adolph Rupp had proclaimed confidently to reporters, "Gentlemen, I'll guarantee you this: The gamblers couldn't touch our boys with a ten-foot pole." Yet just two months later, three former Kentucky Wildcats, Alex Groza, Ralph Beard, and Dale Barnstable—stars of the legendary squad that won the 1948 Olympic gold medal and was later awarded its own NBA franchise—were arrested and charged with having shaved points in two games during the 1948–49 season, including a first-round loss to Loyola of Chicago in the National Invitation Tournament.

In New York, Rupp-hating basketball fans noted that the gamblers must have found eleven-foot poles.

In the fall of 1952, Milton Gross of the *New York Post* accompanied Floyd Layne as he took a group of children from Forest House on a tour of the American Museum of Natural History. Floyd held two of the kids by the hand while they climbed the stairs to the entrance. "Watch your step," he called to those behind him. "Be careful you don't stumble. Stay right with me."

"I like this work," he told Gross. "I've always had pleasure working with kids, but now it means more to me than ever. This is my future, but I'd like to get the past cleared up a little more."

Gross asked if that meant he was interested in playing in the NBA.

"I wouldn't want to embarrass anybody," Floyd said. "I'd like to wait and see how the league feels about it. I wouldn't want to embarrass the league or myself. I don't know how people in basketball would take to me, but I'd like to find out. All I want is maybe five, ten minutes on the floor. Five minutes could change the whole outlook of my life."

At that time the National Basketball Association was still in its infancy, its finances fragile, and league officials hoped to capitalize on the scandal by presenting the professional game as an untainted alternative to the collegians. After the arrests of the former Kentucky players, Commissioner Maurice Podoloff called an emergency meeting at which the three players, now members of the Indianapolis Olympians, were banned from the league for life.

It was clear that the National Basketball Association would not be accepting any of the other implicated college players anytime soon. In any event, Floyd was drafted in 1953, and for the next twenty-one months he served at a succession of Army bases, playing service basketball while performing his military duties. After receiving his honorable discharge in January 1955 he returned to the Bronx. By that time President Buell Gallagher had decided that the players implicated in the basketball scandal should be allowed to reapply to CCNY, though they would be ineligible for athletic activity. "We consider that they have paid their debt to society," he told *The Campus*. "I'm sure that none of them are proud of what they have done." In February, Floyd reentered City College, where his classmates now included Eddie Roman.

After the sentencing by Judge Saul Streit, Eddie had worked a succession of odd jobs, in a men's haberdashery, a luncheonette, a TV distributing house, enduring what he characterized as "a tremendous depression." It was a period of his life that later on he would find he had mostly blocked from memory, a blur of shame and anger. He had committed a crime, of course; he had confessed to it and pleaded guilty, had even given up his teammates to the district attorney's investigators, but despite everything he was still marked by the scandal, scorned as a dumper, a money-grubber, a traitor to his school and his city. One time he was playing pickup basketball in the neighborhood, a three-on-three game with a crowd gathered around to watch, and during a break in the action a kid wearing jeans and a leather jacket tossed a couple of pennies in his direction. The kid seemed to have intended it less as a dare than a joke— he just stood there with an idiot grin on his face—but at that moment, with the coins still lying at his feet, Eddie understood that he could not escape his reputation even here, in his own schoolyard, and something snapped inside him and without even thinking about it he grabbed the kid by the front of the jacket and pushed him up against a wall and smashed him in the face, hard enough that he thought he heard something break; then, still seething, he simply turned and waited for the ball.

He had always been quiet, cheerful, slow to anger; it had never been in his character to fight, but now it was not so clear to him what his character was. Most of his time he preferred to spend by himself, or with guys who had known him before City College; in public he had to face too many questions he was tired of answering, too many conversations he did not wish to have. Always shy by nature, he now shrank from introducing himself to anyone new, in dread of the dawning awareness in the other person's eyes, that terrible moment of recognition.

Finally he enlisted in the Army, where he was assigned to a tank unit at Fort Lawton in Washington. One night at a USO dance Eddie was introduced to a young telephone switchboard operator named Donna Laruhn. She was from Minnesota originally, blond and vivacious and direct in her manner, and he found to his amazement that he was able to talk to her. (She would describe him later as having been "shy and depressed" and "ashamed and devastated.") That year a reporter from *Sport* magazine tracked him down for a story on the basketball fixers; Eddie said that he preferred to remain out of the public eye, although he did volunteer that "I met a very wonderful girl here and plan to get married as soon as I get settled in civilian life."

He and Donna did get married, and before long she gave birth to a boy they named Mark. Eddie took several courses at the University of Seattle on the GI Bill; soon, though, his father got sick with cancer and he and Donna and the baby moved back east, into the house on Teller Avenue, so they could help his mother take care of him. Almost immediately he reenrolled at CCNY for the fall 1954 semester.

He had worried about unpleasant encounters with fellow students, but to his relief, none of that happened. He told *The Campus* that he was "very happy to be back at the college, and I feel that I've been treated very fairly in being given the opportunity to get my degree." Asked about the recent exoneration of Nat Holman, Eddie sidestepped the issue, saying diplomatically, "I'm very glad to see that the affair has finally settled itself and that the college will receive no more unfavorable publicity."

In a 1954 *Sport* article, "The Basketball Fixers—Three Years After," Floyd Layne was quoted as saying, "I'll never stop praying that somehow I, as well as the other fellows, will someday get another chance to play in the Garden. We know now what a great mistake we made, but I think we have paid for it sufficiently. I know as far as I'm concerned, it will always remain with me like a bad nightmare."

The NBA had never issued any sort of formal announcement; as far as Floyd knew, there was no piece of paper with his name printed alongside those of the others involved in the point-shaving scandal. The blacklist was apparent only in absence: in the canceled meetings, the invitations that didn't come, the phone calls that were never returned. Floyd had always believed in his own powers of persuasion; he was sure that if he could just talk to Commissioner Maurice Podoloff, explain his side of the story, he would be granted the opportunity to play. Somehow a meeting could never be arranged, but finally Podoloff agreed to speak with him on the phone. Though the commissioner was evasive, not wanting to commit to anything, Floyd came away with the impression that his best course of action would be to persuade one of the teams to give him a tryout. Eagerly he wrote to five NBA clubs; he also spoke to Bobby Wanzer, the coach of the Rochester Royals (and a fellow graduate of Benjamin Franklin High School), and a tryout with the Royals was in the works until one day Floyd received another call from Maurice Podoloff, who said that he was sorry but the NBA's board of governors had vetoed the idea. "Mr. Podoloff told me that if the league allowed me to have a tryout, then it would have to allow tryouts to all the others involved in the scandal," Floyd explained disappointedly to a reporter. "It didn't want to be put in that position."

Instead, Floyd began playing for the Hazleton Hawks of the Eastern League, a weekend league based in Pennsylvania; the team owners had decided that they could boost attendance by bringing in the college players implicated in the gambling scandal, not just Floyd Layne but also Eddie Roman, Ed Warner, and Sherman White, along with several others. (And not only players: For many years Bobby Sand coached in the Eastern League.) They traveled to Scranton, Reading, Sunbury, Pottsville, declining industrial towns built around steel mills and coal mines, playing in dimly lit gyms and armories, usually for only a few hundred people. On Saturday mornings they would pile into cars for the long drive to Pennsylvania; after the game they took rooms in local motels and then set out the next day for whatever town was next on the schedule. For this they earned perhaps fifty dollars per game, though the league's finances were always precarious and veteran players demanded to be paid in cash and right after the final buzzer, when the ticket revenue was still in the box office. They were in the prime of their careers, playing as hard as ever, working the give-and-go, running the weave to perfection, just as they had under the spotlights of Madison Square Garden, though now they were performing before sparse crowds in high school gyms, much as they had when they were only high schoolers themselves. Still, they endured the low pay and long car rides, and the constant companionship of wistfulness and regret, all on the thin hope that by playing in the Eastern League they might demonstrate to NBA owners that despite the transgressions of their past they had been accepted by the fans and their other teammates and were thus worthy of a second chance.

But the years passed and still the calls from the NBA didn't come. Eddie Roman began teaching in a public school inside a Bronx detention center called the Youth House for Boys. Floyd, too, continued to work with kids, as director of the Woodstock Community Center in the Bronx. He graduated from City College with a bachelor of science degree in education; a CCNY official described him to a reporter as having a "superior record and superior personality." By this time he had gotten married and hoped to begin raising a family. He said, "One thing that keeps running through my mind is the effect this stigma will have on my children. I'm afraid they'll be hurt. I don't want my kids to be hurt."

Sometimes he thought that it would be better if he could just leave well enough alone, as the others did, but something inside kept pushing him. It had been six years now since the scandal, and still he seemed no closer than he had been that day at the American Museum of Natural History when he told Milton Gross that he wished only for five minutes on an NBA court. Finally, not knowing where else to turn, Floyd approached Sid Friedlander, the *Post*'s veteran basketball writer. He came "with a question," Friedlander wrote. "With a whole string of questions, in fact."

"When does it end?" Floyd asked. "When does the punishment end? I did a bad thing and I've been paying for it. Do I pay for it for the rest of my life or can I get a second chance—a chance to show the world that I realize my mistake and clear myself of this thing that's over my head?"

Floyd asked Friedlander to help him present his case to the NBA. "If only I could talk to the board of governors myself," he said. "Or if I could talk to Ned Irish." Irish was the Madison Square Garden basketball promoter who was now president of the New York Knicks; surely he remembered Floyd from City College and might be willing to put in a word for him with the owners. Friedlander promised to speak with them.

Commissioner Maurice Podoloff told Friedlander that he was too concerned about a possible public outcry to let in any of the players involved in the scandal. "The league is just beginning to go well," he said. "We can't take the slightest chance. The wolves in the two-bit seats would murder us. They're heartless."

Ned Irish, for his part, adamantly refused to speak with Floyd. "After what he did," Irish said, "I don't want to see him. I don't want to talk to him. I don't want any of them in the Garden."

So Floyd went back to playing on weekends for the Hawks of Hazleton, Pennsylvania; that year Phil Sarno of Hazleton's paper, *The Plain Speaker*, noted that Floyd "has fit in well and has many followers, as well as Sherman White, Ed Roman, and Ed Warner, who were also involved in the so-called 'game fixes.' They all have acted in a gentlemanlike manner ever since they entered the circuit. Fans throughout the region have long forgotten the scandal blemish and are now cheering their performances. . . . The NBA would do well to amend its way of thinking."

Time, though, was the players' enemy; they were already approaching their thirties, when most basketball players see a decline in their skills. By 1958, Floyd admitted to a reporter from the *New York Amsterdam News*, "I don't think my chances of getting into pro ball now are any good. In fact, none of the boys involved look forward to anything but what we're doing right now. I was the only optimistic one, anyway."

CHAPTER 34

Late one Sunday night in February 1960, Ed Warner, star forward for the Williamsport Billies of the Eastern League, was driving back to New York after a game with Wilkes-Barre. His Billies teammate and longtime friend Carl Green was in the front seat beside him, and in the back seat was another teammate, Zeke Sinicola, and the Williamsport coach, Bobby Sand. Usually in the Eastern League, players shared the long-distance driving, but this was Ed's car, a cream-colored Oldsmobile, and he didn't like anyone else to drive it. He was driving fast, the way he always did, and the Pennsylvania Turnpike was slippery from a recent snowfall and the car seemed to be shimmying just a bit, and at one point Sand called to him from the back to slow down.

"I know *my* car," Warner said, and for a while there was no sound but the steady, soothing hum of the tires on the highway, and for just a moment he may have fallen asleep, because the big car started fishtailing, its back end describing ever wider arcs, and suddenly something seemed to catch and the car began to spin, and in a dreamlike moment it slid through the guardrail and tumbled forty feet down a hillside, turning over several times before finally landing on its roof. Upside down, Carl Green managed to push himself through a window that had been smashed and bent, and when he landed outside he realized that the impact had knocked off one of his shoes and his foot was wet and freezing in the snow, and blindly he began walking back up the hill, in a panic because he thought the car might catch fire and blow up; then he heard Bobby Sand shouting "Carl! Carl!" like a voice cutting through a dream, and he snapped to and limped back to the car and with his one shod foot he managed to kick in a window and the others crawled out, first Bobby and then Zeke and finally Ed from the front seat, and somehow they dragged themselves back up the snowy hill to the road and eventually a flatbed truck came by and transported them to the nearest hospital, Gnaden Huetten Memorial in Lehighton, where they remained for three days.

The article in the *Williamsport Sun-Gazette* reported that the four had "nearly met death" that night. All three of the players were badly injured and missed the remainder of the season. Bobby Sand suffered a concussion and extensive facial bruising, and when he returned home, still sore all over and with both eyes blackened, he told Sylvia that he would never coach again in the Eastern League; the following season his position was taken by Eddie Roman.

By that point Eddie was already planning to retire, despite the fact that he was still an All-Star with the Scranton Miners; he had sustained a number of injuries, including a ruptured blood vessel in his leg, and was finding it harder to stay in shape. He was too busy anyway to keep going away on weekends, despite the extra money the games brought in. He and Donna now had three young children, and they had moved out of his parents' house to a place of their own in Queens. He was still teaching physical education at the Bronx Youth House—a residential facility that some who didn't know any better casually derogated as "Juvie Hall"—working with kids most of whom were black or Puerto Rican, all of whom seemed poorer and more hopeless than he had been only a couple of decades earlier, growing up a couple of dozen blocks to the north. Eddie had decided that he wanted to become a school psychologist, and he enrolled at Columbia University in a master's program in education.

For years after the scandal he had been choked by bitterness and the guilt of having cost his family the chance for financial security offered by the corporate teams of the American Athletic Union. Still, excelling in the Eastern League turned out to have been good for his self-esteem; unexpectedly, too, some of that earlier bitterness seemed to dissolve in teaching and new fatherhood, devoting attention to others who knew little or nothing of his history. Now, in his thirties, he was able to take a longer view of the basketball scandal, to understand it as more than just a personal cataclysm. "The American people have a romanticized view of athletics," Eddie told an interviewer. "They want to identify with the fantasy that the world of sports has come to represent. Whenever you break some kind of moral code, when you do something to the basic fiber of something people believe in, you face wrath that is much stronger than an ordinary crime. It's more acceptable to commit burglary or assault than to accept money for shaving points. People think, How can they do that to a fan? It's an illusion that it's a sport—they get angry at anyone breaking that illusion. People identify with athletes and have a romanticized view of them, and anyone who breaks that code and doesn't fit into that image—they reject him. And then the owners, out of self-protection, shove you under the carpet. . . . The point is that the name of the game is, and always has been, money."

They had all suffered for what they had done, Eddie often mused, each in his own way. Norm Mager had been released by the Baltimore Bullets of the NBA after the arrests; now he worked as a salesman, soliciting accounts for his father's office cleaning business. In the years after the scandal, the constant sense of shame Mager felt had expressed itself in a form of agoraphobia: He would leave for work at six in the morning to avoid the rush hour crowds, then stay inside the officc all day and late into the evening; sometimes just being on the subway, exposed to what he imagined were the stares of his fellow New Yorkers, was so painful that by the time he got home he was in tears. Al Roth routinely denied his identity when someone happened to recognize him. He, too, had re-enrolled at City College, earning a business degree at the downtown campus; he had done very well in the construction business, but even now he hesitated before saying his name to a potential client. Irwin Dambrot had built a thriving dental practice in Forest Hills, Queens. Though he had taken a bribe from gamblers just once, he never got over the remorse he felt for having gone along with the crowd in doing something that he knew was wrong; when he spoke of the scandal he always referred to it as a *shande*—the Yiddish word for shame.

Ed Warner was the only one of the City players who went to prison, and the only one who never got a college degree. He did four months and four days at Rikers Island, and when he got out, the word was that the Boston Celtics had their eye on him. In the beginning Ed was optimistic about being allowed into the NBA, telling a reporter that he thought he had "a fighting chance they'll say okay." He got a job on the assembly line at a Chevrolet plant in Tarrytown, driving up each morning from Harlem, waiting to see what would happen; over time, though, it became apparent that a call from an NBA team was not forthcoming, and eventually he quit the Chevy plant and began running numbers full time—going, in a sense, into his father's business.

Ed worked for a ring that operated out of a candy store on 142nd Street. He was tall and muscular and widely known, and over time, when the heroin trade came to Harlem, he began to serve as an enforcer, going out on the deals to make sure no problems arose. He never carried a gun but he always had a knife, a long flip blade that he kept in his back pocket, and he brought to his work the tough, unsmiling intensity that had served him well on the basketball court; away from business, though, he became a fun-loving guy with a playful demeanor. He liked to turn the music up loud on the radio when he drove around town, and when he stopped for a red light he would sometimes hop out and dance right there in the street, breaking up the guys who always seemed to be riding in the back. "He was the prince of Harlem," recalls Sonny Hill, who played with Ed in the Eastern League. "The crowds up there would part when he walked by—that's the kind of respect people had for him."

Ed's legend in Harlem had been burnished by his performance in the Rucker League, a tournament held each year at a playground on 128th Street. In 1954 he decided to put together his own team, the Ed Warner Big Five, which advanced to the championship game, playing against a team sponsored by a luncheonette called Snookie's Sugar Bowl. That afternoon hundreds of spectators crammed into bleachers and hundreds more pressed themselves up against the chain-link fence that surrounded the park; cars were double-parked up and down Seventh Avenue, and for once the cops didn't hand out tickets, just closed off the street to traffic and settled in to watch the game with the rest of the crowd. The founder of the tournament, a Parks Department official named Holcombe Rucker, had scheduled the game to start at five o'clock, the time suggested by the owner of Snookie's; Ed had wanted it to start at five thirty, because five o'clock was when the day's winning number was announced and he had to be available afterward to distribute any payouts. So the game had already begun when Ed swooped up in his black Oldsmobile, jumping from the car and pulling open the trunk while yelling in feigned outrage, "Rucker sold out to Snookie! Rucker sold out to Snookie!" and the crowd laughed and pointed out Big Ed, as he was known, as he stripped off his button-down shirt to his under-shirt and rolled up his black pin-striped dress pants, then threw on a pair of high-top sneakers and tied a bandanna around his head to pro-tect his marcelled hairdo.

That was how Ed Warner played in the Rucker finals, with the ban-danna and rolled-up trousers, but he led his team to the championship, bringing out the moves that had once captivated the Garden; he seemed to be leaping higher than everyone else on the court, and with that ban-danna tied around his head, Carl Green, who was playing for Snookie's, thought he looked like a genie popping out of a bottle, and that day a new nickname for Ed was born: the Genie.

The coach of the Ed Warner Big Five, John Isaacs, recalled later, "We won the game, and we were thrilled. But you know, I thought about that game as the years went on, and I got to thinking that it was actu-ally kind of sad, because Ed Warner should have been making all those moves in the pros, and not just at the Rucker." Floyd was still plugging to get into the NBA, and Ed hoped he would someday make it, but by this time he was resolved to the fact that the NBA was never going to let in someone like him; he and Sherman White might well have been the two best college players of their time, but they had been sent to prison, and instead of playing for the Celtics and the Knicks their basketball horizons now extended no farther than Hazleton and Williamsport, the team for which Ed was playing in 1960 when he totaled his car on a snowy Pennsylvania highway in the dead of night.

Ed didn't talk much about the injuries he suffered in the crash, but he never seemed quite the same afterward, and although he had been an All-Star in 1959, by 1962 he was out of the league. It was around that time that he begun experimenting with cocaine, a drug that, un-like marijuana or heroin, he considered appropriately glamorous. "He said, 'Kings and queens do this stuff, man,'" says Carl Green. "I said, 'I don't care if God does it.'" He was also, for the first time, selling drugs, and one night in 1963, while having a drink in a Harlem bar called Dot's, he was seized by a group of plainclothes policemen and charged with selling $150 worth of heroin to an undercover narcotics agent. Two months later he pleaded guilty and was sentenced to two and a half to four years in Green Haven Prison, maximum security.

Floyd Layne and Eddie Roman would often drive up to visit Ed in Green Haven, eighty miles north on the turnpike and then onto a two-lane country road, feeling each time that clutch in the stomach as farmland gave way to a clearing where suddenly, like a cathedral in a medieval landscape, the prison rose dark against the sky: thirty-foot-high walls punctuated by guard towers, looking like the Big House in the gangster movies they used to watch on Saturday afternoons as kids. It was strange and sad to see Ed in his green prison uniform, hair razored short, but they always talked with him for as long as the guards would allow, joking and telling stories and doing what they could to keep up his spirits. When Ed was paroled and working as a referee for some of the Harlem tournaments, Floyd and Eddie made sure to attend the games. Afterward Eddie would teasingly berate him, using the players' slang for someone who doesn't run much: "You've got to move more! You're standing on a dime."

It was funny because Eddie himself had always been the least mobile man on the court, even when he was in playing shape. Now, in retirement, he had put on a lot of weight, and his only basketball came in after-dinner shootarounds with his son on the hoop he had installed in the backyard. Floyd, on the other hand, was as slim and limber as ever. He still believed he could compete with anyone, had never lost the eagerness to test himself against the best that the sport had to offer, keeping alive the hope that the NBA might even now relent, might give him, as he had once wished for, five minutes on the court.

All through the 1960s, Floyd Layne continued to work with children in the community centers of the Bronx, watching with anger and dismay as blight crept into his beloved neighborhoods. One of the centers was only a few blocks from the apartment building on Prospect Avenue in which he had grown up. At the time, the East Bronx had been a model of integration, with racially mixed housing projects, parents' associations, and community centers; two decades later, it was unusual to see white faces on the street or the subway, anywhere other than in cars, the doors locked and windows rolled up, looking for the on-ramp to the expressway. Federally funded highways had drawn white families from the Bronx to the suburbs as blacks and Puerto Ricans arrived in larger numbers; they came looking for work, but the union jobs that had lifted earlier generations into the middle class were fast disappearing. The garment industry in which Floyd and Bobby Sand had found refuge after the scandal was already mostly gone; innumerable manufacturing plants had likewise decamped for the suburbs, or abandoned the region entirely, and eventually the Bronx seemed to have but one thriving industry: drugs. The streets were riddled with potholes, concrete reduced to rubble, as though a series of earthquakes had recently moved through. Many of the buildings that still remained had been picked over by junkies for their pipes and copper wire, like ghouls rifling through a corpse's pockets; once the buildings had been rendered uninhabitable, landlords could hire arsonists to torch them for the insurance money. The children who were left behind played in abandoned buildings or lots choked with weeds and garbage; free entertainment came from pulling the alarm in a fire box and watching the commotion that resulted, the noisy, rollicking arrival of the fire trucks like circus wagons. Nights were mostly silent but for the wail of police sirens, the streets mostly dark but for the warming glow from the recreation centers, among the few establishments still willing to stay open late, where kids might get some exercise, make friends, do homework, find an adult who would listen to their problems.

During the week, Floyd was in the centers afternoons and evenings. He kept up a constant banter as he circulated among the kids; sometimes he took one or two aside to ask about their families or their grades, making sure they understood that he was keeping track of them. He thought of his work as a kind of lifesaving operation, but over the years he had lost plenty of kids to drugs and violence. He still wore the gold championship ring he had received as a member of the City College Beavers; it sometimes provided an opportunity to talk about college to a kid who might never have considered going. One teenager who had expressed a desire to quit high school recalled Floyd telling him, "You know what's out there on every street corner—drunks and drug addicts sprawled in the gutters. And you know how a lot of them got there? They said they would quit high school and get a job. They got the job, worked their backs off for a little money for a few years. Then they got tired and gave up. Now they got nothing but a bad habit and one foot in the grave."

That teenager was an aspiring basketball player named Nate Archibald, known to everyone as Tiny. In high school his father had walked out on the family, and in the aftermath Tiny's grades suffered so dramatically that for a while he became ineligible to play basketball. "That was the roughest year of my life," Archibald would say later. "I don't know where I would have ended up with no father to help me, to tell me what to do. I was lucky to get a father—a Floyd Layne." Floyd counseled him all through high school and college—doing what he could to make sure Tiny would have the opportunity that he never had: to play in the NBA.*

For those who showed the desire to go on with their education, Floyd would seek out college administrators and registrars, athletic directors and coaches, anyone who might make a difference; he found scholarships to pay for tuition, sources of funding for books and transportation. He once estimated that he had helped four hundred kids get into college, although the number might well have been higher. One of his colleagues, ironically enough, was Junius Kellogg, the Manhattan College player who had blown the whistle on point shaving, and who in later years organized youth programs with the city's Community Development Agency. "Floyd has salvaged at least a thousand kids that I know of," Kellogg once said. "No overstatement can be made of his work."

It often occurred to Floyd that while he had been entrusted with thousands of the city's kids, NBA commissioner Maurice Podoloff would not allow him to play a game with a small group of adults. Over the years he had seen powerful men commit worse crimes than he had ever been charged with, and then, having performed the appropriate penance, or none at all, return to public life. America, it seemed, demanded a higher moral standard of its ballplayers than it did of its policemen or politicians.

* Nate "Tiny" Archibald would play in the National Basketball Association for fifteen seasons. He was a six-time All-Star, and in 1991 he was inducted into the Naismith Memorial Basketball Hall of Fame.

He was now approaching his forties. By this time half his life had been lived in shadow; there was great pain in that, but finally, he had come to recognize, there was pleasure too. Sometimes he was able to see himself as fortunate, could acknowledge, as he was to say years later, that "I would be unreachable and untouchable in the NBA. Instead, I got to touch the lives of an unimaginable number of kids." For him the scandal had been a tragedy, but through him, for so many of the city's children, it had been a kind of blessing.

Frustrated as an athlete, Floyd increasingly directed his competitiveness, his love of teamwork, and his knowledge of the game into coaching. On summer weekends he participated in Harlem's Rucker Tournament, where over the years he coached dozens of future NBA players, many of whom he would bring to the Bronx to scrimmage with the kids. Like Eddie Roman, Floyd had enrolled at Columbia University and earned a master's degree in education. In 1965 he took a one-year hiatus to serve as a physical education instructor and basketball coach at the College of the Virgin Islands. Returning to the Bronx, he resumed his work with young people while applying wherever he could for coaching jobs; almost always he received only a form letter in reply. Once, when the position of basketball coach became available, he inquired at his alma mater, Benjamin Franklin High School, but was informed that officials at the New York City Board of Education would not agree to hire him.

Finally, in 1970, he got a break: The basketball coach at Queensborough Community College was going on leave, and the chairman of the physical education department, a former CCNY classmate named Al Kahn, offered Floyd the position. "I know about his background," Kahn told a reporter who asked about the scandal, "and I am sure many of those involved in bringing him here also knew the story. But that's a dead issue. You don't have to open everyone's closet to find what type of person they are." After two years, however, the previous basketball coach returned to Queensborough and Floyd was once more out of a job.

Word of his success with young basketball players had gotten around, and sometimes NBA general managers sent their drafted players to him to learn the nuances of the game. Yet still he could not find a place in the NBA itself; he applied for assistant coaching positions with the Seattle SuperSonics under Bill Russell and the Portland Trail Blazers under Lenny Wilkens, but nothing ever came of it.

Then one morning in August 1974, Floyd was sitting at his breakfast table reading the Sunday *New York Times*. He turned to the Help Wanted section, as he always did, and scanned the page with the heading "Teacher Openings." There, at the bottom of the page, was a small boxed notice that read BASKETBALL COACH, beneath it a single sentence: "C.C.N.Y. needs a Men's Varsity Basketball Coach."

The position had come open once before, in 1970. Floyd had expressed an interest in applying, and several of his former teammates, Eddie Roman and Irwin Dambrot among them, met with the chairman of the department of physical and health education to convince him of Floyd's merits. The chairman, though, told them that he was sorry, but the reality of the situation was that City College would have nothing to do with Floyd Layne; there were still old-timers in the department, he explained, whose votes would never be swayed.

Four years later, Floyd had no reason to be optimistic, but even so, he sent in his application to the address he knew so well. In all, City College received seventy-five applications for the position. The composition of the department was different now—several of the older members had retired, as had college president Buell G. Gallagher—and the basketball program had been languishing for several years; the search committee was looking for a dynamic candidate, a person with extensive experience, who understood the special mission of the City College of New York, who could encourage student involvement with the team and work with alumni to contribute to the program. The final decision was made just before the start of the fall semester.

Twenty-three years earlier, Floyd Layne had been escorted off the campus by two of District Attorney Frank Hogan's detectives; now he would return to City College as its varsity basketball coach.

The press conference to announce the hiring was held on September 5, 1974. Over the years City College had been steadily expanding; the cluster of five original Gothic buildings remained, like a historic city center surrounded by suburban sprawl, but the campus now included several hulking office towers, and Lewisohn Stadium, that grand classical amphitheater, was being demolished to make way for a modern academic complex. The students were more diverse than they used to be, their hair longer, their clothes more relaxed and colorful, but they still lounged in the sun before classes and smoked cigarettes by the flagpole, and just inside the main gate Raymond Haber was still hawking his pragels, his twenty-eighth year on the job. "Layne will be a good coach," he assured a customer in his familiar rasping voice. "He's had some hard knocks in his life but he will be very thorough."

City College had a new athletic center, too, inside a sleek thirteen-story science building; this press conference, though, was to be held in the old gymnasium in Wingate Hall, described by a reporter for *The Campus* as "the scene of many a victory in Floyd Layne's life." The gym had not been well kept up, its paint peeling, some of the concrete crumbling, but on the basketball court a large, buoyant crowd milled about, and the mood and the setting made the event seem less a press conference than a class reunion, a sort of homecoming.

Floyd Layne was the seventh varsity basketball coach in the history of City College, and the first African American. The third of those seven coaches had held the job for forty years, and while Floyd saw himself as a different kind of coach, less aggressive with his players, he also believed he had learned a toughness from Nat Holman that had served him well. He had always counseled young people to focus on the positives rather than the negatives, and this was an opportunity for him to do so; he felt it would best, for him and for the college, to reconcile with the past and move forward. So earlier in the week Floyd had called Nat and said to him, "Will you do me a favor? There's going to be a press conference. Come up and say a few words."

Nat Holman was now seventy-eight years old. His hair was white but it was thick and brushed neatly back, and his eyebrows were dark and he still seemed sturdy and vigorous; as always, he was impeccably dressed, with a neatly folded pocket square tucked into the breast pocket of his suit. Floyd wore brightly checked pants and a dark sports jacket with a loud patterned tie, the lapels very wide in the seventies style; at forty-five his face showed only the slightest traces of age and sorrow, his smile as broad and infectious as ever. He rested his hand lightly on the

older man's shoulder as they stood beaming for the cameras, so far removed now from that terrible night on the platform at Pennsylvania
Station when Nat Holman had turned away from his arrested players
and Floyd Layne had turned away too, feeling himself miraculously
spared but also knowing that miracles didn't last and that soon enough
he would be called to account for his mistakes.

*Floyd Layne and Nat Holman at the press conference that announced Layne's hiring as head
basketball coach of City College.* Associated Press/Ron Frehm

Floyd and Nat took their seats at a small table crowded with mi-
crophones and recording equipment, and the City College president,
Robert Marshak, welcomed everyone and officially announced the appointment of Floyd Layne as varsity basketball coach and physical education instructor. When it was his turn to speak, Holman said that he
was sure that Floyd would make a good coach. He mentioned his many
admirable qualities, how he had been a heady basketball player and a
superb ball handler and had "always accepted criticism gracefully." He
didn't expect Floyd to give 100 percent, he said; he expected him to give
110 percent.

The microphone was now passed in front of Floyd Layne. "Thank you very much," he began, speaking slowly and deliberately, as he often did, as if needing to make sure of each word before moving on to the next one. "It certainly is a pleasure to be here today, appointed the head basketball coach at City College."

The crowd stood attentively as photographers' cameras clicked, and Floyd talked about how education and coaching went hand in hand and how he hoped to do the same job at City College that he had been doing in the community with the youngsters. He vowed that in the coming year the Beavers would emphasize defense and teamwork. Basketball was a team game, he reminded them, and players who truly understood that could achieve great things; it was a lesson that had been demonstrated long ago by twelve kids from the streets of New York who together accomplished something that no other team ever had.*

The year after the scandal broke, at the age of twenty-two, he had written an article for *Sport* magazine with a young writer named Jimmy Breslin, entitled "Don't I Deserve Another Chance?" In that article Floyd had vowed, "I'm never going to rest until I'm back in the place where I made my mistake," and now, at last, he was.

"We were kids who made a mistake," he said, "and we paid a heavy price for that mistake over the next twenty years. For me, that incident in 1951 really put my feet on the ground. It cemented a lot of things, taught me about adversity, and led me to dedicate myself to kids, so that they wouldn't make the same kind of mistake, and pay the same terrible price in terms of their personal and professional lives." Saying that, he could not help but think of the price that had been exacted on his own life, the many disappointments, the rejections, the broken promises, the long exile that seemed now to have come to an end, right here, on the very court on which he used to play, and for a few moments he fell silent, gathering himself as he wiped away tears. "Words cannot describe my feelings at this time," he finally said. "The shortest distance between two points is a straight line, and I've traveled in a wide circle, but I got back home."

---

* Nor would any other: In 1953 the National Collegiate Athletic Association ruled that in the future a team could play in either the NIT or NCAA tournament in a single year, but not both.

EPILOGUE

Though he lived for another three decades, Harry Gross would be remembered only for a brief period in the early 1950s, when his exploits fascinated and appalled New York, appearing day after day on the front pages of the city's newspapers.

In September 1951, after refusing to testify against the eighteen indicted police officers, he was sentenced to seventeen years in prison—twelve years for his bookmaking activities and another five for the contempt he had shown in Judge Samuel Leibowitz's court. He served eight years; when he got out he moved to California, the state that had provided a haven for him once before, after he torpedoed his bookmaking syndicate by means of his own reckless betting. He emerged from prison a changed man, less shrewd than he had once been, less calculating, his legendary guile having been displaced by volatility and rage. Not long after his release he was charged with beating his wife's eighty-four-year-old grandfather to death in an argument; he did three more years in jail for manslaughter, and in his later life—no longer protected from arrest by generous expenditures of "ice"—he would be imprisoned twice more for bookmaking offenses. In 1986, at the age of sixty-nine, he was arrested for trying to purchase thirteen pounds of heroin. A month later he slashed his wrists in the modest home in which he lived alone in Long Beach; his suicide note explained that he would rather die than return to prison.

It was an especially sad and terrible end to a disreputable life, one defined by events that had taken place long before; the *New York Times* article about the suicide was headlined THE LONELY DEATH OF A MAN WHO MADE A SCANDAL.

"He was a smooth, suave individual with gentlemanly manners," recalled the former Brooklyn district attorney Miles McDonald. At the close of 1953, McDonald had been appointed a state supreme court justice—the job that his father had always wanted for him—an appointment earned in large part from the renown and goodwill he had earned from the Harry Gross case. When the trial of the eighteen police officers collapsed, District Attorney McDonald shared the information that his rookie squad had collected with Police Commissioner George Monaghan; under its new leadership the NYPD initiated departmental trials of officers suspected of taking bribes, and this time Gross, having been promised some clemency, actually did testify. On the basis of his testimony twenty-three policemen were removed from the police force, the largest mass dismissal in the history of the department.

During the departmental trials, Harry Gross would testify that his payoffs had gone to the very top—that he had personally given bribes to Police Commissioner William P. O'Brien and his two highest-ranking officers, Chief Inspector August Flath and Chief of Detectives William Whalen. Even so, no investigation of those allegations was ever pursued. When a reporter asked him why he thought this was, Gross merely shrugged. All he would say was, "Maybe some money changed hands."

In 1952, Bobby Sand moved with his family to Clearview Gardens in Queens, the same housing cooperative to which Eddie Roman moved five years later. Bobby would never get over the sadness he felt for Eddie and the other City players involved in the scandal, thinking of the pain they brought to their families, the sharply diminished futures they had faced at such a young age. That awful night when he called the players' parents to tell them the news was to stay with him forever; even decades later, near the end of his life, he would tell Robert Lipsyte of *The New York Times*, "I cried my heart out. I still do."

He, too, had suffered for his part in the scandal, had admitted his mistakes and paid a heavy price for them. In the years afterward he wrote several articles for *Scholastic Coach* magazine; he scouted for the

NBA's Rochester Royals and in the summers conducted basketball clinics around the country and overseas. Still, he yearned to return to the classroom; in 1958, after President Buell Gallagher denied his request to resume teaching, an op-ed in the student newspaper *The Campus* asked, "How much longer must he remain a second-class citizen in the academic community?"

In 1959 Bobby appealed the president's decision to the state's commissioner of education, who ruled against him, explaining that a work assignment could not be appealed "after serving in it for more than five years without complaint." He refused to give up, though: He filed a petition with the New York State Supreme Court, asserting that City College's ongoing deprivation of his teaching rights under tenure far exceeded any reasonable punishment. In February 1961 Justice Russell Hunt agreed, instructing the Board of Higher Education to review Sand's employment status. "Even a felon has the right to be apprised of his minimum and maximum penalties," Hunt noted, and Sand "ought to receive consideration not less than that accorded a felon."

By this time Bobby Sand had been in administrative exile for nearly a decade; he was forty-four years old, but in truth he felt far older. Between scouting and coaching he had been away from home almost every weekend, it seemed, for years, and the accident in Ed Warner's car had left him deeply shaken; for the rest of his life he could not sit in a car without reflexively bracing his hand against the roof. He didn't think he could bear to spend more time discussing appeals with attorneys, waiting for months on end for the phone to ring, living with the constant swings of anticipation and disappointment. By the summer of 1961, the Board of Higher Education had not yet responded to the justice's order, and Bobby announced that he would drop all litigation, saying that he was "tired of fighting." The following year, though, he decided to make one last appeal to the board, "in a spirit of no pressure and no litigation." Finally, in April 1962, the BHE relented, ordering City College to reinstate Bobby Sand as an instructor. "I feel wonderful," Bobby told a reporter from *The Campus* after the decision was announced. "The whole family feels wonderful and of course I'm looking forward to teaching again."

He was assigned to teach three courses in the hygiene department: two introductory physical education classes as well as a required course

called Personal Hygiene. Over time he would resume teaching economics as well. He also served as an adviser to the school's House Plan Association (the City College version of fraternities), developed counseling
programs for minority students, and provided career guidance for the
school's student athletes. The Personal Hygiene course he taught was
coed, and as the sixties progressed, Bobby began presenting information designed to help female students take greater control of their bodies, encouraging them to make their own decisions about their health
and to seek a fulfilling balance between family and work life. ("The husbands and boyfriends were not always thrilled with that," notes his
daughter Wendie.) In 1969, when more than two hundred black and
Puerto Rican students demanding increased minority enrollment shut
down the campus, occupying buildings for two weeks, he saw to it that
the college gym remained open all night long, offering students a safe
place to relax, exercise, blow off steam. In 1971 the college's alumni association presented him with its Faculty Service Award; only nine years
earlier he had been banned from the classroom.

That same year the former CCNY downtown business school, now
renamed Baruch College, announced the appointment of its new head
basketball coach: Bobby Sand.

All through the 1960s, Eddie Roman worked in New York City's notorious "600 schools" (so called because of the Board of Education code assigned to them), schools composed entirely of students who had been
suspended for aggressive or otherwise disruptive acts or intractable be-
havioral problems. Chaotic and chronically understaffed, the 600
schools were such difficult, demanding places to work that the teachers
received an annual bonus sardonically referred to as "combat pay." Eddie's assignment was to meet with students who had just arrived from
the regular system, and try as best he could to evaluate their problems
and identify the school program in which they should be placed. Thus
he was encountering the students when they first understood themselves to be lastingly stigmatized—when they tended to be either fearful
and silent or crackling with anger, defensive and mistrustful and unsure what their future held: the very moment when they were likely the
most resistant to adult intervention. "He was a very warm person," says

Marty Groveman, a former City College basketball player who also worked in the 600 schools, "but even more than that, he seemed to understand the issues that faced the black population of the inner city, recognized how tough it was for so many of these kids to overcome their environment—impoverishment, often single-parent families, alcoholism, drug addiction. He understood all of that very well."

Eventually Eddie returned to graduate school once more, this time at New York University, where he entered a part-time doctoral program in adolescent psychology. His older brother, Mel, was a psychologist and his younger brother, Richard, a college professor; he was the only one of the Roman sons not to have his Ph.D., and it was important to him to earn one as well. Still, he had always been a perfectionist, and he never seemed to have enough time to finish the dissertation. Perhaps it was the influence of his late father, Julius, the house painter, but Eddie had discovered to his surprise that he was good with his hands, and sometimes after work he would go to a school wood shop and build furniture for the house: a bed for one of the kids, a set of bookshelves, a partition for the living room to turn a two-bedroom apartment into a three-bedroom. His mother still lived on Teller Avenue, now all alone on the bottom floor of their old house; the neighborhood was increasingly dangerous, and Eddie often tried to persuade her to move, but she was adamant, so he often drove up to the Bronx to visit her. In the 1970s he began working as a school psychologist with emotionally disturbed children at a special program in Queens. Shocked to discover that some of the kids were arriving hungry in the mornings, he bought a set of brightly colored plastic bowls for his office; afterward he would regularly bring in boxes of cereal and cartons of milk so that the students might have something to eat before classes began. He was the union representative for his United Federation of Teachers local, and his daughter Tammy remembers that he was often "up to two o'clock in the morning talking to someone who had a problem. He was always helping somebody."

He rarely mentioned the scandal to his children, and when he did it was only in the most general terms. He had been young and foolish, he would tell them; he didn't get much money and had only wanted to help his mother out. Still, the impact of the scandal came across in all sorts of ways. Even decades later he couldn't bear to be thought of as at all unethical; his son Mark says, "He was the most honest person I ever met. He would never take anything for free, never accept extra change from a cashier, always made sure to return money if somebody dropped it."

Now in Queens, as before in the Bronx, the house in which he lived was far too small. The two girls shared what would have been the master bedroom, he and Donna taking the bedroom that had been carved out of the living room. There was constant anger and tension between the two of them, marital arguments made even more stressful by the lack of privacy; finally they separated, after nearly twenty years of marriage, and Eddie moved to an apartment nearby.

Afternoons during basketball season, if he had some free time, Eddie liked to go by the City College gym when Floyd held practices there; sometimes he even shot around a bit with the team. His weight was now up to about 270 pounds and he had suffered a bout of phlebitis in his leg, but he still had a piercingly accurate outside shot, one that now could only metaphorically be referred to as a "jumper." (Floyd, nearing fifty, remained as fit as ever.) In middle age Eddie seemed at last to have settled into himself. His hair was longer now, and he had grown a beard that was streaked with gray; he bore almost no resemblance to the

eager, awkward eighteen-year-old who had once been one of those kids on the court, his hips too wide, shoulders too narrow, a knotted handkerchief dangling from a belt loop. He had made sure to attend Floyd's first game as head coach of the Beavers, telling a reporter from *The New York Times* that the hiring was "a validation of Floyd's life" and that "as long as Floyd is here, I'll be here." It was, he said, the first City College basketball game he

Eddie Roman in his late forties. Tammy Cantatore   had seen since 1951.

Over the years, he and Floyd and Ed Warner had remained as close as ever. Floyd had found Ed a job in a community center in the Bronx, and Eddie often drove up there to talk with the kids. "He was warm, he was understanding," Ed was to say later. "The kids would listen to him. They knew he made an error as a youngster, but they saw how he picked up his life."* Warner supplemented his income by refereeing college and semipro basketball games in Manhattan and the Bronx. One night in April 1984, on his way home from a doubleheader, he was stopped at a red light on the Harlem River Drive when another car smashed into him from behind. For the second time in his life he almost died in his car. Unconscious, he was rushed by ambulance to the intensive care unit of a nearby hospital; later he was transferred to the Rusk Institute of Rehabilitation Medicine, where he remained for six months. For the longest time Ed could move only his head. Floyd and Eddie often came to visit, as they had when he was in Green Haven Prison; they sat for hours at his bedside, took turns feeding him. Ultimately, through grueling physical therapy, Ed would regain the use of his arms, but he remained paralyzed below the waist. It was the cruelest irony of all: Perhaps the most gifted athlete in City College history would spend the rest of his life in a wheelchair.

In 1985, Eddie completed his dissertation, "Racial Differences and Attributions: Black and White Male Students' Judgments of Causation, Future Success, and Affect for the Success and Failure of Black and White Peers on Stereotype-Linked Tasks." He had designed and undertaken a set of experiments with 720 male students from parochial schools in New York City, half of them black and half of them white, to examine their perceptions of success and failure regarding "academic" and "athletic" tasks. In his introduction to the dissertation, Eddie noted that "professional athletes make powerful role models and inadvertently nurture the false hopes which misdirect many black youngsters

---

* Ed Warner picked up his life as well, getting off drugs and working with young people at a Harlem social service agency, and later becoming a drug counselor. In his forties he began a relationship with a coworker named Natalie Higgens; he was fifty years old when his youngest son, Dana, was born, and he was present as a father for Dana in a way that he had not been with his previous six kids. Many years later Dana would tattoo his right arm with his father's initials and date of birth, but not the date of his death, because, he would explain, "He still lives through me."

into placing greater expenditures of time and effort into sports than into academic achievement." Instead, he argued, "coordinated attempts should be made to emphasize education as the most realistic option for preparing black youth for the future."

In 1967, when he earned his master's degree, Eddie had joked in a letter to Richie that "I might get my PhD by the time I'm 50 years old." In fact he was fifty-five. Soon he could retire from the school system, and when he did he was going to set up his own practice as a psychologist. He thought one day he might try to get some money together and move to the Catskills, maybe near Bushville Paradise, the bungalow colony in which his family had spent many summers when he was a boy. After being single for several years he had begun seeing a woman named Joyce and they were happy together; in all ways his life seemed at last to be opening up. At a ceremony in 1986 the City College Alumni Association inducted him into the CCNY Athletic Hall of Fame; Floyd had previously been given that honor, as had Irwin. By this time college basketball had suffered two more bookmaking scandals, in 1961 and 1979. Little by little, it seemed, the blot of their own scandal was fading away. He was thinking about traveling again; after his separation from Donna he had traveled by himself through Europe, staying in youth hostels the whole time, and he was looking forward to going back. "You had the feeling that he was finally going to have some enjoyment in his life," says his brother Richard, "and then he fucking got leukemia."

Just after Thanksgiving in 1986 he was painting the interior of his daughter JoAnn's house and she was shocked to see that he was as white as a ghost, barely able to stand. He had been experiencing pain in his bones for a while but had not wanted to admit anything. Finally he went to a doctor and after a series of tests received the grim diagnosis: He had, at best, a 30 percent chance to survive.

When Eddie told him the news, Floyd reminded him that he was a fighter, and that they had faced odds worse than 30 percent once before and beaten them. He was admitted to a hospital on Long Island, where he went once a month for treatments, staying for a week at a time. He told his daughter Tammy, "I thought I had problems before. Now I have a real problem and those other problems don't matter, and they wouldn't have mattered then if I had known about this."

Over time the chemotherapy took a lot out of him; he was tired and nauseated and appeared somehow shrunken, his enormous bulk no longer seeming to overflow the narrow hospital bed. Floyd and Ed frequently came to the hospital; once when they were visiting he told them, "I'm not taking any more treatments. It's too hard. I can't do it anymore." And Ed leaned forward in his wheelchair and said, "You fucking listen to me. You've got to fight. You wouldn't quit on me. We're not quitting on you."

He continued with the treatments, and eventually he went into remission. He felt more and more like himself, his energy and good spirits starting to return. His first grandchild, Joseph, was born that year, and he was besotted with happiness and pride; he bragged to all of his friends about his grandson's large hands—the hands, he would say, of a basketball player. Tammy lived nearby, and he would come by her house every afternoon at three o'clock to see the baby. "He was so happy," she recalls. "It was like his life was starting up again."

Before long, though, the cancer returned, and Eddie was transferred to a hospital in Westchester County; he was staying in a special facility that the patients called the Last Chance Ward, but in fact he was optimistic about his prognosis. When he was in remission the doctors had removed some of his bone marrow, and now they were going to re-inject it into him. First, though, he required more chemotherapy treatments, and after one of them he was alone in his room and he went into cardiac arrest and died before anyone could get to him. He was fifty-seven years old.

A memorial service was held two days after Eddie's death, on March 3, 1988, at Sinai Chapels in Queens. "I'm getting us all together for this," Floyd told a reporter who called from the *New York Post*. "That's always been my job, in good times and bad."

The chapel was a large room, but it barely held the 250 friends and relatives who had come to mourn together that evening. The eleven rows of polished wooden pews were filled, and many people stood in the back and along the walls. Eddie's coach from Taft High School, Bernie Schiffer, sat with the members of the team; again and again he shook his head and said in disbelief, "I thought he'd be coming to *my* funeral." Ed Warner sat in a wheelchair at the back of the room; he had driven in that morning with Floyd Layne and Sherman White. Dave Anderson of *The New York Times* called the memorial service "a spontaneous reunion of so many basketball players of their era"; one of those present that day would recall it as "the tallest funeral I've ever been to."

The eulogy was delivered by Arthur Kotel, a childhood friend from the Bronx who had become a rabbi. Afterward a long line of mourners rose to pay tribute and deliver their goodbyes. Several school colleagues spoke of Eddie's unstinting care for angry and troubled children, children who had "more problems than they had solutions for." He was, one said, "the righteous of the righteous," who "gave us his sense of excellence: Always do the best you can."

Finally Floyd Layne stepped to the lectern; for a long while he stood struggling to gather himself. "He was my friend for life," he said at last, his voice breaking. "He and I and Ed Warner were brothers together. Some people thought we had adversity in our lives. Not so. We were blessed." Floyd spoke of the beautiful days when they would play basketball together and afterward his mother would feed them, when she would put her arms around his friends and say, "These are my two Eddies. These are my other sons." He asked those in the audience to look around and notice how many people there had played with Eddie, to see the loyalty he inspired, because they all knew what kind of teammate he was, intelligent, dedicated, generous, a player who understood that he didn't have to shoot to make a basket. "If you needed a score you went through Eddie for either a shot or a pass," he said. "You knew you'd be okay as long as somewhere along the line Eddie touched the ball."

They had been joined first by a shared love of the game; later, too, they would be joined by another bond, of hardship and suffering. "In 1950," Floyd said, "God told us, 'You're a champion.' But the next year He told us, 'Now let Me see what kind of champion you really are. Let Me knock you to your knees and see if you can get up and be a champion again.'" Over the years he and Eddie, each in his own way, had worked to redeem their lives, dedicating themselves to education, for themselves and for others, doing whatever they could to help young people in the poorest and most despairing corners of the city. "We were not blind," Floyd said pointedly, "but we never saw color. We saw only teammates and friends."

That had been true from the earliest days, when Eddie would walk to his house on weekend afternoons, crossing the streetcar tracks on Webster Avenue that divided Floyd's neighborhood from his. They had first played together on a youth club called the Bronx Wildcats, its emblem a cross inside a Star of David. Later, of course, they would be part of another team, one composed entirely of black and Jewish players, kids who had learned the game on cracked asphalt courts with rusted metal backboards and hoops long since stripped of nets: always moving, always looking for the open man, helping each other out, working together at all times. It was an example that Floyd had tried to follow on and off the court, and in later years he would have his business cards inscribed with the motto "Basketball is a microcosm of life."

Over time he and his City College teammates would come to be remembered more for their achievements than for their failings. He would serve as City College varsity basketball coach for fourteen years, the longest continuous term of anyone in the college's history other than Nat Holman. The NIT and NCAA trophies were permanently displayed in a glass case in the college athletic center; Floyd passed them every day on his way to the office, beside the rows of City College Athletic Hall of Fame plaques that included his own name as well as Eddie's and Irwin's. Later Al Roth, Norm Mager, Joe Galiber, and finally, in 1994, Ed Warner would join them there; that same year the team as a whole would be inducted into the New York City Basketball Hall of Fame, the first college team ever to be so chosen. In 2009, a panel of sportswriters and coaches would name the 1950 City College double-championship victory the greatest college basketball moment in the history of Madison Square Garden.

What a shame it was that Eddie was not alive to see any of that. Still, all of those decades later, an old man now, when Floyd thought about Eddie he found that what he remembered most warmly was not any specific moment of triumph and exultation; instead, he reveled in the constancy of their friendship, its dependability in good times and bad ("If Eddie Roman was your pal," he liked to say, "you had quite a pal"), the very ordinariness of it, phone calls made from one kitchen to another, or long car rides through the Pennsylvania hills, or, further back, fall evenings when the two of them left City College basketball practice together, heading to the uptown subway. Carrying their schoolbooks in their gym bags, they would bound out of Wingate Hall—whimsical little terra-cotta acrobats beaming down at them as they passed—and then walk along the edge of the campus toward St. Nicholas Terrace, the high bluff overlooking the Hudson River where once, long before, George Post had stood and envisioned a college, and where now the city seemed to spread itself out below them, silver and still as a photograph and blurring fast in the fading light.

ACKNOWLEDGMENTS

A book such as this one is truly the product of a community, and in writing *The City Game* I have relied on the intelligence, enthusiasm, and generosity of a great many people. First thanks, of course, must go to the surviving members of the 1949–50 City College Beavers double-championship team, all of whom graciously consented to speak with me for this book: Herb Cohen, Arthur Glass, Floyd Layne, Ron Nadell, and Mike Wittlin. They recalled their team, and their teammates, with great pride and affection, sharing memories that were often pleasurable but sometimes, even at such a remove, painful to bring to mind. Well into their eighties, these men continue to exemplify the enduring virtues of teamwork and cooperation; in so many ways, this book could never have been written without them.

Thanks, as well, to those many players on other City College basketball squads, both before and after the double-championship season, who through their conversations gave an outsider a glimpse behind the heavy wooden doors of the Main Gym: Harold Bauman, Irwin Buchalter, Ed Chenetz, Ira Citron, Bernie Cohen, Jerry Domershick, Marty Groveman, Marty Gurkin, Bernard Laterman, Maurice Silverstein, Arnie Smith, and Sid Trubowitz.

Eddie Roman's younger brother, Dick Roman, and Dick's wife, JoAnne Maikawa, warmly welcomed a stranger into their home, and for days Dick answered all of my questions with his characteristic perceptiveness, compassion, and honesty. Later, he introduced me to other

Roman family members, accompanied me on a field trip to his family's former home on Teller Avenue in the Bronx, and read the manuscript in draft form. For me, one of the greatest of this project's many pleasures is the opportunity it afforded to become friends with Dick and JoAnne. Nat Holman's nephew Bruce Holman likewise welcomed me into his home and spent hours telling me stories of his uncle, sharing family mementos with me, and answering my many follow-up questions; he is a warm and gracious man and I thank him deeply for his enthusiastic assistance. Bobby Sand's daughter Wendie Sand spoke to me on numerous occasions; I am indebted to her not only for her generosity, but also for her remarkable powers of recall. To these other relatives of the players and coaches, who kindly spoke with me for this book, I additionally offer grateful thanks: Tammy Cantatore, Marilyn Cassotta, Katrin Dambrot, Eva Hall, Alexander Holman, Scott Mager, Mark Roman, Cary Roth, Gloria Roth, Pam Roth, Adam Sand, Dana Warner, Ed Warner, Jr., LeRoy Watkins, Jr., and Ruby Wint.

Many longtime friends and colleagues of the players, coaches, and other central figures of the story spoke with me for this book, and I thank them for their recollections, which were fond, often amusing, and unfailingly illuminating: Alvin Apfelberg, Herb Bard, Aaron Carton, Julian Cohen, Mike Fleischer, Dorian Fliegel, Carl Green, Marty Groveman, Sheldon Kastner, Elliott Loeb, Nancy Helfand Loeb, Fortune Macri, Bob McCullough, Leroy Moorehead, Ernesto Morris, Leo Warren Morrison, Joe Potozkin, Murray Richman, Joanne Roddy, Sonny Rollins, Al Rothman, Ron Schechter, Morty Schwartz, Arnold Stein, Howard Stein, and Richard Tobias. Thanks, as well, to those players who competed with and against the members of the City College team, in college, in the Catskills, or in the Eastern League: Stacey Arceneaux, Art Goldberg, Sonny Hill, Jack Laub, Hal Lear, Barry Love, Frank Mulzoff, Cal Ramsay, Satch Sanders, Dolph Schayes, and Dick Schnittker.

A host of others gave generously of their time, sharing with me their stories of City College, New York City, and the Catskills in the middle decades of the twentieth century: Marvin Abraham, Gus Alfieri, Ed Argow, Marty Bernstein, Avery Corman, Irwin Danz, Leonard Dauer, Lucia Edmonds, Greta Facey, Philip Gittleman, Larry Gralla, Ruth Relkin Green, Gerry Grob, Robert Gurland, Mel Herman, Jerry Houston, Jerry Jacobson, George Jordan, Renee Kahn, Dick Kaplan, Norma Keller,

Justin Kodner, Richard Kor, Jerry Koral, Eugene Kramer, Leonard Kreuter, Mark Maged, Jonathan Malamed, Al Mantis, Alan Miller, Myron Neugeboren, Rayner Pike, Anita Friedman Plaxe, Herb Pollack, Patti Posner, Alan Rubin, Ed Rudetsky, Martin Schaum, Philip Scheffler, Emil Scheller, Gloria Schulman, Sherwood Schwartz, Stuart Schwartz, Ina Segal-Gonick, Mort Sheinman, Dorothy Steinmetz, Eleanor Talisman, Pamela Talisman, Raphael Thelwell, Esther Tuchman, Morris Tuchman, Gerald Walpin, Selma Wassermann, Michael Weinberg, Marty Weintraub, Morton Weiser, and Gloria Mandels White.

At my hesitant request Charley Rosen, author of *Scandals of '51*, shared the research materials—newspaper clippings, photographs, interview transcripts—that he had compiled for the earlier book. He did so cheerfully and without reluctance, explaining to me that other writers in the past had similarly helped him; I have every intention of carrying on his honorable example. George Roy, codirector of the HBO documentary *City Dump: The Story of the 1951 CCNY Basketball Scandal*, also generously shared his research materials with me. Anthony Fletcher provided invaluable legal and other assistance. Three estimable New York–based sportswriters recalled the era with warmth, humor, and insight: Dave Anderson, Jerry Izenberg, and George Vecsey. Additionally I offer posthumous tribute to another illustrious sportswriter, Pete Axthelm, who wrote a celebrated book about New York City basketball that was also entitled *The City Game*.

I conducted research for this book in many libraries and archives, but primarily at the City College of New York, the New York Public Library, the Brooklyn Historical Society, the Columbia University Rare Book and Manuscript Library, the Main Library of St. John's University, the New York County District Attorney's Office, and the New York County Lawyers Association. I owe a special debt to Professor Sydney C. Van Nort, the deeply knowledgeable and dauntingly capable archivist of the City College Archives and Special Collections Library, and Professor William Gibbons, chief of reference of City College's Cohen Library (who has himself written about Nat Holman), each of whom spent many hours patiently answering my questions and directing me to relevant transcripts, photos, newspapers, yearbooks, letters, and other items of interest in the college's collections.

During the years of work on this book numerous friends offered literary advice, editorial suggestions, collegial support, and congenial conversation over Manhattans or plates of Chinese food. I'm privileged to know them, and I hope someday to be able to return their many favors: Karen Abbott, Lenny Benardo, Josh Broder, Dan Conaway, Marty Dobrow, Raymond Granger, Kevin Hogan, Karen Leiner, Deborah Schupack, Adam Sexton, David Vyorst (of blessed memory), and Jennifer Weiss.

At Ballantine Books, it has been my great good fortune to work with Susanna Porter as an editor for a second time. Over a course of years Susanna helped to shape the manuscript with characteristic insightfulness, acumen, thoughtfulness, and sensitivity; this book would be a far poorer one without her editorial ministrations. Also at Ballantine, Emily Hartley handled myriad details of scheduling and production with admirable skillfulness and unflagging good cheer. I offer heartfelt thanks, as well, to publisher Kara Welsh, deputy publisher Kim Hovey, and editor in chief Jennifer Hershey for their continuing support, and to the talented team that turned a manuscript into a book: art director Paolo Pepe, cover designer Greg Mollica, and interior designer Susan Turner; Penguin Random House general counsel Linda Friedner; publicist Greg Kubie; and production editor Loren Noveck and copy editor Emily DeHuff, who scrutinized the manuscript with remarkable care and precision.

As ever, I am so very thankful to my wise and wonderful literary agent, Henry Dunow. I shared with Henry the notion of a book about the City College basketball team before I had committed a single word to paper; his excitement about the idea spurred me to write *The City Game*, and his dedication to it since then has been nothing short of inspiring.

I am deeply grateful to my parents, Burton and Joellyn Goodman, and my in-laws, Steve and Nancy Schwerner, for their enthusiastic support. Finally, I offer this book, as always, with love to my children, Ezra and Vivian (who by now have heard about as much as they need to about mid-century college basketball), and to my wife, Cassie Schwerner: wisest counsel, truest guide, and the reader for whom I write all my books.

SOURCES

None of the scenes in this book have been imagined, and no dialogue invented. Every quotation is taken from either a published source or an interview and has been cited in the book's endnotes, which can be found at matthewgoodmanbooks.com. In doing the research for this book I conducted interviews with more than 130 people, including players, coaches, writers, and fans; the full interview list can likewise be found at the above Web address.

In multiple interviews and phone conversations Floyd Layne talked to me about his upbringing, his education, his life on the court as player and coach, and his participation in point shaving. As a young man, Floyd produced his own anguished account of the City College scandal for *Sport* magazine entitled "Don't I Deserve Another Chance?" in which he described his motivations for shaving points, the overwhelming numbness and guilt he felt afterward, and his determination not to rest "until I'm back in the place where I made my mistake." Floyd's long and fruitless struggle to enter the National Basketball Association was chronicled in a number of newspaper articles, most notably a two-part column by Sid Friedlander of the *New York Post* in January 1957, the second half of which was an "open letter" to NBA commissioner Maurice Podoloff asking for Floyd to be allowed into the league. Frank Gifford's book *Gifford on Courage* (1976) includes a chapter on Layne that poignantly describes his work with young people and his return to City College as its head basketball coach. Floyd's return to CCNY was also the subject of an episode of the short-lived syndicated television series *Comeback;* the show includes scenes of a bearded Eddie Roman speaking fondly of his old teammate and friend.

I interviewed, as well, all of the other surviving members of the City College double-championship squad: Herb Cohen, Ron Nadell, Arthur Glass, and Mike Wittlin. For those players who are no longer alive—notably Eddie Roman, Ed Warner, Al Roth, Irwin Dambrot, Joe Galiber, Norm Mager, and Leroy Watkins—I conducted interviews with family members and close friends. Especially illuminating were the many conversations I had with Eddie Roman's younger brother, Richard Roman; with his children Mark Roman and Tammy Cantatore, who provided valuable information about Eddie's later years; and with his cousin Marilyn Cassotta, who also happened to be a City College student at the time of the scandal. Both Richard Roman and Marilyn Cassotta were in the Roman home on the day after the arrests. Reminiscences of Eddie Roman's childhood in the Bronx came from family members as well as his lifelong friends Howard Stein, Al Rothman, Bernie Cohen, Arnold Stein, and Ron Schechter. Dick Kaplan, who was a sportswriter for the City College student newspaper the *Observation Post,* recalled for me the story of his encounter with Eddie Roman in the college cafeteria.

Ed Warner's family background and his life in the years after the scandal were recounted by his longtime partner, Eva Hall; additional memories were provided by Ed's friends and classmates Leroy Moorehead, Ernesto Morris, and Leo Warren Morrison, as well as his sons Ed Warner, Jr., and Dana Warner. His Harlem neighborhood was described in an article in the newspaper *The Afro-American,* "Ed Warner, Ex-Altar Boy at St. Phillips Church," published shortly after his arrest. Information about Warner's exploits in Harlem's Rucker League championship game came from the book *Pickup Artists: Street Basketball in America* (1998), by Lars Anderson and Chad Millman, as well as interviews with his friends Bob McCullough and Carl Green. Green also provided a firsthand account of the car accident that occurred during their stint in the Eastern League, which was supplemented by news accounts in local Pennsylvania newspapers and conversations with Bobby Sand's daughter Wendie.

City College's response to the basketball scandal is lavishly related in the transcripts of the disciplinary hearing held by the Board of Higher

Education of the City of New York. *In the Matter of Charges Preferred Against Nat Holman and Harry Robert Sand* (held in the City College Archives) comprises more than 3,600 pages, and includes testimony from both Holman and Sand, as well as from faculty manager of athletics Sam Winograd and players including Floyd Layne, Ed Warner, and Norm Mager. Among other subjects, Layne and Warner spoke of their gratitude to Bobby Sand for his efforts to obtain employment for them in the wake of the scandal. For his part, Mager spoke of how Sand helped him with his studies and expressed concern about his mental state during the championship season, going so far as to suggest that Mager leave the team for a while; in his testimony Mager also mentioned Holman's regular admonitions that the Beavers were supposed to be playing "major league basketball."

Nat Holman recounted his early life on the Lower East Side in a long interview he gave to the American Jewish Committee in 1978 as part of its oral history collection; he also covered that material in a chapter of the 1974 anthology *From Eminently Disadvantaged to Eminence*, edited by Harold Geist. Both of those sources, along with much other biographical information, can be found in the Nat Holman Papers, which are held in the archives of the Morris Raphael Cohen Library at the City College of New York. The papers as a whole comprise a treasure trove of Holmaniana, including photographs, magazine advertisements, congratulatory letters written to him after the double championship, even articles that Nat clipped from newspapers to use as material for the after-dinner speeches he was often asked to give. "He ran his own clipping service," noted his nephew Alexander Holman, who in an interview provided a good deal of Holman background, including specifics about Nat's wardrobe (which went to Alexander after his death) as well as the detail about how he discovered ahead of time the answer to one of the questions for the radio quiz show on which Nat was about to appear.

Much more Holman family information came from numerous conversations with Nat's nephew Bruce Holman. The descriptions of Nat's coaching style were drawn from interviews with his players at City College—members of the championship team and those of previous and subsequent squads—as well as newspaper and magazine articles, among them the 1950 *Newsweek* profile "Drive, Drive, Drive!" and an article in *Collier's* magazine, "Basketball's Nat Holman: Easy Doesn't Do

It," written by Stanley Frank, who in addition to being a talented reporter was a City College graduate. Writing for *The Saturday Evening
Post*, Frank also produced indelible portraits of Madison Square Garden
basketball impresario Ned Irish ("Basketball's Big Wheel") and City College campus life ("College Without Frills or Fun").

Nat Holman's byline appears on three books, *Winning Basketball*
(1932), *Championship Basketball* (1942), and, most significantly, *Holman
on Basketball* (1950). In fact the primary author of *Holman on Basketball*
was the CCNY assistant basketball coach, Bobby Sand. (This was acknowledged even by Nat Holman. During the disciplinary hearings, for
instance, Sand's attorney asked Holman, "Did you give Bobby a bonus
for writing the book?" and he replied, "That was all part of the bonus.
Originally, it was $800, and I made it $1,000 because I was well pleased,
and the fact that we got it out on time and the job was out of the way.")
More than three hundred pages long, *Holman on Basketball* is the most
thorough and thoughtful description of City College basketball strategy
and tactics—the "City game." It also contains the "Fifty Morale Builders" that Floyd Layne was still handing out to participants in his basketball clinics six decades later.

Descriptions of City College basketball games are drawn from interviews with players and spectators, as well as from accounts in all
the major New York newspapers of the period, including the *Times,
Post, Daily News, Daily Mirror, Daily Compass, World-Telegram and Sun,
Journal-American, Herald Tribune,* and *Brooklyn Daily Eagle*. The City College student newspapers—*The Campus* and the *Observation Post* of the
main campus, and *The Ticker* of the downtown business school—were
extraordinarily useful for the close-up views they provide of the basketball team; at least as valuable was their in-depth coverage of the scandal and its aftermath, including genuinely thoughtful, searching, and
compassionate editorials and letters to the editor. Happily, microfilmed
copies of the newspapers have been digitized and are now available
online, the first two at digital-archives.ccny.cuny.edu and the third at
academicworks.cuny.edu.

The March 29, 1950, issue of the student newspaper *The Scout*,
available at the Cullom-Davis Library of Bradley University, provides lit-
erally a shot-by-shot summary of the NCAA championship game. Film

clips of that game, as well as the previous tournament game against North Carolina State, can be seen in Universal International and Warner-Pathé newsreels held in the Motion Picture and Television Reading Room in the Library of Congress. Silent films of the NIT and NCAA tournament games, made by an anonymous member of the crowd at Madison Square Garden, are today held in the City College Archives.

In 1987, author Peter Levine conducted a lengthy interview with Bobby Sand for his book on American Jews and sport, *Ellis Island to Ebbets Field*. In the interview Sand vividly described his life and career, from his upbringing in Brownsville, Brooklyn, to his family's health troubles, the double championship and the point-shaving scandal, and his complicated relationship with Nat Holman. Sand's efforts to return to the classroom were reported in the City College newspapers; the arc of his career was summarized in a press release issued by the college's Office of Public Relations in October 1971 announcing his hiring as the basketball coach for the former downtown business school, now renamed Baruch College. Sand family history was provided by his grandson Adam and, especially, by his daughter Wendie; in numerous conversations and emails, Wendie Sand was able to recall almost everything I asked her about, even including the type of pen—brown-and-green tortoiseshell with a gold nib—that her father used to write the letter to Ed Warner in the City College cafeteria. ("It became verboten," Wendie recalled of that pen. "We kept it in the drawer like it was some sort of juju charm doing terrible things to us.")

Two excellent books have previously been written about the 1951 point-shaving scandal, Stanley Cohen's *The Game They Played* (1977) and Charley Rosen's *Scandals of '51* (1978). Cohen's beautifully written book was especially valuable for his incisive analysis of Judge Saul Streit's legal reasoning. (Excerpts from Streit's ruling were published in many of the New York papers.) The book begins with a description of the incident in which Eddie Roman, in the weeks after the scandal, punched an observer who tossed pennies at him during a local pickup game; Roman is not there cited by name (he is referred to simply as "the big man"), but his identity is hardly disguised, and in a phone conversation, Stanley Cohen confirmed that it was Eddie Roman and that he had witnessed the confrontation. Charley Rosen generously gave me transcripts of several interviews he conducted while researching *Scandals of '51*, including interviews with Floyd Layne and Eddie Roman.

The 1998 HBO documentary *City Dump: The Story of the 1951 CCNY Basketball Scandal* contains clips taken from interviews with several people involved in the scandal; it also features a great deal of rare archival footage, including Ed Sullivan's introduction of Nat Holman on his show *Toast of the Town*. The codirector of *City Dump*, George Roy, graciously provided me with several boxes of research material that had been compiled for the documentary, in which I discovered photocopies of detectives' notes listing wiretaps that had been placed on the phones of Salvatore Sollazzo, Eddie Roman, and Bob Zawoluk, as well as copies of District Attorney Frank Hogan's own notes regarding the arrests. The boxes also yielded a partial transcript of Ed Warner's interrogation by detectives. Additional descriptions of the interrogations can be found in Frank Hogan's *Report of the District Attorney, County of New York: 1949–1954* and in the memoir *The D.A.'s Man* (1957) by Harold Danforth, one of Hogan's investigators. Among other details, the book reveals that one of the players tried to leap out a window when confronted with his crimes; Danforth did not indicate which player it was, but Frank Hogan's diary entry for that day indicated it was Al Roth. Hogan's diaries, as well as a wealth of other material spanning his legal and political careers, can be found in the Frank Smithwick Hogan Papers, which are held in the Rare Book and Manuscript Library of Columbia University.

The New York district attorney's office under Frank Hogan is described in Barry Cunningham's book *Mr. District Attorney: The Story of Frank S. Hogan and the Manhattan D.A.'s Office* (1977), as well as in Richard Rovere's 1947 *New Yorker* profile, "Father Hogan's Place." (Cunningham's book also makes intriguing note of Hogan's "wire vault" on the ninth floor of the Criminal Courts Building, a climate-controlled, vacuum-sealed, permanently locked room containing thousands of secretly recorded tapes; according to Cunningham, "These secret tapes were said to incriminate scores of politicians, judges, entertainers, sports figures, and other prominent individuals—men and women who escaped indictment only because Hogan lacked enough corroborative evidence to convict them.")

City College player Ron Nadell, whom I interviewed for this book, was mistakenly arrested with the other players at Penn Station and described being brought to the district attorney's office for questioning. Additional firsthand reminiscences of that evening came from Ina Segal-Gonick, a City College student who worked in the Athletic Association office and had been given tickets to the Temple game; she was with the basketball team—and, as it turned out, two detectives—on the train returning to New York from Philadelphia.

The document *Outline of Proof as to Various Counts of the Indictment*, produced by the district attorney's office of the County of New York in 1951 in preparation for possible trials, contains detailed descriptions of interviews conducted with many of the figures involved in the case, as well as information from detectives and associates of Salvatore Sollazzo and Eddie Gard. Gard himself declined to speak with me for this book. He was amply remembered, though, by teammates and associates, among them Gloria Roth, Al Roth's wife; Gard had introduced them to each other before the point-shaving scandal. His early life is summarized in the dossier *Background Material on Eddie Gard, 79 Avenue Z, Brooklyn, N.Y.*, produced by the New York County district attorney's office shortly after his arrest. Gard's point-shaving activities were also described by Ed Warner, Eddie Roman, and Al Roth in the aforementioned *Outline of Proof*, as were those of his partner Salvatore Sollazzo. The most thorough discussion of Sollazzo's life and crimes can be found in Robert Rice's book *The Business of Crime* (1956).

The City College double-championship team was a phenomenon that had not been seen before in New York, and for more than a year the exploits of the team—on the court and, subsequently, off it—appeared in the city's sports pages on nearly a daily basis. The most penetrating investigations into the point-shaving scandal were produced by two young sportswriters, Ben Gould of *The Brooklyn Daily Eagle* and Stan Isaacs of *The Daily Compass*. (The *Compass* was being run on a shoestring and would fold the following year; to hide the fact that he provided virtually the entirety of the paper's sports coverage, Isaacs published many of his articles under pseudonyms.) Additional information about the scandal came from interviews I conducted with sportswriters including George Vecsey, Jerry Izenberg, and Dave Anderson, the estimable sports columnist for *The New York Times*, who as a cub reporter for the *Journal-*

American worked alongside editor Max Kase and remembered him well and fondly, including the regular pinochle games Kase ran in the back office of the sports department.

Family background and personal information about Miles McDonald were taken from an interview with his daughter, Joanne Roddy, as well as from Violet Brown's five-part profile that ran in *The Brooklyn Daily Eagle* in October 1950. The Harry Gross scandal was itself the subject of two books. *Pay-Off: The Inside Story of Big City Corruption* (1951), by Walter Arm, maintains a close focus on the Gross affair. *The Big Fix* (1954), written by a pair of New York newspaper reporters, Norton Mockridge and Robert H. Prall, provides a wider view of the life and work of Miles McDonald and his staff, as well as the political career of William O'Dwyer; the scene at Gracie Mansion between O'Dwyer and the Bronx Democratic boss Ed Flynn is drawn primarily from their account. The full scope of McDonald's grand jury investigation can be seen in volume 4 of *New York City Police Corruption Investigation Commissions, 1894–1994* (1997), edited by Gabriel J. Chin. The volume extensively covers the Harry Gross case, from the undercover work of the rookie squad to the surveillance of Gross's Inwood wire room; it also includes a section on John M. Murtagh, Mayor O'Dwyer's highly accommodating commissioner of investigation, who later on, as a chief magistrate, set bail for the accused players and gamblers.

William O'Dwyer's history of dealings with shady characters (including Frank Costello and James Moran) is covered extensively in George Walsh's *Public Enemies: The Mayor, the Mob, and the Crime That Was* (1980). Additional accounts of O'Dwyer's career can be found in *What Have You Done for Me Lately? The Ins and Outs of New York City Politics* (1967), written by the *New York Times* reporter Warren Moscow; *New Yorker* correspondent Philip Hamburger's *Mayor Watching and Other Pleasures* (1958); and Robert Caro's magisterial *The Power Broker: Robert Moses and the Fall of New York* (1975), which contains a section on the O'Dwyer mayoralty. O'Dwyer himself wrote movingly of his Irish upbringing in his memoir *Beyond the Golden Door*, published posthumously in 1987.

In 1953, Ed Reid of *The Brooklyn Daily Eagle*—who received a Pulitzer Prize for Public Service for his exposé of the links between police and bookmakers—published *The Shame of New York*, the first chapter of which concerns the Harry Gross scandal. Prior to that, in 1951, Reid wrote an article for the men's magazine *True*, "I Broke the Brooklyn Graft Scandal," in which he described how he first heard of the legendary "Mr. G." (Ed Reid can be seen portraying himself in a cameo role in the 1958 movie *The Case Against Brooklyn*, loosely based on his *True* article.) In 1980, James Reardon published a lightly veiled autobiographical novel about his career with Harry Gross, entitled *The Sweet Life of Jimmy Riley*. Harry Gross's life, and his death at his own hand, were sensitively described in a 1986 *New York Times* obituary by Robert D. McFadden, "The Lonely Death of a Man Who Made a Scandal."

Suggestions about St. John's University's involvement with point shaving were repeated time and again in interviews with players and sportswriters of the era. In his book *The Wizard of Odds* (2001), Charley Rosen likewise indicated that "Dozens of metropolitan area coaches and players (including several from Catholic universities), and numerous bookies and sharpsters can all testify to the personal involvement of Cardinal Spellman, head of the archdiocese of New York." (Rosen further alleged that Frank Hogan possessed recordings of conversations between St. John's players and Eddie Gard; I have not been able to verify that, though detectives' notes do indicate that Bob Zawoluk's phone was wiretapped.) Firsthand information about the St. John's basketball team and the friendship between coach Frank McGuire and Police Commissioner William O'Brien came from an interview with the team co-captain Frank Mulzoff. Additional material about McGuire's friendships with policemen and criminals can be found in Bethany Bradsher's *The Classic: How Everett Case and His Tournament Brought Big-Time Basketball to the South* (2011). A 1957 *Sports Illustrated* article by Richard J. Schaap, "Basketball's Underground Railroad," quotes McGuire as boasting of his close relationship with New York's police department and declaring that any coach who wanted to recruit in New York City first needed to obtain a "passport" from him. Marty Glickman described his encounter with an apprehensive St. John's player in his 1996 autobiography *The Fastest Kid on the Block*.

In an interview at his home on Long Island, the former City College player Ron Nadell recalled seeing Bob Zawoluk enter the district attorney's office with an attorney. The career of that attorney, Henry Ughetta, was summarized in Andy McCue's 2014 biography of Walter O'Malley,

Mover and Shaker, and in Ughetta's 1967 *New York Times* obituary; details of his political and charitable activities in Brooklyn can be found in news stories in *The Brooklyn Daily Eagle* (searchable online at bklyn .newspapers.com). Zawoluk's shifting account of his dealings with Eddie Gard and Salvatore Sollazzo can be traced through various newspaper accounts of the time, including especially Ben Gould's investigative articles in *The Brooklyn Daily Eagle* during February and March 1951; the articles "St. John's Star Bares Sollazzo Offer of 'Gift' " in the *World-Telegram and Sun* and "St. John's Star Accuses Sollazzo" in the *Journal-American,* both from March 9, 1951; and Milton Gross's profile in *Sport* magazine, "Zawoluk Wasn't for Sale." Information about Francis Cardinal Spellman's political influence was drawn primarily from John Cooney's biography *The American Pope: The Life and Times of Francis Cardinal Spellman* (1984).

Stefan Kanfer's *A Summer World: The Attempt to Build a Jewish Eden in the Catskills, from the Days of the Ghetto to the Rise and Decline of the Borscht Belt* (1989) is an especially engaging and thoughtful history; the book does not shy away from discussions of point-shaving in the hotels. Life in those hotels—including the Friday night basketball games—was warmly remembered by those who worked and vacationed there in *It Happened in the Catskills* (1991), one of a series of New York–based oral histories compiled by Myra Katz Frommer and Harvey Frommer. In 1950, Catskills basketball was considered significant enough that the *New York Post* assigned a stringer to cover it, and during the summer, Larry Weiner wrote several stories about the games; in August of that year, *Life* magazine produced a photo spread, "Borscht Basketball"; in November, *Scholastic Coach* also covered the phenomenon in an article entitled "A Hoop-Crazy Mountain." Additional information about Borscht Belt basketball came from interviews with Jack Laub, a star college basketball player who worked with Eddie Roman and Bob Zawoluk at the Waldemere Hotel (and who served as a go-between in bringing Roman to the University of Cincinnati); Michael Weinberg, son of the former owner of Scaroon Manor, a favorite summer employment spot for City College players; and Patricia Posner, a descendant of the family that owned the Hotel Brickman, where Eddie Roman and Al Roth worked in the summer of 1950. During interviews at his home in Florida, the former City College player Herb Cohen described his employment, as busboy and basketball player, both at Sca-roon Manor and at the Hotel Brickman.

A great deal has been written about the creation—architectural and intellectual—of the City College of New York. George B. Post's design for the college was insightfully evaluated by Sarah Bradford Landau in *George B. Post, Architect: Picturesque Designer and Determined Realist* (1998), and, contemporaneously, by Arthur Ebbs Willauer in his review "College of the City of New York," which appeared in *The American Architect and Building News* in 1908. James Traub's *City on a Hill: Testing the American Dream at City College* (1994) is a thoughtful and cogent discussion of the college and its mission; Traub describes CCNY as "perhaps the longest-running radical social experiment in American history." James Wechsler vividly portrayed political life on the campus in the 1930s in his book *Revolt on the Campus* (1935); the student activism of the following decade is chronicled by Marvin Engel in "CCNY Student Strikes, 1948–1949," in a 1999 issue of *Jewish Currents*. In 1947 a member of the City College faculty, Samuel Middlebrook, wrote the essay "Pioneer in Democratic Education" for *The American Mercury*; it is an eloquent affirmation of the special role played by CCNY in the life of the city. In addition to the student newspapers, volumes of the college yearbook, *Microcosm*, held in the City College Archives, provide the rich flavor of campus life. The 1983 anthology *City at the Center* contains many fond and often amusing essays by City College graduates, including the great writers Meyer Liben and Vivian Gornick. Morris Freedman's "CCNY Days," for one, provides a colorful reminiscence of campus life, including the story of the English professor who each semester favored his students with a poem he had written in honor of Whirlaway's victory in the Kentucky Derby; the poem had been composed, fittingly enough, in galloping meter, and when recited aloud came to its final line in just a beat over two minutes—precisely the time in which Whirlaway himself had run the race.

Raymond Haber appears selling his pragels in a 1958 CCNY student film called *The Balloon and Five Pence*, which can be found on YouTube; the film, however, is silent, and so viewers must imagine for themselves his deathless call: "They're homogenized! Lavenderized! Beaverized!"

SELECTED BIBLIOGRAPHY

Aamidor, Abraham. *Chuck Taylor, All Star: The True Story of the Man Behind the Most Famous Shoe in History*. Bloomington: Indiana University Press, 2006.

Alfieri, Gus. *Lapchick: The Life of a Legendary Player and Coach in the Glory Days of Basketball*. Guilford, CT: Lyons Press, 2006.

Anderson, Lars, and Chad Millman. *Pickup Artists: Street Basketball in America*. London: Verso, 1998.

Arm, Walter. *Pay-Off: The Inside Story of Big City Corruption*. New York: Appleton-Century-Crofts, 1951.

Ashe, Arthur R., Jr. *A Hard Road to Glory: A History of the African-American Athlete*. 3 vols. New York: Warner Books, 1988.

Bee, Clair. "I Know Why They Sold Out to the Gamblers." *The Saturday Evening Post*, February 2, 1952, 26–27, 76–80.

Bernstein, Lee. *The Greatest Menace: Organized Crime in Cold War America*. Amherst: University of Massachusetts Press, 2002.

Bischoff, John Paul. *Mr. Iba: Basketball's Aggie Iron Duke*. Oklahoma City: Oklahoma Heritage Association / Western Heritage Books, 1980.

Bisher, Furman. "Each Game He Dies." *Collier's*, January 31, 1948, 23, 48.

Bjarkman, Peter C. *Hoopla: A Century of College Basketball*. Indianapolis: Masters Press, 1996.

Board of Higher Education of the City of New York. *In the Matter of Charges Preferred Against Nat Holman and Harry Robert Sand*, 1953. Cohen Archives, Morris Raphael Cohen Library, City College of New York.

Bradsher, Bethany. *The Classic: How Everett Case and His Tournament Brought Big-Time Basketball to the South*. Houston: Whitecaps Media, 2011.

Brown, Phil. *Catskill Culture: A Mountain Rat's Memories of the Great Jewish Resort Area.* Philadelphia: Temple University Press, 1998.

Caro, Robert A. *The Power Broker: Robert Moses and the Fall of New York.* New York: Vintage Books, 1975.

Caute, David. *The Great Fear: The Anti-Communist Purge Under Truman and Eisenhower.* New York: Simon & Schuster, 1978.

Chalk, Ocania. *Black College Sport.* New York: Dodd, Mead, 1976.

Chambers, Bradford. "The Boy Gangs of Mousetown." *Reader's Digest,* August 1948, 144–58.

Chandler, Dan, and Vernon Hatton. *Rupp from Both Ends of the Bench.* Lancer, KY: Lancer Publishers, 1972.

Chansky, Art. *Light Blue Reign: How a City Slicker, a Quiet Kansan, and a Mountain Man Built College Basketball's Longest-Lasting Dynasty.* New York: Thomas Dunne Books, 2009.

Chepesiuk, Ron. *Gangsters of Harlem: The Gritty Underworld of New York's Most Famous Neighborhood.* Fort Lee, NJ: Barricade Books, 2007.

Chin, Gabriel J., editor. *New York City Police Corruption Investigation Commissions, 1894–1994.* Volume 4. Buffalo, NY: William S. Hein, 1997.

Clark, Kenneth. "Candor About Negro-Jewish Relations," *Commentary,* February 1946, 8–14.

Cohen, Stanley. *The Game They Played.* New York: Farrar, Straus and Giroux, 1977.

Cole, Lewis. *A Loose Game: The Sport and Business of Basketball.* Indianapolis: Bobbs-Merrill, 1978.

Cooney, John. *The American Pope: The Life and Times of Francis Cardinal Spellman.* New York: Times Books, 1984.

Corman, Avery. *My Old Neighborhood Remembered.* Fort Lee, NJ: Barricade Books, 2014.

Cunningham, Barry, with Mike Pearl. *Mr. District Attorney: The Story of Frank S. Hogan and the Manhattan D.A.'s Office.* New York: Mason/Charter, 1977.

Danforth, Harold R., and James D. Horan. *The D.A.'s Man.* New York: Crown, 1957.

Davies, Richard O., and Richard G. Abram. *Betting the Line: Sports Wagering in American Life.* Columbus: Ohio State University Press, 2001.

Devaney, John. *Tiny! The Story of Nate Archibald.* New York: G. P. Putnam's Sons, 1977.

"Drive, Drive, Drive!" *Newsweek,* December 4, 1950, 76–78.

Durso, Joseph. *Madison Square Garden: 100 Years of History.* New York: Simon & Schuster, 1979.

Edwards-Lindstrom, Patty. *Victory, Honor and Glory: Celebrating the History of Bradley Basketball*. Peoria, IL: All About Sports, 2007.

Ehrlich, Gerald. "And the Greatest of Them All, Nat Holman," Nat Holman Papers, City College of New York Libraries, Archives and Special Collections, box 5, folder 1.

Ellis, Edward Robb. *The Epic of New York City: A Narrative History from 1524 to the Present*. New York: Coward-McCann, 1966.

Emerson, Thomas I., and David Haber. *Political and Civil Rights in the United States*. Buffalo: Dennis, 1952.

Engel, Marvin. "CCNY Student Strikes, 1948–1949." *Jewish Currents*, December 1999, 4–7, 38.

Fariello, Griffin. *Red Scare: Memories of the American Inquisition*. New York: W. W. Norton, 1995.

Fay, Bill. "They're Balmy over Basketball." *Collier's*, January 13, 1951, 26–27, 65–67.

Federal Writers' Project of the Works Progress Administration in New York City. *New York Panorama: A Companion to the WPA Guide to New York City*. 1938. New York: Pantheon, 1984.

———. *The WPA Guide to New York City: The Federal Writers' Project Guide to 1930s New York*. 1939. New York: New Press, 1992.

Figone, Albert J. *Cheating the Spread: Gamblers, Point Shavers, and Game Fixers in College Football and Basketball*. Urbana: University of Illinois Press, 2012.

Fitzpatrick, Frank. *And the Walls Came Tumbling Down: The Basketball Game That Changed American Sports*. Lincoln: University of Nebraska Press, 1999.

Flath, August William. *Reminiscences of August William Flath: Oral History, 1958–1959*. Rare Book and Manuscript Library, Butler Library, Columbia University.

Flynn, Edward J. "Bosses and Machines." *Atlantic Monthly*, May 1947, 34–40.

Fox, John. *The Ball: Discovering the Object of the Game*. New York: HarperCollins, 2012.

Fox, Stephen. *Big Leagues: Professional Baseball, Football, and Basketball in National Memory*. New York: William Morrow, 1994.

Frank, Stanley. "Basketball's Big Wheel." *The Saturday Evening Post*, January 15, 1949, 25, 132–34.

———. "Basketball's Nat Holman: Easy Doesn't Do It." *Collier's*, February 18, 1950, 19, 65–67.

———. "College Without Frills or Fun." *The Saturday Evening Post*, April 26, 1947, 34–35, 102–108.

Freeman, Joshua B. *Working-Class New York: Life and Labor Since World War II*. New York: New Press, 2000.

Fried, Richard M. *Nightmare in Red: The McCarthy Era in Perspective*. New York: Oxford University Press, 1990.

Frommer, Myra Katz, and Harvey Frommer. *It Happened in Brooklyn: An Oral History of Growing Up in the Borough in the 1940s, '50s, and '60s*. New York: Harcourt Brace, 1993.

———. *It Happened in Manhattan: An Oral History of Life in the City During the Mid-Twentieth Century*. New York: Berkley Books, 2001.

———. *It Happened in the Catskills: An Oral History in the Words of Busboys, Bellhops, Guests, Proprietors, Comedians, Agents, and Others Who Lived It*. New York: Harcourt Brace Jovanovich, 1991.

Geist, Harold, editor. "Nat Holman, 'Mr. Basketball.'" In *From Eminently Disadvantaged to Eminence*. St. Louis: Warren H. Green, 1974, 48–63.

Gibbons, William C. "Is Basketball's Future Its Past? Nat Holman's Lost Legacy." *Encounter: Education for Meaning and Social Justice*, vol. 19:3 (Autumn 2006), 32–38.

Gifford, Frank, with Charles Mangel. *Gifford on Courage*. New York: M. Evans, 1976.

Gildea, Dennis. *Hoop Crazy: The Lives of Clair Bee and Chip Hilton*. Fayetteville: University of Arkansas Press, 2013.

Glazer, Ruth. "West Bronx: Food, Shelter, Clothing." *Commentary*, June 1949, 578–80, 584–85.

Glickman, Marty. *The Fastest Kid on the Block*. Syracuse, NY: Syracuse University Press, 1996.

Gould, Todd. *Pioneers of the Hardwood: Indiana and the Birth of Professional Basketball*. Bloomington: Indiana University Press, 1998.

Gralla, Larry. "Allagaroo's Grand Slam!" *City College Alumnus*, May 1950, 12–15, 21–23.

Gurock, Jeffrey S. *Jews in Gotham: New York Jews in a Changing City, 1920–2010*. New York: New York University Press, 2012.

Guttmann, Allen. *A Whole New Ball Game: An Interpretation of American Sports*. Chapel Hill: University of North Carolina Press, 1988.

Halberstam, David J. *Sports on New York Radio: A Play-by-Play History*. Chicago: Masters Press, 1999.

Hamburger, Philip. *Mayor Watching and Other Pleasures*. New York: Rinehart, 1958.

Hamill, Pete. "The Gardens of New York." Introduction to *Garden of Dreams: Madison Square Garden 125 Years*. New York: Stewart, Tabori & Chang, 2004.

———. "The New York We've Lost." *New York*, December 21–28, 1987.

Handshuh, Pearl, et al. *Boulevard-Prospect Area, Bronx, New York City: A Survey by Honor Students, Hunter College.* Mayor's Committee on Unity, New York, 1946.

Hardin, John A. *Fifty Years of Segregation: Black Higher Education in Kentucky, 1904–1954.* Lexington: University Press of Kentucky, 1997.

Hiner, Jason. *Mac's Boys: Branch McCracken and the Legendary 1953 Hurryin' Hoosiers.* Bloomington: Indiana University Press, 2006.

Hobson, Howard. "How to Stop Those Basketball Scandals." *Collier's,* December 29, 1951, 26–27, 65–67.

Hogan, Frank S. *Report of the District Attorney, County of New York: 1949–1954.* New York: Bar Press, 1954.

Hollander, Zander, editor. *Madison Square Garden: A Century of Sport and Spectacle on the World's Most Versatile Stage.* New York: Hawthorn Books, 1973.

Holman, Nat. *Championship Basketball.* Chicago: Ziff-Davis, 1942.

———. *Holman on Basketball.* New York: Crown, 1950.

———. "How to Score." *Boys' Life,* January 1948, 22, 44.

———. "What to Look For in a Basketball Game." *Nat Holman's 1951 Basket-Ball Annual,* vol. 1, no. 1 (1950), 41–49.

———. *Winning Basketball.* New York: Charles Scribner's Sons, 1932.

Isaacs, Neil D. *All the Moves: A History of College Basketball.* Philadelphia: J. B. Lippincott, 1975.

———. *Vintage NBA: The Pioneer Era, 1946–1956.* Indianapolis: Masters Press, 1996.

Jacobs, Barry. *Across the Line: Profiles in Basketball Courage; Tales of the First Black Players in the ACC and SEC.* Guilford, CT: Lyons Press, 2008.

Jonnes, Jill. *We're Still Here: The Rise, Fall, and Resurrection of the South Bronx.* Boston: Atlantic Monthly Press, 1986.

Kalb, Marvin. "The College Basketball Victory That Seemed Too Good to Be True—and Was." *The Atlantic,* April 25, 2013.

Kanfer, Stefan. *A Summer World: The Attempt to Build a Jewish Eden in the Catskills, from the Days of the Ghetto to the Rise and Decline of the Borscht Belt.* New York: Farrar, Straus and Giroux, 1989.

Kapp, Isa. "By the Waters of the Grand Concourse." *Commentary,* September 1949, 269–73.

Kay, Philip. *"Guttersnipes" and "Eliterates": City College in the Popular Imagination.* Dissertation, Graduate School of Arts and Sciences, Columbia University in the City of New York, 2011.

Keating, William J., with Richard Carter. *The Man Who Rocked the Boat.* New York: Harper & Brothers, 1956.

Koppett, Leonard. *The Essence of the Game Is Deception: Thinking About Basketball.* Boston: Little, Brown, 1973.

————. *The Rise and Fall of the Press Box*. Toronto: Sport Classic Books, 2003.

————. *24 Seconds to Shoot: An Informal History of the National Basketball Association*. New York: Macmillan, 1968.

Lait, Jack, and Lee Mortimer. *New York: Confidential!* Chicago: Ziff-Davis, 1948.

Lancaster, Harry C. *Adolph Rupp as I Knew Him*. Lexington, KY: Jim Host and Associates, 1979.

Landau, Sarah Bradford. *George B. Post, Architect: Picturesque Designer and Determined Realist*. New York: Monacelli Press, 1998.

Lardner, James, and Thomas Reppetto. *NYPD: A City and Its Police*. New York: Henry Holt, 2000.

Layne, Floyd. "Don't I Deserve Another Chance?" *Sport*, September 1952, 52–53, 82–83.

Levine, Peter. *Ellis Island to Ebbets Field: Sport and the American Jewish Experience*. New York: Oxford University Press, 1992.

Liben, Meyer. "CCNY—A Memoir." *Commentary*, September 1965, 64–70.

Lucas, Adam. *The Best Game Ever: How Frank McGuire's '57 Tar Heels Beat Wilt and Revolutionized College Basketball*. Guilford, CT: Lyons Press, 2006.

Mallozzi, Vincent M. *Asphalt Gods: An Oral History of the Rucker Tournament*. New York: Doubleday, 2003.

Martin, Charles H. *Benching Jim Crow: The Rise and Fall of the Color Line in Southern College Sports, 1890–1980*. Urbana: University of Illinois Press, 2010.

McCue, Andy. *Mover and Shaker: Walter O'Malley, the Dodgers, and Baseball's Westward Expansion*. Lincoln: University of Nebraska Press, 2014.

McFadden, Robert D. "The Lonely Death of a Man Who Made a Scandal." *The New York Times*, April 5, 1986.

McMurren, Lionel E. *Frederick Douglass P.S. 139: A Citadel of Inspiration*. Littleton, MA: Tapestry Press, 2005.

Melchiorre, Gene. "How I Fell for the Basketball Bribers." *Look*, January 13, 1953, 62–64.

Menzer, Joe. *Four Corners: How UNC, N.C. State, Duke, and Wake Forest Made North Carolina the Center of the Basketball Universe*. New York: Simon & Schuster, 1999.

Middlebrook, Samuel. "Pioneer in Democratic Education." *American Mercury*, May 1947, 606–13.

Miller, Richard I. *The Truth About Big-Time Football*. New York: William Sloane Associates, 1953.

Minsky, Alan. *March to the Finals: The History of College Basketball's Illustrious Finale*. New York: Metro Books, 1999.

Mockridge, Norton, and Robert H. Prall. *The Big Fix*. New York: Henry Holt, 1954.

Morrow, Elise. "Peoria." *The Saturday Evening Post*, February 12, 1949, 20–21, 119–23.

Moscow, Warren. *The Last of the Big-Time Bosses: The Life and Times of Carmine De Sapio and the Rise and Fall of Tammany Hall*. New York: Stein and Day, 1971.

———. *What Have You Done for Me Lately? The Ins and Outs of New York City Politics*. Englewood Cliffs, NJ: Prentice-Hall, 1967.

"Nat for Just a Day," *Scholastic Coach*, December 1945, 5, 38.

Nelli, Bert, and Steve Nelli. *The Winning Tradition: A History of Kentucky Wildcat Basketball*. Second edition. Lexington: University Press of Kentucky, 1998.

Nelson, Murry R. *Abe Saperstein and the American Basketball League, 1960–1963: The Upstarts Who Shot for Three and Lost to the NBA*. Jefferson, NC: McFarland, 2013.

———.*The Originals: The New York Celtics Invent Modern Basketball*. Bowling Green, OH: Bowling Green State University Popular Press, 1999.

Nitchman, Nelson W. "The NCAA 1950 Basketball Finals." *Athletic Journal*, May 1950, 28–30, 51–53.

O'Connell, Jim. *100 Years of St. John's Basketball*. Jamaica, NY: St. John's University Department of Athletics, 2008.

O'Dwyer, William. *Beyond the Golden Door*. Jamaica, NY: St. John's University, 1987.

Oursler, Fulton. "The Remarkable Story of William O'Dwyer," *Reader's Digest*, May 1952, 1–12.

Packer, Billy, and Roland Lazenby. *The Golden Game*. Dallas: Jefferson Street Press, 1991.

Padwe, Sandy. *Basketball's Hall of Fame*. Englewood Cliffs, NJ: Prentice-Hall, 1970.

Paxton, Harry T. "The Basketball Bug Bites Dixie." *The Saturday Evening Post*, March 10, 1951, 31, 111–14.

Peeler, Tim, and Roger Winstead. *NC State Basketball: 100 Years of Innovation*. Chapel Hill: University of North Carolina Press, 2010.

Peterson, Robert W. *Cages to Jump Shots: Pro Basketball's Early Years*. New York: Oxford University Press, 1990.

Pileggi, Nicholas. "Crime at Mid-Century." *New York*, December 30, 1974, 57–63.

Pritchett, Wendell. *Brownsville, Brooklyn: Blacks, Jews, and the Changing Face of the Ghetto*. Chicago: University of Chicago Press, 2002.

Raab, Selwyn. *Five Families: The Rise, Decline, and Resurgence of America's Most Powerful Mafia Empires*. New York: Thomas Dunne, 2005.

Rappoport, Ken. *The Classic: The History of the NCAA Basketball Championship*. Mission, KS: National Collegiate Athletic Association, 1979.

Reid, David. *The Brazen Age: New York City and the American Empire; Politics, Art, and Bohemia*. New York: Pantheon Books, 2016.

Reid, Ed. "I Broke the Brooklyn Graft Scandal." *True*, February 1951, 25–27, 79–85.

———. *The Shame of New York*. New York: Random House, 1953.

Rice, Robert. *The Business of Crime*. New York: Farrar, Straus and Cudahy, 1956.

Rice, Russell. *Adolph Rupp: Kentucky's Basketball Baron*. Champaign, IL: Sagamore Publishing, 1994.

———. *Kentucky Basketball's Big Blue Machine*. Huntsville, AL: Strode Publishers, 1976.

Riess, Steven A., editor. *Sports and the American Jew*. Syracuse, NY: Syracuse University Press, 1998.

Ritter, Lawrence S. *East Side, West Side: Tales of New York Sporting Life, 1910–1960*. New York: Total Sports, 1998.

Rizzo, Betty, and Barry Wallenstein, editors. *City at the Center: A Collection of Writings by CCNY Alumni and Faculty*. New York: City College of New York, 1983.

Roberts, William. *College Basketball Bribery Scandals, 1947–1951*. Master's thesis, California State Polytechnic University at Pomona, 1979.

Rosen, Charley. *The Chosen Game: A Jewish Basketball History*. Lincoln: University of Nebraska Press, 2017.

———. *Crazy Basketball: A Life In and Out of Bounds*. Lincoln: University of Nebraska Press, 2011.

———. *The First Tip-Off: The Incredible Story of the Birth of the NBA*. New York: McGraw-Hill, 2009.

———. *Scandals of '51: How the Gamblers Almost Killed College Basketball*. 1978. New York: Seven Stories Press, 1999.

———. *The Wizard of Odds: How Jack Molinas Almost Destroyed the Game of Basketball*. New York: Seven Stories Press, 2001.

Rosenblum, Constance. *Boulevard of Dreams: Heady Times, Heartbreak, and Hope Along the Grand Concourse in the Bronx*. New York: New York University Press, 2009.

Rovere, Richard H. "The Decline of New York City." *American Mercury*, May 1944, 526–32.

———. "Father Hogan's Place." *New Yorker*, August 16, 1947, 36–57.

———. "Nothing Much to It." *New Yorker*, October 8, 1945, 28–41.

Rudy, S. Willis. *The College of the City of New York: A History, 1847–1947.* New York: City College Press, 1949.

Rupp, Adolph. *Rupp's Championship Basketball for Player, Coach and Fan.* New York: Prentice-Hall, 1948.

Russell, John. *Honey Russell: Between Games, Between Halves.* Washington, DC: Dryad Press, 1986.

Samtur, Stephen M., and Martin A. Jackson. *The Bronx: Lost, Found, and Remembered (1935–1975).* New York: Back in the Bronx, 1999.

Sand, Bobby. "A Proposal to Revolutionize Basketball." *Sport*, February 1952, 10–11, 85.

Sansone, Gene. *New York Subways: An Illustrated History of New York City's Transit Cars.* Centennial edition. Baltimore: Johns Hopkins University Press, 1997.

Schaap, Richard J. "Basketball's Underground Railroad," *Sports Illustrated*, February 4, 1957, 9–10, 43.

Schneider, Eric C. *Vampires, Dragons, and Egyptian Kings: Youth Gangs in Postwar New York.* Princeton, NJ: Princeton University Press, 1999.

Schuyler, Montgomery. "The College of the City of New York." *Architectural Record*, March 1907, 167–85.

Schwartz, David G. *Cutting the Wire: Gambling Prohibition and the Internet.* Reno: University of Nevada Press, 2005.

Shapiro, Edward. "The Shame of the City: CCNY Basketball, 1950-51." In *Jews, Sports, and the Rites of Citizenship*, edited by Jack Kugelmass. Urbana: University of Illinois Press, 2007.

Shecter, Leonard. *The Jocks.* New York: Warner Books, 1970.

Sheehan, Susan. *A Prison and a Prisoner.* Boston: Houghton Mifflin, 1978.

Small, Collie. "The Crafty Wizard of Lexington." *The Saturday Evening Post*, February 15, 1947, 23, 141–42.

Smith, Carol. "The Dress Rehearsal for McCarthyism." *Academe*, July–August 2011.

Smith, Ronald A. *Pay for Play: A History of Big-Time College Athletic Reform.* Urbana: University of Illinois Press, 2011.

Sokol, Jason. *All Eyes Are Upon Us: Race and Politics from Boston to Brooklyn.* New York: Basic Books, 2014.

Sperber, Murray. *Onward to Victory: The Crises That Shaped College Sports.* New York: Henry Holt, 1998.

Spivack, Robert G. "New York: Backslider." In *Our Sovereign State*, edited by Robert S. Allen. New York: Vanguard Press, 1949.

Stern, Robert A. M., Thomas Mellins, and David Fishman. *New York 1960:*

Architecture and Urbanism Between the Second World War and the Bicentennial. New York: Monacelli Press, 1995.

Surdam, David George. *The Rise of the National Basketball Association.* Urbana: University of Illinois Press, 2012.

Teitelbaum, Stanley H. *Sports Heroes, Fallen Idols.* Lincoln: University of Nebraska Press, 2005.

Thomas, Ron. *They Cleared the Lane: The NBA's Black Pioneers.* Lincoln: University of Nebraska Press, 2002.

Traub, James. *City on a Hill: Testing the American Dream at City College.* Reading, MA: Addison-Wesley, 1994.

———. *The Devil's Playground: A Century of Pleasure and Profit in Times Square.* New York: Random House, 2004.

Ultan, Lloyd. *The Northern Borough: A History of the Bronx.* Bronx, NY: Bronx County Historical Society, 2009.

Van Nort, Sydney C. *The City College of New York.* Charleston, SC: Arcadia Publishing, 2007.

Vincent, Ted. *The Rise and Fall of American Sport: Mudville's Revenge.* Lincoln: University of Nebraska Press, 1981.

Walsh, George. *Public Enemies: The Mayor, the Mob, and the Crime That Was.* New York: W. W. Norton, 1980.

Wechsler, James. *Revolt on the Campus.* 1935. Seattle: University of Washington Press, 1973.

White, Shane, et al. *Playing the Numbers: Gambling in Harlem Between the Wars.* Cambridge, MA: Harvard University Press, 2010.

Whitman, Howard. "New York's Tin Shields Become an Iron Curtain." *Collier's,* March 3, 1951, 18–19, 58–60.

Willauer, Arthur Ebbs. "College of the City of New York." *American Architect and Building News,* May 20, 1908, 163–68.

Wilner, Barry, and Ken Rappoport. *The Big Dance: The Story of the NCAA Basketball Tournament.* Lanham, MD: Taylor Trade Publishing, 2012.

Wingate, Livingston. *The Real HARYOU-ACT Story.* New York, 1966.

Woodward, Stanley. "Basketball Betting: An Open Scandal." *Sport,* January 1951, 14–15, 76–77.

INDEX

Page numbers in *italics* refer to illustrations.

About the Author

MATTHEW GOODMAN is the author of three previous books of nonfiction: *Eighty Days: Nellie Bly and Elizabeth Bisland's History-Making Race Around the World; The Sun and the Moon: The Remarkable True Account of Hoaxers, Showmen, Dueling Journalists, and Lunar Man-Bats in Nineteenth-Century New York;* and *Jewish Food: The World at Table*. A *New York Times* bestseller, *Eighty Days* was a Barnes & Noble Discover Great New Writers and Indie Next Great Reads selection and has been translated into eight languages. His work has appeared in *The American Scholar, Harvard Review, Salon,* and many other publications. He lives in Brooklyn with his wife and two children.

matthewgoodmanbooks.com
Facebook.com/matthew.goodman.395
Twitter: @MGoodmanBooks